CHINA'S BILATERAL RELATIONS AND ORDER TRANSITION IN THE INDO-PACIFIC

CHINA'S BILATERAL RELATIONS AND ORDER TRANSITION IN THE INDO-PACIFIC

Editors

Kai He
Griffith University, Australia

Feng Liu
Tsinghua University, China

World Scientific

NEW JERSEY · LONDON · SINGAPORE · BEIJING · SHANGHAI · TAIPEI · CHENNAI

Published by

World Scientific Publishing Europe Ltd.

57 Shelton Street, Covent Garden, London WC2H 9HE

Head office: 5 Toh Tuck Link, Singapore 596224

USA office: 27 Warren Street, Suite 401-402, Hackensack, NJ 07601

Library of Congress Cataloging-in-Publication Data
Names: He, Kai, 1973–   editor. | Liu, Feng, 1981–   editor.
Title: China's bilateral relations and order transition in the Indo-Pacific /
    Kai He, Griffith University, Australia, Feng Liu, Tsinghua University, China.
Description: Singapore ; Hackensack, NJ : World Scientific, 2025. |
    Includes bibliographical references and index.
Identifiers: LCCN 2024021797 | ISBN 9781800616271 (hardcover) |
    ISBN 9781800616318 (ebook) | ISBN 9781800616325 (ebook other)
Subjects: LCSH: China--Foreign relations--21st century. | Indo-Pacific Region--Strategic aspects. |
    China--Foreign relations--United States. | United States--Foreign relations--China.
Classification: LCC JZ1734 .C543 2025 | DDC 327.51073--dc23/eng/20240826
LC record available at https://lccn.loc.gov/2024021797

British Library Cataloguing-in-Publication Data
A catalogue record for this book is available from the British Library.

Copyright © 2025 by World Scientific Publishing Europe Ltd.

*All rights reserved. This book, or parts thereof, may not be reproduced in any form or by any means,
electronic or mechanical, including photocopying, recording or any information storage and retrieval
system now known or to be invented, without written permission from the Publisher.*

For photocopying of material in this volume, please pay a copying fee through the Copyright Clearance
Center, Inc., 222 Rosewood Drive, Danvers, MA 01923, USA. In this case permission to photocopy
is not required from the publisher.

For any available supplementary material, please visit
https://www.worldscientific.com/worldscibooks/10.1142/Q0480#t=suppl

Desk Editors: Kannan Krishnan/Rosie Williamson/Shi Ying Koe

Typeset by Stallion Press
Email: enquiries@stallionpress.com

© 2025 World Scientific Publishing Europe Ltd.
https://doi.org/10.1142/9781800616318_fmatter

About the Editors

Kai He is a professor of international relations at the School of Government and International Relations, Griffith University. He served as a non-resident senior scholar at the United States Institute of Peace (2022–2023), an Australian Research Council (ARC) Future Fellow (2017–2020), and a postdoctoral fellow in the Princeton-Harvard China and the World Program (2009–2010). He has authored or co-authored seven books and edited or co-edited seven volumes. His latest book is *After Hedging: Hard Choices for the Indo-Pacific States between the US and China* (co-authored with Huiyun Feng, *Cambridge Elements Series in International Relations*, 2023). Correspondence should be sent to k.he@griffith.edu.au.

Feng Liu is a professor at the Department of International Relations, Tsinghua University, China. He is also the co-editor-in-chief of *The Chinese Journal of International Politics*. He served as a visiting scholar at the University of Groningen (2014) and the University of California, San Diego (2014–2015). His current research focuses on international relations theory, international security, and international relations in East Asia. He has authored

vi *About the Editors*

more than 100 journal articles and book chapters. His articles have appeared in various peer-reviewed journals such as *International Affairs, The Chinese Journal of International Politics,* and *Pacific Review.* Correspondence should be sent to liu-feng@tsinghua.edu.cn.

© 2025 World Scientific Publishing Europe Ltd.
https://doi.org/10.1142/9781800616318_fmatter

List of Contributors

Rumi Aoyama is a professor at the Graduate School of Asia-Pacific Studies and the director of the Waseda Institute of Contemporary Chinese Studies at Waseda University. Correspondence should be sent to luming@waseda.jp.

Zheng Chen is a professor at the School of International Relations and Public Affairs, Fudan University. Correspondence should be sent to chenzheng@fudan.edu.cn.

Ja Ian Chong is an associate professor at the Department of Political Science, National University of Singapore, and a non-resident scholar at the Carnegie Endowment for International Peace. Correspondence should be sent to chongjaian@nus.edu.sg.

Bates Gill is a member of the board of governors of the Rajaratnam School of International Studies (RSIS, Singapore) and serves on the board of advisors of the National Bureau of Asian Research. He is a senior fellow in Asian security with The National Bureau of Asian Research and is an honorary professor at the Department of Security Studies and Criminology, Macquarie University. Correspondence should be sent to bates.gill@mq.edu.au.

Li Li is a senior research professor and deputy director of the Institute of International Relations, Tsinghua University, and a non-resident senior fellow of the Institute of South Asian Studies, National University of

Singapore. Correspondence should be sent to lili_thiir@mail.tsinghua.edu.cn.

Ruonan Liu is an associate professor at the School of International Relations, University of International Business and Economics. Correspondence should be sent to liuruonan@uibe.edu.cn.

Harsh V. Pant is a professor of international relations at King's College London, the director (honorary) of the Delhi School of Transnational Affairs at Delhi University, and the vice-president of the Observer Research Foundation. Correspondence should be sent to harsh.pant@kcl.ac.uk.

Andrew Scobell is a distinguished fellow with the China program at the United States Institute of Peace. Correspondence should be sent to ascobell@usip.org.

Shounak Set is FHEA is a Lecturer in Defence Studies at King's College London and the U.K. Defence Academy. Correspondence should be sent to shounak.set@kcl.ac.uk.

Guangtao Wang is an associate professor at the Institute of International Studies, Fudan University. Correspondence should be sent to wangguangtao@fudan.edu.cn.

Minghao Zhao is a professor at the Center for American Studies, Fudan University, and a senior fellow at the Fudan Institute of Belt and Road & Global Governance. Correspondence should be sent to mhzhao@fudan.edu.cn.

Fangyin Zhou is a professor at the School of International Relations, Guangdong University of Foreign Studies. Correspondence should be sent to zhoufangyin@gmail.com.

© 2025 World Scientific Publishing Europe Ltd.
https://doi.org/10.1142/9781800616318_fmatter

Acknowledgments

This volume is based on a special issue entitled "Discerning China's Bilateral Relations in the Indo-Pacific: Views from China and the Region" in *The China Review* (vol. 23, no. 1, February 2023). The editors of this volume would like to thank Zaijun Yuan, the editor of *The China Review*, and The Chinese University of Hong Kong Press for their support and permission to publish the revised versions of the articles in this volume. The editors also thank Weixin Hu, Xiaoyu Pu, Mark Beeson, Todd Hall, Yinan He, Mingjiang Li, Xinbo Wu, and other colleagues for their constructive comments and suggestions on this project. All errors and omissions are the authors' own. This project is supported by the Australian Research Council (DP210102843 and DP230102158) and the United States Institute of Peace (USIP). The opinions, findings, and conclusions or recommendations expressed in this volume are those of the authors and do not necessarily reflect the views of the USIP.

© 2025 World Scientific Publishing Europe Ltd.
https://doi.org/10.1142/9781800616318_fmatter

Contents

About the Editors   v

List of Contributors   vii

Acknowledgments   ix

Introduction: Discerning China's Bilateral Relations
in the Indo-Pacific: Views from China and the Region   xiii
  Feng Liu and Kai He

Chapter 1   China's Bilateral Relations, Order Transition,
             and the Indo-Pacific Dynamics   1
             Feng Liu and Kai He

Chapter 2   Infrastructure Statecraft and Sino–U.S. Strategic
             Competition in the Indo-Pacific   33
             Minghao Zhao

Chapter 3   Parsing Post-Pandemic U.S.–China Competition:
             Mutual (Mis)Perceptions and Dueling Geostrategies   67
             Andrew Scobell

Chapter 4   The U.S. Factor and the Evolution of China–India
             Relations   95
             Li Li

Chapter 5   The Himalayan Barrier: India–China Relations
             since Galwan   123
             Shounak Set and Harsh V. Pant

xii *Contents*

Chapter 6   The Japan's "Free and Open Indo-Pacific" and
Sino–Japanese Relations: A Chinese Perspective   149
Guangtao Wang and Zheng Chen

Chapter 7   Stability and Fragility in Japan–China Relations:
China's Pivotal Power and Japan's Strategic
Leverage   177
Rumi Aoyama

Chapter 8   China–Australia Relations and China's Policy
Choices toward Australia: A Chinese Perspective   201
Fangyin Zhou

Chapter 9   Explaining the Troubled Australia–China
Relationship: A Perspective from Australia   231
Bates Gill

Chapter 10   Reinforcing Wedging: Assessing China's Southeast
Asia Policy in the Context of Indo-Pacific Strategy   263
Ruonan Liu

Chapter 11   Herding Cats: Coordination Challenges in
ASEAN's Approach to China   293
Ja Ian Chong

Index   327

© 2025 World Scientific Publishing Europe Ltd.
https://doi.org/10.1142/9781800616318_0001

Introduction

Discerning China's Bilateral Relations in the Indo-Pacific: Views from China and the Region[*]

Feng Liu[†] and Kai He[‡]

†Tsinghua University, China

‡Griffith University, Australia

The strategic competition between the United States (U.S.) and China has become a defining feature of international relations in the Indo-Pacific. How China interacts with the U.S. and other major players in the Indo-Pacific will shape the nature and process of the potential international order transition, either peacefully or confrontationally, in the future. This volume systematically explores China's bilateral relations with five key players in the Indo-Pacific: the U.S., Japan, India, Australia, and ASEAN. By both theoretically unpacking bilateral relations between states and empirically examining China's strategic interactions with others in the region, this research aims to shed light on the complexity of China's bilateral relationships in the region. Each bilateral relationship is studied from both sides of the coin, i.e., by scholars from within and outside China. This project explores the divergent perspectives between

---

[*]This chapter was originally printed as "Discerning China's Bilateral Relations in the Indo Pacific: Views from China and the Region." *The China Review*, Vol. 23, No. 1 (2023): 1–10. https://www.jstor.org/stable/48717986. Reproduced with kind permission of CUHK Press.

xiv *Introduction*

Chinese scholars and non-Chinese experts on the same bilateral relationship in a pairwise fashion. The insights provided by this study will enrich our understanding of strategic dynamics during the period of potential order transition in the Indo-Pacific against the backdrop of U.S.–China strategic competition.

The rise of China has generated intense strategic competition between the United States (U.S.) and China in the global context. The COVID-19 pandemic, the ongoing Ukrainian War, and the possibility of a global economic recession have further accelerated the potential shift in the international system's order. The U.S. under former President Donald Trump highlighted the Indo-Pacific concept in its 2017 National Security Strategy document and launched an official Indo-Pacific Strategy in 2019 in order to countervail Chinese power and influence in the region. For Chinese leaders, America's Free and Open Indo-Pacific (FOIP) strategy is perceived as an attempt to contain China's rise. The Biden administration has not altered the course of the U.S.–China strategic competition, although it claimed that it would not follow Trump's approach toward China.

In September 2021, the U.S. formed a new military pact—AUKUS—with Australia and the United Kingdom. This represents the latest military initiative by the U.S. against China's expanding military reach in the Indo-Pacific region. While serving as the speaker of the U.S. House of Representatives, Nancy Pelosi visited Taipei in early August 2022, triggering stark opposition from Beijing, which resulted in large-scale military exercises around Taiwan. The Taiwan Policy Act (TPA) proposed by the U.S. might put the bilateral relationship between the U.S. and China on a collision course. The future of the Taiwan Strait will be under the shadow of domestic politics in both China and the U.S. The continuous deterioration of U.S.–China relations has the potential to plunge the whole world into a new Cold War, despite both parties' declarations of intent to avoid such a dangerous confrontation.[1]

The Indo-Pacific region has become a new focal point of the U.S.–China rivalry. Despite the ongoing war between Russia and Ukraine, U.S. policymakers continue to label China as "America's most consequential geopolitical challenge" in the latest Biden–Harris administration's National Security Strategy, released in October 2022. This is so because China is "the only competitor with both the intent to reshape the international order and, increasingly, the economic, diplomatic, military, and technological power to do it."[2] Consequently, the U.S. will "shape the strategic environment around Beijing to advance our vision for an open and inclusive international system."[3]

It is true that, under Xi Jinping, China has changed its previous foreign policy of "keeping a low profile" to one focused on "striving for achievement."[4] China's ambitious, but controversial, Belt and Road Initiative (BRI) has raised eyebrows in many Western countries, especially the U.S. Consequently, in order to counter China's BRI, the U.S. launched the Build Back Better World (B3W) partnership with the other G7 countries in June 2021, focusing on investments in infrastructure and socioeconomic development projects for the developing world in the coming years.[5] China's so-called "wolf warrior" diplomacy is also perceived as a manifestation of its revisionism against the current international order.[6] The future of the Indo-Pacific region in particular and the international order in general largely depends on the strategic competition between the U.S. and China.

Compared with the U.S., China is at the center of the gravity of Indo-Pacific security and prosperity, a position attributed not only to its geographical location but also to its bourgeoning economic and military power. To a certain extent, the manner in which China engages with the U.S. and other major players in the Indo-Pacific will shape the nature and process of the international order transition, either peacefully or confrontationally, into the future. In the short term, most states in the region might want to hedge their bets between the U.S. and China, as this will maximize their security and economic interests.[7] In the long term, however, all key players in the region, especially ASEAN, Australia, India, and Japan, might have to pick sides between the two giants, although it is not in their interests to do so. Alternatively, they might choose the third path, which involves playing a more independent role by avoiding the antagonism between the U.S. and China, similar to how non-aligned countries operated during the Cold War.[8] However, the extent to which they can maintain distance from the two great powers remains a debatable question.

Bilateral Relations Matter

This volume aims to examine the dynamics of a potential order transition in the Indo-Pacific against the background of U.S.–China strategic competition through a unique bilateral-relation perspective. International relations, in essence, are about the "relations" among states, with bilateral xvi *Introduction*

relationships, in particular, serving as the basic building blocks of all the "relations." Some scholars even suggest that more attention should be paid to the "relations" instead of "states" in the "relational turn" of international relations theory.[9] Here, we adopt a more epistemological, rather than ontological, view, recognizing the coexistence of both "states" and "relations." More importantly, we highlight the significant, but sometimes neglected, role of bilateral relationships among states in shaping the dynamics of security and prosperity in the region.

As mentioned before, we positioned China as the center of gravity in the Indo-Pacific region. This project, therefore, focuses on exploring China's bilateral relations with other key players in the Indo-Pacific. China's rise will first and foremost affect its bilateral relations with other players in the region. Should China rise peacefully, its bilateral relations with other nations would be stable and prosperous. On the contrary, should China's rise prove to be confrontational, its bilateral relations are likely to be strained and troubled.[10] By examining China's bilateral relationships with key regional players, we can make sense of the implications of China's rise in the regional order, especially during the potential order transition period. More importantly, how China perceives its bilateral relations may differ from how other countries view theirs with China. The convergence and divergence of perceptions and policies between China and the rest of the world will reflect both opportunities and challenges brought by the rise of China in the Indo-Pacific region.

By inviting leading scholars from China and abroad, this project systematically examines China's key bilateral relations with the five major players in the Indo-Pacific: the U.S., Japan, India, Australia, and ASEAN. Each bilateral relationship is studied from both sides of the coin, i.e., by scholars from inside and outside China. This project does not aim to find convergent views between Chinese and non-Chinese scholars, although this might happen at times. The major task of this project is to explore the divergent perspectives between Chinese scholars and non-Chinese experts on the same bilateral relationship in a pairwise fashion.

Readers are encouraged to independently compare and contrast the distinctive views of a Chinese scholar and a non-Chinese scholar on a specific bilateral relationship. They may or may not reach the same conclusion due to their own theoretical inclinations and empirical experiences. However, the academic insights generated from this intellectual exercise will contribute to our understanding of the complexity of China's bilateral relationships in the region as well as shed some light on the

Introduction xvii

implications of China's rise for a potential order transition in the Indo-Pacific region.

A Glance at Key Arguments

The first theoretical chapter by Feng Liu and Kai He unpacks the concept of bilateral relationship through two of its dimensions: identity and behavior. The identity feature refers to "rivalry" or "partnership," while the behavioral one means "cooperative" or "competitive" action. They innovatively typologize four types of bilateral relationships: competitive rivalry, cooperative rivalry, competitive partnership, and cooperative partnership. Taking these four types of bilateral relationships as dependent variables, they introduce an interest–threat nexus model to explain under what conditions China will establish a specific bilateral relationship with key players in the region. In particular, they argue that the perceptions of heightened threat and diminished economic interest have shaped a competitive rivalry between China and the U.S. under the Trump administration. This bilateral relationship has not changed since Biden came to power in early 2021. Historical issues and territorial disputes have placed the China–Japan relationship as one oscillating between cooperative and competitive rivalries.

The border disputes and strategic competition in South Asia have changed the China–India relationship from a previously cooperative partnership to a competitive rivalry under Modi. The high-level threat perceptions between Australia and China have driven their bilateral relationship toward competitive rivalry, despite the highly complementary economic and trade structures between the two countries. Their "interest–threat nexus" model suggests that how China behaves matters in shaping the perceptions of others regarding both threats from and shared interests with China. How to utilize its diplomatic means to alleviate threat perceptions and increase shared interests with regional actors will be the toughest task for the Chinese government in the future.

Two chapters on China–U.S. relations written by Minghao Zhao from China and Andrew Scobell from the U.S. examine the strategic competition between the two nations from different perspectives. While Zhao focuses on U.S.–China competition and rivalry in the infrastructure arena, with China's BRI as a focal point, Scobell examines how perceptions and misperceptions shape the strategic competition between the two states in

xviii *Introduction*

multiple dimensions and arenas. Both share a relatively pessimistic view that U.S.–China relations have taken a turn toward "competitive rivalry."

However, Zhao points out that the infrastructure competition between these two powers is not necessarily a zero-sum game. The "good competition" can bring benefits to the regional countries and open up more opportunities for U.S.–China collaboration with third parties. Scobell argues that for qualitative improvement in U.S.–China relations, the two states need to directly address their mutual hostility, misperceptions, and negative images. This, however, seems to be an extremely difficult task in the immediate future.

Two chapters on China–Japan relations are contributed by Zheng Chen and Guangtao Wang from China and Rumi Aoyama from Japan. While Chen and Wang's chapter focuses on China's assessments and policy responses toward the Japan's FOIP concept and strategy, Aoyama examines Japan's delicate foreign policy strategies toward China. Chen and Wang suggest that Chinese officials and analysts have tried to carefully differentiate Japan's Indo-Pacific strategy from America's. However, the COVID-19 pandemic and the recent domestic changes in Japan and the U.S. have further complicated geopolitical and geoeconomic tensions between China and Japan.

Aoyama introduces a modified strategic triangle model that positions Japan–China relations within the strategic interplay between Japan, China, and the U.S. Her analysis suggests that the asymmetry of threat perceptions among the three players—with Japan perceiving China as its most significant security concern and China perceiving its greatest security threat emanating from the U.S.—gives Japan strategic leverage over China. Consequently, Japan can maintain ostensibly stable but substantially fragile relations with China. It is clear that the two chapters share a similar view regarding the rival nature and competitive orientation of the bilateral relationship between China and Japan.

The two chapters on China–India relations are written by Li Li from a Chinese perspective and by Harsh Pant and Shounak Set from an Indian viewpoint. Li examines how the U.S. factor has played an important role in shaping China–India relations, especially in the context of the 2020 Galwan Valley border dispute. Li argues that since the U.S. has identified China as a strategic competitor and introduced the Indo-Pacific strategy, India has significantly tilted toward the U.S. and embraced the Quadrilateral Security Dialogue (Quad). Consequently, China has gradually perceived India as a threat to its security. The mutually enhanced threat perceptions between China and India in the context of U.S.–China strategic competition might entrap China and India into a dangerous, hard-balancing, competitive course in the future.

In a similar vein, Pant and Set also highlight that the 2020 Galwan Valley clash between India and China marks a turning point in shaping the Indian elite and public opinion toward China. However, they argue that India's main approach to dealing with China's security challenge has been "internal balancing," i.e., strengthening its national capabilities, instead of "external balancing"—forming alliances. According to their analysis, India's involvement in the Quad is ambiguous and evasive in nature. Although both chapters envision a competitive direction in India–China relations in the future, they hold different views on how the two countries will compete.

The two chapters on China–Australia relations are contributed by Fangyin Zhou from China and Bates Gill from Australia. Both chapters focus on explaining the dramatic downward spiral of the bilateral relationship after 2016. Zhou examines how Chinese scholars perceive the reasons for the deterioration of bilateral relations, attributing them to U.S. influence and pressure on Australia, Australia's unique threat and interest perceptions of China, and Australia's domestic political factors. In addition, China's limited economic coercion also contributes to the deterioration of bilateral relations.

Taking a neoclassical realist perspective, Gill argues that Australia's distrustful and defensive policies toward China are rooted in changes in the international power structure driven by the rise of China, as well as the transitional impacts of these structural changes on Australian domestic norms, worldviews, processes, and incentives. As Gill mentions, for the Australian public, Beijing's actions at home and abroad, including those directly targeting Australians, are the primary factors contributing to the downward shift in bilateral relations.

Zhou and Gill not only disagree on the key reasons for the worsening relationship between China and Australia in recent years but also hold slightly different views on future bilateral relations. Zhou appears somewhat optimistic about a relatively stable bilateral relationship between China and Australia in the future under the Labor Government, although it has yet to materialize at present. In comparison, Gill anticipates troubled bilateral relations, characterized by a prolonged period of tension and distrust between the two nations in the future.

The last two chapters focus on China's relationships with ASEAN states, written by Ruonan Liu from China and Ja Ian Chong from

Singapore. From a Chinese perspective, Liu examines China's different strategies toward ASEAN, including the self-restraint and strategic reassurance policies from the 1997 Asian financial crisis to 2000, as well as the wedging strategy between ASEAN and the U.S., after 2010. Liu argues that the primary goal of China's foreign policy toward ASEAN is to reduce the possibility of ASEAN countries embracing the U.S.' FOIP strategy of countervailing China's influence and power in the region. China, however, faces three challenges: ASEAN's desire for China to accept its outlook on the Indo-Pacific, the emergence of a quasi-alliance under the FOIP framework, and the weakening friendly sentiment toward China in ASEAN societies. According to Liu, the future ASEAN states' attitudes and policies toward China mainly depend on whether China can win over the trust of Southeast Asian governments and people.

According to Chong, the ASEAN–China relationship might be considered the most difficult bilateral relation to analyze in this collection simply because ASEAN comprises 10 countries. It remains a debatable question whether ASEAN can exercise agency as a unit in dealing with China. Challenging the popular hedging argument in explaining ASEAN states' policy behavior toward China, Chong argues that ASEAN's current behavior toward China features a certain haphazardness that differs from the more considered and concerted action of hedging. ASEAN states face challenges in achieving consensus on adopting a unified position toward outside powers, including China. Through an examination of both historical and contemporary cases, Chong suggests that ASEAN member states are more likely to overcome coordination problems when engaging China on less contentious issues and when they agree on focal points establishing clear pathways for cooperation.

China's Bilateral Relations in Perspective

China's rise is a defining political event for world politics in the 21st century. How China develops bilateral relationships with its neighbors in the Indo-Pacific will shape the security and prosperity of the region as well as the nature and outcome of a potential transition in the international system's order. This volume sheds some light on the diverse and complex nature of the bilateral relations between China and five key players (the U.S., Japan, India, Australia, and ASEAN) in the Indo-Pacific. It is not our intention to find consensual views between scholars within and outside

Introduction xxi

China on a specific bilateral relation. Instead, we highlight the importance of adopting pluralistic and eclectic approaches in examining bilateral relations between China and its neighboring states.

Some takeaways are worth noting. A bilateral relationship between two countries is not solely determined by either side, regardless of any asymmetry in power between them. However, a country's adverse attitude and aggressive policy toward another will inevitably have negative impacts on the bilateral relationship between the two. More importantly, a strained and troubled bilateral relationship, if not properly managed or promptly fixed, is more likely to fall into a downward spiral, as we have seen from China and Australia in recent years.

The agency of regional actors under the Sino–U.S. strategic competition is an issue that merits more attention. Though a particular bilateral relationship between China and a regional actor may largely be shaped by structural forces such as power transition or U.S. pressure, some chapters in this volume reveal that regional middle and small powers also try to seize opportunities to realize their own international as well as domestic agendas. As two great powers continue to pursue competitive economic, security, and technological initiatives, this may allow other states more room for maneuvering. The third-party issues could complicate the management of Sino–U.S. competition.

This volume illustrates the challenges and difficulties for China to forge a true "cooperative partnership" with others in practice, although China has rhetorically formed various partnerships with many countries. The structural power shift in the international system driven by the rise of China is one of the key variables in explaining the growing rivalry and competition between China and other states, especially with the U.S. In addition, how other leaders perceive and interpret China's rise, as either a threat or an opportunity, also plays an important role in shaping their bilateral relations with China. Amid the shifting power balance in the region, perception gaps over capabilities, interests, and appropriate strategies are naturally widening. Nevertheless, in order to ensure a conducive external environment for a peaceful rise, Chinese leaders must consider how to shape external perceptions and images of China's power and influence in the region. What China says on the world stage is certainly important. However, other states pay more attention to what China does. Fine-tuning its policy behavior to reshape other countries' perceptions and images regarding its rise is the key for China to go ahead and forge true cooperative partnerships with others, including the U.S.

xxii *Introduction*

Endnotes

1 A. Blinken, "The administration's approach to the People's Republic of China," Speech delivered at the George Washington University, 26 May 2022. https://www.state.gov/the-administrations-approach-to-the-peoples-republic-of-china/; The Ministry of Foreign Affairs of China, "Wang Yi delivers a speech at Asia Society," 23 September 2022. https://www.fmprc.gov.cn/eng/zxxx_662805/202209/t20220924_10770946.html.

2 The White House, *National Security Strategy*, October 2022. https://www.whitehouse.gov/wp-content/uploads/2022/10/Biden-Harris-Administrations-National-Security-Strategy-10.2022.pdf.

3 *CBS News*, "Blinken says China is greater long-term threat than Russia," 26 May 2022. https://www.cbsnews.com/news/blinken-says-china-is-greater-long-term-threat-than-russia/.

4 Xuetong Yan, "From keeping a low profile to striving for achievement," *The Chinese Journal of International Politics*, 7(2), 153–184 (2014).

5 The White House, "President Biden and G7 leaders launch build back better world (B3W) partnership," 12 June 2021. https://www.whitehouse.gov/briefing-room/statements-releases/2021/06/12/fact-sheet-president-biden-and-g7-leaders-launch-build-back-better-world-b3w-partnership/.

6 P. Martin, *China's Civilian Army: The Making of Wolf Warrior Diplomacy* (Oxford: Oxford University Press, 2021).

7 On hedging strategies by regional powers, see D. J. Lim and Z. Cooper, "Reassessing hedging: The logic of alignment in East Asia," *Security Studies*, 24(4), 696–727 (2015); J. D. Ciorciari and J. Haacke, "Hedging in international relations: An introduction," *International Relations of the Asia-Pacific*, 19(3), 367–374 (2019).

8 J. J. Carafano, M. Primorac and D. Negrea, *The New Non-aligned Movement*, The Heritage Foundation, 17 May 2022. https://www.heritage.org/global-politics/commentary/the-new-non-aligned-movement.

9 P. T. Jackson and D. H. Nexon, "Relations before states: Substance, process and the study of world politics," *European Journal of International Relations*, 5(3), 291–332 (1999).

10 B. Buzan, "China in international society: Is 'peaceful rise' possible?" *The Chinese Journal of International Politics*, 3(1), 5–36 (2010).

© 2025 World Scientific Publishing Europe Ltd.
https://doi.org/10.1142/9781800616318_0002

Chapter 1

China's Bilateral Relations, Order Transition, and the Indo-Pacific Dynamics[*]

Feng Liu[†] and Kai He[‡]

[†]*Tsinghua University, China*
[‡]*Griffith University, Australia*

The shifting balance of power and the growing strategic competition between China and the United States have accelerated the transition in the international system's order. The nature and process of the transition, whether peaceful or confrontational, largely depend on how China interacts with the United States and other regional players, especially Australia, Japan, and India. In this chapter, we introduce an "interest–threat nexus" model to shed light on why China has formed different types of bilateral relations with key players in the region. We argue that China's bilateral relations are shaped by two perceptual factors: security threats and economic interests. While the threat perception shapes the "identity" feature of the bilateral relationship as either a partnership or rivalry, the "behavioral" feature of the relationship—either cooperative or competitive in action—is largely influenced by the economic interests between the two countries. A systematic and nuanced analysis of China's

---

[*]This chapter was originally printed as "China's Bilateral Relations, Order Transition, and the Indo-Pacific Dynamics." *The China Review*, Vol. 23, No. 1 (2023): 11–43. https://www.jstor.org/stable/48717987. Reproduced with kind permission of CUHK Press.

bilateral relations with major regional players will help us understand the changing dynamics of the order transition in the Indo-Pacific.

The power transition between China and the United States (U.S.) has led to a gradual order transition in the Indo-Pacific region, which is further accelerated by the intensifying Sino–U.S. strategic competition in the context of COVID-19.[1] The process and outcome of a regional order transition are often shaped by two factors. The first is the nature of the competition between the ruling power or hegemon and a rising power. Whether the ruling state is willing to cede its dominance to the rising power and what strategies the rising power would adopt to compete for domination largely determine how the regional order transition would play out. The second factor is how other regional states react to the potential order transition. The legitimacy of a new order comes from the recognition and support of the members within the order. In other words, hegemony or any regional leadership needs to secure support from others. Therefore, the attitudes of other regional states toward the hegemon and the rising power will also affect the process and outcome of the order transition.

China's bilateral relationships with other powers are at the core of these two factors, shaping the order transition in the Indo-Pacific region. Besides the evolution of Sino–U.S. relations, bilateral relations between China and other major regional actors, especially Australia, Japan, and India, must also be considered when contemplating how the rise of China fosters the regional order transition. To a certain extent, the nature and process of the order transition, whether peaceful or confrontational, largely depend on how China interacts with the U.S. and other key players in the region. For example, if other regional powers support U.S. hegemony, China's efforts to reshape the regional order will face more hindrances. However, if others side with China to challenge U.S. hegemony, it will accelerate the order transition in the Indo-Pacific.[2]

Bilateral relations between China and the above key players have undergone dramatic changes over time. For example, China established a "constructive strategic partnership" with the U.S. in the 1990s. The U.S., under the Bush administration, encouraged China to become a "responsible stakeholder" after the 9/11 terrorist attacks. The two countries claimed to build a "constructive relationship of cooperation," but the word "strategic" was dropped from the official documents. During the Obama administration, China promoted a "new type of great power relationship" with the U.S. despite receiving the cold shoulder from the U.S. Former U.S. President Donald Trump waged a trade war with China, which was labeled as a "strategic competitor" of the U.S.

Defining and characterizing a bilateral relationship with a foreign country is simply not a matter of diplomatic rhetoric. Instead, it reflects the nature and expectations of the bilateral relationship. One of the most notable features of China's foreign policy is the so-called "strategic partnership diplomacy."[3] It is reported that China has established 18 types of "partnerships" with over 100 countries in the world, mostly since the early 2000s.[4] A bilateral relationship is a basic building block of international relations among states.[5] How to explain the nature and rationale of China's bilateral relationships beyond diplomatic rhetoric is the key to understanding the process and outcome of the order transition in the region. If China's relations with other states were characterized by partnership, the order transition among the states in the context of China's rise would more likely be peaceful than widely believed. However, if the relations were to feature rivalry, the order transition would more likely be conflictual in nature.

This chapter focuses on characterizing and explaining China's bilateral relationships with key powers in the Indo-Pacific. It suggests that China's bilateral relationships are a function of convergent or divergent threat perceptions and economic interests between China and other states. Depending on the levels of threat perception and economic interests, China's bilateral relations can be characterized as "cooperative partnership," "cooperative rivalry," "competitive partnership," or "competitive rivalry." We first introduce a typology of bilateral relationships and elaborate an "interest–threat nexus" framework of bilateral relations. We argue that perceptual changes in security threat and economic interest levels shape the evolution of a state's bilateral relationships with others. The perceptions of threat and interest are mutually constituted through the interaction between the two countries. Applying our "interest–threat nexus" framework, we conduct brief case studies to analyze China's bilateral relations with some key regional actors, including the U.S., Japan, India, and Australia. Finally, we suggest that China should consider how to reduce the security concerns of other powers and increase economic openness with them, including the U.S., so that the future order transition in the Indo-Pacific will unfold among partners instead of rivals.

1.1. Defining Bilateral Relations: An Analytical Framework

1.1.1. *Typologizing bilateral relations*

A state's bilateral relations with another state are not static. Rather, they will vary along with changes in the external environment and a state's perceptions. Two factors need to be considered when defining state-to-state relations. The first is the "identity" feature of the relationship, while the second is the "behavioral" feature of the relationship. Here, we borrow Alexander Wendt's definition of identity as a subjective "property of intentional actors that generates motivational and behavioral dispositions."[6] In other words, the identity of the relationship defines the fundamental nature of a country's relationship with others. It should be noted that this type of identity is also called "role identity," which exists "only in relation to Others" through an intersubjective process.[7] It means that a state's relationship with others is not solely determined by its own subjective perceptions. Instead, it is a mutually constitutive process of "Self" and "Others" between two countries.

According to Wendt, there are three cultures of anarchy, characterized by "enmity," "rivalry," and "friendship," rooted in the three philosophical views of Thomas Hobbes, John Locke, and Immanuel Kant, respectively.[8] These three anarchic cultures represent three types of relationships among states. We argue that the categories of enmity and friendship are too extreme in defining China's bilateral relationships with other countries, given its deep integration into international society. For example, NATO's Secretary-General Jens Stoltenberg recently stated, "We don't regard China as an adversary or an enemy."[9] Nevertheless, we do not rule out the possibility of China falling into deadly enmity or forging friendships with others in the future.

Therefore, we use two less extreme categories, "rival" and "partner," to define the "identity" feature of bilateral relationships in this research. Rivalry means that two countries view each other as threats, especially in the security domain, because security is the primary concern of states in anarchy.[10] Although some security threats might not seriously threaten a state's survival in the international system, the existence of any security threat tends to cause two states to treat each other as rivals instead of partners. On the other hand, if there is no or a low-level security threat, the bilateral relationship between two countries can be categorized as "partnership," which means they can co-exist within the anarchic international system.[11]

The other factor in defining the bilateral relationship is its "behavioral" feature, which can be categorized as either "cooperation" or "competition." This division signifies the bilateral tendencies in coordinating the pursuit of their national interests, as manifested in the policy approaches of conformity and conflict resolution. As Robert Keohane clarifies, "discord sometimes prevails even when common interests exist."[12] He also notes that "[c]ooperation occurs when actors adjust their behavior to the actual or anticipated preferences of others, through a process of policy coordination."[13] Competition, on the other hand, means that conflicting policies are adopted when an actor refuses or resists another party's efforts to coordinate their policies. It is worth noting that, by definition, the identity feature of a relationship might influence how states behave, i.e., either cooperate or compete, with one another. However, this does not mean that identity *determines* behavior. In other words, two rivals may cooperate in some arenas, while two partners might engage in serious competition on some issues.

For instance, both France and Germany are U.S. security allies and can be treated as partners of the U.S. However, both partners openly opposed the U.S. war with Iraq in 2003. Similarly, the U.S. has not hesitated to impose economic sanctions on its own allies, such as Japan and Canada. It is clear that a mere "partnership" does not preclude competition between two countries. On the other hand, although Trump openly labeled China as a strategic competitor or rival, he still sought cooperation with China in dealing with the nuclear crisis on the Korean Peninsula. In a similar vein, the Biden administration also openly stated that it would seek cooperation with China on the issue of climate change.[14] This means that cooperation can occur between two rivals.

Based on the "identity" and "behavioral" features of bilateral relationships, we can typologize four kinds of bilateral relationships between two states: competitive rivalry, cooperative rivalry, competitive partnership, and cooperative partnership, as shown in Table 1.1. Competitive rivalry refers to the most intense bilateral relationship between two countries in

Table 1.1   Typologies of bilateral relationships.

The behavioral feature The identity feature	Competition	Cooperation
Rival	Competitive rivalry	Cooperative rivalry
Partner	Competitive partnership	Cooperative partnership

our typology, as they not only harbor security threats to each other but also compete with one another. However, as previously mentioned, two rivals can also cooperate in some areas to form a cooperative rivalry. A partnership implies little or no security threat. However, two partners can either cooperate or compete with one another as cooperative or competitive partners. Indeed, compared to competitions between rivals, those between partners are usually short-lived, feature fewer agendas, or are less intense. In short, those traits mandate that partners are less likely to become rivals due to competition. Accordingly, constrained by the competitive nature of the bilateral relationship, cooperation between rivals cannot be as extensive and deep as that between partners.

Three caveats are worth noting. First, these four types of bilateral relationships represent a set of ideal and intermediate relationships against the background of globalization and economic interdependence. This does not deny that states can view each other as adversaries or even enemies in world politics. If a state faces an existential threat from another, it typically considers the threatening state as its enemy. For example, in the eyes of North Korea, the U.S. might be viewed as an enemy because it threatens the survival of the regime. An adversarial relationship is situated between enmity and rivalry because it embodies less antagonism than enmity but more confrontational elements than rivalry. To simplify our model, we exclude enmity and adversariness from our typology, treating both as extended and extreme forms of rivalry.

In a similar vein, we acknowledge that the behavioral feature of bilateral relationships does not only include cooperation and competition. Two states can engage in confrontation and alienation. While confrontation means that the two states resort to conflict to resolve disputes, alienation refers to a situation in which two states stay away from one another with limited engagement. Again, we treat both confrontation and alienation as two extremes in our analysis, excluding them from our typology. Our typological model of bilateral relations aims to explain China's bilateral relationships with key states in the Indo-Pacific. Since the end of the Cold War, China has not engaged in military conflict with others, and the interactions between China and other regional states can hardly be characterized as confrontational, despite some diplomatic and even military tensions in disputed territories. Similarly, alienation does not apply to China's bilateral relationships because of its deep integration into international society. Therefore, our model does not include confrontation or alienation, although we do not rule out, either in theory or practice, the possibility of two countries engaging in such behaviors toward one another.

Moreover, the two sides may have different perceptions of the bilateral relationship. Bilateral relations between states are usually composed of interactive processes with different agendas. Differences in the priorities of national interests and the distinctive features of domestic political institutions may lead to different positionings of bilateral relations as conceived by each party. Even if one party regards the other as a cooperative partner, the latter may still view the former as a competitive rival. Out of these cognitive and perceptual differences, the eventual type of bilateral relations will be shaped by the diplomatic interactions between the two states.

1.1.2. An "interest–threat nexus" model of bilateral relations

These four types of bilateral relationships can be seen as the four variations of the dependent variable (DV) in this research. Here, we introduce an "interest–threat nexus" model to explain why a state forges different bilateral relations with others. Applying a rationalist approach, we highlight two factors that shape a state's bilateral relations. The first is common interests, which are the basis for cooperation.[15] Only when the two states share common interests can they cooperate with one another and positively drive their bilateral relations. Here, we emphasize economic interests while recognizing the importance of other interests, such as political and ideological ones.[16] Without common interests, two states will remain competitive with one another because of the anarchic nature of the international system, in which states inevitably rely on themselves.

The second factor is threat perception, which shapes the "identity" or nature of the relationship.[17] If one state regards another as a threat to its national security or survival in the international system, their relationship is more likely to become a rivalry. If this threat perception worsens, the two states might become involved in adversarial relations or even enmity. Some may argue that the economy and security are not independent of one another. Indeed, in some cases, the economy is closely related to security, and policymakers might securitize some economic issues in bilateral relations.[18] However, economy and security are distinctive goals for a state. While security mainly refers to the survival of a state against possible military invasion from others in the international system, the economic

8   *F. Liu & K. He*

Table 1.2.   Economic interest, security threat, and bilateral relations.

Perceptions of security threat \ Perceptions of economic interest	High	Low
High	1 Cooperative rivalry	2 Competitive rivalry
Low	3 Cooperative partnership	4 Competitive partnership

goal focuses on the well-being and development of a state concerning its own population. States need to maintain domestic development and social stability through economic progress. Under certain circumstances, a state might even choose to maintain vital economic ties with an enemy posing grave threats to its security.[19] That is why we choose to distinguish a state's security from its economic goals in our "interest–threat nexus" model, although we acknowledge that some economic behaviors could be securitized in practice.[20]

Both economic interests and threat perceptions are coded as high or low. As Table 1.2 shows, the interplay between economic interests and threat perceptions shapes a state's bilateral relationships. It is worth noting that both these factors are examined through perceptual lenses. It means that how a state defines its bilateral relationships is primarily shaped by its *perceptions* of economic interests and security threats regarding others. According to Stephan Walt's balance of threat theory, power, geographic proximity, and offensive capabilities are the main sources of threats.[21] Although these are material in nature, we argue that threat is a subjective perception of a state regarding others. In a similar vein, economic interests are also material in nature and relate to a state's economic development and trade structure in comparison with others. However, whether a state shares a high-level economic interests with another is not only driven by the material nature of their economies but also shaped by the perceptions of their leaders. For example, two countries might be natural trading and economic partners if their economies are highly complementary and inter-dependent. However, if one country refuses to *perceive* the common economic interests, it will not pursue a cooperative relationship with the other. Empirically, the current relationship between Australia and China might fall into this tragedy of manipulated perceptions, despite their materially complementary economic interests.

Table 1.2 indicates how a state's perceptions of economic interests and security threats shape its bilateral relations with others. Cell 1 refers to a situation in which a state perceives high-level security threats but, at the same time, high-level economic interests regarding the other state. The high-level security threats will make the other country a rival to this state. However, the high economic interests encourage them to cooperate. Therefore, this state is more likely to form a "cooperative rivalry" relationship with the other state in this high-threat and high-economic-interest situation.

Cell 2 indicates a situation in which a state perceives high security threats and low economic interests regarding the other state. Of course, the high level of threat perceptions make them rivals by nature, while the low level of economic interests encourage more competition than cooperation between the two. Therefore, it is more likely that these two countries will form a "competitive rivalry" relationship.

Cell 3 represents a scenario in which a country perceives a low level of security threat but a high level of economic interest. The low-level threat perceptions lead them to become partners instead of rivals. The high-level economic interests encourage more cooperation between the two. Therefore, in this low-security and high-economic-interest situation, the two countries are more likely to form a "cooperative partnership."

Cell 4 indicates a situation in which a country perceives a low level of security threat as well as a low level of economic interest. The low-level threat perceptions will encourage these two countries to develop partnership relations. However, the low-level economic interests might preclude more cooperation between the two. Consequently, these two countries might engage in a "competitive partnership" because of the natural tendency of states under anarchic conditions toward self-help and self-interest.

It is worth noting that this "interest–threat nexus" model of relationship mainly focuses on examining how mutual perceptions of threat and economic interests shape different types of bilateral relations between two states. A bilateral relationship is an intersubjective process of mutual constitution of "Self" and "Others" between two countries. It means that the establishment of any relationship is built on two countries' joint policy efforts. If country A tries to form a cooperative partnership with country B, but the latter refuses to respond in a similar way, then we will see a perception gap between the two regarding their bilateral relations. In other words, the bilateral relationship between these two will not reach the intended outcome of a cooperative partnership, as country A had expected. Simply put, convergent perceptions of economic interests and threats are prerequisites for establishing a certain type of bilateral relationship, as specified by the model. Divergent perceptions, on the other hand, will lead to a perception gap between two countries in their relationship, potentially causing misunderstandings and diplomatic tensions.

In addition to the perceptual differences between the two countries, a country's perceptions of security threats and economic interests might also evolve over time. There are two scenarios that can induce such changes. The first is leadership transition. As different leaders have different power sources, their preferences in foreign policy will also vary, leading to distinctive interpretations of the nature of national interests and threats. The second is a diplomatic or military crisis, which might alter the mutual perception of security threats and economic interests between two states. According to our "interest–threat nexus" model, shifting perceptions of states will lead to respective policy changes in bilateral relations.

Applying our model, we briefly examine China's bilateral relations with key players in the Indo-Pacific: the U.S., Japan, India, and Australia. For each case study, we discuss how the interplay of threat perceptions and economic interests has shaped the evolution of China's bilateral relationships with these key regional players. It is worth emphasizing that a state's perceptions of security threats and economic interests are mutually constituted through diplomatic behaviors and interactions with others. It means that a state's perception is not static, but dynamic in nature, shaped by interactive behaviors with others. In addition, we measure a state's threat perception by examining the public statements of leaders and high-ranking officials, as well as government documents. For the perception of economic interests, we also use some empirical data collected for analytical purposes.

1.2. Sino–U.S. Relationship: From Cooperative Partners to Competitive Rivals

In terms of the nature, or "identity," of the relationship, the Sino–U.S. relationship has evolved from enmity to partnership during the Cold War era. China was a *de facto* ally of the U.S. against the Soviet Union in the 1980s. In the post-Cold War period, China's strategy of integrating into the international system corresponded with the U.S.' engagement policy toward China. However, since 2012, the Sino–U.S. strategic competition has intensified. China's bilateral relations with the U.S. have been shaped by changing perceptions of security threats and economic interests between the two.

During Obama's first term, the two states maintained a cooperative partnership because of their shared low-level threat perceptions and high-level economic interests. In April 2009, the leaders of the two states held their first meeting on the sidelines of the G20 London Summit and agreed to work together to build a positive, cooperative, and comprehensive China–U.S. relationship for the 21st century.[22] In the 2010 *National Security Strategy*, the Obama administration welcomed China's role as a responsible stakeholder, cooperating with the U.S. and the international community on issues such as economic recovery and climate change.[23] Although the two countries had disputes over certain specific issues during this period, such as those discussed in the 2009 Copenhagen Climate Conference, their mutual threat perception remained at a low level. As mentioned earlier, China proposed to build a "new type of great power relationship" with the U.S. during Xi's meeting with Obama in 2013. The first "new" aspect of China's proposal was to emphasize "no conflict, no confrontation" between the two nations.[24] The implication is that China did not expect a high-level security threat from the U.S. under the Obama administration.

The cooperative trend of Sino–U.S. bilateral relations during Obama's first term was also guided by their shared common interests. Economically, China has become increasingly integrated into the international economic order since the 2000s. Its large population has proved advantageous in the transformation of the international industrial structure. China has become the "world's factory," helping it to achieve rapid economic development. As the world's largest economy, the U.S. has deepened its economic ties with China. From 2007 to 2015, the total trade volume between China and the U.S. rose from US$302.1 billion to US$557 billion, with an annual growth rate of 10 percent. China became the largest trading partner of the U.S. in 2015, while the U.S. remained China's second-largest trading partner, the largest market for exports, and the fourth-largest market for imports. In terms of investment flows, China's investment in the U.S. shot up from US$460 million in 2008 to US$8.03 billion in 2015.[25] Overall, the two states were highly economically interdependent during this period.

Since Obama's second term, China's bilateral relations with the U.S. have gradually shifted from cooperative partnership to competitive rivalry, primarily due to changing threat perceptions between the two. The U.S. tends to view China as a "revisionist power" and a usurper of the U.S.-led global order. It thus shifted from the longstanding "rapprochement policy" to containment, which aims to curtail and wear down the rise of China.[26] In 2011, the Obama administration launched a "rebalance" policy for Asia, through which the U.S. strengthened its security alliances and military cooperation with countries around China.[27] Although Obama publicly assured China that the rebalance policy did not target it, Chinese leaders viewed it as a containment strategy against China's rise.[28] At the 2013 Shangri-La Dialogue, the U.S. Secretary of Defense stated that the U.S. would deploy 60 percent of its navy fleet and air power to the Asia-Pacific, a move that was seen as clearly targeting China. The 2015 *National Security Strategy* specifically posited that the U.S. "will manage competition from a position of strength while insisting that China uphold international rules and norms on issues ranging from maritime security to trade and human rights."[29] After Trump came to power, his 2017 *National Security Strategy* further identified China as a "strategic competitor."[30] As a leverage against Chinese competition, the Trump administration also recruited India into its geopolitical framework under the guidelines of the "Indo-Pacific Strategy," whose initiative was elaborated in the "U.S. Strategic Framework for the Indo-Pacific" of 2018 and the *Indo-Pacific Strategy Report: Preparedness, Partnerships and Promoting a Networked Region* of 2019. Furthermore, as one of the most important instruments under the "Indo-Pacific Strategy," the Trump administration rekindled and elevated the level of geopolitical partnership under the Quad, which boosted the security partnership between the U.S. and its regional allies and partners in an attempt to encircle China. Therefore, we can confidently argue that during Obama's second term and the Trump administration, China and the U.S. became rivals instead of partners.

At the same time, economic interests between the two countries began to diverge, driving the behavioral feature of their bilateral relationship from "cooperation" to "competition," especially during the Trump administration. The first problem is the trade deficit. According to the U.S. Commerce Department, the gap between Chinese goods imported by the U.S. and American goods exported to China reached US$375.2 billion in 2017, accounting for 47 percent of the U.S. foreign trade deficit.[31] This huge trade deficit was an important reason for the U.S. to wage the trade war with China. The second problem is technological competition. The 2017 *National Security Strategy* accused China of stealing U.S. intellectual property worth hundreds of billions of dollars, thereby eroding U.S. competitive advantages in the long term.[32] As a result, the U.S. has stepped up efforts to suppress Chinese technology companies, for instance by prohibiting U.S. companies from selling components to the Chinese telecom firm ZTE and adding Huawei and its affiliates to the Entity List. The Trump administration also attempted to overhaul the global supply chain by promoting the "Economic Prosperity Network" to accelerate the economic decoupling process between China and the allies and partners of the U.S.[33]

Generally, since Obama's second term, Sino–U.S. bilateral relations have gradually experienced a transformation from cooperative partnership to competitive rivalry. The trade war initiated by the Trump administration further deepened the divergence of economic interests between the two. On the security front, the U.S. has cooperated closely with China with regard to counterterrorism. However, China's rapid rise and the relative decline of the U.S. after the Global Financial Crisis, combined with China's increasingly proactive strategic stance, have led the U.S. to increasingly perceive China as a potential threat.[34] Coincidentally, Chinese leaders have also been fully aware of the increasing threats from the U.S. toward China's own security and that of its regime, especially after some high-ranking officials in the Trump administration publicly criticized the political legitimacy of the Chinese Communist Party (CCP).[35]

After Biden came to power, the U.S. did not reset its relationship with China. While recognizing the immediate threat posed by Russia after the outbreak of the war in Ukraine, the U.S.' 2022 *National Security Strategy* still deems China as its "most consequential geopolitical challenge." Furthermore, the U.S. perceives a closer alignment between Beijing and Moscow as a challenge to the "rule-based order."[36] The U.S., as articulated in its *National Security Strategy* as well as various statements by high-level officials of the Biden administration, is set to engage in a long-term competition with China through both internal development and external alignment in the Indo-Pacific region and around the globe.[37]

In contrast to Trump's unilateral approach, coalition-building is a notable feature of the Biden administration's great-power competition strategy. The U.S. attempts to rally its allies and partners to form various counter-China coalitions across technological, economic, and military domains. For example, in the security realm, the Biden administration has formed AUKUS with the U.K. and Australia—a mechanism deemed by U.S. Indo-Pacific Affairs Coordinator Kurt Campbell as the "most important strategic innovation," in addition to bolstering existing security partnerships and mechanisms.[38] In the technological realm, Biden has also proposed to develop a "Chip 4" alliance and excluded China from the semiconductor supply chain.[39] Also noteworthy was NATO's designation of China as an adversary on the same level as Russia in its "Strategic Concept of 2022." These developments signified the U.S.' efforts to mobilize its European and Asian allies in countering the security challenges posed by China.

Finally, in the economic field, the Biden administration's proposal of the Indo-Pacific Economic Framework (IPEF) was the most essential move to counter China's influence. The four pillars of IPEF are "Connect Economy," "Resilient Economy," "Clean Economy," and "Fair Economy," all of which cover hot topics in the China–U.S. economic competition, including the areas of the digital economy, supply chains, and technology transfers. As the U.S. relinquished its membership in the Trans-Pacific Partnership (TPP) and considered the prospect of joining the Comprehensive and Progressive Agreement for Trans-Pacific Partnership (CPTPP), it has groomed the IPEF as its economic game-changer; once activated, this could exclude China from the global economy and restore U.S. leadership in the Indo-Pacific. Undoubtedly, the Biden administration's de-risking approach has already produced effects in diversifying supply chains away from China and reducing outbound investments to China, especially in high-tech and sensitive sectors. Partially due to the worsening economic relationship, Mexico replaced China as the biggest U.S. trade partner in 2023 for the first time in twenty years. More importantly, the U.S. has continued to challenge China's core interests in Taiwan, Xinjiang, and Hong Kong. It seems that this competitive rivalry relationship between the two nations is likely to persist for a relatively long time unless they can change their threat perceptions as well as find new convergent economic interests.[40]

1.3. Sino–Japanese Relationship: Between Competitive and Cooperative Rivalries

Due to historical reasons, the territorial disputes between China and Japan in the East China Sea have not been effectively resolved. In the security domain, as a military ally of the U.S., Japan is also viewed by China as part of its security threats. Therefore, China and Japan have viewed each other as rivals since the end of the Cold War. However, as neighboring states, the two have also maintained close cooperation in the economic arena. Because of the relatively static security perceptions together with dynamic economic interest perceptions between the two countries, we have witnessed frequent alternations between competitive rivals and cooperative rivals between them in the 2000s.

The territorial disputes as a legacy of World War II have constantly hindered the development of bilateral relations as well as the establishment of mutual trust between China and Japan. As China surpassed Japan to become the world's second-largest economy in 2010, Japan's "strategic anxiety" and its perception of China as a threat have further intensified. In the *2013 Defense of Japan*, the Japanese Ministry of Defense contends that China's military activities in its surrounding waters and airspace "are a matter of concern for the region and the international community, including Japan."[41] Its *2016 Defense of Japan* further condemns China's actions in the East and South China Seas and expresses "great concerns over Chinese military activities."[42] In order to countervail China's rise, the Abe government primarily adopted three balancing strategies. The first is internal balancing by enhancing domestic military capabilities. In July 2014, the Abe administration proposed a resolution to lift the ban on the right to collective self-defense and ease restrictions on the development of military forces. The second strategy is external balancing by strengthening the U.S.–Japan alliance. In April 2015, Japan and the U.S. revised the Guidelines for Japan–U.S. Defense Cooperation. At the Japan–U.S. Summit Meeting in February 2017, the two states reaffirmed that Article 5 of the Japan–U.S. Security Treaty covers the Senkaku/Diaoyu Islands. Besides, Japan also escalated its level of security partnership with the Philippines and Vietnam, intending to pose a more formidable check on China regarding disputes in the South China Sea.[43] Third, Japan conducted institutional balancing by forging informal security institutions and sought to counter China's influence in the region. From 2015 to 2017, Japan signed a series of military cooperation documents with India, South Korea, Australia, and the U.K. In particular, it formed a quasi-alliance with Australia and revived the Quad—a security dialogue mechanism involving the U.S., Australia, and India.

Both the incumbent Kishida administration and its predecessor, the Suga administration, have deemed China as Japan's chief security threat.

Accordingly, in April 2021, Prime Minister Suga issued a joint statement with the U.S., chastising Chinese actions that "undermine the regional peace and prosperity of the Indo-Pacific."[44] Furthermore, at the Shangri-La Security Dialogue in June 2022, Prime Minister Kishida criticized China's efforts to change the status quo in the East China Sea, South China Sea, and Taiwan Strait in his remarks.[45] In its December 2022 *National Security Strategy*, the Kishida administration described China as "the greatest strategic challenge" for Japan and planned to significantly increase the defense budget in order to bolster its counterstrike capabilities.[46] Regarding their security strategies, both the Suga and Kishida administrations inherited policies from the previous Abe administration and sought to strengthen Japan's coordination with the U.S., on the one hand, and attempted to increase its military might, on the other hand.

In the eyes of Chinese leaders, Japan's security cooperation with the U.S. and its active security engagements with China's neighbors, especially India, are seen as a containment strategy against China's rise, thereby posing serious threats to China's national security. Therefore, the high-level threat perceptions between the two countries have engraved a mutual rivalry into the "identity" feature of their bilateral relationship.

As mentioned above, rivals can also cooperate, especially when they share common economic interests. Japan's economy was severely impacted by the Global Financial Crisis in 2008. While the "Abenomics" proposed by Shinzo Abe contributed to the recovery of the Japanese economy in 2013, it also resulted in the continuous depreciation of the yen as well as the widening of the fiscal deficit. In addition, Japanese economic circles expressed their dissatisfaction with the government in relation to the damage to Sino–Japanese economic relations. Hiromasa Yonekura, the then chairman of Japan Business Federation, said that the Japanese government had deeply harmed the friendly relations between the companies and people of Japan and China that had been built with painstaking efforts over many years.[47]

In this context, Abe recognized the common economic interests, especially the importance of economic cooperation with China for Japan's economic development. Japan's changing perceptions of economic interests with China are well reflected in its modified attitudes toward the Belt and Road Initiative (BRI) proposed by China. Japan had previously followed the U.S.' proposal to boycott the BRI and refused to join the Asian Infrastructure Investment Bank (AIIB). However, faced with the pressure of recovering the Sino–Japanese political relationship and the faltering

Japanese economy, Abe sent Toshihiro Nikai, secretary-general of the Liberal Democratic Party, as the prime minister's special envoy to attend the Belt and Road Forum for International Cooperation in May 2017, expressing hopes to enhance Sino–Japanese economic cooperation. In November 2017 and September 2018, large delegations of Japanese business and entrepreneurial groups visited China to discuss the possibility of strengthening China–Japan economic cooperation under the framework of the BRI. Thanks to the joint efforts of both sides, 52 deals worth US$18 billion were inked at the China–Japan Third-party Market Cooperation Forum held in October 2018, putting bilateral economic relations back on the track of cooperation.[48]

Although China and Japan resumed some economic cooperation, there remains an unreconciled problem between the two countries—the leadership contestation in the economic domain. As mentioned before, China's economic rise has encouraged it to take on a more important and even leadership role in regional financial and economic affairs.[49] In recent years, China has increased its investment in infrastructure construction in Southeast Asia. In 2015, China established the first China-led financial institution—the AIIB, which is seen as a direct challenge to U.S.-led global financial governance, especially the International Monetary Fund (IMF) and the World Bank. More importantly, the success of AIIB has cast a shadow over Japan's leadership status as well as the Asian Development Bank (ADB) in regional infrastructure financing. Before the AIIB, Japan had long been the largest source of investment, including infrastructure financing in the Asia-Pacific. The establishment of AIIB and China's increasing infrastructure investments through its BRI have inevitably challenged and even eroded Japan's influence in the region. Consequently, Japan launched its own version of infrastructure development aid with a total of US$110 billion in funding, openly confronting the AIIB. As the U.S. announced its withdrawal from the TPP, Japan took the initiative to finalize the CPTPP based on the existing framework of the TPP, aiming to control the formulation of trade regulations in the Asia-Pacific region. Japan played a major role in the Biden administration's intensified economic competition with China. Serving as an ardent supporter of the IPEF, Japan collaborated with the U.S. and its allies and partners to contain China across various domains, including semiconductors and global supply chains. Therefore, the leadership contestation between China and Japan in the economic and financial domain is expected to further intensify in the future.

The academic and policy circles have long used the phrase "hot economy, cold politics" to describe China–Japan relations, indicating that the two countries have a difficult political relationship but a positive economic relationship. In fact, this expression has oversimplified the dynamics of the Sino–Japanese relationship. Due to the conflicting interests, including territorial disputes and the strategic anxiety of Japan as a result of China's rise, the two states have often engaged in competition in the realm of security. Although they share some common economic interests, the economic leadership contestation also increases the competitive elements in their bilateral relations.[50] In addition, diplomatic tensions and maritime disputes have constantly resulted in adverse spillover effects on their economic cooperation. The economic relationship between the two countries is ambiguous and mixed with elements of both competition and cooperation. Therefore, China–Japan bilateral relations have often switched between competitive and cooperative rivalry.

1.4. Sino–Indian Relationship: From Cooperative Partners to Competitive Rivals

Since Narendra Modi came to power in 2014, Sino–Indian relations have experienced dramatic changes. Before the Doklam crisis in 2017, the threat perception between the two remained at a relatively low level. In addition, China and India engaged in active cooperation under a number of multilateral frameworks. India contributed US$8.4 billion to become a founding member of the AIIB at China's invitation. India was officially granted membership status at the Shanghai Cooperation Organization (SCO) Summit held in June 2017. As emerging powers, the two states stand in the same position in promoting reforms of international institutions such as the United Nations, the IMF, and the World Bank. During the meeting between President Xi Jinping and the then President Pranab Mukherjee in May 2016, the two states also agreed to "deepen China-India strategic cooperative partnership for peace and prosperity, and build a closer development partnership."[51] According to our framework, China–India relations before the Doklam crisis can be categorized as a cooperative partnership.

The bilateral relations took a nosedive after the Doklam crisis, with the 72-day border standoff at one point bringing the two nations close to war.[52] Although the crisis was resolved in the end, China and India remained suspicious of each other. In order to repair the ruptured bilateral relations, leaders from the two states met for an informal meeting in Wuhan, where they reached the "Wuhan consensus," providing strategic guidance for the improvement of bilateral relations. The consensus stressed that "both sides agreed to properly manage and control their differences. Both sides possess the maturity and wisdom to resolve their differences through peaceful discussions while respecting each other's concerns and aspirations."[53] Since then, the leaders of the two states have held bilateral talks at occasions such as the SCO Summit, the BRICS Summit, and the G20 Summit, fostering the recovery of China–India relations. However, the outbreak of conflict in the Galwan Valley in 2020 again seriously damaged the relationship. It is unlikely that the bilateral relationship will return to its previous cooperative partnership status after the Galwan standoff.

The dramatic changes in Sino–Indian relations are closely related to strategic shifts on both sides. Since 2012, China has been pursuing an outward-oriented strategy, especially through cooperation with many countries via the BRI. In South Asia, China has increased assistance to relevant states, including investments in infrastructure development. For example, China signed BRI memoranda of understanding (MoUs) with Bangladesh and Nepal, promising to provide funds for infrastructure construction. In April 2015, China launched the construction of the China–Pakistan Economic Corridor, and a 43-year lease of Gwadar Port in Pakistan was granted in September. In July 2017, China signed an agreement worth US$1.12 billion with Sri Lanka, which allowed China Merchants Port Holdings Company Limited to build and operate the Hambantota Port in Sri Lanka. The promotion of the BRI has comprehensively improved bilateral relations between China and South Asian states. China has not only become a major trading partner and source of foreign capital for these states but also provided them with a large amount of military equipment, thereby greatly enhancing its influence in South Asia.

From India's perspective, China's behavior in South Asia could potentially threaten its national security. As a traditional regional power, India has been striving to build an "Indian order" in South Asia and promote its own version of the Monroe Doctrine.[54] The rise of China's regional influence undoubtedly implies a decline in India's influence. Therefore, India has refused to support and join the BRI. Before the 2017 BRI Forum held in Beijing, the spokesperson of the Indian External

Affairs Ministry stated, "no country can accept a project that ignores its core concerns on sovereignty and territorial integrity."[55] Other than the concern about the China–Pakistan Economic Corridor passing through the India-claimed sovereignty, India worries more about China's increasing influence in the region. Moreover, India is concerned about the military implications of China's infrastructure construction in South Asian states for its own security. Ever since China launched its first overseas military base in Djibouti in July 2017, India has been increasingly wary of China's growing influence in the Indian Ocean. The construction of the Gwadar port has accelerated, India's concerns about China's potential military presence in the northern Indian Ocean and the Strait of Hormuz have intensified further, as this would threaten its national security and regional dominance.[56]

To balance against China's challenge, India has been actively developing closer relationships with regional countries.[57] Through economic plans such as the "Spice Route Project" and the "Asia–Africa Growth Corridor," the two major regional cooperation mechanisms—the Bangladesh, Bhutan, India, and Nepal (BBIN) Initiative and the Bay of Bengal Initiative for Multi-Sectoral Technical and Economic Cooperation (BIMSTEC)—as well as the Indian Ocean Rim Association (IORA), India seeks to compete with China for regional influence. India has also continuously strengthened its security cooperation with Indo-Pacific states. On the one hand, India has taken an active part in the U.S.-led containment of China via the Quad platform. On the other hand, it has also signed a series of security treaties with Japan, Australia, Singapore, and Indonesia as the "major military partner" of the U.S.

New Delhi's close security cooperation with China's neighboring countries has also raised security concerns in Beijing. In the eyes of Chinese leaders, India is seen as aiding the U.S. in containing China's rise. The Doklam crisis and the Galwan standoff have further ignited strong nationalism in China. There is no doubt that China possesses stronger national power than India. However, since China's national security priorities unequivocally lie in the western Pacific, India's resolve and focus on China are significantly stronger than those of China toward India. This asymmetric "resolve" seems to strengthen India's threat to China.[58] China's threat perceptions of India, therefore, have also reached a relatively high level, although the "Wuhan consensus" between Xi and Modi temporarily eased the diplomatic tensions between the two.[59] In recent years, these mutual high-threat perceptions have driven the change in bilateral relations between China and India from the previous partnership to a rivalry.

In the economic domain, China has been India's largest trading partner since 2007. The two states have had convergent economic interests for a long time. Economic ties between them have further tightened in the early days of the Modi administration. During Xi's visit to India in September 2014, China announced its plans to invest US$6.8 billion in building two industrial parks in India. Companies from the two states also signed 24 MoUs, worth a total of US$3.4 billion.[60] During Modi's visit to China in May 2015, the two sides signed 24 documents for cooperation, worth a total of US$22 billion. However, at the same time, the trade balance between China and India has become an increasingly prominent issue. In 2016, although bilateral trade between the two reached US$71.18 billion, India's trade deficit with China hit US$47.68 billion. India then realized that it needed to become more economically independent. During Modi's first term in office, India launched 54 anti-dumping investigations against China.[61] India also proposed "Supply Chain Initiative" with Japan and Australia while cooperating with the U.S. on supply chains via the framework epitomized by the IPEF.[62] Through these initiatives, India aims to alleviate its dependence on China and promote economic decoupling between the two. After the Galwan Valley conflict, India stepped up efforts to restrict trade with China by suspending customs clearance of Chinese goods, banning hundreds of Chinese mobile apps, speeding up anti-dumping investigations against China, and prohibiting Chinese companies from bidding for infrastructure projects in India. It seems that the diplomatic and military crises have influenced India's perceptions of economic interests with China. The previous cooperative economic ties have been hindered by some competitive sentiments and policies.

To sum up, in light of the BRI project as well as the unresolved border disputes, India has regarded China as a threat to its security. Similarly, India's security cooperation with the U.S., Japan, and other neighboring countries of China has also increased the threat perceptions of China toward India. With the rising trade deficit between China and India, the previously shared economic interests have been overshadowed by trade restrictions and disputes. This situation has further deteriorated due to the rising nationalism in each state following conflicts resulting from territorial disputes. Therefore, according to our model, China and India have transitioned from being cooperative rivals to competitive rivals, and this relationship may continue in the future.

1.5. Sino–Australian Relationship: From Cooperative Partners to Competitive Rivals

Under the broad context of regional power transition and Sino–U.S. strategic competition, the relationship between China and Australia has gone through several phases. From 2007 to 2015, the bilateral relationship was fairly stable and friendly. Both sides agreed to "foster a strategic partnership built upon mutual trust and mutual benefit" and "build an annual meeting mechanism between their prime ministers" during the meeting between President Xi and Australian Prime Minister Julia Gillard in April 2013.[63] The bilateral relationship was then upgraded to a "comprehensive strategic partnership" in November 2014, serving as guidance for future cooperation. The two states further deepened their economic cooperation. Australia announced that it would join the AIIB in March 2015 and signed a free-trade agreement with China in June 2015. Since there were no conflicting core interests between China and Australia and China's rising economic development had also provided Australia with many opportunities, the two states strengthened their cooperation in an all-round way. The bilateral relationship during this period could be defined as a cooperative partnership. From 2015 onward, under the Turnbull and Morrison administrations, the Sino–Australian relationship has seriously deteriorated from a partnership with little or no security threats to a rivalry with substantial threats.

Until the end of Abbott's term, according to our model, China–Australia relations remained a cooperative partnership because of the mutual perceptions of low-level security threats and high-level economic interests. During the Turnbull and Morrison administrations, Australia's security perceptions of China began to change. Not only did it start to regard China as a security threat, but it also began to change its previously positive attitudes toward China in the economic realm. Although Australia still regarded China's economic development as an opportunity, it gradually became concerned about China's investments. The Australian government increased its scrutiny of Chinese investments and canceled several Chinese investment deals, which has led to a huge decline in Chinese investment in Australia.[64] More importantly, Australia started to view China's behavior in recent years as a threat to regional security, the stability of the international order, and Australia's political security. The government's *2017 Foreign Policy White Paper* regarded China as challenging the U.S., which "has been the dominant power in our region throughout

Australia's post-Second World War history."[65] In June 2017, Prime Minister Turnbull criticized China for implementing the Monroe Doctrine in Asia.[66] In December, Turnbull openly condemned China for interfering with Australia's domestic affairs and declared that "Australia will stand up to China" in Mandarin.[67] In June 2018, the Australian Parliament passed resolutions on counter espionage and foreign interference, as well as the Foreign Influence Transparency Scheme Act.

In late 2019, Australia's Home Affairs Minister Peter Dutton publicly criticized the CCP, "accusing it of conduct 'inconsistent' with Australian values," as well as for "cyber-attacks, theft of intellectual property, and undue influence at universities."[68] During the pandemic, Foreign Minister Marise Payne publicly questioned China's transparency on the COVID-19 outbreak and announced that Australia would push for an investigation into the origins and spread of COVID-19 in April 2020.[69] In the security arena, Australia has devised multiple ways to balance against China. On the one hand, it has strengthened its relationship with the U.S. It proposed to work with the U.S. and Papua New Guinea to upgrade the Lombrum naval base on Manus Island to counter the multi-use port facility built by China there. Australia also coordinated its cooperation with the U.S. in security via multilateral policy frameworks, including Quad and AUKUS. On the other hand, Australia has also strengthened its ties with Japan. It signed the Reciprocal Access Agreement and established a quasi-alliance with Japan in order to contain China.[70]

Australia's negative views on and balancing strategies against China received strong responses from China. Regarding Australia's accusations of China's interference in its affairs, the Chinese government called them "shocking and baseless."[71] China also criticized Australia's call for an open investigation into the origin of COVID-19, labeling it a "political attack" aimed at the legitimacy of the CCP. Hu Xijin, the then chief editor of the leading Chinese newspaper *Global Times*, attacked Australia on his Weibo social media account by referring to it as "chewing gum stuck on the sole of China's shoes" because "Australia is always there, making trouble."[72] Partially as a response to Canberra's obvious balancing actions, Beijing has increased its strategic involvement in Australia's neighborhood, the South Pacific Islands. The recent security cooperation pact between China and the Solomon Islands is a particular case which raises serious security concerns for Australia.

In sum, bilateral relations between China and Australia are largely shaped by the leaders' perceptions of security threats and economic interests between the two countries. During the Rudd, Gillard, and Abbott administrations, China and Australia maintained all-round cooperative relations due to their shared perceptions of low-security threats and high economic interests, although the two countries held divergent views on specific issues, such as the South China Sea. The bilateral relationship during this period could be characterized as a cooperative partnership. During the Turnbull and Morrison administrations, Australia's threat perception of China gradually increased and expanded from the security realm to the economic realm. Consequently, the escalating diplomatic tensions have deepened the mutual perceptions of high-level security threats and low economic interests between the two countries. According to our model, bilateral relations between China and Australia have dropped from the previous cooperative partnership to competitive rivalry since the Turnbull administration. As Hugh White notes, Australia is now even more hostile toward China than states such as Japan.[73] The tension between China and Australia did not abate even after the ascension of the newly elected Albanese administration. On the contrary, Albanese openly stated that his government would not respond to China's four points of instruction on alleviating bilateral tensions and stated that the sole guideline of Australia's China policy was its national interest.[74] This stance implies that the incumbent Australian administration is expected to continue the tough approach toward China inherited from its predecessors. In the foreseeable future, this competitive rivalry relationship between China and Australia will continue, despite their economic structures remaining highly complementary and interdependent in nature.

1.6. Conclusion

By introducing an "interest–threat nexus" model of bilateral relations, this chapter sheds some light on how China has formed different types of bilateral relationships with other key regional players. It argues that the perceptions of security threat and economic interests are two variables in accounting for the variations in different bilateral relations between China and others. China's bilateral relationship with the U.S. changed to competitive rivalry after Trump came to power and will remain the same during the Biden administration. The historical issues and territorial disputes have placed the China–Japan relationship somewhere between cooperative and competitive rivalry. The border disputes and strategic competition in South Asia have changed the China–India relationship from the previous cooperative partnership to competitive rivalry under Modi. The high-level threat perceptions between Australia and China have driven their bilateral relationship into competitive rivalry, despite the highly complementary economic and trade structures between the two countries.

As the China–U.S. strategic competition intensifies, China's relations with Japan, India, and Australia have also dived along the same downward trajectory. However, by contrast, Southeast Asian countries, including U.S. allies Thailand and the Philippines, still retain stable relations with China. Notably, the China–Philippines relationship significantly improved during the Duterte administration. Both sides not only successfully managed disputes over the South China Sea and established a bilateral consultation mechanism but also emphasized their economic and commercial partnership. The newly elected Marcus administration in the Philippines also openly announced the initiative to promote the development of China–Philippine relations. These staggering discrepancies between Southeast Asian countries and the U.S. in terms of their China policies carry a twofold meaning: first, they reflect that the regional security framework the U.S. aspired to build is yet to form a coordinated stance among its immediate and potential member states, resulting in apparent differences in terms of their China policies; second, such discrepancies are in part due to varying security concerns among U.S. regional allies and partners. For instance, powerhouses such as Japan, India, and Australia aspire to play leading roles in their affiliated regions, generating greater resentment to China's rise as their neighbor. On the contrary, Southeast Asian countries are reluctant to take sides and are more accommodating to the rise of China. Their stance affirms that China has acquired a certain amount of legitimacy to reshape the regional status quo in the process of regional power transition.

As a rising power, China is seen as a challenger to the existing regional order by default. It is rational for other states to view China as a challenger to the order or even a threat to their national security. However, how China behaves also matters in shaping the threat perceptions of others regarding its rise. To a certain extent, China has successfully alleviated the threat perceptions of some ASEAN states in the South China Sea through constant negotiations, consultations, and dual-track diplomatic efforts. In a similar vein, the Xi–Modi meeting in Wuhan after the Doklam crisis somewhat reset the bilateral relations, albeit temporarily. During their first in-person meeting at the G20 summit in Bali in November 2022, Xi and Biden agreed to resume some communication mechanisms that were cut off after the then U.S. House Speaker Nancy Pelosi's visit to Taiwan. Although these positive efforts to manage China–U.S. competition were temporarily halted by the Chinese balloon episode earlier in 2023, Xi and Biden's second face-to-face meeting in San Francisco accelerated the resumption of many dialogue channels between the two countries. How to utilize its diplomatic means to alleviate the threat perceptions of regional actors will be the most challenging task for the Chinese government in the future.

Shared economic interests remain the key for China in maintaining a cooperative relationship with other powers. Although many countries might view China as a rival presenting high security threats, they are still willing to cooperate with it in the economic arena. In other words, so long as rivals can still trade with one another, cooperative rivalry will be more peaceful than competitive rivalry. However, China–Australia relations suggest that we should not take economic interdependence between two countries as a given because political and diplomatic tensions can indeed poison and even damage economic ties. Therefore, it is important for China to continue reforming its domestic economic structure as well as to retain its openness in trade and investment. This economic attractiveness will then encourage others to pursue a cooperative rather than competitive relationship with China.

To a certain extent, the regional order transition is a process of changing dynamics of bilateral relationships among major powers in the Indo-Pacific. If all states treat each other as "competitive rivals," i.e., with high-threat and low-economic perceptions, the order transition is more likely to trigger military conflicts among great powers. Rivals can easily become adversaries and even enemies. However, if states treat each other as partners or even cooperative partners, the order transition among partners might be different and more peaceful than what has been widely perceived by power transition theorists throughout history.

Acknowledgment

This project is supported by the Australian Research Council (DP 210102843) and (DP230102158) and the United States Institute of Peace (USIP). The opinions, findings, and conclusions or recommendations expressed in this chapter are those of the authors and do not necessarily reflect the views of the USIP.

Endnotes

1 R. Haass, "The pandemic will accelerate history rather than reshape it," *Foreign Affairs*, 7 April 2020. https://www.foreignaffairs.com/articles/united-states/2020-04-07/pandemic-will-accelerate-history-rather-reshape-it; Kai He and Mingjiang Li, "Understanding the dynamics of the Indo-Pacific: US–China strategic competition, regional actors, and beyond," *International Affairs*, 96(1), 1–7 (2020).

2 It is worth noting that the U.S. and China are not the only actors that matter in the order transition process. Other powers might take a more independent role in shaping a "multiplex world order" after the U.S.-led liberal hegemony as Amitav Acharya suggests. See A. Acharya, "After liberal hegemony: The advent of a multiplex world order," *Ethics & International Affairs*, 31(3), 271–285 (2017).

3 Zhongping Feng and Jing Huang, "China's strategic partnership diplomacy: Engaging with a changing world," *Working Paper 8*, European Strategic Partnerships Observatory (2014); G. Struever, "China's partnership diplomacy: International alignment based on interests or ideology," *Chinese Journal of International Politics*, 10(1), 31–65 (2017).

4 China.org, "China-Russia partnership upgraded again, and what else is China's 'partners,'" 6 June 2019. http://guoqing.china.com.cn/2019zgxg/2019-06/06/content_74861984.html; *Xinhua Net*, "180 Countries has establishing diplomatic relations, 112 partnerships: China's friends are all over the world," 9 October 2020. http://www.xinhuanet.com/world/2020-10/09/c_1126586666.htm.

5 For the importance of relationality in international relations, see Chih-yu Shih, "Affirmative balance of the Singapore–Taiwan relationship: A bilateral perspective on the relational turn in international relations," *International Studies Review*, 18(4), 681–701 (2016); A. H. M. Nordin, G. M. Smith, R. Bunskoek, Chiung-chiu Huang, Yih-jye (Jay) Hwang, P. T. Jackson, E. Kavalski, L. H. M. Ling, L. Martindale, M. Nakamura, D. Nexon, L. Premack, Yaqing Qin, Chih-yu Shih and D. Tyfield, "Towards global relational theorizing: A dialogue between sinophone and anglophone scholarship on relationalism," *Cambridge Review of International Affairs*, 32(5), 570–581 (2019).

6 A. Wendt, *Social Theory of International Politics* (Cambridge: Cambridge University Press, 1999), p. 224.

7 *Ibid.*, p. 227.

8 *Ibid.*, Chapter 6.

9 R. Heath, O. Reingold and I. Noguchi, "NATO head: China is not an enemy," *Politico*, October 6, 2021. https://www.politico.com/news/2021/10/06/global-insider-nato-china-ties-515188.

10 K. N. Waltz, *Theory of International Politics* (Reading, Mass: Addison-Wesley, 1979), pp. 88–93.

11 Please note that here we assume that two countries always tend to perceive the nature of their bilateral relationship accordingly. In other words, our model leaves out the rare scenario where one perceives the relationship as rivalry and the other perceives partnership.

12 R. O. Keohane, *After Hegemony: Cooperation and Discord in the World Political Economy* (Princeton: Princeton University Press, 1984), p. 12.

13 *Ibid.*, p. 51.

14 J. Ruwitch, "U.S. and China agree to cooperate on climate crisis, despite fraught relationship," *NPR*, 20 April 2021. https://www.npr.org/2021/04/20/989015638/u-s-and-china-agree-to-cooperate-on-climate-crisis-despite-fraught-relationship.

15 Keohane (1984), *Op. cit.*; R. O. Keohane and J. S. Nye, *Power and Interdependence* (Boston: Longman, 2012); L. Martin, "Interests, power, and multilateralism," *International Organization*, 46(4), 765–792 (1992).

16 As Steve Chan claims, economic performance is the key element of elite legitimacy and regime survival for East Asian states, so economic interests can be the most important consideration for these countries to cooperate with China. See S. Chan, *Looking for Balance: China, the United States, and Power Balancing in East Asia* (Stanford: Stanford University Press, 2012).

17 S. M. Walt, *The Origins of Alliances* (Ithaca: Cornell University Press, 1994).

18 H. Farrell and A. L. Newman, "Weaponized interdependence: How global economic networks shape state coercion," *International Security*, 44(1), 42–79 (2019).

19 K. Barbieri and J. S. Levy, "Sleeping with the enemy: The impact of war on trade," *Journal of Peace Research*, 36(4), 463–479 (1999); A. Skonieczny, "Trading with the enemy: Narrative, identity and US trade politics," *Review of International Political Economy*, 25(4), 441–462 (2018).

20 Some scholars use the concept of the "economic-security nexus" when discussing the East Asian regional order, which mainly emphasizes the differentiation or integration of bilateral economic and security relations between regional countries, and is essentially a system-level concept. Our analysis of the "interest-security nexus," which is a unit level concept, focuses on how two countries' perceptions of economic interest and security threat shape bilateral relations. On "economic-security nexus," see T. J. Pempel, "Soft balancing, hedging, and institutional Darwinism: The economic-security nexus and East Asian regionalism," *Journal of East Asian Studies*, 10(2), 209–238 (2010); A. Goldstein and E. D. Mansfield (eds.) *The Nexus of Economics, Security, and International Relations in East Asia* (Stanford: Stanford University Press, 2012); Feng Liu and Ruonan Liu, "China, the United States, and order transition in East Asia: An economy-security nexus approach," *The Pacific Review,* 32(6), 972–995 (2019).

21 Walt (1994), *Op. cit.*, Chapter 2.

22 *Xinhua Net*, "Hu, Obama meet in London," 1 April 2009. http://www. xinhuanet.com/world/2020-10/09/c_1126586666.htm.

23 The White House, National Security Strategy 2010, p. 43. https://nssarchive. us/wp-content/uploads/2020/04/2010.pdf.

24 Qi Hao, "China debates the 'new type of great power relations,'" *Chinese Journal of International Politics*, 8(4), 349–370 (2015).

25 Data available at National Bureau of Statistics of China. https://data.stats. gov.cn/english/.

26 For the debate on the changing perception of China in the United States, see A. I. Johnston, "The failures of the 'failure of engagement' with China," *The Washington Quarterly*, 42(2), 99–114 (2019); Kai He, Huiyun Feng, Steve Chan and Weixing Hu, "Rethinking revisionism in world politics," *Chinese Journal of International Politics*, 14(2), 159–186 (2021).

27 P. Harris and P. Trubowitz, "The politics of power projection: The pivot to Asia, its failure, and the future of american primacy," *Chinese Journal of International Politics*, 14(2), 187–217 (2021).

28 K. Lieberthal and Wang Jisi, *Addressing US-China Strategic Distrust*, Vol. 4 (Washington DC: Brookings, 2012); see also Yan Xuetong, "Strategic cooperation without mutual trust: A path forward for China and the United States," *Asia Policy*, 15(1), 4–6 (2013).

29 The White House, *National Security Strategy 2015*, p. 24. https://obamawhitehouse.archives.gov/sites/default/files/docs/2015_national_security_strategy_2.pdf.

30 The White House, *National Security Strategy 2017*. https://trumpwhitehouse.archives.gov/wp-content/uploads/2017/12/NSS-Final-12-18-2017-0905.pdf.

31 *The New York Times*, "US-China trade deficit hits record, fueling trade fight," 6 February 2018. https://www.nytimes.com/2018/02/06/us/politics/us-china-trade-deficit.html.

32 The White House, *National Security Strategy 2017*, p. 21. https://trumpwhitehouse.archives.gov/wp-content/uploads/2017/12/NSS-Final-12-18-2017-0905.pdf.

33 H. Pamuk and A. Shalal, "Trump administration pushing to rip global supply chains from China: Officials," *Reuters*, 4 May 2020. https://www.reuters.com/article/us-health-coronavirus-usa-china-idUSKBN22G0BZ.

34 Avery Goldstein analyzed the potential crisis in US-China relations, see A. Goldstein, "First things first: The pressing danger of crisis instability in U.S.-China relations," *International Security*, 37(4), 49–89 (2013).

35 For example, see Secretary M. R. Pompeo, "Communist China and the free world's future," Remarks at the Richard Nixon Presidential Library and Museum, 23 July 2020. https://sv.usembassy.gov/secretary-michael-r-pompeo-remarks-at-the-richard-nixon-presidential-library-and-museum-communist-china-and-the-free-worlds-future/.

36 The White House, *National Security Strategy 2022*, p. 11. https://www. whitehouse.gov/wp-content/uploads/2022/10/Biden-Harris-Administrations-National-Security-Strategy-10.2022.pdf.

37 *Ibid.*, pp. 23–24; A. Blinken, "The administration's approach to the People's Republic of China," Speech Delivered at the George Washington University, 26 May 2022. https://www.state.gov/the-administrations-approach-to-the-peoples-republic-of-china/.

38 S. B. Canales, "AUKUS 'most important strategic innovation' as China looks to 'break' Australia: US President Joe Biden Advisor Kurt Campbell," *The Canberra Times*, 1 December 2021. https://www.canberratimes.com.au/story/7533455/aukus-not-doomed-to-fail-as-china-wants-to-break-australia-biden-advisor/.

39 C. Davies, Song Jung-a, K. Inagaki and R. Waters, "US struggles to mobilise its East Asian 'Chip 4' alliance," *Financial Times*, 13 September 2022. https://www.ft.com/content/98f22615-ee7e-4431-ab98-fb6e3f9de032.

40 As recent national surveys have demonstrated, the strategic rivalry between China and the United States has the potential to develop into antagonism between two societies that in turn intensifies and prolongs their confrontation. See L. Silver, K. Devlin and C. Huang, "Most Americans support tough stance toward China on human rights, economic issues," Pew Research Center, 4 March 2021. https://www.pewresearch.org/global/2021/03/04/most-americans-support-tough-stance-toward-china-on-human-rights-economic-issues/; Songying Fang, Xiaojun Li and A. Y. Liu, "Chinese public opinion about US-China relations from Trump to Biden," *Chinese Journal of International Politics*, 15(1), 27–46 (2022).

41 Japan Ministry of Defense, *Defense of Japan 2013*, p. 40. https://www.files. ethz.ch/isn/172496/Japan%20Defense%202013-Full.pdf.

42 Japan Ministry of Defense, *Defense of Japan 2016*, p. 43. https://warp. da.ndl.go.jp/info:ndljp/pid/11591426/www.mod.go.jp/e/publ/w_paper/pdf/2016/DOJ2016_1-2-3_web.pdf.

43 B. E. M. Grønning, "Japan's security cooperation with the Philippines and Vietnam," *The Pacific Review*, 31(4), 533–552 (2018).

44 The White House, "U.S.-Japan joint leaders' statement: 'U.S.-Japan global partnership for a new era,'" 16 April 2021. https://www.whitehouse.gov/briefing-room/statements-releases/2021/04/16/u-s-japan-joint-leaders-statement-u-s-japan-global-partnership-for-a-new-era/.

45 Prime Minister's Office of Japan, "Keynote address by Prime Minister Kishida Fumio at the IISS Shangri-La Dialogue," 10 June 2022. https://japan.kantei.go.jp/101_kishida/statement/202206/_00002.html.

46 The National Security Council of Japan, *National Security Strategy of Japan*, December 2022. https://www.cas.go.jp/jp/siryou/221216anzenhoshou/nss-e.pdf.

47 "People worry that the trend of 'cold politics and cool economy' between China and Japan will last forever," 26 September 2012. http://japanese.china. org.cn/jp/txt/2012-09/26/content_26640289.htm.

48 Ministry of Commerce (PRC), "The first China-Japan third-party market cooperation forum held in Beijing," 28 October 2018. http://english.mofcom.gov.cn/article/newsrelease/significantnews/201810/20181002801052.shtml.

49 China's rise accompanied by Japan's decline, especially in some international institutions, see H. Dobson, "Japan and the changing global balance of power: The view from the summit," *Politics*, 30(S1), 33–42 (2010).

50 C. W. Hughes, "Japan's 'resentful realism' and balancing China's rise," *Chinese Journal of International Politics*, 9(2), 109–150 (2016).

51 Ministry of Foreign Affairs (PRC), "Xi Jinping holds talks with President Pranab Mukherjee of India," 26 May 2016. https://www.fmprc.gov.cn/mfa_eng/zxxx_662805/t1367581.shtml.

52 S. Ganguly and A. Scobell, "The Himalayan impasse: Sino-Indian rivalry in the wake of Doklam," *The Washington Quarterly*, 41(3), 177–190 (2018).

53 *Xinhua Net*, "China, India reach broad consensus in informal summit," 29 April 2018. http://www.xinhuanet.com/english/2018-04/29/c_137145546.htm.

54 J. R. Holmes and Toshi Yoshihara, "India's 'Monroe Doctrine' and Asia's maritime future," *Strategic Analysis*, 32(6), 997–1011 (2008).

55 *India Today*, "India skips China's Belt and Road Summit over CPEC 'sovereignty' concerns," 14 May 2017. https://www.indiatoday.in/india/story/belt-and-road-initiative-china-president-xi-jinping-976944-2017-05-14.

56 Xiaoyu Pu, "The status dilemma in world politics: An anatomy of the China–India asymmetrical rivalry," *Chinese Journal of International Politics*, 15(3), 227–245 (2022).

57 R. Rajagopalan, "Evasive balancing: India's unviable Indo-Pacific strategy," *International Affairs*, 96(1), 75–93 (2020).

58 Yun Sun, "China's strategic assessment of India," *Texas National Security Review*, 25 March 2020. https://warontherocks.com/2020/03/chinas-strategic-assessment-of-india/.

59 H. Pant and P. Saha, "India, China, and the Indo-Pacific: New Delhi's recalibration is underway," *The Washington Quarterly*, 43(4), 191–193 (2020).

60 R. J. Nair, "Xi sees factory China and back office India as global engine," *Reuters*, 17 September 2014. https://www.reuters.com/article/china-southasia-india-idINKBN0HB2J520140917.

61 Directorate General of Trade Remedies, "Anti-dumping cases." https://www.dgtr.gov.in/anti-dumping-cases.

62 Department of Foreign Affairs and Trade (Australia), "Joint statement on the supply chain resilience initiative by Australian, Indian and Japanese trade ministers," 27 April 2021. https://www.dfat.gov.au/news/media-release/joint-statement-supply-chain-resilience-initiative-australian-indian-and-japanese-trade-ministers.

63 Ministry of Foreign Affairs (PRC), "Xi Jinping meets with Australian Prime Minister Julia Gillard, agreeing to build China-Australia strategic partnership of mutual trust and mutual benefit," April 7, 2013. https://www.fmprc.gov.cn/mfa_eng/topics_665678/boao_665692/t1029404.shtml.

64 *BBC News*, "Chinese investment in Australia plummets 61%," 1 March 2021. https://www.bbc.com/news/business-56234776.

65 Department of Foreign Affairs and Trade (Australia), *2017 Foreign Policy White Paper*, 23 November 2017, p. 1. https://apo.org.au/sites/default/files/resource-files/2017-11/apo-nid120661.pdf.

66 M. Turnbull, "Keynote address at the 16th IISS Asia security summit, Shangri-La dialogue," 3 June 2017. https://www.malcolmturnbull.com.au/media/keynote-address-at-the-16th-iiss-asia-security-summit-shangri-la-dialogue.

67 *The Guardian*, "Turnbull says Australia will 'stand up' to China as foreign influence row heats up," 9 December 2017. https://www.theguardian.com/australia-news/2017/dec/09/china-says-turnbulls-remarks-have-poisoned-the-atmosphere-of-relations.

68 F. Hunter, "Dutton takes aim at Chinese communist party for hostile conduct," *The Sydney Morning Herald*, 11 October 2019. https://www.smh.com.au/politics/federal/dutton-takes-aim-at-chinese-communist-party-for-hostile-conduct-20191011-p52zsm.html.

69 L. Kelly, "Australia demands coronavirus enquiry, adding to pressure on China," *Reuters*, 19 April 2020. https://www.reuters.com/article/us-health-coronavirus-australia/australia-demands-coronavirus-enquiry-adding-to-pressure-on-china-idUSKBN221058?edition-redirect=ca.

70 Prime Minister of Australia, Australia-Japan Leaders' Meeting Joint Statement, 22 October 2022. https://www.pm.gov.au/media/reciprocal-access-agreement.

71 Hunter (2019), *Op. cit.*

72 H. Davidson, "'Chewing gum stuck on the sole of our shoes': The China-Australia war of words—timeline," *The Guardian*, 29 April 2020. https://www.theguardian.com/world/2020/apr/29/chewing-gum-stuck-on-the-sole-of-our-shoes-the-china-australia-war-of-words-timeline.

73 H. White, "Malcolm Turnbull condemns China but has no alternative plan," *The Australian Financial Review*, 4 June 2017. https://www.afr.com/opinion/malcolm-turnbull-condemns-china-but-has-no-alternative-plan-20170604-gwk1un.

74 "Australia 'doesn't respond to demands,' Anthony Albanese tells China," *The Guardian*, 11 July 2022. https://www.theguardian.com/australia-news/2022/jul/11/australia-doesnt-respond-to-demands-anthony-albanese-tells-china.

© 2025 World Scientific Publishing Europe Ltd.
https://doi.org/10.1142/9781800616318_0003

Chapter 2

Infrastructure Statecraft and Sino–U.S. Strategic Competition in the Indo-Pacific[*]

Minghao Zhao

Fudan University, China

Major powers are advancing strategic competition in infrastructure building in the developing world. They cultivate their infrastructure statecraft by securing financial and technological resources, making institutional arrangements, and managing infrastructure-related consequences. The infrastructure statecraft, which covers physical and digital infrastructure as well as hard and soft infrastructure, carries connotations of geopolitics, geoeconomics, and geotechnology. The strategic competition between China and the United States (U.S.) in the infrastructure of the Indo-Pacific has intensified in recent years. China has been proactively advancing infrastructure cooperation under the banner of the Belt and Road Initiative (BRI). The U.S. has proposed the "Free and Open Indo-Pacific Strategy" and "Partnership for Global Infrastructure and Investment," and it competes with China in the infrastructure field by building networked coalitions with its allies and partners. The infrastructure competition illustrates the development–security nexus challenge of U.S.–China rivalry over connectivity in the Indo-Pacific. China has taken measures to readjust the manner in which it advances the BRI and

---

[*]This chapter was originally printed as "Infrastructure Statecraft and Sino-U.S. Strategic Competition in the Indo-Pacific." *The China Review*, Vol. 23, No. 1 (2023): 45–77. https://www.jstor.org/stable/48717988. Reproduced with kind permission of CUHK Press.

enhances its infrastructure statecraft. This chapter argues that Sino–U.S. competition over regional infrastructure is not necessarily a zero-sum game.

With the competitive strategy toward China pursued by the Trump and Biden administrations, United States (U.S.)–China relations have experienced the most significant transformation since the establishment of diplomatic ties in the 1970s.[1] As Kai He and Feng Liu argue in this volume, since Obama's second term, China's bilateral relations with the U.S. have been gradually changing from "cooperative partnership" to "competitive rivalry" (see Chapter 1). Chinese observers increasingly worry that this trend may lead to the emergence of a U.S.-led bloc, reminiscent of the Cold War, which excludes China. In recent years, U.S.–China strategic competition in the Asia-Pacific region has intensified.[2] China strives to promote the Belt and Road Initiative (BRI) proposed by President Xi Jinping, which features international cooperation on infrastructure development. As of October 2023, more than 180 countries and international organizations have inked BRI-related cooperation agreements with the Chinese government. In fact, BRI is the embodiment of China's emerging connectivity-oriented foreign policy, mainly based on its infrastructure statecraft. Many countries in the Indo-Pacific region have collaborated with China to implement BRI and proceed with numerous infrastructure projects.[3]

However, China's infrastructure statecraft has also led to concerns and speculations among regional countries regarding China: they are worried about a China-centric regional order as well as overdependence on China economically and politically.[4] The BRI also fuels U.S.' negative perceptions of China's strategic intentions and its foreign policy. American policy elites are increasingly concerned about the geopolitical implications of China's infrastructure offensive, with many viewing it as Beijing's power play to dominate Eurasia and surrounding areas economically and strategically.[5] In response, the U.S. proposed the Free and Open Indo-Pacific Strategy (FOIP) in November 2017 and vowed to further engage in regional infrastructure development. There is conspicuous continuity in U.S.' China policy after Joe Biden came to power, with his administration attaching greater emphasis to building up coalitions with America's allies and partners to counterbalance Chinese influence. In June 2021, the Biden administration unveiled the Build Back Better World (B3W) initiative, together with like-minded democracies, aiming to meet developing countries' high demand for infrastructure. B3W is perceived as a strategic counterbalance against BRI. In June 2022, the U.S. and its G7 partners announced the Partnership for Global Infrastructure and Investment (PGII), which is a repackaging of B3W.

As Andrew Scobell points out in this volume, the U.S.–China competition encompasses multiple dimensions and arenas, with a considerable number of contentious issues and significant diverging interests (see Chapter 3). Indeed, rivalry over infrastructure has become the focal point of U.S.–China strategic competition in the Indo-Pacific. The U.S. is building a multilayered and networked coalition with its allies and partners to check Chinese infrastructure statecraft and geoeconomic influence. As Rory Medcalf observes, "the Indo-Pacific is being posited in some quarters as a counter or alternative to the China-centric view of regional order being pursued by Beijing under the rubric of the Belt and Road Initiative."[6] Moreover, the interplay on infrastructure between China and the U.S. may indicate some key features of U.S.–China strategic competition, such as the salience of the development–security nexus.[7] It also has to do with the institutional balancing in U.S.–China relations, which means that the two countries compete within and through international institutions such as the Asian Infrastructure Investment Bank (AIIB).[8]

This chapter aims to explore Sino–U.S. strategic competition over infrastructure in the Indo-Pacific through the analytical framework of infrastructure statecraft, which centers on resources, institutions, and management. It argues that for China, the infrastructure associated with BRI is a double-edged sword. China faces numerous and daunting challenges in implementing infrastructure projects, mitigating host countries' concerns about overdependence, and dealing with counterbalancing moves adopted by other countries. It also discusses America's infrastructure statecraft, which features its efforts to construct a networked coalition by combining with allies and partners as well as public and private sectors. Although the U.S. seeks to intensify its competition *vis-à-vis* China over infrastructure, American commitments remain questionable in the eyes of regional countries. Moreover, the U.S. lacks effective policy instruments given the Trump administration's "America First" doctrine and the Biden administration's "Foreign Policy for the Middle Class." The final section offers some thoughts on how to manage the Sino–U.S. infrastructure competition.

2.1. Infrastructure Statecraft and China's BRI

For major powers in the world, the capacity for infrastructure building is vital to their national strength and international influence, given the huge demand for infrastructure in the developing world.[9] As research by the Asian Development Bank (ADB) shows, the Asia-Pacific region needs an annual investment of US$1.7 trillion for infrastructure development. In recent years, major powers have attached greater importance to competition with regard to infrastructure building in third countries.[10] With the BRI, China has become one of the most proactive and capable players in the infrastructure race.[11] The U.S. decided to take on China in this regard by proposing the Build Back Better World (B3W)/Partnership for Global Infrastructure and Investment (PGII) initiative. The European Union (EU) and Japan have also joined the power game by advancing the Global Gateway plan and the Partnership for Quality Infrastructure initiative, respectively. Hence, a networked coalition of democracies, led by the U.S., is emerging against China in the area of infrastructure building.[12]

In order to better understand the interaction between infrastructure building and great power competition, this chapter proposes an analytical framework of infrastructure statecraft. There has been increasing discussion on the economic statecraft of major powers, including China, the U.S., and Japan. Like economic statecraft, infrastructure statecraft involves major powers leveraging their capacities in infrastructure building as a means of exerting power and international influence, which are essential for the strategic competition among them.[13] There are three components of infrastructure statecraft. First, country A needs to provide financial and technological resources to effectively and efficiently meet the infrastructure demands of recipient countries. Country A also needs to ensure the sustainability of its assistance, which depends on the complementarity between its domestic and international policy goals. Second, country A is expected to be able to make institutional arrangements bilaterally and multilaterally to implement infrastructure cooperation with recipient countries. It has to do with setting rules and norms in the infrastructure field, which is fundamental to country A's power and influence on soft connectivity.[14] Third, country A needs to manage the political, security, and reputational risks at different stages of infrastructure building in the recipient countries.[15]

In the era of great power competition, infrastructure statecraft serves as the vehicle through which country A may deal with strategic competition with country B and the coalition led by country B.[16] Infrastructure statecraft, which covers physical and digital infrastructure as well as hard and soft infrastructure, carries geopolitics, geoeconomics, and geotechnology connotations.[17] Infrastructure can play a vital role in the power projection of major countries and influence the foreign policy of recipient countries, alliance management, and coalition building.[18] Infrastructure is a significant instrument of geoeconomic competition. Moreover, the technological consequences of the infrastructure race among major powers have gained greater saliency, largely due to the expansion of digital infrastructure, such as wireless and fixed broadband, date centers, and undersea cables, in the 21st century.[19] In essence, infrastructure statecraft sits at the confluence of development and security, or is a product of the development–security nexus, adding complexity to great power competition. Some scholars, such as T. J. Pempel, have proposed the concept of the economic–security nexus to analyze East Asian regionalism. Given the increasing importance of infrastructure in the era of major power competition and its role as an enabler for the relevant nations' development, it is more appropriate to reframe the concept as the development–security nexus.[20]

In September and October 2013, Chinese President Xi Jinping unveiled the two parts of the BRI: the Silk Road Economic Belt and the 21st Century Maritime Silk Road in Central Asia and Southeast Asia, respectively. As Christopher Johnson points out, this bold initiative is quite personal to President Xi, and it can be viewed as the Chinese Communist Party's (CCP's) roadmap for China's global resurgence.[21] The BRI is not only a foreign policy concept in China's "new era" but also one of the major national development strategies in the aftermath of the 18th National Congress of the CCP. The BRI addresses the interaction of domestic and foreign policies and aims to tackle the internal and external challenges facing China, boost its economic development, and ensure a favorable international environment.

The BRI, with infrastructure building as a key pillar, is expected to help keep China's economic boom alive while deepening economic ties with related countries. In recent years, China's GDP growth has decreased to less than 6 percent, and the country faces challenges such as soaring labor costs, an aging population, growing energy demands, and overcapacity in manufacturing sectors.[22] The BRI is instrumental in addressing those challenges. For instance, by facilitating energy infrastructure building in related countries, China can enhance market access for its energy and construction enterprises and secure its own energy supply.

According to an estimate by Cecilia Joy-Perez and Derek Scissors, 44 percent of the BRI-related construction pertains to the energy sector.[23]

Through the BRI, China might better tackle the internal development imbalances that may otherwise lead it to the risk of getting caught in a "middle-income trap." This domestic rationale is critical for China to sustain the BRI. Some cross-border infrastructure projects are beneficial to its ethnic minority areas in the borderland, which may help realize national security goals. BRI adds an international policy pillar for the 'Go West' (西部大開發, *xibu da kaifa*) drive, which was previously regarded as a domestic endeavor in China. In the early 1990s, the Chinese government launched a 'Go West' campaign aimed at addressing the development disparity between the coastal areas and its vast western region. Wealthier provinces in the eastern part of the country were required to aid poorer ones such as Xinjiang, Ningxia, and Qinghai in the west by providing financial support, co-developing large-scale business projects, and transferring advanced human resources. By participating in the BRI, those western and bordering provinces, such as Yunnan and Inner Mongolia, may become the new frontier of opening up. As Wang Jisi points out, China is waking up to the huge potential of its ties with its neighboring countries to the west.[24] Chinese corporations and subnational governments in those provinces are optimistic about the BRI and are keen to leverage the opportunities it offers to enhance their own infrastructure and expand economic openness to bordering countries.

From the Chinese perspective, the BRI could be a solution to "development deficits, security deficits and governance deficits," which lead to the quagmire in which the world finds itself.[25] In order to fix globalization and regionalization in the Asia-Pacific region, it is essential to find new growth engines that largely depend on infrastructure, especially digital. The BRI has the potential to boost the world economy and meet the huge demands of the developing world for infrastructure. As Andrew Elek asserts, the BRI responds to demands for reducing traditional trade barriers and narrowing gaps in transport and communications infrastructure through "cooperation on capacity-building and adding vital economic infrastructure is a positive-sum game," and the BRI can push relevant countries to "promote a creative new approach to global economic integration."[26]

Since its inception in 2013, more than 180 countries and international organizations have inked agreements with the Chinese government to promote various forms of cooperation associated with the BRI.[27] China has made efforts to strengthen institutional arrangements. In the past few years, the BRI Forum for International Cooperation (BRF) has been hosted twice in Beijing. China strives to integrate the BRI with the development needs and plans of participating countries bilaterally, and government-to-government coordination mechanisms have been established between China and Laos, Pakistan, and Hungary, among other countries.[28] In the meantime, multilateral institutions have been deemed more important in implementing the BRI, and China seeks to take advantage of resources, networks, and the experience of international organizations. The BRI aligns with the UN 2030 Agenda for Sustainable Development, and a number of UN specialized agencies, such as the World Health Organization (WHO) and the International Labour Organization (ILO), have established partnerships with Chinese governmental bodies.[29] The BRI is inextricably tied up with China's expanding aspirations for global governance. Yang Jiechi, the then member of the Political Bureau of the CCP Central Committee and director of the Office of the Foreign Affairs Commission of the CCP Central Committee, states that the BRI may serve as an important and innovative platform through which "a community with a shared future for humanity" (人類命運共同體, *renlei mingyun gongtongti*) can be realized.[30] Obviously, the BRI with infrastructure as a priority has become an overarching concept of China's foreign policy, especially toward its neighboring countries.

Without a doubt, the Asia-Pacific region stands to greatly benefit from the BRI if the project is carried out properly. The Asia-Pacific has been a priority in Chinese foreign policy. China has become more proactive in overhauling its diplomatic activities with its neighbors since 2013, and it considers infrastructure cooperation as a significant policy instrument. In October 2013, Xi Jinping presided over a high-level conference on China's relations with neighboring countries. He emphasized new diplomatic principles in dealing with these countries: intimacy, honesty, generosity, and inclusiveness.[31] The essence of the new good neighborhood policy is to achieve win-win relations with neighboring countries in light of their growing apprehensions of a rising China and a potentially Sino-centric regional order. Admittedly, in the past few years, territorial disputes between China and countries such as the Philippines and Vietnam have indicated Beijing's diplomatic challenges; consequently, the critical task for Chinese leadership is to promote mutual accommodation between a powerful China and its neighboring countries. China expects its efforts in deepening economic ties by means of the BRI and infrastructure cooperation will be instrumental in mitigating those tensions. Notably, the maritime component of the BRI demonstrates China's willingness to deepen ties with maritime Asia. China is located at the eastern end of the Eurasian landmass, and it has been viewed geographically and traditionally as a continental power. But under Xi's leadership, China has vowed to gain a powerful maritime position in the coming decades, attaching more importance to boosting regional maritime infrastructure, including ports and undersea fiber-optic cables.[32]

According to the BRI blueprint, together with relevant stakeholders, China seeks to build up the China–Indochina Peninsula Economic Corridor, the China–Pakistan Economic Corridor (CPEC), the China–Central Asia–West Asia Economic Corridor, the China–Bangladesh–China–India–Myanmar Economic Corridor, and the China–Mongolia–Russia Economic Corridor, which are all located in the Asia-Pacific. For every economic corridor, infrastructure is the most salient component. In addition, China collaborates with Indonesia, Myanmar, Sri Lanka, and other littoral countries of the Pacific and Indian oceans to construct the 21st Century Maritime Silk Road. A variety of specific infrastructure projects have been implemented.[33] For instance, the construction of the China–Laos railway, part of the Pan-Asia Railway Network, has been operationalized. In order to improve infrastructure utilization, several overseas economic and trade cooperation zones have been established in Malaysia, Cambodia, and Vietnam. China proposed a package of infrastructure modernization, industrialization, and urbanization to those countries. It is noteworthy that, as the developed country in ASEAN, Singapore has been quite proactive in constructing the New International Land–Sea Trade Corridor, which connects western China to Southeast Asia under the China–Singapore (Chongqing) Connectivity Initiative (CCI-ILSTC). Singapore has played a critical role in facilitating the development of economic special zones in China, and the related experience and know-how are an important intellectual asset for the BRI. The two countries have vowed to enhance cooperation on regional infrastructure.[34] Moreover, China seeks to take advantage of regional multilateral institutions such as ASEAN. The BRI supports the ASEAN Community Vision 2025 and the Master Plan on ASEAN Connectivity 2025, which center on bridging the huge infrastructure gap in the region.[35]

However, China's infrastructure statecraft is problematic. Many observers argue that, although infrastructure-building under the BRI may add to China's geopolitical advantages, it in fact renders China's geopolitical situation more complex, if not disadvantageous. Chinese efforts to expand its footprint in the infrastructure field and galvanize international cooperation face a number of risks and challenges.

Although many countries in the Asia-Pacific region are supportive of the BRI's infrastructure drive, they are still concerned about potential side effects, such as the debt burden and China's excessive influence on their own critical infrastructures and economies.[36] Appropriate mechanisms are needed to uphold financial sustainability, which becomes more severe and urgent in the post-COVID-19 era. The Chinese government has stated that it has no intention of creating any debt traps for participating countries; however, many partners in the region, including Laos, Cambodia, and Malaysia, face financial difficulties. In order to avoid overdependence on external borrowing, Myanmar has renegotiated deals with China on some projects, such as the deep-sea port in Kyaukpyu at the Bay of Ben.[37] Malaysia reduced the cost of the East Coast Rail Link from US$16 billion to US$10.7 billion.[38] It also began investigations into corruption and fiscal mismanagement related to the BRI projects.[39] Some countries are becoming wary of corruption related to Chinese corporations. In January 2018, Bangladesh blacklisted a Chinese construction firm for alleged bribery.[40] In planning and implementing infrastructure projects in host countries, Chinese companies have found it challenging to enhance their capabilities in dealing with political, societal, and cultural risks locally. In addition, ensuring the security of BRI infrastructure projects and workers is a pressing problem for China. Thousands of Chinese have been sent to work on the CPEC projects in Gwadar and other places in Pakistan. Although a special force has been set up by Islamabad for the security of the Chinese workers and the CPEC projects, there is still a long way to go in finding truly feasible and sustainable solutions to instabilities and dangers posed by local separatism, terrorism, and extremism. Transnational crime is another threat to Chinese companies. The role that China's government and security forces should play in addressing these issues remains a complex challenge for China's infrastructure statecraft.

For China, the BRI and its infrastructure drive are a double-edged sword in terms of geopolitics, and China's infrastructure statecraft faces competing pressures from the U.S. and other major powers in the Indo-Pacific. On the one hand, infrastructure cooperation is conducive to enhancing China's influence in regional economic and security affairs if it can be well implemented. On the other hand, it is inevitable that China's expanding interests in the infrastructure field will be at odds with those of other regional giants. Although China claims that the BRI infrastructure cooperation is a development-oriented endeavor, other regional powers are wary of a China-centric regional order stemming from the BRI and Chinese influence on infrastructure in the Indo-Pacific. Japan, India, and Australia each have their own visions of regional connectivity and economic integration. They intend to counterbalance China's ever-growing infrastructure footprint and its commercial, security, and geopolitical implications.[41]

To compete with China, the Japanese government proposed the "Quality Infrastructure" initiative, backed by over US$200 billion, and former Prime Minister Abe stated that "Infrastructure cannot be cheap and poor. We look at cost and effectiveness through the total life cycle of the project."[42] In addition, Japan and India are jointly promoting the Asia Africa Growth Corridor (AAGC) and supporting Iran's Chabahar port to counterbalance the China-financed Gwadar port in Pakistan. The Modi government insists on maintaining an opposing attitude toward the CPEC and BRI in general. Australia remains vigilant to China's deepening ties with Pacific Island countries, and it has markedly increased its development and security assistance to Papua New Guinea, Fiji, and the Solomon Islands, among others. In November 2018, Canberra unveiled a US$1.5 billion infrastructure fund for the region, and the then Prime Minister Scott Morrison asserted that "Australia has an abiding interest in the Southwest Pacific that is secure strategically, stable economically and sovereign politically."[43]

The Chinese government has been keenly aware of the challenges and backlashes against its infrastructure statecraft. In August 2018, Xi Jinping likened the BRI to a "fine brush painting" (工筆畫, *gongbihua*), an analogy meant to stress that BRI projects should be of high quality and employ high standards to meet the real needs of host countries.[44] Some readjustments aiming to smooth the implementation of BRI have been unveiled. More efforts are proposed to push for progress on infrastructure projects that aim to deliver tangible benefits for local communities and attract more private capital. China has vowed to pay more attention to the corruption and safety issues of infrastructure projects in BRI-participating countries. In addition, China has pledged to undertake more cooperation projects in the fields of education, healthcare, culture, and environmental protection to promote the development of soft infrastructure in relevant countries, especially by helping them train more talent. The investments and operations of Chinese construction companies are subject to stricter regulations so that they can better fulfill their social responsibilities.

Aiming to mitigate major power pressures on its infrastructure statecraft, China seeks to further expand third-party market cooperation with developed countries and large multinational corporations. China has realized that there are multidimensional benefits if it can successfully turn competition into cooperation. It would not only improve the international image of BRI projects but also be helpful in burden-sharing and risk management. A new approach to positively interacting with regional giants could be explored by promoting such third-party cooperation. For example, China–Japan Third-Party Market Cooperation Working Mechanism has been set up, with both the Chinese and Japanese governments pledging to cooperate on Thailand's "Eastern Economic Corridor" among other projects. In addition, China's Silk Road Fund and American conglomerate General Electric plan to jointly invest in the energy infrastructures of several countries participating in the BRI, such as Pakistan. The Third-Party Market Cooperation Guidelines and Cases were released by China's National Development and Reform Commission, the country's most important government agency for implementing the BRI.[45] To reassure other countries, Xi Jinping emphasized on many occasions that the BRI is an initiative for economic cooperation rather than a geopolitical or military alliance. He explained that the BRI is an open and inclusive initiative rather than an exclusive bloc or a "China club."[46]

2.2. America's Counterbalance against China's Infrastructure Statecraft

The U.S. views itself as a "resident power" in the Indo-Pacific region and has deep concerns about the BRI and China's infrastructure offensive. The response of the Obama administration to BRI was relatively mild, although the U.S. strongly boycotted the AIIB.[47] China was deemed the most significant threat to the U.S. by the Trump administration, and there have been heated debates on how to formulate competitive strategies *vis-à-vis* the BRI in American policy circles. In the eyes of American strategists, the BRI is an Indo-Pacific strategy with Chinese characteristics—China is using it to launch an infrastructure race throughout the Eurasian continent as well as expand its security and political influence, which will in turn threaten the U.S.-led international order.[48]

In late 2017, the Trump administration released its first *National Security Strategy*, claiming that the U.S. was facing a new era of global competition. The document characterizes Beijing as "the revisionist power" and "strategic competitor" and calls for the adoption of a whole-of-government strategy toward China.[49] In his private exchanges with some prominent business leaders and senior White House colleagues in August 2018, Donald Trump was quoted as saying that China's BRI was both aggressive and potentially disruptive to global trade.[50] American senior officials often accuse China of being an economic predator in sharply worded statements. They portray the infrastructure projects sponsored by China as "debt traps," alleging that the initiative would compromise the sovereignty and interests of participating countries and undermine regional security in general.[51] In November 2018, at the Asia-Pacific Economic Cooperation Summit, then U.S. Vice President Mike Pence stated, "We don't drown our partners in a sea of debt. We don't coerce or compromise your independence. We do not offer a constricting belt or a one-way road."[52] Moreover, Congress has urged the American Executive to take more countervailing measures against BRI. In August 2018, some 16 U.S. senators sent a letter to Treasury Secretary Steve Mnuchin and Secretary of State Mike Pompeo expressing their concerns about and disapproval of the BRI, calling it a scheme aimed at building a global economic order ultimately dominated by China.[53]

The U.S. counterbalances China's infrastructure statecraft by advancing the Free and Open Indo-Pacific Strategy (FOIP), which was formally announced by Donald Trump during his first official trip to Asia in November 2017. According to the *National Security Strategy* released by the Trump administration in late 2017, the "Indo-Pacific" region refers to "the vast area that stretches from the west coast of the Indian Ocean to the eastern shores of the United States, representing the most populous and economically dynamic part of the world."[54] Indeed, the Indo-Pacific has become a concept with geographical and strategic significance. FOIP was initiated by the Trump administration, but it is the result of continuous adjustments to U.S. policy toward the Asia-Pacific region over the past decades. In fact, the Bush administration had already declared that the strategic focus of the U.S. would shift from the Atlantic and Pacific oceans to the Pacific and Indian oceans in its *Cooperative Strategy for 21st Century Seapower* as early as 2007. By the time Barack Obama took office, the U.S. began to clearly conceive its regional strategy based on the framework of the Indo-Pacific.[55] In particular, the American government was consistent in fully expanding its relations with India. Former Secretary of State Hillary Clinton once stated, "We are expanding our work with the Indian navy in the Pacific Ocean, because we understand how important the Indo-Pacific basin is to global trade and commerce."[56] In January 2015, the U.S. and India jointly released the U.S.–India Joint Strategic Vision for the Asia-Pacific and Indian Ocean.[57]

The FOIP in its current form was finalized during the Trump administration. To a large extent, FOIP serves as a counterbalance to "the Indo-Pacific Strategy with Chinese characteristics"—the BRI.[58] The U.S. believes that the BRI and its infrastructure drive in particular have the potential to put China in a central position in the Indo-Pacific region, where "Chinese dominance risks diminishing the sovereignty of many states in the Indo-Pacific."[59] After the end of World War II, one of the core objectives of the U.S. grand strategy was to prevent a hegemon from emerging in the region.[60] FOIP is backed up by a distinct underlying current of maritime power and aims to check the emergence of potential hegemons on the Eurasian continent from both the eastern and western frontlines of the Pacific and Indian oceans.

The American government seeks to criticize China's infrastructure statecraft and provide alternatives to regional countries. In August 2018, Mike Pompeo visited Malaysia, Singapore, and Indonesia. On the eve of his visit, Pompeo delivered a speech, entitled "Remarks on 'America's Indo-Pacific Economic Vision,'" at the Indo-Pacific Business Forum held by the U.S. Chamber of Commerce, stating that the U.S. "does not invest for political influence, but rather practices partnership economics." Pompeo also emphasized that "we believe in strategic partnerships, not strategic dependency."[61]

The U.S. has not entered into a competition with China in terms of scale and funding but rather has focused on funding for the development of digital and energy infrastructures. The American government has invested US$113 million in advance funding to mobilize more private capital for concrete action plans such as the Enhancing Development and Growth through Energy (EDGE). The U.S. Department of Commerce, the Department of Energy, and the Agency for International Development have also launched a series of initiatives and mechanisms to promote the expansion of links between the U.S. business community and the Indo-Pacific infrastructure market.[62] The U.S. seeks to take advantage of the private sector more robustly when competing with China's infrastructure statecraft in which state-owned enterprises (SOEs) play a leading role.

A new infrastructure and development financing institution—the U.S. Development Finance Corporation (DFC)—was established in 2019 to modernize American economic statecraft in counterbalancing Chinese influence in infrastructure construction and other sectors.[63]

Moreover, in the infrastructure competition against China, the U.S. has built a networked coalition through closer alignment with Japan and Australia, along with other allies and partners. For instance, the U.S.– Japan Strategic Energy Partnership, set up in 2017, aims to facilitate high-standard investment in energy projects, such as liquefied natural gas (LNG) infrastructure, and create synergy with America's EDGE program. The U.S. has also set up minilateral institutions to push forward the infrastructure competition with China. In November 2018, the U.S. Overseas Private Investment Corporation (OPIC), Japan Bank for International Cooperation (JBIC), and Australia's Department of Foreign Affairs and Trade (DFAT) and Export Finance and Insurance Corporation (EFIC) signed a Memorandum of Understanding (MoU) to operationalize the Trilateral Partnership for Infrastructure Investment in the Indo-Pacific, which prioritizes digital connectivity and energy infrastructure.[64] The networked coalition is also based on America's utilization of civilian power. With strong support from the American government and led by the U.S. Chamber of Commerce, the Indo-Pacific Business Forum becomes a potent platform for unleashing the potential of public–private partnerships in promoting infrastructure building in the Indo-Pacific.

America's counterbalance against China's infrastructure statecraft is closely linked to its security policy tools under the FOIP. The Indo-Pacific region is seen as a "priority theater" by the Pentagon, given that Chinese influence on regional infrastructure is believed to have military and security consequences, such as hindering the American military's capacity to project power and enhancing China's ability to collect intelligence. Using its security leverage, the U.S. seeks to alter the considerations of related countries when it comes to infrastructure cooperation with China. According to Mike Pence, the U.S. poured US$500 million in security assistance to countries in the Indo-Pacific region in 2018, of which US$400 million was invested in the military, an amount higher than the sum of investments from the last three years combined.[65] In particular, the U.S. focuses on four major areas of maritime security: humanitarian aid, disaster control, enhancing peacekeeping capacities, and cracking down on transnational crime, with an emphasis on Southeast Asia and Pacific Island countries, as well as increasing investments in coastal countries.[66]

Infrastructure Statecraft and Sino–U.S. Strategic Competition in the Indo-Pacific 47

The Trump administration also dispatched Defense Secretary Jim Mattis to Vietnam, Indonesia, and other Asian countries. Mattis described Vietnam as a "natural partner" and offered to facilitate Indonesia in becoming a "global maritime axis."[67]

As the geostrategic position of the Bay of Bengal becomes increasingly prominent, and with countries such as Sri Lanka becoming important partners in BRI ports and other infrastructure projects, the U.S. has increased its attention on Colombo. Moreover, the U.S. has invested more in its competition against China in the Pacific Island countries because it is increasingly worried about China gaining security influence by engaging in infrastructure construction in the Pacific Island countries, even establishing military bases there. In August 2019, during his visit to Micronesia, Mike Pompeo claimed that China wanted to "redraw" the lines in the Pacific Ocean. A director-level position in charge of the affairs of Pacific Island countries was created within the White House National Security Council to enhance cross-agency coordination among the U.S. Department of State, Department of Defense, and others. The goal was to make "whole-of-government" efforts to counterbalance China's influence in the Pacific Island countries. The U.S. Department of State channeled US$7 million in security aid to Papua New Guinea, Fiji, and Tonga via the "Foreign Military Financing" project. Defense attachés were also assigned to U.S. embassies in countries such as Papua New Guinea and the Federated States of Micronesia, all possible sites for more intense strategic competition between China and the U.S. In addition, the U.S. and Australia have jointly constructed the Manus Island military base with Papua New Guinea.[68] The U.S., Japan, and Australia have deepened their trilateral cooperation in infrastructure building in the Pacific Island countries. For instance, they jointly support Papua New Guinea's goal of raising its electricity supply to 70 percent of the country by 2030. The Australian Infrastructure Financing Facility for the Pacific, among other initiatives, can be very helpful for the U.S. to cultivate allied power in curbing Chinese infrastructure statecraft.[69]

Another counterbalance of the U.S. lies in its values-oriented diplomacy and ideological competition with China in a high-profile manner. FOIP has one pillar on democracy and governance, which is key in forming more comprehensive and effective checks against BRI and China's infrastructure offensive. As Francis Fukuyama contends, the U.S. is worried that Beijing might export its state-driven China model to other developing countries through the BRI projects.[70] Mike Pence attended the

APEC Leaders' Meeting in November 2018 and announced the Indo-Pacific Transparency Initiative at a cost of more than US$400 million.[71] He emphasized that good governance is a core component of the U.S. vision for the Indo-Pacific region. The U.S. pledges to support initiatives that respect individual rights, guarantee freedom of religion and expression, and fight corruption. The Indo-Pacific Transparency Initiative aims to strengthen the good governance of countries in the region, improve their ability to safeguard sovereignty, and help them avoid falling into debt traps. Mike Pence stated that "authoritarianism and aggression have no place in the Indo-Pacific region."[72]

The Biden administration has vowed to undertake long-term, strategic competition *vis-à-vis* China and views the Indo-Pacific as the central area for U.S.–China "stiff competition."[73] The Biden administration has upgraded coalition-driven efforts to confront China's infrastructure statecraft in great power competition.[74] The B3W initiative, jointly launched by the U.S. and the G7 countries in June 2021, emphasizes that advanced democracies will cooperate to support infrastructure development in developing countries to address the infrastructure financing gap of more than US$40 trillion. B3W focuses on four major issues: climate change, health security, digital technologies, and gender equity and equality. B3W will have a global scope, spanning from Latin America and the Caribbean to Africa to the Indo-Pacific. The Biden administration emphasized that B3W is values-driven and will be "carried out in a transparent and sustainable manner—financially, environmentally, and socially." It stated that "[i]nfrastructure investment by a responsible and market-driven private sector, paired with high standards and transparency in public funding, is crucial for long-run development effectiveness and sustainability."[75] In June 2022, the Biden administration, together with America's core allies, replaced B3W with the PGII. They vowed to mobilize public and private resources to meet the key infrastructure needs of low- and middle-income countries and offer them "a comprehensive, transparent, values-driven financing choice for infrastructure development to advance climate and energy security, digital connectivity, health and health security, and gender equality and equity priorities."[76]

With the push from the Biden administration, the Quadrilateral Security Dialogue (known as Quad), comprising the U.S., Japan, India, and Australia, is becoming the central platform for allied advantage in infrastructure competition. In September 2021, the first-ever in-person Quad Leaders' Summit was held in Washington. Building on the B3W, the

Quad pledged to launch the Quad Infrastructure Coordination Group, which is instrumental to "share assessments of regional infrastructure needs and coordinate respective approaches to deliver transparent, high-standards infrastructure."[77] In the future, the Quad mechanism may serve as a basis for a larger networked coalition composed of the EU, the United Kingdom, and South Korea, among other players, which have commercial and security interests in Indo-Pacific infrastructure.[78] For instance, the EU has released its own Indo-Pacific strategy. In December 2021, the EU unveiled the Global Gateway plan, which aims to support infrastructure development around the world. This plan would mobilize €300 billion between 2021 and 2027 for connectivity projects, notably in the digital, climate, energy, transport, health, and other sectors.[79] When talking about the purpose of the Global Gateway, European Commission President Ursula von der Leyen openly acknowledged its competitive stance toward China. She stated, "We want to create links and not dependencies."[80]

The Biden administration also seeks to impose more reputational costs on China's infrastructure statecraft through political instruments. In December 2021, Secretary of State Antony Blinken gave a speech in Jakarta, Indonesia. He criticized "Beijing's aggressive actions" in the Indo-Pacific and stated that "we're hearing increasing concerns from government officials, industry, labor, and communities in the Indo-Pacific about what happens when infrastructure isn't done right, like when it's awarded through opaque, corrupt processes, or built by overseas companies that import their own labor, extract resources, pollute the environment, and drive communities into debt." Blinken claimed that the Indo-Pacific countries deserve "a better kind of infrastructure."[81]

Moreover, the Biden administration is trying to consolidate American dominance in setting standards and rules in the infrastructure area. The U.S. continues to operationalize the Blue Dot Network in certifying high-quality infrastructure projects that meet standards defined by advanced democracies, such as Japan and Australia. In terms of specific projects, the U.S., Japan, and Australia announced a partnership with the Federated States of Micronesia, Kiribati, and Nauru to build a new undersea cable to improve internet connectivity in December 2021. In 2022, the Biden administration established new projects on regional infrastructure within the Indo-Pacific Economic Framework (IPEF). The IPEF is viewed as America's new policy tool to advance geoeconomic competition against China in the Indo-Pacific region. It has four pillars: trade; supply chains; clean energy, decarbonization and infrastructure; and tax and anti-corruption. The IPEF is supported by many Indo-Pacific countries, including seven of the ten ASEAN members. The Biden administration has made consistent efforts to promote consultations among IPEF member states on the rules governing infrastructure building.[82] In addition, to shore up anti-corruption in infrastructure, in partnership with the OECD, the Biden administration proposed the Connecting the Dots initiative in October 2021.[83] The Biden administration held the Summit for Democracy in December 2021, and a series of initiatives were set up to support journalists, human rights activists, and civil society organizations. More funds would be used by the American government to encourage media coverage of China-related scandals in implementing the BRI and related infrastructure projects.[84]

2.3. Managing Sino–U.S. Infrastructure Competition in the Indo-Pacific

The BRI and China's infrastructure statecraft are viewed as one of the frontlines in the unfolding U.S.–China strategic competition. The infrastructure rivalry between China and the U.S.-led networked coalition will have significant impacts on the evolution of regional order. Most countries in the Indo-Pacific are experiencing economic, political, and social transitions, and many are struggling with infrastructure deficits. There is an emerging U.S.-led alliance system against China in the region that is issue-based and task-oriented. The ASEAN-centered institutions, which were developed in the post-Cold War period, are increasingly incapable of regulating competition among regional giants. In the meantime, middle powers such as South Korea and Vietnam are striving to reposition themselves in the changing strategic landscape. To a large degree, regional order in the Indo-Pacific is influenced by geoeconomic power and institutional balancing, and it remains a contested project.[85]

Without doubt, as China kept rising, renewed U.S. efforts to align with Japan, India, and other powers in the Indo-Pacific region to check Beijing's influence in all domains, including infrastructure, sounded an alarm for Chinese policy planners. The U.S.-led coalition is a major source of Beijing's insecurity in its home region, and it is viewed by most Chinese observers as an "Asian NATO" and an "Economic NATO." In particular, institutional balancing surrounding infrastructure has become more salient in U.S.–China strategic competition. Many American policymakers and strategists increasingly perceive BRI's infrastructure push as confrontational, if not in a zero-sum manner. The U.S. has developed a number of minilateral mechanisms focusing on infrastructure in Southeast Asia and the Pacific Island countries. As for the norms governing regional infrastructure connectivity, there are also major disagreements between the U.S. and China, especially with regard to digital infrastructure.[86] The U.S. intends to provide a competing vision *vis-à-vis* BRI for the Indo-Pacific region and an alternative to China's infrastructure offer.[87]

The implications of U.S.–China strategic competition have led to pervasive anxiety in the region. As Gurpreet S. Khurana, director of India's National Maritime Foundation, said, America's attempt to set up a new Cold War alliance in line with FOIP could be exceptionally dangerous for countries in the region.[88] In fact, Japan, India, and Australia want neither a G2 made up of the U.S. and China nor a major power confrontation. For instance, the Japanese government uses "Indo-Pacific concept" rather than "Indo-Pacific strategy." Japan has made efforts to work with China in facilitating regional infrastructure, as evidenced by their joint support for the Eastern Economic Corridor in Thailand. As U.S.–China tensions soar, Canberra worries about being caught in the crossfire. Australian Prime Minister Scott Morrison stated that, "Inevitably, in the period ahead, we will be navigating a higher degree of U.S.–China strategic competition." He made it clear that "it is important that U.S.–China relations do not become defined by confrontation."[89] During his visit to the U.S. in September 2019, Morrison mentioned Canberra's "strategic and comprehensive partnerships" with Beijing and said that "China's economic growth is welcomed by Australia." India seeks to strike a delicate balance in its ties with the U.S. and China, emphasizing its principle of strategic autonomy. In June 2018, Indian Prime Minister Narendra Modi emphasized in his keynote speech at the Shangri-La Dialogue that India will promote the "free, open, and inclusive" Indo-Pacific, based on the five S principles in Hindi: *samman* (respect), *samvad* (dialogue), *sahyog* (cooperation), *shanti* (peace), and *samriddhi* (prosperity).[90]

ASEAN countries have also cast doubts on FOIP and America's commitment to the region. Southeast Asian countries such as Indonesia and Thailand believe that the core of FOIP lies within the Quad, whereas the centrality of ASEAN in this regional arrangement will be challenged. ASEAN has realized that FOIP is likely to trigger confrontation between China and the U.S. and drag Southeast Asia into a dilemma over which side to take. In January 2019, the involved parties conducted in-depth discussions on the launch the *ASEAN Outlook on the Indo-Pacific* at the ASEAN Foreign Ministers' Meeting in Chiang Mai, Thailand, emphasizing the need to protect the centrality of ASEAN. As Indonesian Minister of Foreign Affairs Retno Marsudi said, it is important to ensure that "the Indian and Pacific oceans do not become a site of battle for natural resources, regional conflicts and maritime supremacy."[91] ASEAN countries are not willing to become victims of intensifying U.S.–China competition. As Singapore's Prime Minister Lee Hsien Loong stressed, Southeast Asia is no stranger to the great game of nations, and "the rest of the world too has to adjust to a larger role for China. Countries have to accept that China will continue to grow and strengthen, and that it is neither possible nor wise for them to prevent this from happening." He added that there is no strategic inevitability about a U.S.–China face-off, and "nor is it possible to create NATO or Warsaw Pact equivalents with a hard line drawn through Asia, or drawn down the middle of the Pacific Ocean."[92]

From the above, we could find that the complex interplay between the BRI and FOIP might not only drive the negative trajectory of the U.S.–China relationship, which is now at risk of sliding into disastrous confrontation, but may also significantly affect the evolving regional order. It is imperative to control U.S.–China geopolitical and geoeconomic competition in the region, particularly by navigating their infrastructure rivalry.[93] Some conceptual frameworks and practical mechanisms are needed to ensure U.S.–China competitive coexistence and "good competition" in regional infrastructure connectivity.[94]

First, the U.S. and China need to consider holding thematic in-depth dialogues on the infrastructure issue. When participating in the Raisina Dialogue in India in January 2019, U.S. Admiral Philip Davidson, Commander of the U.S. Indo-Pacific Command, said that the "free and open Indo-Pacific is not a containment strategy for China. … We are not asking people to choose between the U.S. and China."[95] Many Chinese strategists also argue for a restrained and delicate response to FOIP, and there is room for the Chinese side to influence the implementation of FOIP. Through U.S.–China dialogues, both sides can notify each other about the developments of the BRI and FOIP, find ways to mitigate mutual concerns on infrastructure projects, and even explore opportunities for cooperation.[96] As a matter of fact, General Electric, Honeywell, and Caterpillar, among numerous other American corporations, have significantly benefited from the BRI and the energy infrastructure in particular. American finance institutions, such as Citibank and Bank of America, are interested in furthering their engagement with BRI infrastructure projects.[97]

Second, the U.S. and China must ensure diffuse reciprocities among regional countries. Secretary Antony Blinken stated in December 2021, "It's not about a contest between a U.S.-centric region or a China-centric region. The Indo-Pacific is its own region."[98] Regional countries, especially ASEAN, are reluctant to pick a side in the event of a China–U.S. rivalry, and they want stronger economic and investment relations with both powers.[99] Southeast Asian countries seek to promote diversified infrastructure cooperation. With the U.S.' announcement of the IPEF, Southeast Asian countries are concerned about new risks of taking sides. In the meantime, they also doubt how much financial support the Biden administration can provide, given the partisan politics in the U.S. In order to ensure various connectivity initiatives in complementing efforts, Indonesia has proposed to establish the ASEAN Indo-Pacific Infrastructure and Connectivity Forum.[100] The U.S. and China need to respect ASEAN's leadership in setting infrastructure rules and standards. In addition, the economic decoupling between Beijing and Washington will not only result in greater Sino–U.S. confrontation but also have sophisticated and far-reaching impacts on regional economic health and the sustainability of infrastructure development. The U.S. and China should open their strategic apertures and rebalance their bilateral economic ties in a more prudent and constructive manner.

Third, it is necessary to address common challenges related to infrastructure connectivity, such as fiscal constraints. A report released by the Harvard Kennedy School claims that China is using "debtbook diplomacy" to expand its strategic clout by providing exorbitant volumes of credit to developing economies in the Asia-Pacific, with significant ramifications for U.S. foreign policy.[101] Such exaggeration might scare people away from China, but it will do nothing to help U.S. competitiveness. Admittedly, infrastructure calls for massive investments, and usually, such projects are initiated by the host countries themselves, who would then choose to enter into contracts on terms they deem appropriate. As China is a latecomer to the global capital market, the debts it issues are not high in percentage terms. According to the 2017 annual report by the Central Bank of Sri Lanka, the country had a total external debt of over US$50 billion, out of which only about 10 percent was financed by China, and over 60 percent of China-financed debts came with interest rates lower than the international level.[102] However, China is aware of the financing risks and has endorsed the Guiding Principles on Financing the

Development of the Belt and Road with the ministries of finance of 25 countries. In April 2018, the China–IMF Capacity Development Center was established to provide training for officials and business communities from BRI-participating countries in order to improve the financial sustainability of related projects. Together with other stakeholders, China and the U.S. could further discuss international rules, norms, and procedures that can mitigate debt risks while meeting their huge demands for investments.

Last but not least, the U.S. and China must seriously tackle the development–security nexus challenges associated with infrastructure construction and establish some deconfliction and confidence-building measures in addressing the securitization of infrastructure connectivity.[103] The U.S. is more attentive to the geostrategic implications of infrastructure connectivity projects related to China in the Indo-Pacific region. For instance, Randall Schriver, U.S. Assistant Secretary of Defense for Indo-Pacific Security Affairs, accused China of employing the BRI projects as a means for both economic and military expansion, including turning several ports in Cambodia, Sri Lanka, and Vanuatu into Chinese naval bases. However, those accusations have been refuted by the related countries. The U.S. and China may consider promoting the International Development and Security Dialogue to identify ways to manage the security implications of infrastructure projects and ensure mutual access to them. In terms of digital infrastructure, there is a pressing need to build international rules. It is not legitimate to exclude China from the rule-making process, and third parties such as ASEAN need to play a leading role in this regard.[104] Facing the pressure from U.S.–China competition in digital connectivity, ASEAN is making efforts to push forward its "Digital Integration Framework Action Plan." Those moves are expected to reduce the fragmentation risks of digital infrastructure and industries in the Indo-Pacific.[105]

2.4. Conclusion

The Communist Party of China has proposed a two-stage strategic plan to realize "socialist modernization" and pursue global leadership by 2049. The U.S. seems to be firm in safeguarding its hegemonic position in world politics. The "competitive rivalry" relationship between China and the U.S. is likely to persist for decades to come. Indeed, the

Russia–Ukraine armed conflict that started in early 2022 is expected to intensify U.S.–China rivalry, as the Biden administration vowed to build a new Bretton Woods system and push its allies and partners to decrease their economic reliance on China.[106] In the foreseeable future, U.S.–China strategic competition over infrastructure connectivity will intensify across the globe and particularly in the Indo-Pacific. Although China still labels itself as a developing country, it has demonstrated extraordinary capabilities in physical and digital infrastructure construction. A state-led model to address infrastructure deficits is often necessary for a developing country, which could make China's approach more attractive. However, China's infrastructure statecraft has met with challenges and setbacks. Recipient countries are worried about their overdependence on China, while financial sustainability issues, among other economic, societal, and political difficulties, in the post-COVID-19 era have forced China to shrink its BRI footprint and enhance its infrastructure statecraft.

Infrastructure connectivity has embedded security and military implications. The U.S. is determined to compete with China in the infrastructure race in the Indo-Pacific. Limited financial resources and a reluctant private sector weaken America's infrastructure statecraft. Through building networked coalitions with allies and partners, as evidenced by the Quad, B3W/PGII, and U.S.–Japan–Australia Trilateral Partnership for Indo-Pacific Infrastructure Investment, the U.S. seeks to gain a "position of strength" against China. However, whether this approach will be successful remains uncertain.

The infrastructure statecraft of China and the U.S. each have their respective constraints. The infrastructure competition between these two powers is not necessarily confrontational. The "good competition" can bring benefits to regional countries and open up more opportunities for U.S.–China collaboration with third parties. China needs to address American concerns and carefully manage the security implications of BRI infrastructure projects. In the meantime, there is no need for the U.S. to view China's expanding infrastructure footprint in the region through a Cold War lens or consider it a zero-sum game. As a report by AidData of the College of William & Mary contends, the BRI would help weak and conflict-prone countries meet their infrastructure needs and ease development imbalances, thereby improving political stability. This would allow the U.S. and other Western countries to focus more resources on global threats and crises.[107]

Efforts by other regional players to mitigate U.S.–China infrastructure competition are critical. There is deep-rooted suspicion of and resistance to China-centric regional order infrastructure connectivity in the Indo-Pacific.[108] Given intractable domestic hurdles in boosting infrastructure investments in the U.S., regional countries are doubtful of America's resolve and resource availability in confronting infrastructure competition. With their respective constraints in exercising infrastructure statecraft, China and the U.S. need a new great power bargain to effectively manage their competitive coexistence in infrastructure in the Indo-Pacific.[109]

Endnotes

1. Suisheng Zhao, "Engagement on the defensive: From the mismatched grand bargain to the emerging US-China rivalry," *Journal of Contemporary China*, 28(118), 6–11 (2019); White House, "Remarks by President Biden on America's place in the world," 4 February 2021. https://www.white house.gov/briefing-room/speeches-remarks/2021/02/04/remarks-by-president-biden-on-americas-place-in-the-world/.

2. A. Denmark, "A new era of intensified US-China competition," Asia Dispatches, Asia Program, The Wilson Center, 4 January 2018. https://www.wilsoncenter.org/blog-post/new-era-intensified-us-china-competition.

3. Mingjiang Li, "The Belt and Road Initiative: Geo-economics and Indo-Pacific security competition," *International Affairs*, 96(1), 160–187 (2020).

4. Yunling Zhang, "China and its neighbourhood: Transformation, challenges and grand strategy," *International Affairs*, 92(4), 835–848 (2016).

5. E. Ratner, "Testimony before the U.S.-China economic and security review commission," Hearing on China's Belt and Road Initiative: Five Years Later, Council on Foreign Relations, 25 January 2018. https://www.uscc.gov/sites/default/files/Ratner_USCC%20Testimony%20CORRECTED.pdf; G. Taylor, "Steve Bannon in Japan, rails against China's 'hegemonic' ambitions," *The Washington Times*, 15 November 2017.

6. R. Medcalf, "Indo-Pacific visions: Giving solidarity a chance," *Asia Policy*, 14(3), 81 (2019).

7. R. Foot and A. King, "Assessing the deterioration in China—U.S. relations: U.S. governmental perspectives on the economic-security nexus," *China International Strategy Review*, 1(1), 39–50 (2019); D. Chandler, "The security-development nexus and the rise of 'anti-foreign policy,'" *Journal of International Relations and Development*, 10(4), 362–386 (2007).

8. Kai He, "Role conceptions, order transition and institutional balancing in the Asia-Pacific: A new theoretical framework," *Australian Journal of*

International Affairs, 72(2), 92–109 (2018); Jue Wang and M. Sampson, "China's multi-front institutional strategies in international development finance," *The Chinese Journal of International Politics*, 15(4), 374–394 (2022).

9 J. Hillman, *Influence and Infrastructure: The Strategic Stakes of Foreign Projects*, Center for Strategic and International Studies (CSIS), Washington DC, 22 January 2019.

10 M. Goodman and D. Parker, "Eurasia's infrastructure rush: What, why, so what?" *CSIS Global Economic Monthly*, 5(1), 1–2 (2016).

11 Selina Ho, "Infrastructure and Chinese power," *International Affairs*, 96(6), 1468–1474 (2020).

12 M. Jamrisko, "China no match for Japan in Southeast Asia infrastructure race," *Bloomberg*, 23 June 2019. https://www.bloombergquint.com/china/china-no-match-for-japan-in-southeast-asia-infrastructure-race.

13 J. Hillman and E. Yayboke, *The Higher Road: Forging a U.S. Strategy for the Global Infrastructure Challenge*, Center for Strategic and International Studies (CSIS), Washington DC, 23 April 2019; T. Dadabaev, "Japanese and Chinese infrastructure development strategies in Central Asia," *Japanese Journal of Political Science*, 19(3), 542–561 (2018); R. Borah, "India responds to Belt & Road Initiative with infrastructure push," *Nikkei Asian Review*, 13 August 2019. https://asia.nikkei.com/Opinion/India-responds-to-Belt-and-Road-Initiative-with-infrastructure-push.

14 M. P. Goodman, G. de Brouwer, S. Armstrong and A. Triggs, "Delivering prosperity in the Indo-Pacific: An agenda for Australia and the United States," CSIS Briefs, Center for Strategic and International Studies (CSIS), Washington DC, pp. 8–9, April 2019; D. Kliman and A. Grace, *Power Play: Addressing China's Belt and Road Strategy*, Center for a New American Security, Washington DC, pp. 25–27, September 2018.

15 D. Shambaugh, "U.S.-China rivalry in Southeast Asia: Power shift or competitive coexistence?" *International Security*, 42(4), 85–127 (2018).

16 M. Fisher and A. Carlsen, "How China is challenging American dominance in Asia," *The New York Times*, 9 March 2018.

17 Gerald Chen, *Understanding China's New Diplomacy: Silk Road and Bullet Trains* (Cheltenham: Edward Elgar Publishing, 2018).

18 Xue Gong, "The Belt & Road Initiative and China's influence in Southeast Asia," *The Pacific Review*, 32(4), 635–665 (2019).

19 E. Kania, *Securing Our 5G Future: The Competitive Challenge and Considerations for U.S. Policy*, Center for a New America Security, Washington DC, p. 10, 7 November 2019; B. Harding, "China's digital Silk Road and Southeast Asia," Commentary, Center for Strategic and International Studies (CSIS), Washington DC, 15 February 2019. https://www.csis.org/analysis/chinas-digital-silk-road-and-southeast-asia.

20 T. J. Pempel, "Soft balancing, hedging, and institutional Darwinism: The economic-security nexus and East Asian regionalism," *Journal of East Asian Studies*, 10(2), 209–238 (2010).

21 C. K. Johnson, *President Xi Jinping's 'Belt and Road' Initiative*, Center for Strategic and International Studies (CSIS), Washington DC, 28 March 2016. https://www.csis.org/analysis/president-xi-jinping%E2%80%99s-belt-and-road-initiative.

22 Li Wei, "Zhongguo weilai nengyuan fazhan zhanlue tanxi (The future of China's energy strategy)," *Renmin wang (People's Daily Online)*, 12 February 2014. http://politics.people.com.cn/n/2014/0212/c1001-24329909.html.

23 C. Joy-Perez and D. Scissor, "Be wary of spending on the Belt and Road," American Enterprise Institute, 14 November 2018. http://www.aei.org/publication/be-wary-of-spending-on-the-belt-and-road/.

24 Wang Jisi, "Xijin: zhongguo diyuan zhanlue de zaipingheng (March westward: The rebalancing of China's geopolitical strategy)," *Huanqiu shibao wang (Global Times Online)*, 17 October 2012. https://opinion.huanqiu.com/article/9CaKrnJxoLS.

25 Xi Jinping, "Xieshou tuijin yidaiyilu jianshe (Promoting the Belt and Road Initiative together)," *Xinhua wang [Xinhua Net]*, 14 May 2017. http://www.xinhuanet.com/2017-05/14/c_1120969677.htm.

26 A. Elek, "China takes the lead on economic integration," *East Asia Forum*, 7 July 2015. https://www.eastasiaforum.org/2015/07/07/china-takes-the-lead-on-economic-integration.

27 Ye Qiong, "Gaozhiliang gongjian yidaiyilu shuoguo huiji shijie (High-quality cooperation of the BRI benefits the world)," *Zhongguo yidaiyilu wang (China and the BRI Web)*, 11 October 2021. https://www.yidaiyilu.gov.cn/xwzx/gnxw/189005.htm.

28 Bowen Yu, "Cognitive evolution and China's international development cooperation," *The Chinese Journal of International Politics*, 14(4), 481–505 (2021).

29 *"The Belt and Road Initiative: A New Means to Transformative Global Governance towards Sustainable Development,"* United Nations Development Programme and China Center for International Economic Exchanges, pp. 55–59. https://www.undp.org/content/dam/china/docs/Publications/UNDP-CH-GGR%202017.pdf.

30 Yang Jiechi, "Yi Xi Jinping waijiao sixiang wei zhidao shenru tuijin xinshidai duiwai gongzuo (Advancing the diplomatic work of the new era with Xi Jinping's thought)," *Renmin wang (People's Daily Online)*, 2 August 2018. http://theory.people.com.cn/n1/2018/0802/c40531-30192489.html.

31 "Xi Jinping zai zhoubian waijiao gongzuo zuotanhui shang fabiao zhong-yao jianghua (Xi Jinping made important speech at the conference on China's relations with neighboring countries)," *Renmin wang* (*People's Daily Online*), 25 October 2013. http://politics.people.com.cn/n/2013/1025/c1024-23332318.html.

32 Wang Hong, "Haiyang qiangguo jianshe zhutui shixian zhongguomeng (Building up the maritime power can help realize the China dream)," *Renmin ribao (People's Daily)*, 20 November 2017; J. Bradford, "PRC investments in global maritime infrastructure: Implications for port access, Center for International Maritime Security," 5 May 2021. https://cimsec.org/prc-investments-in-global-maritime-infrastructure-implications-for-port-access/.

33 M. Jamrisko, "China no match for Japan in Southeast Asia infrastructure race," *Bloomberg*, 23 June 2019. https://www.bloombergquint.com/china/china-no-match-for-japan-in-southeast-asia-infrastructure-race.

34 Industry Week, "China, Singapore vow trade cooperation, infrastructure investment," 12 June 2017. https://www.industryweek.com/the-economy/trade/article/22019429/china-singapore-vow-trade-cooperation-infrastructure-investment.

35 "Master Plan on ASEAN Connectivity 2025," ASEAN Secretariat, September 2016. https://asean.org/wp-content/uploads/2016/09/Master-Plan-on-ASEAN-Connectivity-20251.pdf.

36 Zhaohui Wang and Yufeng Fu, "Local politics and fluctuating engagement with China: Analysing the Belt and Road Initiative in maritime Southeast Asia," *The Chinese Journal of International Politics*, 15(2), 163–182 (2022).

37 "Myanmar signs smaller Chinese port deal amid 'debt trap' fears," *South China Morning Post*, 9 November 2018. https://www.scmp.com/news/asia/southeast-asia/article/2172442/myanmar-signs-smaller-chinese-port-deal-amid-debt-trap.

38 "Fast track: Indonesia, Malaysia rail projects may give China more deals," *The Strait Times*, 23 April 2019. https://www.straitstimes.com/asia/se-asia/fast-track-indonesia-malaysia-rail-projects-may-give-china-more-deals.

39 B. Berge, "Malaysia's canceled Belt and Road Initiative projects and the implications for China," The Diplomat, 27 August 2018. https://thediplomat.com/2018/08/malaysias-canceled-belt-and-road-initiative-projects-and-the-implications-for-china/.

40 "Bangladesh blacklists Chinese construction firm, cancels highway deal after bribe claim," *South China Morning Post,* 18 January 2018. https://www.scmp.com/news/asia/south-asia/article/2129493/bangladesh-blacklists-chinese-construction-firm-cancels-highway.

41 J. Smith, "China's Belt and Road Initiative: Strategic implications and international opposition," *Backgrounder*, No. 3331, The Heritage Foundation, August 2018.

42 "Japan's Prime Minister: Japan will pour $200 billion into global infrastructure," *Nikkei Asian Review*, 9 June 2016. https://asia.nikkei.com/Economy/Japan-s-prime-minister-Japan-will-pour-200-billion-into-global-infrastructure.

43 S. Morrison, "Australia and the Pacific: A new chapter," Speech, Lavarack Barracks, Townsville, Queensland, 8 November 2018. https://www.pm.gov.au/media/address-australia-and-pacific-new-chapter.

44 "Xi Jinping: tuidong gongjian yidaiylu zoushen zoushi zaofu renmin (Xi Jinping: Strengthening the BRI cooperation and benefiting the people)," *Xinhua wang [Xinhua Net]*, 27 August 2018. http://www.xinhuanet.com/politics/leaders/2018-08/27/c_1123336562.htm.

45 Third-Party Market Cooperation Guidelines and Cases, National Development and Reform Commission, China, August 2019. https://www.yidaiyilu.gov.cn/wcm.files/upload/CMSydylgw/201909/201909051015041.pdf.

46 "Xi pledges to bring benefits to people," *China Daily*, 28 August 2018. http://www.chinatoday.com.cn/ctenglish/2018/ttxw/201808/t20180828_800139306.html.

47 A. Blinken, "An enduring vision for Central Asia," Remarks at the Brookings Institute, 31 March 2015. http://www.state.gov/s/d/2015/240013.htm; M. Wolf, "A rebuff of China's AIIB is folly," *Financial Times*, 24 March 2015. https://www.ft.com/content/0dff595e-d16a-11e4-86c8-00144feab7de.

48 T. P. Cavanna, "What does China's Belt and Road Initiative mean for US grand strategy?" *The Diplomat*, 5 June 2018. https://thediplomat.com/2018/06/what-does-chinas-belt-and-road-initiative-mean-for-us-grand-strategy/.

49 White House, *National Security Strategy of the United States of America*, Washington DC, pp. 2–3, 25 December 2017.

50 A. Karni, "Trump rants behind closed doors with CEOs," *Politico*, 8 August 2018. https://www.politico.com/story/2018/08/08/trump-executive-dinner-bedminster-china-766609; and M. Pence, "Remarks by Vice President Pence on the administration's policy toward China," White House, 4 October 2018. https://trumpwhitehouse.archives.gov/briefings-statements/remarks-vice-president-pence-administrations-policy-toward-china/.

51 A. Panda, "Is the Trump administration about to take on China's Belt and Road Initiative?" *The Diplomat*, 19 October 2017. https://thediplomat.com/2017/10/is-the-trump-administration-about-to-take-on-chinas-belt-and-road-initiative/.

52 Charissa Yong, "Pence warns Indo-Pacific region against China's debt diplomacy, says US offers 'better option'," *The Straits Times*, 8 November 2018. https://www.straitstimes.com/world/united-states/pence-slams-china-says-us-offers-countries-better-option.

53 C. Grassley, "Grassley, senators express concerns over China's 'debt trap' diplomacy with developing countries," United States Senate, 10 August 2018. https://www.grassley.senate.gov/news/news-releases/grassley-senators-express-concerns-over-china-s-debt-trap-diplomacy-developing.

54 White House (2017), *Op. cit.*, pp. 45–46.

55 P. Harris and P. Trubowitz, "The politics of power projection: The pivot to Asia, its failure, and the future of American primacy," *The Chinese Journal of International Politics*, 14(2), 191–199 (2021).

56 H. R. Clinton, "America's engagement in the Asia-Pacific, remarks," Hawaii, 28 October 2010. https://2009-2017.state.gov/secretary/20092013clinton/rm/2010/10/150141.htm.

57 White House, "U.S.-India joint strategic vision for the Asia-Pacific and Indian ocean region," Press Release, 25 January 2015. https://obamawhitehouse.archives.gov/the-press-office/2015/01/25/us-india-joint-strategic-vision-asia-pacific-and-indian-ocean-region.

58 Z. Cooper and A. Shearer, "Thinking clearly about China's layered Indo-Pacific strategy," *Bulletin of the Atomic Scientists*, 73(5), 305–311 (2017).

59 White House (2017), *Op. cit.*, p. 46.

60 Z. Khalilzad, D. T. Orletsky, J. D. Pollack, K. L. Pollpeter, A. Rabasa, D. A. Shlapak, A. N. Shulsky and A. J. Tellis, *The United States and Asia: Toward a New US Strategy and Force Posture*, RAND Corporation, Santa Monica, California, 2001, pp. 43–48. https://www.rand.org/pubs/monograph_reports/MR1315.html.

61 M. R. Pompeo, "Remarks on 'America's Indo-Pacific economic vision'," US Department of State, Washington DC, 30 July 2018. https://www.state.gov/remarks-on-americas-indo-pacific-economic-vision/.

62 US Department of Commerce, "Secretary of commerce Wilbur Ross announces programs to increase US commercial engagement in the Indo-Pacific region," Press Release, Office of Public Affairs, 30 July 2018. https://www.commerce.gov/news/press-releases/2018/07/us-secretary-commerce-wilbur-ross-announces-programs-increase-us.

63 R. W. Washburne, "A better economic development model," *The New York Times*, 28 June 2018. https://www.nytimes.com/2018/06/28/opinion/letters/development-model.html.

64 White House, *US-Japan Joint Statement on Advancing a Free and Open Indo-Pacific through Energy, Infrastructure and Digital Connectivity*

Cooperation, 13 November 2018. https://www.whitehouse.gov/briefings-statements/u-s-japan-joint-statement-advancing-free-open-indo-pacific-energy-infrastructure-digital-connectivity-cooperation/.

65 M. Pence, "The United States seeks collaboration, not control, in the Indo-Pacific," *The Washington Post*, 9 November 2018. https://www.washingtonpost.com/opinions/mike-pence-the-united-states-seeks-collaboration-not-control-in-the-indo-pacific/2018/11/09/1a0c330a-e45a-11e8-b759-3d88a5ce9e19_story.html.

66 US Department of State, *US Security Cooperation in the Indo-Pacific Region*, Fact Sheet, Office of the Spokesperson, 4 August 2018. https://www.state.gov/u-s-security-cooperation-in-the-indo-pacific-region/.

67 Zhao Minghao, "The 'Indo-Pacific strategy' and China-US geopolitical competition," China-United States Exchange Foundation, 21 August 2018. https://www.chinausfocus.com/foreign-policy/the-indo-pacific-strategy-and-china-us-geopolitical-competition.

68 R. D. Fisher Jr, "Testimony before the house permanent select committee on intelligence," Hearing on China's Global Military Power Projection Challenge to the United States, pp. 10–12, 17 May 2018. https://docs.house.gov/meetings/IG/IG00/20180517/108298/HHRG-115-IG00-Wstate-FisherR-20180517.pdf; and D. Cave, "A new battle for Guadalcanal, this time with China," *The New York Times*, 23 July 2018.

69 S. McLeod, "Deepening Japan's cooperation with Papua New Guinea," *East Asia Forum*, 20 October 2020. https://www.eastasiaforum.org/2020/10/20/deepening-japans-cooperation-with-papua-new-guinea/.

70 F. Fukuyama, "Exporting the Chinese model," *The Straits Times*, 30 December 2015.

71 "Remarks by Vice President Pence at the 2018 APEC CEO summit," Port Moresby, Papua New Guinea, 16 November 2018. https://www.white-house.gov/briefings-statements/remarks-vice-president-pence-2018-apec-ceo-summit-port-moresby-papua-new-guinea/.

72 Pence (2018), *Op. cit.*

73 K. M. Campbell and E. Ratner, "The China reckoning: How Beijing defied American expectations," *Foreign Affairs*, 97(2), 60–70 (2018).

74 Cheng Li, *Biden's China Strategy: Coalition-driven Competition or Cold War-style Confrontation?* The Brookings Institution, May 2021, pp. 2–4.

75 The White House, *Fact Sheet: President Biden and G7 Leaders Launch Build Back Better World (B3W) Partnership*, 12 June 2021. https://www.whitehouse.gov/briefing-room/statements-releases/2021/06/12/fact-sheet-president-biden-and-g7-leaders-launch-build-back-better-world-b3w-partnership/.

76 The White House, *Memorandum on the Partnership for Global Infrastructure and Investment*, 26 June 2022. https://www.whitehouse.gov/briefing-room/presidential-actions/2022/06/26/memorandum-on-the-partnership-for-global-infrastructure-and-investment/.

77 The White House, *Fact Sheet: Quad Leaders' Summit*, 24 September 2021. https://www.whitehouse.gov/briefing-room/statements-releases/2021/09/24/fact-sheet-quad-leaders-summit/.

78 US Department of Defense, *Indo-Pacific Strategy Report: Preparedness, Partnerships, and Promoting a Networked Region*, pp. 44–48, 1 June 2019. https://media.defense.gov/2019/Jul/01/2002152311/-1/-1/1/DEPARTMENT-OF-DEFENSE-INDO-PACIFIC-STRATEGY-REPORT-2019.PDF.

79 S. Tagliapietra, "The global gateway: A real step towards a stronger Europe in the world?" *Bruegel Blog*, 7 December 2021. https://www.bruegel.org/2021/12/the-global-gateway-a-real-step-towards-a-stronger-europe-in-the-world/.

80 S. Lau and H. Cokelaere, "EU launches 'global gateway' to counter China's Belt and Road," Politico, 15 September 2021. https://www.politico.eu/article/eu-launches-global-gateway-to-counter-chinas-belt-and-road/.

81 A. Blinken, "A free and open Indo-Pacific," US Department of State, 14 December 2021. https://www.state.gov/a-free-and-open-indo-pacific/.

82 The White House, *Fact Sheet: In Asia, President Biden and a Dozen Indo-Pacific Partners Launch the Indo-Pacific Economic Framework for Prosperity*, 23 May 2022. https://www.whitehouse.gov/briefing-room/statements-releases/2022/05/23/fact-sheet-in-asia-president-biden-and-a-dozen-indo-pacific-partners-launch-the-indo-pacific-economic-framework-for-prosperity/.

83 US Department of State, *U.S. and OECD Co-host Panel on Quality Infrastructure and the Blue Dot Network*, 5 October 2021. https://www.state.gov/u-s-and-oecd-co-host-panel-on-quality-infrastructure-and-the-blue-dot-network/.

84 The White House, *Fact Sheet: Announcing the Presidential Initiative for Democratic Renewal*, 9 December 2021. https://www.whitehouse.gov/briefing-room/statements-releases/2021/12/09/fact-sheet-announcing-the-presidential-initiative-for-democratic-renewal/.

85 A. Acharya, "Asia after the liberal international order," *East Asia Forum*, 10 July 2018. https://www.eastasiaforum.org/2018/07/10/asia-after-the-liberal-international-order/.

86 E. Medeiros, "The changing fundamentals of US-China relations," *The Washington Quarterly*, 42(3), 100–101 (2019); J. Hemmings, "Reconstructing order: The geopolitical risks in China's digital silk road," *Asia Policy*, 15(1), 15–16 (2020); Kliman and Grace (2018), *Op. cit.*, pp. 12–13.

87 Washburne (2018), *Op. cit.*; J. Zumbrun and S. Fidler, "White House sets aside skepticism, backs funding increase for World Bank," *Wall Street Journal*, 22 April 2018. https://www.wsj.com/articles/white-house-sets-aside-skepticism-backs-funding-increase-for-world-bank-1524344235; C. Edel, "How to counter China's influence in the South Pacific," *Foreign Affairs*, 13 November 2018. https://www.foreignaffairs.com/articles/china/2018-11-13/how-counter-chinas-influence-south-pacific.

88 G. S. Khurana, "Trump's new cold war alliance in Asia is dangerous," *The Washington Post*, 14 November 2017. https://www.washingtonpost.com/news/theworldpost/wp/2017/11/14/trump-asia-trip/.

89 S. Morrison, "The beliefs that guide us," Keynote Address to Asia Briefing Live, Prime Minister of Australia and his Cabinet, Sydney, 1 November 2018. https://www.pm.gov.au/media/keynote-address-asia-briefing-live-beliefs-guide-us.

90 Indian Ministry of External Affairs, "Prime Minister's keynote address at Shangri La Dialogue," 1 June 2018.

91 L. Yulisman, "Indonesia wants ASEAN to be axis of Indo-Pacific strategy," *The Straits Times*, 10 January 2019.

92 "PM Lee Hsien Loong gave the keynote address at the International Institute for Strategic Studies (IISS) Shangri-La Dialogue opening dinner on 31 May 2019 at the Shangri-La Hotel, Singapore," Singaporean PM Office, 31 May 2019. https://www.pmo.gov.sg/Newsroom/PM-Lee-Hsien-Loong-at-the-IISS-Shangri-La-Dialogue-2019.

93 T. R. Heath and W. R. Thompson, "Avoiding US-China competition is futile: Why the best option is to manage strategic rivalry," *Asia Policy*, 13(2), 91–120 (2018).

94 K. M. Campbell and J. Sullivan, "Competition without catastrophe: How America can both challenge and coexist with China," *Foreign Affairs*, 98(5), 97–98 (2019); U.S. Department of State, "A free and open Indo-Pacific," 14 December 2021. https://www.state.gov/a-free-and-open-indo-pacific/.

95 D. Peri, "Free Indo-Pacific not against China: U.S. admiral," *The Hindu*, 9 January 2019. https://www.thehindu.com/news/national/free-indo-pacific-not-against-china-us-admiral/article25952614.ece.

96 T. R. Heath, K. Gunness and C. A. Cooper, *The PLA and China's Rejuvenation*, RAND Corporation, December 2016, Summary xiii. http://www.rand.org/content/dam/rand/pubs/research_reports/RR1400/RR1402/RAND_RR1402.pdf.

97 "Western firms are coining it along China's One Belt, One Road," *Economist*, 3 August 2017. https://www.economist.com/business/2017/08/03/westernfirms-are-coining-it-along-chinas-one-belt-one-road.

98 A. Blinken, "A free and open Indo-Pacific," US Department of State, 14 December 2021. https://www.state.gov/a-free-and-open-indo-pacific/.

99 Lee Hsien Loong, "The endangered Asian century: America, China, and the Perils of confrontation," *Foreign Affairs*, 99(4), 61–64 (2020).

100 A. R. Darmawan, "Reformulating ASEAN's outlook on the Indo-Pacific," *East Asia Forum*, 29 September 2021.

101 S. Parker and G. Chefitz, *Debtbook Diplomacy: China's Strategic Leveraging of Its Newfound Economic Influence and the Consequences for U.S. Foreign Policy*, Belfer Center, Harvard Kennedy School, May 2018.

102 China's Ministry of Foreign Affairs, "Transcript of Vice foreign Minister Le Yucheng's exclusive interview with the *Financial Times*," 26 September 2018. https://www.fmprc.gov.cn/mfa_eng/wjbxw/t1598897.shtml.

103 W. Pacatte, *Competing to Win: A Coalition Approach to Countering the BRI*, Center for Strategic and International Studies (CSIS), p. 10, Washington DC, December 2019.

104 M. Manantan, "US, Japan, and Southeast Asia cooperation: Building a data governance blueprint," *Asia-Pacific Bulletin*, 505, East-West Center, pp. 1–2, 30 April 2020.

105 A. Anuar, "ASEAN's digital economy: Development, division, disruption," RSIS Commentary, No. 046, Singapore: S. Rajaratnam School of International Studies, Nanyang Technological University, p. 3, 18 March 2019.

106 R. Foroohar, "It's time for a new Bretton woods," *Financial Times*, 18 April 2022. https://www.ft.com/content/b437fd60-7817-490e-b456-eb7ef1565f13.

107 R. Bluhm, A. Fuchs, A. Strange, A. Dreher, B. Parks and M. J. Tierney, "Connective financing: Chinese infrastructure projects and the diffusion of economic activity in developing countries," *Working Paper* No. 64, AidData, September 2018.

108 Feng Zhang and Barry Buzan, "The relevance of deep pluralism for China's foreign policy," *The Chinese Journal of International Politics*, 15(3), 268–271 (2022).

109 Shambaugh (2018), *Op. cit.*

© 2025 World Scientific Publishing Europe Ltd.
https://doi.org/10.1142/9781800616318_0004

Chapter 3

Parsing Post-Pandemic U.S.–China Competition: Mutual (Mis)Perceptions and Dueling Geostrategies[*]

Andrew Scobell

United States Institute of Peace, United States

As the world navigates the third decade of the 21st century, relations between the United States (U.S.) and the People's Republic of China can best be characterized as elevated great power competition or rivalry. Indeed, at the midpoint of the Joseph R. Biden administration, there appears to be greater continuity than change in the U.S.' China policy and no indication of change in Beijing's policy toward the U.S. Thus, a condition of heightened great power competition is likely to extend into the foreseeable future. This competition encompasses multiple dimensions and arenas with a considerable number of contentious issues and significant diverging interests. Key challenges in the bilateral relationship include overcoming deep mutual distrust and suspicion and reconciling competing geostrategies. For qualitative improvement, not only must the two states address perceptions and misperceptions, but each also needs to fundamentally alter its image of the other.

---

[*]This chapter was originally printed as "Parsing Post-Pandemic U.S.-China Competition: Mutual (Mis)Perceptions and Dueling Geostrategies." *The China Review*, Vol. 23, No. 1 (2023): 79–105. https://www.jstor.org/stable/48717989. Reproduced with kind permission of CUHK Press.

3.1. Introduction

Relations between the United States (U.S.) and the People's Republic of China (PRC) are currently at their lowest point in decades. What is the best way to characterize the relationship? How can we explain the evolution and current condition of bilateral ties? What are the central challenges in U.S.–China relations? I posit the following answers. First, the relationship is best characterized as one of heightened great power competition or rivalry. Second, the trajectory of U.S.–China relations can be best understood by viewing it through a political psychology lens and using a geopolitical rubric. Third, the central challenges include addressing deep mutual distrust and reconciling competing geostrategies.

What explains the dramatic deterioration in relations between the U.S. and China in recent years? Neither realism nor liberalism by themselves seem to offer strong explanatory value. Realism alone would anticipate elevated great power competition between the U.S. and China commencing much earlier than it actually did—by at least a decade or two.[1] Liberalism alone would expect that, as Washington and Beijing engage more, both diplomatically and economically, with each other in the global system, increasing common interests would lead these two great powers to find greater cooperation mutually beneficial.[2]

Not long ago, the framework of U.S.–China relations appeared stable and durable, with an overall climate that seemed cordial. When a turn for the worse occurred toward the end of the 2010s, it appeared sudden and abrupt.[3] What happened, and what explains the dramatic turnaround? The U.S.–China dyad had long been troubled, yet the outward appearance of comity persisted because the dominant image each side maintained of the other remained positive despite a rising undercurrent of tensions and an accumulation of unresolved disputes. Images are slow to change, even in the face of perceptions to the contrary. Moreover, until relatively recently, the predominant strategic focuses of the U.S. and China were on different geographic arenas: the former in the Greater Middle East, while the latter focused on the Western Pacific.

Political psychology highlights the significance of images and "perceptual factors" (see Chapter 1) in international relations. One state's image of another state tends to be enduring, while its perceptions of that state may change based on specific actions taken by it. Robert Jervis noted, "the strong tendency for people to see what they expect to see and assimilate incoming information to pre-existing images."[4] Geopolitics, meanwhile, underscores the impact of geography on international politics, particularly on the strategic topography of a country's surroundings.[5] A state's conception of its threat environment and strategic formulation is influenced by the contours of its geographic environment. This geostrategic outlook tends to be somewhat static, but it can also fluctuate as a state's capabilities and ambitions rise or fall.

After defining key terms, this chapter proceeds to assess the current state of U.S.–China relations and explain how the relationship reached its present condition. Next, it analyzes the cases of COVID-19 and Ukraine to highlight the condition of contemporary ties and assess where the dyad might be headed. Lastly, the chapter offers some conclusions about and implications derived from the foregoing research and analysis.

3.1.1. *Definitions*

A rivalry can be said to exist when a relationship between two states is antagonistic, characterized by "long-term hostility" and intense competition. Interstate rivalry manifests itself as the persistence of "multiple disputes, continuing disagreements and the threat of the use of force."[6] U.S.–China competition encompasses multiple dimensions and arenas, with a considerable number of contentious issues, significant diverging interests, and the persistent military confrontation at multiple political-military flashpoints in the Western Pacific, which threaten to escalate into actual armed conflict. While no widely accepted definition of what constitutes a great power exists, it seems evident that both the U.S., with the world's largest economy and most potent armed forces, and China, possessing the world's second-largest economy and a sizeable military, merit this label.

"Image" refers to a state's standing in the eyes of another state's elites. Image is important for assessing a state's disposition *vis-à-vis* another state. "Perception," meanwhile, refers to the cognitive processing of information by a state's elites. Images in international relations are overarching and enduring, whereas perceptions of state rhetoric and actions are specific and immediate. As Robert Jervis observed, "when a statesman has developed a certain image of another country he will maintain that view [even] in the face of large amounts of discrepant information."[7] For an image to change, national elites must be inundated with *overwhelming* "amounts of discrepant information" to overcome the impact of cognitive dissonance.[8]

3.2. Where Are U.S.–China Relations?

In 2022, U.S.–China relations were characterized as elevated great power competition, or what Feng Liu and Kai He dub "competitive rivalry" (see Chapter 1). Although it is also unclear what "great power competition" means, beyond heightened tensions and increased potential for conflict, it is evident that this term is foremost in the minds of elites in Washington and Beijing.[9] Yet, American policymakers and analysts are far more forthright about openly using the word "competition" than their Chinese counterparts.

3.2.1. *Joe Biden: Building back for the better?*

Midpoint in the Joseph R. Biden administration, there appears to be considerable continuity with the hardline China policy of the Donald J. Trump administration. Yet, the continuity between the Trump and Biden administrations lies in the realm of negative images and perceptions of China rather than in their approaches. While under Trump, U.S.' China policy was filled with inflated rhetoric and high-profile confrontational posturing, Biden has adopted measured verbiage and a more subdued approach. Moreover, the Biden administration has adopted a more holistic and strategic approach both at home and abroad. In the foreign policy arena, this entails not only focusing solely on hard-nosed dialogue with Beijing but also actively engaging with allies and partners throughout the Indo-Pacific and beyond. Moreover, these efforts extend beyond the military realm by strengthening security cooperation and collaborating to enhance the capabilities of others. A prime example of this enhanced military cooperation is the Biden administration's effort to devise an agreement that enables technical cooperation with Australia and the United Kingdom in the design and construction of nuclear-powered submarines for Canberra's navy, better known by the acronym "AUKUS."[10] The Biden administration has also focused on expanding consultation and coordination with like-minded states in the diplomatic and economic spheres. The prime example of this is the revitalization of the Quadrilateral Security Dialogue between Washington, Canberra, New Delhi, and Tokyo, better known as the "Quad."[11] Beyond these initiatives, as Indo-Pacific Coordinator at the National Security Council Kurt Campbell has observed, is the need for the U.S. to articulate a "positive economic vision" for the region.[12]

Over the years, America's China policy has generally been under the purview of senior officials in successive administrations who assumed that Washington's relationship with Beijing was obviously special and inherently valuable to the U.S. This tendency prompted successive administrations to make maintaining positive or at least cordial bilateral ties a high priority in and of itself rather than considering comprehensively U.S. foreign policy and asking how China fit within the bigger picture and related to Washington's overarching priorities. Hence, U.S.' China policy was sometimes viewed in a vacuum and frequently divorced from its relations with other states, including its key allies and partners. The Biden administration is consciously working to avoid this trap by widening Washington's foreign policy outlook and embedding the China strategy within a broader Indo-Pacific strategy. According to Kurt Campbell, "The best China policy is a good Asia policy."[13]

Domestically, the Biden administration recognizes that for America to succeed in long-term competition with China, it must invest in itself and its future. Biden's Build Back Better plan aims to invest billions of dollars in extensively upgrading U.S. infrastructure. However, the fate of this effort has been hampered by hyper-partisanship and political gridlock in Washington.[14]

3.2.2. *Xi Jinping: The logic of dual circulation?*

Continuity also seems to characterize China's confrontational policy toward the U.S., with President Xi Jinping continuing a hard-hitting approach. This tough-nosed strategy also appears to be in effect across the board in Beijing's foreign relations with other states in the Asia-Pacific.

For decades, Beijing had never adopted a regional policy; instead, it was focused on balancing against, band-wagoning with, or standing equidistant between the two superpowers of the time: the U.S. and the Soviet Union. Yet, with the end of the Cold War and the disintegration of the Soviet Union, China found itself in an uncomfortable geopolitical situation but faced unparalleled opportunities to expand its influence across Asia-Pacific. In acting upon these opportunities in Central Asia, Southeast Asia, and elsewhere, China developed a neighborhood strategy that remained undefined until Xi Jinping's tenure. In 2017, Beijing published its first white paper on its home region, stating that "China has all along taken advancement of regional prosperity and stability as its own responsibility."[15] This rhetoric implies that China considered this region its own "sphere of influence," and Beijing's strategy is focused on limiting U.S. access in this region and restricting U.S. access at China's immediate periphery.[16]

In 2013, shortly after taking office, Xi, looking beyond Beijing's home region, launched his signature foreign policy initiative aimed at engaging with the wider world. The Belt and Road Initiative (BRI), which largely targeted developing countries, was intended to present China as an economic opportunity for the entire globe, eager to lend a helping hand by building and financing massive and much needed infrastructure projects, including highways, railways, pipelines, and ports.[17]

Along with the increased international economic activity, China began to act more assertively, particularly in its immediate neighborhood. This increased use of coercion occurred in various locations, including the South China Sea, the East China Sea, the Taiwan Strait, and the high Himalayas. Military and paramilitary activities were aimed at strengthening China's territorial claims in these locations, including maintaining a persistent presence and the building of permanent structures, especially on islands and reefs in the South China Sea. Further afield, trade, investment, and other economic activities also increased alongside a growing diplomatic presence and military activity. Under Xi, China has made extensive use of diplomatic and economic tools to exert coercive measures on various countries. In addition, China's armed forces have engaged in more military field exercises with other armed forces at greater distances from home, and in 2017, the People's Liberation Army established its first official overseas base in the small African state of Djibouti.[18]

Meanwhile, at home, under Xi's leadership, Beijing tightened its control over the defense establishment and restructured China's economy to strengthen central planning.[19] A key concept in the Chinese Communist Party's (CCP's) efforts to recalibrate the economy is "dual circulation." This term refers to an initiative aimed at countering China's considerable dependence on global trade and investment by giving greater attention to domestic factors that drive its economic growth, thereby stimulating the economy.[20] How successful this initiative will be remains unclear; however, it appears to be Beijing's attempt at achieving a limited "decoupling" of the Chinese and U.S. economies.[21]

Beijing also focused funding and resources on military modernization and technological innovation. In addition, Xi has presided over harsh crackdowns on dissent not only in China's Han heartland but also in the country's far-flung regions, including Hong Kong, Tibet, and Xinjiang.

The overarching trend of the past decade has been a reassertion of central control across all spheres, including the military, economics, politics, technology, and society.

3.3. How Did U.S.–China Relations Get Here?

To recap, relations between the U.S. and China seem to have experienced swift and sudden deterioration in the late 2010s. But in reality, the rift had been building for many years, although the animosity and tension simmered just below the surface. Yet, at an immediate and pragmatic level, both Washington and Beijing strived to keep up appearances, as leaders in both capitals sought cordial bilateral relations since each side benefited from continued U.S.–China comity. Moreover, at a deeper level, cognitive factors delayed the emergence of open conflict as geostrategic thinking in both countries evolved slowly. The following two sections focus on these two areas, explaining how each separately had culminated to a tipping point by 2019 and the onset of the COVID-19 pandemic.

3.3.1. *Sudden image shift, slow perception drift*

U.S. and Chinese images of the other have remained largely positive over the past few decades, even as perceptions of the other's actions became increasingly negative. Yet, the tipping point appears to have been in 2019, when Washington's and Beijing's images of each other became unmistakably negative. Each side had finally come to view the other in adversarial terms, perceiving elevated security threats and endangered economic interests (see Chapter 1). Although the exact year marking the shift is a matter of debate, it became undeniable toward the end of the Trump administration.[22]

Following U.S.–China rapprochement in the early 1970s, both Washington and Beijing maintained largely positive images of one another for more than three decades as elites in the two capitals were inclined to see what they expected and wanted to see.[23] In the 1970s and 1980s, objective conditions—notably, a U.S.–Chinese alignment against the Soviet Union—reinforced these upbeat perspectives. In the aftermath of the 1989 Tiananmen Square massacre, despite a shaken bilateral relationship in search of a post-Cold War rationale, a facade of positivity endured for at least another decade. Although suspicions and distrust accumulated in Washington and Beijing, these sentiments often remained suppressed as both sides were "pretending to be friends."[24] However, these sensitivities began surfacing with increasing frequency in the 2000s and 2010s as the U.S.–China power gap was perceived to narrow quite suddenly and dramatically: first militarily, then economically, and finally technologically.[25] With these power shifts, new and more negative images gradually emerged, replacing the prior positive ones.

Military: Significant U.S. concerns about China's growing military power first emerged decades ago during the 1990s, when the official PRC defense budget began to grow annually by double digits. Negative perceptions of China's armed forces first stemmed from the PLA's direct involvement in the bloody suppression of the 1989 protests in Beijing. These dark scenes were reinforced by a series of provocative missile tests and military exercises that China conducted in the vicinity of the Taiwan Strait during the 1995–1996 crisis. By the mid-2000s, U.S. concerns about the growing strength of Chinese capabilities led to the Department of Defense embracing a new term: "anti-access and area denial," or "A2/AD." This addition to the Pentagon's lexicon signaled that the U.S. military had begun taking Chinese military modernization more seriously, especially its ability to hold at risk American air and naval assets operating within the so-called "First Island Chain"—the East China Sea, the Yellow Sea, the Taiwan Strait, and the South China Sea. Yet, A2/AD revealed more about Pentagon "psychology" than it did about actual improvements in PLA capabilities.[26]

However, the emergence of periodic political-military crises, such as the Hainan Island incident of April 2001, failed to alter Washington's overall and pervasive positive image of China. Finally, by the mid-2010s, Chinese actions began chipping away at the largely favorable image that Washington had held. China's 2013 unilateral declaration of an expansive air defense identification zone (ADIZ) in the East China Sea, along with Beijing's massive island-building initiative and construction of military facilities in the South China Sea that began in 2014, grabbed U.S. attention.[27] Moreover, the massive military parade held in September 2015 to commemorate the end of the Second World War in Asia also served to erode Washington's enduring positive image of a cooperative, non-threatening China. During this decade, the PLA continued to conduct bilateral military exercises with Russian forces; some involved tens of thousands of Chinese troops, while others were conducted in provocative locations.

By 2019, the cumulative effect of all these developments ultimately produced a fundamental change in Washington's image of China.

Meanwhile, Chinese post-Mao perceptions of a threatening U.S. military first emerged in 1989, when Washington froze arms sales as part of sanctions imposed in the aftermath of the Tiananmen crackdown. These Chinese perceptions were reinforced during the 1995–1996 Taiwan Strait crisis, when Beijing was caught by surprise when the U.S. dispatched not one but two carrier battle groups to the vicinity of island.[28] Although this move served as a wake-up call to China that the PLA needed greatly improved operational capabilities to effectively counter U.S. military intervention in a Taiwan contingency, the crisis did not fundamentally alter the pervasive positive image of the U.S. held by Beijing.

In 1999, when the U.S. military bombed the PRC embassy in Belgrade, killing three Chinese civilians and wounding some twenty others, Beijing was convinced that the act was intentional and refused to accept American insistence that it was a tragic accident; however, the attack did not shift the overall positive image of the U.S. held by most Chinese leaders. This image inertia was all the more remarkable given that Beijing found it impossible to believe that the high-tech superpower could accidentally strike the clearly marked diplomatic compound of a neutral third country within a warzone.[29]

Beijing also interpreted any American efforts to strengthen its alliances in Asia and reconfigure its military posture in the region as being hostile to China. Beijing interpreted the Obama administration's "rebalance to Asia" in this light, seeing it as part of a ramped-up U.S. strategy to contain China. The Trump administration's decision to rename its combatant command with geographic responsibility for the Pacific region was viewed similarly (see the following). Moreover, U.S. military responses to other threats in the wider region—whether in Afghanistan and Central Asia or North Korea—were almost always interpreted as being really about China.[30]

Economic: America's overall image of China's economic posture has remained largely positive for decades, despite repeated negative perceptions. The predominant U.S. narrative continued to be that China was opening up—albeit in fits and starts—and the main trend was the transformation from a closed, centralized economy to an open, free-market system that would one day become fully integrated into the global economic system. Driven by the dream of hundreds of millions of Chinese consumers eager to purchase American brands, U.S. businesses continued to believe that greater market access and a more level playing field in China were within reach. This narrative and dream received a huge boost in December 2001, when China joined the World Trade Organization (WTO).[31] Beijing, however, never fully implemented the package of commitments it made as a condition for entering the WTO. Despite this absence of Chinese follow through, many Washington bureaucracies and U.S. corporations maintained a largely positive image of Beijing and a hopeful view of China's economic trajectory for nearly two decades.[32]

However, in the 2010s, the U.S. observed an economically dynamic China that began acting more assertively and autonomously on the international stage. These activities and initiatives generated concerns and negative perceptions. Beijing was no longer perceived as supportive of the existing U.S.-led global financial and trading system. Instead, China began to be seen as dissatisfied with the existing order and intent on establishing a rival set of institutions. To many U.S. constituencies, Beijing appeared to be creating a parallel universe that it would dominate in an opaque and arbitrary fashion, in contrast to the existing transparent and rules-based system led by the U.S. These new Chinese-initiated institutions include the Asia Infrastructure Investment Bank (AIIB) and the BRICS' New Development Bank. But the highest-profile, most ambitious, and hence most alarming of all was China's launch of the Belt and Road Initiative (BRI). At best, BRI was seen as a manifestation of great power competition in "infrastructure statecraft" and viewed in zero-sum terms (see Chapter 2). In the U.S., this worldwide effort is often depicted in more ominous terms: as a highly coordinated scheme aiming to dominate the world economy by seizing control of one national economy at a time. The widely used pejorative term "debt trap diplomacy" implied that Beijing's deliberate strategy is to entice developing countries into signing onerous loans from Chinese financial institutions, which they would never be able to repay, to finance highly desirable domestic infrastructure projects.[33] According to this interpretation, when the country inevitably defaulted, China as the creditor would step in to recoup the unpaid debt and end up "owning" the country.

By 2019, many years of accumulated American negative perceptions had reached a tipping point, fundamentally transforming Washington's positive and conciliatory image of China into a negative and confrontational one. The upshot was strong support within both the U.S. national security community and the U.S. business community for a

Parsing Post-Pandemic U.S.–China Competition   77

confrontational economic policy initiative toward Beijing. The Trump administration obliged.[34]

Meanwhile, for decades, Beijing perceived the U.S. as being strongly supportive of China's reform and opening policy. Gradually, however, Beijing began interpreting U.S. actions as hostile to China and Chinese companies. With Beijing's hosting of the 2008 Olympics and China's successful weathering of the Global Financial Crisis, many Chinese thought that China's economy had become one of the world's great power houses. This perception was only reinforced when, two years later, China surpassed Japan to become the world's second-largest economy.[35]

Within China, a widely held perception emerged that the U.S. was increasingly acting to thwart China. One scholar opined: "When China was rising as an economic power, the United States tolerated it. Now that China is strong … [the United States] cannot tolerate it anymore."[36] In the mid-2010s, Beijing perceived the Trans-Pacific Partnership (TPP), spearheaded by the Obama administration, as a deliberate U.S. effort to establish an economic bloc aimed at excluding and containing China.[37] By 2019, Chinese businesses and economic bureaucracies were deeply concerned about increased upheaval and uncertainty in U.S.–China relations and wondered whether the two countries could continue to conduct business together.[38]

Technology: For several decades, the U.S. has been extremely supportive of developing science and technology in China. Initially, this support was provided in the form of education and training for Chinese scientists and technical personnel, who arrived in waves to study science, technology, engineering, and mathematics (STEM) at U.S. universities. Support also came in the form of technology transfers from U.S. companies to their Chinese joint venture partners. Gradually, however, negative perceptions of Chinese actions began to mount in the 1990s. What American companies had long tolerated as the cost of doing business in China came to be resented and seen as being "forced to hand their technology to the Chinese and essentially train Chinese companies to become their competitors."[39]

Moreover, China was accused of the theft of U.S. technology. This was among the main findings of a 1999 report issued by the U.S. House of Representatives Select Committee on *U.S. National Security and Military/Commercial Concerns with the People's Republic of China.*[40] Concerns about Chinese commercial and industrial espionage only increased during the first two decades of the 21st century.[41]

By the mid-2010s, China appeared to be advancing rapidly in fields such as artificial intelligence and quantum computing, rivaling industry leaders in the U.S.[42] Meanwhile, Chinese tech companies had become extremely competitive globally; a prime example was Huawei, which was at the time the only multinational information technology company offering all components of 5G technology wireless networks at affordable prices to subscribers globally.[43] Eventually, Chinese students studying STEM fields in the U.S. came to be perceived as engaging in espionage and stealing U.S. technology.[44] Meanwhile, Chinese tech firms, including Huawei, were perceived as appendages of the CCP and were accused of engaging in unauthorized data collection and spying. Ultimately, by 2019, the accumulation of perceived hostile actions fundamentally altered the pervasive U.S. image of China from a positive one to a negative one.

China reveres the U.S. as a high-technology superpower; indeed, Washington's technological prowess makes it for Beijing both a valued partner and a feared adversary. Beijing has long respected America's technical prowess in the military realm, even when demonstrated in the nearby Pacific in 1950s Korea and again in 1960s Vietnam. However, in the aftermath of U.S.–China rapprochement in the early 1970s, Washington came to enjoy a positive image in Chinese eyes. This favorable image continued through the 1980s and subsequent decades, despite periodic crises and tensions in bilateral relations, as China benefited from U.S. cooperation, sharing of technology, and access to education and research in STEM subjects.

Perceptions of U.S. technology as threatening periodically emerged, but this did not alter the overarching positive image of Washington held in Beijing. Chinese leaders were awed by the precision-guided munitions showcased in the First Persian Gulf War in 1991. The impact triggered a major transformation in China's military strategic guidelines.[45] Other impactful defense technology-related developments included extensive U.S. attention to outer space, which signaled to the PLA that space is a key domain in high-tech warfare.[46]

Beijing also perceived the U.S. as a cyber superpower with extensive internet capabilities in both the civilian and military realms. China was keen to learn from the U.S. and acquire its hardware and software technologies and improve upon them, but at the same time Beijing became wary of Washington. Beijing feared that software companies such as Apple and Microsoft might have "backdoors" that could be exploited by the U.S. government to engage in high-tech spying.[47] Moreover, Beijing also grew concerned that Washington was engaging in active influence operations to undermine popular support for the ruling CCP and assumed cyberspace to be a critical domain through which the U.S. would penetrate China to foment domestic upheaval. Beijing's response involved constructing the "Great Firewall of China."[48] Beijing's alarm over Washington's perceived efforts to instigate color revolutions around the world and within the PRC heightened in the mid-2010s, with Hong Kong becoming a particular concern.

By 2019, an accumulation of multiple perceived technological threats from the U.S. ultimately triggered a transformation in Beijing's image of Washington from positive to negative.

In general, once the image of the other shifts from positive to negative, three cognitive features of great powers amplify the impact of the transformation.[49] First, great powers find it difficult to empathize with each other, producing particularly acute cases of the security dilemma. Second, great powers tend to be quick to presume malevolent intentions on the part of other great powers. Third, threat perceptions tend to spike when power differentials are perceived as narrowing. The issue that crystalized the image shift and amplified the image transformation in the case of the U.S. and China was the COVID-19 pandemic. Emerging in China in late 2019, the coronavirus disease became a global pandemic by mid-2020. Most relevant to our analysis was the adverse impact of the pandemic on U.S.–China relations.

3.3.2. COVID-19 and U.S.–China competition

Initially, COVID-19 seemed to provide the impetus for an improvement in bilateral relations, or at least a reason for increased great power cooperation. Yet, weeks of mostly hopeful and positive gestures between Washington and Beijing were followed by months—and years—of burgeoning confrontation, punctuated by mutual finger-pointing and inflated rhetoric.

Washington found it difficult to appreciate the complex nature of the challenge that COVID-19 posed to the ruling CCP. The opaque and secretive nature of the political system encourages local officials to suppress information and downplay its seriousness to central leaders as they seek to manage the crisis themselves. Attention in the U.S. focused on CCP efforts to quash public efforts to raise the alarm and penalize whistleblowers such as Dr. Li Wenliang.[50] U.S. frustration with Beijing's reluctance to share information about the origins of the virus and transparency regarding its spread produced a prominent narrative that the CCP deliberately exported the virus to the U.S.[51] A less malevolent narrative involved a cover-up intended to hide the regime's incompetence.[52] Both narratives included competing theories about the virus escaping from a lab in Wuhan alongside the official story of the virus originating at a so-called "wet market" in the same city.[53] The nefarious narrative variant essentially interpreted the overseas spread of the virus as Beijing intentionally "weaponizing" a biological agent, while the more charitable narrative variant interpreted the spread as a horrific accident which could have been prevented if China were a more safety-conscious society with more stringent attention to regulations and protocols.[54] The nefarious narrative gained greater resonance in an environment where the power differential between China and the U.S. appeared to have narrowed significantly. American threat perceptions of China rose as Beijing was seen as far more economically, militarily, and technologically capable and more driven to supplant Washington as the capital of the world's preeminent power.[55]

Beijing, meanwhile, also found it difficult to understand Washington's perspective and priorities *vis-à-vis* COVID-19. On the one hand, CCP leaders considered their own draconian "zero-tolerance" strategy at home to be perfectly reasonable; on the other hand, they seemed to find U.S. leaders' efforts to block COVID-19 from entering the U.S. unreasonable.[56] In early February 2020, Xi Jinping called his American counterpart Donald Trump and reportedly urged him to rescind his 31 January order that suspended air travel between China and the U.S.[57] Xi reportedly assured Trump that Beijing had COVID-19 under control and that it was not highly contagious. Hence, it was not necessary for the U.S. to halt U.S.–China travel. When the Trump administration ordered the suspension of air travel from China, Beijing interpreted this move as intended to hurt China rather than designed to protect America. Moreover, when the U.S. head of state and other officials began explicitly or implicitly to blame China for the virus—labeling it as the "China virus" or the "Wuhan virus"—these verbal salvos were perceived as a well-coordinated effort to embarrass Beijing, and it interpreted U.S. actions and rhetoric as deliberate, orchestrated, and malevolent.[58] These threat perceptions were heightened by Beijing's belief that China was closing the gap with the U.S. in terms of comprehensive national power.

Moreover, Beijing actively encouraged—or at least did almost nothing to discourage—conspiracy theories suggesting that the U.S. was responsible for COVID-19.[59] Two virulent rumors were perpetuated by

Chinese officials and media outlets. One was that the virus was unleashed by a delegation of U.S. soldiers traveling to Wuhan for the World Military Games in October 2019. The second rumor was that the virus had escaped from the U.S. Army's Medical Research Institute of Infectious Diseases at Fort Detrick, Maryland.[60]

The contrast with how the two great powers managed the last major global pandemic could not have been starker: the severe acute respiratory syndrome (SARS) outbreak in 2002–2004 produced notable cooperation between the U.S. and China.[61] While both SARS and COVID-19 originated in China and spread beyond China's borders, the impact of each on U.S.–China relations was dramatically different. Why? A key reason appears to be the condition of bilateral relations at the time. The responses were not just almost 20 years apart but occurred against the backdrop of polar opposite images of each other. SARS emerged during an era of positive mutual images and a climate of great power cooperation. By comparison, COVID-19 played out when U.S. and Chinese perceptions of each other had become extremely negative, combined with a set of interrelated cognitive factors which served to exacerbate bilateral tensions and elevate great power competition (see Chapter 1).

3.3.3. *From the geography of peace to the geography of conflict*

As the U.S. continued to think in global terms about its core national security interests, China shifted from focusing primarily on its periphery to expanding attention first to its wider neighborhood and then to global and far-flung maritime interests. What Mearsheimer describes as the "stopping power of water" is real, but it has its limits.[62] Although the U.S. and China are separated by vast expanses of ocean, technological advances and ambition have shrunk distances and fueled this geostrategic rivalry.

Since China's transition from a consuming attention to continental security to a preoccupation with the oceanic realm, a "geography of conflict" has usurped the "geography of peace." This is not to say that Beijing had pivoted from a focus on land power to a singular focus on sea power. Indeed, China is in search of what Wang Jisi dubbed a "geostrategic rebalance."[63] Hence, while not neglecting continental concerns, China has paid far greater attention to expanding its maritime interests, including territorial claims in the "Near Seas" and sea lanes in the "Far Seas"—the expansive Pacific Ocean, Indian Ocean, and beyond. This geostrategic shift has elevated U.S.–China tensions, with the South China Sea, East China Sea, and Taiwan Strait becoming more acute political-military flashpoints,[64] as well as expanding the arena of confrontation beyond China's periphery.

The issue of Taiwan has come to the fore of U.S.–China relations in recent years. The August 2022 visit to Taipei by then Speaker of the House of Representatives Nancy Pelosi heightened already elevated cross-strait tensions, prompting Beijing to launch coordinated military exercises in multiple locations all around the island of Taiwan that were unprecedented in scope and scale. This episode, dubbed the Fourth Taiwan Strait Crisis, established the Taiwan Strait as geostrategic "ground zero" in what has become a worldwide U.S.–China great power competition.[65] More recently, the outcome of the January 2024 presidential election ensured that Taiwan will remain a highly contentious issue for Beijing in the foreseeable future. The victory of Democratic Progressive Party (DPP) candidate William Lai Ching-te means that the DPP will control Taiwan's executive branch for another four years, much to China's chagrin since Beijing perceives the DPP as a party of independence, is deeply distrustful of the new Lai administration, and is certain to rachet up the pressure.[66]

Beijing's increasingly global outlook and expanded geostrategic ambitions are highlighted by China's BRI. While many of the infrastructure projects are located within China's own neighborhood, others extend far beyond its borders across the world. Beijing has a nested security conception of China's geostrategic posture, and when Xi and his politburo colleagues look out at the world, they think in terms of Beijing being encircled by four concentric rings of insecurity.[67] The first and innermost ring contains all territories within the boundaries of the PRC that they either claim or control. A second ring extends about 50–100 miles beyond these borders around the PRC's immediate periphery. A third ring encompasses China's entire extended Asia-Pacific neighborhood, including five distinct regions: Northeast Asia, Southeast Asia, Oceania, South Asia, and Central Asia. A fourth outermost ring extends over the rest of the world. The most important of these continue to be the inner rings because of their paramount importance in ensuring internal stability and peripheral security, which are vital for regime security and border defense.

And yet, especially since the 1990s, Chinese leaders see the world well beyond the PRC's borders and even beyond its neighborhood as increasingly important. This is largely due to the recognition that in a globalized world, "thinking locally demands acting globally."[68]

Indeed, this has become Beijing's unofficial foreign policy mantra. As a result, PRC documents emphasize the importance of "overseas interests" and Chinese scholars and analysts now speak of China's expanding "interest frontiers."[69]

The upshot is that China's geostrategic thinking and national security interests increasingly overlap and even directly conflict with those of the U.S. Washington conceives of the U.S. as a global superpower with national interests spanning the world. Indeed, the U.S. possesses the only military capable of dividing the entire planet—not just the country's homeland and/or home continent—into geographic combatant commands. Moreover, since the end of the Cold War, the U.S. Department of Defense has become accustomed to having its forces and platforms operating in oceans and airspace around the world largely unchallenged. Yet in recent years, this has changed as multiple states have improved their standoff and precision strike technologies. Although China is not the only great power competitor with growing military capabilities that give the U.S. pause, it is the most important one. This growing concern prompted the Pentagon to formulate the concept of A2/AD."[70] Not surprisingly, these enhanced Chinese abilities have grown most notably in its home region. However, China's power projection capabilities and military activism have gone global. Certainly, while these worldwide activities and presence may be modest, there is every indication that trends point toward greater worldwide involvement and sustenance. This means that U.S.–China military competition will not only grow within the Asia-Pacific region but also extend well beyond it. Certainly, the Trump and Biden administrations took note.[71]

Furthermore, the U.S.–China military rivalry will only continue to heighten within the Asia-Pacific. This is signaled by the emergence in Washington of the "Indo-Pacific" geostrategic construct. In mid-2018, the U.S. Pacific Command, headquartered at Camp Smith on a hilltop overlooking Honolulu, Hawaii, formally changed its name to "Indo-Pacific Command." The following year, the Trump administration produced glossy documents titled "Indo-Pacific Strategy" and "Indo-Pacific Vision" and regularly repeated the slogan "a free and open Indo-Pacific."[72] This was not merely a name change but was intended to signal that the U.S. had awakened to the seriousness of the China challenge.[73] In addition, the use of "Indo-Pacific" is meant to highlight the maritime nature of the region—a combination of two great bodies of water—the Indian Ocean and the Pacific Ocean. Moreover, it explicitly suggests the importance of India as

84 A. Scobell

a U.S. security partner and implicitly hints at the importance of Australia, an ally strategically located between the two oceans.[74] Indeed, "Indo-Pacific" reportedly resonates with multiple countries within the region.[75]

3.4. Where Are U.S.–China Relations Headed?

A recent think tank report sketched out three possible trajectories for the future of U.S.–China relations.[76] The first is one in which the two great powers work together side by side but separately without close cooperation—labeled "parallel partners." The second possible trajectory is a future in which the U.S. and China are in a heightened state of tension, with significant potential for confrontation and conflict—"colliding competitors." A third potential trajectory is a future in which the two great powers engage in independent actions and pursue separate paths in different strategic directions with little potential for confrontation—"diverging directions."

The first scenario aptly describes bilateral relations prior to 2019; the second scenario is an appropriate characterization of the current state of U.S.–China relations, while the third outlines a possible future scenario if the two great powers manage competition and redefine their respective geostrategies away from confrontation. Yet, the most likely forward trajectory in U.S.–China relations for the foreseeable future—the next five years—is a continued state of heightened great power competition. How Washington and Beijing have handled the COVID-19 pandemic, how this impact has affected their bilateral relations, combined with the respective U.S. and Chinese reactions to Russia's invasion of Ukraine, strongly suggest that this forecast will turn out to be accurate.

3.4.1. *Two contrasting cases of U.S. and Chinese responses to non-traditional security threats*

On its face, COVID-19 should have provided an opportunity for U.S.–China cooperation. As a global pandemic, it is a non-traditional security threat that endangers all countries and there ought to be incentives for the U.S. and China to work together to contain its spread and collaborate on vaccine development and distribution. Yet, this was not to be. The contrast between the way Washington and Beijing responded to COVID-19 and 11 September 2001 is stark. The terrorist attacks on the U.S. served as the impetus for a qualitative improvement in U.S.–China relations following the chill from the EP-3 incident of April 2001. PRC President Jiang Zemin was one of the first foreign leaders to call President George W. Bush to offer his country's support after the attacks. Bush reciprocated the gesture by traveling to Shanghai in October 2001 to attend the APEC Summit, when he could have easily justified staying home. The result of this exchange of signals was warmer relations between Washington and Beijing and cooperation on countering terrorism—albeit in limited ways as "parallel partners."[77]

What explains the differing outcomes? Back in 2001, leaders in Washington and Beijing viewed each other as partners who although didn't always agree completely should and could cooperate in spite of their differences. Meanwhile, in 2022, leaders in Washington and Beijing saw each other as rivals who, although they could cooperate, did not find it in their respective national interests to actually do so. The way COVID-19 played out for U.S.–China relations serves as a testament to the dismal state of bilateral relations, warning us about how difficult cooperation is likely to be in an era of great power competition where images of the other are adversarial and threatening.

3.4.2. *The fallout from Ukraine on U.S.–China relations: One war, two interpretations*

Russia's invasion of Ukraine launched in February 2022—Europe's most consequential conventional conflict since the Second World War—has highlighted the serious mutual misperceptions and conflicting geostrategies of the U.S. and China. For Washington, Beijing has adopted "a stance of pro-Russian pseudo-neutrality."[78] Whereas, as recently as a decade ago, the U.S. perceived China–Russia ties with modest concern,[79] in the aftermath of Russia's 2014 seizure of Crimea and the U.S.' fundamental image shift of China by 2019, the Moscow–Beijing axis began to be viewed with far more concern as American scholars and analysts spoke of an "axis of authoritarians" and the specter of a "two-front war."[80] Moreover, many in the U.S. publicly voiced concerns that Russia's aggression against Ukraine might embolden China to launch a military operation against Taiwan,[81] elevating an already heightened concern over Beijing's near-term forceful designs on Taiwan. In March 2021, then INDOPACOM Commander Admiral Philip Davidson testified before Congress that he believed China was preparing to seize Taiwan by 2027.[82]

For Beijing, Moscow's "special military operation,"[83] was not an invasion but rather seemingly inexorable, conducted in response to decades of hostile U.S. and NATO anti-Russian activities. From China's perspective, the eastward advance of NATO was designed to contain Russia. This interpretation resonates powerfully with Beijing's perspective that Washington seeks to contain China through a strengthened network of Asia-Pacific allies and new security arrangements such as the Quad and AUKUS. From this mindset, Russia is merely reacting in self-defense, and the real blame for the conflict in Ukraine rests squarely on the shoulders of the U.S.[84] Since Beijing considers itself neutral regarding Ukraine and aloof from the conflict, Washington and other Western capitals are assessed to be unfairly victimizing China with their economic sanctions on Russia.

3.5. Conclusion

China's rise has long attracted the attention of Washington, although the current elevated level of alarm is a more recent phenomenon. Meanwhile, in Beijing, although the U.S. has long been a preoccupying concern, the threat perception has recently elevated. Why? This chapter suggests two reasons. First, cognitive factors in Washington and Beijing produced heightened threat perceptions of each other, consistent with the analysis of Liu and He (see Chapter 1). Second, U.S. geostrategic inertia and an evolving Chinese geostrategy put the two great powers on a collision course in the Western Pacific, as perceived in both capitals.

Bilateral relations had been troubled for many years, although both sides outwardly acted as if all was well. Hence, a period of pretense persisted, during which both sides acted as if the relationship were in decent shape, despite periodic tensions and underlying issues. Meanwhile, difficult disputes went unaddressed and unresolved as new issues—the protracted global COVID-19 pandemic and the ongoing war in Ukraine—flared up and proved highly contentious U.S.–China relations. Washington, as the capital of the world's most powerful nation, continues to see itself as "a global force for good."[85] This means that U.S. geostrategy generates a mission for the Pentagon to police the global commons and uphold the international system. Hence, the term "Free and Open Indo-Pacific" emerged to conceptually frame America's approach to the region and the wider world. In the meantime, Beijing, as the capital of a rapidly rising power, has expanded its geostrategic outlook beyond its immediate neighborhood to a growing global perspective and shifted from what was almost exclusively a continental stance to an increasingly maritime posture. In this context, the Middle East has emerged in recent years as a geostrategic region of increasing importance to China. The region is not only an important source of petroleum but also a critical nexus for global sea lanes. Despite the greater significance attached to the Middle East, Beijing has been exceedingly cautious in exerting its influence in the region, at least in the non-economic realm.[86] In the aftermath of the horrific terrorist attack on Israel and the subsequent harsh and extended Israeli military intervention in Gaza on 7 October 2023, China has been remarkably aloof and uninvolved in seeking to end the conflict and/or address the massive humanitarian crisis, beyond mouthing platitudes and criticizing Israel and the U.S.[87] Moreover, Beijing has also been strangely quiet in its international efforts to counter the Houthi missile strikes on commercial shipping in the Red Sea.

Beijing's greater attention to the world beyond its immediate periphery has manifested itself in U.S.–China "strategic competition in infrastructure building" in the Indo-Pacific and beyond (see Chapter 2). For qualitative improvement in U.S.–China relations, not only must hostile perceptions and misperceptions be addressed directly, but the images of each other must be fundamentally reshaped and respective geostrategic outlooks reconciled. Unfortunately, the analysis above suggests that the near-term prospects for reshaping and reconciliation are almost zero.

Endnotes

1   A. L. Friedberg, *A Contest for Supremacy: U.S., China, and a Struggle for Mastery in Asia* (New York: W.W. Norton, 2012).

2   G. J. Ikenberry, *Liberal Leviathan: The Origins, Crisis, and Transformation of the American World Order* (Princeton, NJ: Princeton University Press, 2012).

3   D. M. Lampton, "Reconsidering U.S.-China relations: From improbable normalization to precipitous deterioration," *Asia Policy*, 14, 43–60 (2019).

4   R. Jervis, *Perception and Misperception in International Politics* (Princeton, NJ: Princeton University Press, 1979), p. 117.

5   See the seminal writings of Sir Halford J. Mackinder (1861–1947) and Nicholas J. Spykman (1893–1943).

6 W. R. Thompson, "Identifying rivals and rivalries in world politics," *International Studies Quarterly*, 45, 557–586 (2001), p. 574.

7 Jervis (1979), *Op. cit.*, p. 146.

8 On cognitive dissonance, see Jervis (1979), *Op. cit.*, pp. 382–406.

9 See, for example, the extended discussion in U. Friedman, "The new concept everyone in Washington is talking about," *The Atlantic*, 6 August 2019.

10 "Joint leaders statement on AUKUS," 15 September 2021. https://www.whitehouse.gov/briefing-room/statements-releases/2021/09/15/joint-leaders-statement-on-aukus/.

11 "Quad leaders' joint statement: 'The spirit of the Quad,'" 12 March 2021. https://www.whitehouse.gov/briefing-room/statements-releases/2021/03/12/quad-leaders-joint-statement-the-spirit-of-the-quad/.

12 "White House top Asia policy officials discuss U.S. China strategy at APARC's Oksenberg conference." Stanford University, 27 May 2021. https://fsi.stanford.edu/news/white-house-top-asia-policy-officials-discuss-us-china-strategy-aparc%E2%80%99s-oksenberg-conference.

13 *Ibid.*

14 "Statement from President Biden on the build back better act," 16 December 2021. https://www.whitehouse.gov/briefing-room/statements-releases/2021/12/16/statement-from-the-president-on-the-build-back-better-act/.

15 *China's Policies on Asia-Pacific Security Cooperation* (Beijing: State Council Information Office of the People's Republic of China, 2017).

16 See Table 2.1: "The geostrategy of China's concentric circles" in A. Scobell, B. Lin, H. J. Shatz, M. Johnson, L. Hanauer, M. S. Chase, A. S. Cevallos, I. W. Rasmussen, A. Chan, A. Strong, E. Warner and L. Ma, *At the Dawn of Belt and Road: China in the Developing World* (Santa Monica, CA: RAND, 2018), p. 26.

17 See World Bank, "Belt and Road Initiative brief," 29 March 2018. https://www.worldbank.org/en/topic/regional-integration/brief/belt-and-road-initiative.

18 For comprehensive lists of China's expanding array of military exercises in different regions of the world, see, for example, Scobell *et al.* (2018), *Op. cit.*, pp. 66–67, 85–86, 110–114, 140–142, 163, 203, 239. On China's new base in Djibouti, see P. A. Dutton, I. B. Kardon and C. M. Kennedy, *Djibouti: China's First Overseas Strategic Strongpoint*, China Maritime Report No. 6 (Newport, RI: U.S. Naval War College China Maritime Studies Institute, 2020).

19 A. Scobell, E. R. Burke, C. A. Cooper III, S. Lilly, C. J. R. Holland, E. Warner, J. D. Williams and L. Ma, *China's Grand Strategy: Trends, Trajectory, Long-Term Competition* (Santa Monica, CA: RAND, 2020), p. 28ff.

20 F. Tang, "What is China's dual circulation economic strategy and why is it important?" *South China Morning Post*, 19 November 2020. https://www.scmp.com/economy/china-economy/article/3110184/what-chinas-dual-circulation-economic-strategy-and-why-it.

21 F. Lavin, "This is what U.S.-China decoupling looks like," *Forbes*, 8 December 2021. https://www.forbes.com/sites/franklavin/2021/12/08/this-is-what-us-china-decoupling-looks-like/?sh=e77fc6b3b391.

22 He and Liu identify the date as 2012. See Chapter 1.

23 This paragraph draws upon A. Scobell, "Perception and misperception in U.S.-China relations," *Political Science Quarterly*, 135(4), 637–664 (2021–2022), p. 640.

24 Yan Xuetong quoted in Minghao Zhao, "Is a new cold war inevitable? Chinese perspectives on U.S.-China strategic competition," *Chinese Journal of International Politics*, 12, 1–24 (2019), p. 7.

25 Scobell (2021–2022), *Op. cit.*, pp. 649–659.

26 T. J. Christensen, *The China Challenge* (New York: W.W. Norton, 2015), p. 99.

27 Scobell (2021–2022), *Op. cit.*, p. 652.

28 *Ibid.*, p. 649.

29 D. M. Lampton, *Following the Leader: Ruling China from Deng Xiaoping to Xi Jinping* (Berkeley, CA: University of California Press, 2014), pp. 117–118.

30 See, for example, A. Scobell, "Crouching Korea, hidden China: Bush administration policy toward Pyongyang and Beijing," *Asian Survey*, 42, 343–368 (2002).

31 Scobell (2021–2022), *Op. cit.*, pp. 653–654.

32 A. Scobell, "Constructing a U.S.-China rivalry in the Indo-Pacific and beyond," *Journal of Contemporary China*, 30, 74–75 (2021).

33 "Remarks by Vice President Pence on the administration's policy toward China," 4 October 2018, Hudson Institute. https://www.whitehouse.gov/briefings-statements/remarks-vice-president-pence-administration-policy-toward-china/.

34 Lampton (2019), *Op. cit.*, pp. 54–55.

35 Scobell (2021–2022), *Op. cit.*, p. 654.

36 Professor Shen Dingli of Fudan University quoted in K. Bradsher and S. L. Myers, "China scorns U.S. threats," *The New York Times*, 29 May 2020. https://www.nytimes.com/2020/05/28/world/asia/china-united=states.html.

37 Scobell (2021–2022), *Op. cit.*, p. 655.

38 Scobell (2021), *Op. cit.*, p. 77.

39 J. Pomfret, *The Beautiful Country and the Middle Kingdom: America and China, 1776 to the Present* (New York: Henry Holt, 2016), p. 578.

90   *A. Scobell*

40   *The Report of the Select Committee on U.S. National Security and Military/ Commercial Concerns with the People's Republic of China* (Washington, DC: U.S. Government Printing Office, 1999).

41   W. C. Hannas, J. Mulvenon and A. B. Puglisi, *Chinese Industrial Espionage: Technological Acquisition and Military Modernization* (New York: Routledge, 2013).

42   Kai-Fu Lee, *AI Superpowers: China, Silicon Valley and the New World Order* (New York: Houghton Mifflin Harcourt, 2018).

43   Scobell (2021–2022), *Op. cit.,* p. 659.

44   *Ibid.,* p. 656.

45   See M. T. Fravel, "The 1993 strategy: Local wars under high-technology conditions," in *Active Defense: China's Military Strategy since 1949* (Princeton, NJ: Princeton University Press, 2019), pp. 182–216.

46   J. Johnson-Freese, *Space as a Strategic Asset* (New York: Columbia University Press, 2007), p. 223.

47   Scobell (2021–2022), *Op. cit.,* p. 656.

48   A. Segal, *The Hacked World Order: How Nations Fight, Trade, Maneuver, and Manipulate in the Digital Age* (New York: Public Affairs, 2016), pp. 29–32.

49   For more on these three elements, see Scobell (2021–2022), *Op. cit.,* pp. 640–643.

50   A. Su, "A doctor was arrested for warning China about the coronavirus. Then he died of it," *Los Angeles Times*, 6 February 2020. https://www.latimes.com/world-nation/story/2020-02-06/coronavirus-china-xi-li-wenliang.

51   For a less insidious assessment, see G. Sands, K. Atwood, S. Collinson and K. Bohn, "US government report assesses China intentionally concealed severity of coronavirus," *CNN*, 4 May 2020. https://www.cnn.com/2020/05/03/politics/mike-pompeo-china-coronavirus-supplies/index.html.

52   T. Junio, "Cracks in the 'great firewall': China's incompetent COVID-19 response," *The Hill*, 29 June 2022. https://thehill.com/opinion/international/504503-cracks-in-the-great-firewall-chinas-incompetent-covid-19-response.

53   "Covid origin: Why the Wuhan lab-leak theory is being taken seriously," *BBC*, 27 May 2021. https://www.bbc.com/news/world-asia-china-57268111.

54   J. Rogin, "Opinion: State department cables warned of safety issues at Wuhan Lab studying bat coronaviruses," *The Washington Post*, 14 April 2021. https://www.washingtonpost.com/opinions/2020/04/14/state-department-cables-warned-safety-issues-wuhan-lab-studying-bat-coronaviruses/.

55   This is one of the central presumptions of a recent RAND report. See T. R. Heath, D. Grossman, and A. Clark, *China's Quest for Global Primacy: An Analysis of Chinese International and Defense Strategies to Outcompete the United States* (Santa Monica, CA: RAND, 2021). https://www.rand.org/

content/dam/rand/pubs/research_reports/RRA400/RRA447-1/RAND_ RRA447-1.pdf.

56 Huizhong Wu, "Omicron tests China's 'zero-tolerance' COVID approach weeks ahead of Beijing Olympics," *The Diplomat*, 14 January 2022. https:// thediplomat.com/2022/01/omicron-tests-chinas-zero-tolerance-covid-approach-weeks-ahead-of-beijing-olympics/.

57 J. Rogin, "The opinions essay: How Covid hastened the decline and fall of the U.S.-China relationship," *The Washington Post*, 4 March 2021. https:// www.washingtonpost.com/opinions/2021/03/04/covid-trump-xi-josh-rogin/.

58 In fact, the effort was poorly coordinated and more focused on deflecting blame for the virus away from the Trump administration than on casting blame on Beijing. See Rogin (2021), *Op. cit.*

59 E. Kinetz, "Anatomy of a conspiracy: China took the leading role," *Associated Press*, 15 February 2021. https://apnews.com/article/pandemics-beijing-only-on-ap-epidemics-media-122b73e134b780919cc1808f3f6f16e8.

60 N. Gan and S. George, "China doubles down on baseless 'US origins' Covid conspiracy as delta outbreak worsens," *CNN*, 6 August 2021. https://www. cnn.com/2021/08/06/china/china-covid-origin-mic-intl-hnk/index.html.

61 J. Bouey, "From SARS to 2019-Coronavirus (nCoV): U.S.-China collaborations on pandemic response," Testimony Presented before the House Foreign Affairs Subcommittee on Asia, the Pacific, and Nonproliferation on 5 February 2020. https://www.rand.org/pubs/testimonies/CT523.html.

62 J. Mearsheimer, *The Tragedy of Great Power Politics* (New York: W.W. Norton, 2001), p. 84.

63 Wang Jisi, "'Xijin': Zhongguo diyuan zhanlue de zai pingheng ('Marching West': China's geostrategic rebalance)," *Huanqiu Shibao* (*Global Times*), 17 October 2012.

64 B. Taylor, *The Four Flashpoints: How Asia Goes to War* (Melbourne, Australia: La Trobe University Press, 2018).

65 A. Scobell, "What Pelosi's trip to Taiwan tells us about U.S.-China relations," U.S. Institute of Peace, 5 August 2022. https://www.usip.org/publications/ 2022/08/what-pelosis-trip-to taiwan-tells-us-about-us-china-relations.

66 J. Staats and N. Kuo, "After Taiwan's election, China is now ratcheting up the pressure," U.S. Institute of Peace, 5 March 2024. https://www.usip.org/ publications/2024/03/after-taiwans-election-china-now-ratcheting-pressure.

67 A. J. Nathan and A. Scobell, *China's Search for Security* (New York: Columbia University, 2012), pp. 3–7.

68 *Ibid.*, p. 35.

69 A. Ghiselli, *Protecting China's Interests Overseas: Securitization and Foreign Policy* (New York: Oxford University Press, 2021).

70 Scobell (2021–2022), *Op. cit.*, p. 650.

71 For the analysis of the Trump administration's Pentagon, see "The PLA's growing military presence," in *Military and Security Developments Involving the People's Republic of China* (Washington DC: Office of the Secretary of Defense, 2020). https://media.defense.gov/2020/Sep/01/2002488689/-1/-1/1/2020-DOD-CHINA-MILITARY-POWER-REPORT-FINAL.PDF. For the analysis of the Biden administration, see "The PLA's growing military presence," in *Military and Security Developments Involving the People's Republic of China* (Washington DC: Office of the Secretary of Defense, 2021). https://media.defense.gov/2021/Nov/03/2002885874/-1/-1/0/2021-CMPR-FINAL.PDF.

72 The Trump administration launched this slogan, and the Biden administration has run with it. For two Trump articulations, see *Department of Defense Indo-Pacific Strategy Report* (Washington DC: Department of Defense, 1 June 2019). https://media.defense.gov/2019/Jul/01/2002152311/-1/-1/1/DEPARTMENT-OF-DEFENSE-INDO-PACIFIC-STRATEGY-REPORT-2019.PDF and *A Free and Open Indo-Pacific: Advancing a Shared Vision* (Washington DC: Department of State, 4 November 2019). https://www.state.gov/wp-content/uploads/2019/11/Free-and-Open-Indo-Pacific-4Nov2019.pdf/. For a Biden administration articulation, see Secretary of State Anthony Blinken, "A free and open Indo-Pacific," 14 December 2021 speech in Jakarta, Indonesia assessed. https://www.state.gov/a-free-and-open-indo-pacific/.

73 Scobell (2021), *Op. cit.*, p. 83.

74 *Ibid.*, p. 83.

75 R. Medcalf, "Indo-Pacific visions: Giving solidarity a chance," *Asia Policy*, 14(3), 79–95 (2019).

76 Scobell *et al.* (2020), *Op. cit.*, pp. 114–116.

77 *Ibid.*, p. 115. This characterization draws from D. Shambaugh, *China Goes Global: The Partial Power* (New York: Oxford University Press, 2013).

78 "China and Russia: Testing the 'limitless,'" *The Economist*, p. 37, 19 March 2022.

79 See, for example, R. Weitz, *China-Russia Security Relations: Strategic Parallelism without Partnership or Passion?* (Carlisle Barracks, PA: U.S. Army War College Strategic Studies Institute, 2008).

80 R. J. Ellings and R. Sutter (eds.), *Axis of Authoritarians: Implications of China-Russia Cooperation* (Seattle: National Bureau of Asian Research, 2018).

81 On the differences between the situations, see A. Scobell and L. Stevenson-Yang, "China is not Russia. Taiwan is not Ukraine," U.S. Institute of Peace, 4 March 2022. https://www.usip.org/publications/2022/03/china-not-russia-taiwan-not-ukraine.

82 M. Shelbourne, "Davidson: China could try to take control of Taiwan in 'next six years,'" *USNI News*, 9 March 2021. https://news.usni.org/2021/03/09/davidson-china-could-try-to-take-control-of-taiwan-in-next-six-years.

83 Reuters, "China and Russia hold first military exercise since Ukraine invasion," 24 May 2022. https://www.reuters.com/world/asia-pacific/china-russia-hold-first-military-since-ukraine-invasion-2022-05-24/.

84 See, for example, J. Thomas, "China 'opposes any act' of war; Blames U.S. for sending weapons to Ukraine," *Newsweek*, 24 February 2022. https://www.newsweek.com/china-opposes-any-act-war-blames-us-sending-weapons-ukraine-1682550. Conversations with multiple Chinese scholars and analysts amplify and reinforce this narrative.

85 This phrase was the recruiting slogan used by the U.S. Navy between 2009 and 2015. While "a global force for good" was not particularly popular within the Navy or elsewhere in the Pentagon for that matter, the mantra seems to capture the essence of a dominant and enduring U.S. elite perception of America's role in the world.

86 A. Scobell, "China's search for security in the Greater Middle East," in J. Reardon-Anderson (ed.), *The Red Star and the Crescent: China and the Middle East* (New York: Oxford University Press, 2018), pp. 13–36.

87 A. Scobell, "What China wants in the Middle East," U.S. Institute of Peace, 1 November 2023. https://www.usip.org/publications/2023/11/what-china-wants-middle-east.

© 2025 World Scientific Publishing Europe Ltd.
https://doi.org/10.1142/9781800616318_0005

Chapter 4

The U.S. Factor and the Evolution of China–India Relations[*]

Li Li

Tsinghua University, China

China–India relations are at a crossroads. Since May 2020, the two neighbors have been locked in a protracted border standoff. The format of bilateral engagement, which is based on the delinking of the boundary dispute from cooperation in other areas, is under challenge. This chapter argues that the United States (U.S.) factor has been playing a significant role in the evolution of China–India relations since 1988. The U.S. factor impacts China's perception of India and India's policy toward China. Prior to the U.S. strategic shift to great-power competition, China viewed India as a partner and focused on engaging with India. Designating China as a major competitor, India used the U.S. as leverage in its relations with China. However, India was suspicious of the cooperative side of Sino–U.S. relations and chose to hedge between China and the U.S. Since the U.S. has identified China as a strategic competitor and introduced the Indo-Pacific strategy, India has significantly tilted toward the U.S. and embraced the Quad. As the U.S. Indo-Pacific strategy presents China with two-front challenges, China's security concerns regarding

---

[*] This chapter was originally printed as "The U.S. Factor and the Evolution of China-India Relations." *The China Review*, Vol. 23, No. 1 (2023): 107–133. https://www.jstor.org/stable/48717990. Reproduced with kind permission of CUHK Press.

India have largely increased. The asymmetry in mutual security perceptions between China and India is decreasing. Since India's China policy is moving from hedging to balancing and China is introducing balancing into its India policy despite its commitment to engagement, the two Asian powers might be trapped in mutual balancing in an era of great-power competition.

Since the 1988 path-breaking visit to Beijing by Rajiv Gandhi, the then Indian Prime Minister, China and India have not only normalized their bilateral relations but also established a new format of interaction under which cooperation has been invigorated and differences have been effectively managed. Despite the brief hiatus after the 1998 Indian nuclear tests and short-lived border standoffs in 2013 and 2014, China and India were committed first to establishing the Strategic and Cooperative Partnership for Peace and Prosperity in 2005 and then to building a *Closer Developmental Partnership* in 2014. Even after a 72-day face-off at Donglang/Doklam in 2017, subsequent two informal summits between Xi Jinping and Modi (one in Wuhan and the other in Mamallapuram) seemed to reconfirm their respective commitments to the established format for dealing with each other, with cooperation dominating and differences sidelined.

However, the latest standoff that began in May 2020 seems to be different and has left bilateral relations in a protracted crisis. It happened simultaneously in multiple areas and primarily in the western sector of the China–India border. It was reported that troop deployments reached their highest level in decades as the two sides sent tens of thousands of soldiers and advanced military equipment to the border. On 15 June 2020, the first deadly clash between the two sides since 1975 occurred in the Galwan Valley, claiming the lives of at least 20 Indian and four Chinese soldiers. On 8 September 2020, China and India accused each other of firing warning shots; this was the first such incident in their border dispute in 45 years. Meanwhile, the Indian government has banned over 200 Chinese apps and introduced specific restrictions on Chinese companies. The strategic community in New Delhi has begun discussing India's decoupling from China,[1] its top trading partner, with an annual bilateral trade volume exceeding US$100 billion in 2021.

Since the Galwan violence, both governments have endeavored to de-escalate the situation. Up until the end of February 2024, 21 rounds of

Corps Commander talks and 14 rounds of Working Mechanism for Consultation and Coordination (WMCC) meetings have been held. The two troops have disengaged in areas such as Galwan Valley, Pangong Tso, and Gogra-Hotsprings (known as Jianan Daban by China), but their respective heavy military deployments in the border areas continue. Meanwhile, despite there being only two brief but direct conversations between Xi and Modi (one during the 2022 Bali G20 Summit and the other during the 2023 Johannesburg BRICS Summit), bilateral relations have returned to normal. As the border stalemate has lasted for almost four years, differences seem to be centered around how they deal with each other. While China insists on "an appropriate position" for the border issue and handling the disputes through negotiation and cooperation, India emphasizes that cooperation is impossible as long as border tensions continue.[2]

What has led to the deterioration of China–India relations to such a point? What does the future hold? These are the basic questions hotly debated in academic circles, including those from China and India. Scholars may diverge in their views on the driving forces, but they seem to converge on the view that this relationship is at a crossroads. While Indian experts argue that the very basis of relations that have been built since 1988 "has been shaken,"[3] Chinese scholars believe that, "without a reconstruction, the China–India relations are not able to be reset."[4]

This research seeks to join the current debates as it attempts to understand the logic behind the ups and downs of China–India relations since 1988. It finds that the U.S. factor, usually regarded as "a third-party factor," has been playing a significant role. The U.S. factor has largely impacted how China and India perceive each other and has partly shaped their interactions as a result. This analytical approach provides a reasonable explanation for the coincidence of the deterioration of China–India relations and the emergence of great-power competition between the U.S. and China. It may also help predict the triangular interaction among China, India, and the U.S. and its effects on the evolving world order.

4.1. Literature Review: Factors Affecting the China–India Relations

Explanations for the reasons behind the current crisis in China–India relations are highly divergent, but they can be divided into the following four perspectives: the evolving balance of power, mutual perceptions, change in the international environment, and domestic factors.

The balance of power, a perspective of political realism, is often used in exploring China–India relations. S. Kalyanaraman attributes "the series of crises since 2013" to the power disequilibrium between India and China, represented by the fact that the latter's GDP is five times larger than that of the former.[5] In 1990, they were roughly equivalent. Peter Robertson, Jingdong Yuan, and Harsha Konara Mudiyanselage assume that the simultaneous but asymmetric rise of China and India has led to a security dilemma. China's upper hand in national strength (economic growth) may embolden it and, in turn, provoke India to deepen cooperation with other countries, particularly Japan, to contain China.[6]

Some scholars believe that the respective quests of China and India for great power status have prompted their competition for influence in Asia and beyond.[7] Igor Denisov, Ivan Safranchuk, and Danil Bochkov suggest that competition for "the redistribution of spheres of influence in Asia" plays a significant role in the deterioration of China-India relations. India is increasingly concerned about China's growing influence and presence in South Asia and the Indian Ocean region through the Belt and Road Initiative. At the same time, China is becoming increasingly suspicious of the potential threats to its security posed by the reactivated Quadrilateral Security Dialogue (Quad) among the U.S., Japan, Australia, and India.[8] Jiadong Zhang and Qian Sun support this argument by stating that geopolitical factors (involving national strength, geographical features, and international status) "have begun to play [a] more important role in the bilateral relationship of the two rising countries in the past few years, leading to their strategic competition."[9]

The role of mutual perceptions is another popular lens for analyzing China–India relations. Tien-sze Fang posits that relations between the two are largely defined by their asymmetric threat perceptions, with India's concerns about China being far more acute than China's about India.[10] Being dissatisfied with the status quo, "India's threat perception might have a destabilising effect on bilateral relations as it strives to remove the asymmetry."[11] Haiqi Zheng finds that India perceives China as "its main strategic rival," while "China has always regarded India as a reliable trade partner." As the (power) gap between them continues to widen, "border issues have become more prominent, leading to escalations." It also prompts China to see "limited space for cooperation" in the security field.[12]

Vijay Gokhale attributes the end of "the Rajiv Gandhi–Deng Xiaoping consensus" era to the "rampant" misperception and mistrust, which "became a pervasive feature of Sino-Indian relations" by 2018. Each side has misinterpreted the other's international position and ambitions, "yielding the fear that their foreign policies are targeted against the other."[13] Xiaoyu Pu argues that status concerns contribute to the misperceptions between China and India. Due to the asymmetry in status and perceptions, "China is less sensitive about India's concerns, while India might sometimes overreact to China's behaviour and policies."[14]

Third, the transformation of the international system, representing the return of great-power competition (or rivalry), is increasingly perceived as a determinant shaping China–India relations. Chinese analysts generally believe that "India's aggression is closely related to the deterioration of China–U.S. relations."[15] Lin Wu finds that India observes more opportunities than challenges in the emerging U.S.–China strategic competition. As a party from which both the U.S. and China would like to gain support, India enjoys more room for gains.[16] Minwang Lin perceives that India is taking advantage of the transforming international environment and aspires to be a leading power (*"Vishwa Guru"*) rather than merely a balancing power. It is the repositioned national objective that makes India more aggressive in its dealings with China. The more intense the U.S.–China strategic competition becomes, the more determined India is to contain China.[17] Shisheng Hu and Jue Wang partly attribute India's provocative policy toward China to the changing geopolitical context. India is using its neutrality in the U.S.–China competition as a leverage to maximize its gains in its territorial disputes with China. To put it another way, the border standoffs are used by India to test China's strategic bottom line and leeway in terms of concessions.[18]

Some Indian scholars also emphasize the impacts of the changing international system, but they provide different narratives. Zorawar Daulet Singh insists that the U.S.–China relationship is currently a key factor shaping India–China relations, and "a U.S. policy adjustment on China will impact India–China relations by changing the calculus and thinking in Delhi and Beijing."[19] Sujan R. Chinoy attributes India's tilt toward the U.S. and embrace of the Quad to its belief in "a multipolar Asia," which, from India's perspective, is challenged by the unfolding Chinese dominance. He also emphasizes that "unequivocal support from Quad partners for its land boundary disputes with China will strengthen India's commitments to maritime cooperation beyond the Malacca Strait."[20]

The fourth broadly used perspective includes domestic factors such as strong leadership and intensified nationalism on both sides. Vijay Gokhale explores how China and India's new leadership "hardened mutual suspicions about the other's foreign policy."[21] Jagannath P. Panda assumes that India's negative perception of China is shaped by the latter's "mounting national security ambitions" and "its rapidly growing but insecure nationalism under Xi Jinping and the ambition to succeed over competing powers including India."[22] Shyam Saran contends that, under Xi, China's sensitivity to India's concerns has diminished, and the relationship has changed as a result.[23] Meanwhile, after the Doklam (Donglang) standoff, Kanti Bajpai attributed "the unprecedented spoiling of relations" to Modi's more assertive policy toward China. He even predicted "the possibility of more Doklams around the corner." In his mind, Modi's China policy has two pillars: one "to deepen strategic diplomatic and military relations with a coalition of Asia-Pacific powers against China" and the other "to change the approach to the border conflict," which means pushing for clarification of the Line of Actual Control (LAC), linking further normalization to substantive progress in border negotiations, and injecting "a greater sense of urgency" into the search for a final settlement.[24]

Chinese analysts could not agree more with Kanti Bajpai on Modi's role in the continued deterioration of China–India relations. However, they place greater emphasis on the Hindu nationalist ideology than on Modi's strongman leadership. According to Chunhao Lou, the influence lies in three aspects: first, aiming for national revival, under the Bharatiya Janata Party (BJP), India seeks to become a leading power and views China as a competitor. Second, since the Hindutva agenda deepens religious confrontation between India and Pakistan, India is becoming angrier at China's growing support for Pakistan. Third, the BJP and the Rashtriya Swayamsevak Sangh (RSS) are more sensitive to territorial integrity and reluctant to make any concessions.[25] The RSS is a powerful Hindu nationalist organization in India. Founded in 1925, the RSS has been promoting the ideology of Hindutva, or "Hindu-ness," and the idea that India should be a Hindu Rashtra (Hindu nation). In spite of representing itself as a cultural or a social organization, the RSS is believed as the parent organization or the ideological mentor of India's ruling party Bharatiya Janata Party (BJP). Some of the major political leaders of BJP, including Narendra Modi, were or still are members of the RSS.

4.2. Hypotheses and Analytic Framework

According to a Chinese proverb, "It takes more than one cold day for the river to freeze three feet deep." The above four categories of explanations generally agree with the fact that "long before the present border dispute occurred, Sino–Indian relations had been steadily declining."[26] However, if the current crisis is the result of a quantitative change, none of the perspectives provide a convincing explanation as to why the qualitative change has occurred at this juncture.

Moreover, each of the above perspectives has its own obvious limitations in explaining the ups and downs of this relationship. It was in 2013 that China's GDP overtook India's by fivefold for the first time, but the 2017 Doklam/Donglang face-off occurred at a time when this ratio had shrunk to 4.6.[27] And since 2014, India has been replacing China as the world's fastest-growing economy, as its annual growth rate outpaced China's in 2014, 2015, 2016, and 2018. The latest standoff occurred when China was still haunted by the aftershocks of the first wave of the COVID-19 pandemic. Therefore, it is not very convincing to attribute the deterioration of China–India relations to power disequilibrium. In terms of domestic factors, strong leadership on both sides seems to have only increased the fluctuations in China–India relations. It cannot solely explain why the good chemistry between Modi and Xi does not translate into good relations between the two nations.

Even though the asymmetric threat perceptions might provide reasons for the persistent misunderstandings between the two sides, they do not explain why India has taken different approaches to managing its perceived challenges from China. Highlights on the role of the transforming international system seem to be heading in the right direction. However, India's China policy has long been affected by the nature of China–U.S. relations. India views competitive Sino–U.S. relations as an opportunity to strengthen its position in dealing with China,[28] while cooperative Sino–U.S. relations undermine its capabilities *vis-à-vis* China.[29] Therefore, the crucial impact of the emerging China–U.S. strategic competition on China–India relations deserves further exploration.

Apart from the domestic prism, the other three perspectives highlight the role of the U.S. factor: its impact on the balance of power between China and India, their mutual perceptions, and each side's aspirations for position in a new world order. This chapter attempts to examine the logical linkage between the U.S. factor and the evolution of China–India relations since 1988. It investigates not only how the U.S. factor affects China's perception of India and India's China policy but also how the respective consequences interact and subsequently lead to the ups and downs of China–India relations.

The hypotheses are as follows: first, prior to the emergence of U.S.–China great-power competition (hereafter "the pre-strategic

Table 4.1. The U.S. factor and the evolution of India's policy toward China.

		U.S.–China relationship	
		Competitive	Cooperative
U.S. attitude toward India	Not good	1990s: hedging (engagement & internal balancing)	
	Good	2010 onward: from hedging to balancing	2000s: hedging (engagement, internal balancing & limited external balancing)

competition era"), there was a perception gap between China and India. China's strategic focus was on the East, and it viewed India as a partner, while China was prioritized in India's strategic calculus and designated as a competitor. The asymmetric perceptions may have led to mutual misunderstandings, but they (especially China's positive perceptions of India) have also prevented China–India relations from derailing.

Second, the ups and downs of China–India relations during the pre-strategic competition era were mainly driven by adjustments to India's China policy (Table 4.1). The U.S. attitude toward India and the U.S.–China relationship are the two variables that determine India's approach to dealing with China. Just as Feng Liu and Kai He argued in Chapter 1, identity might influence but not necessarily determine behavior (see Chapter 1). India, which constantly represents China more as a rival, can still choose between cooperation and competition.

Third, as the great-power competition unfolds, India's position in China's strategic calculus is changing because India is getting involved in the Indo-Pacific, the core arena where the U.S. contends with China. China's perception of India is becoming increasingly influenced by India's response to the U.S. Indo-Pacific strategy. Their perception gap has decreased, leading to increased mutual distrust and a major deterioration of the bilateral relationship (Table 4.2).

To better depict policy choices by competing states, this chapter employs the classifications proposed by Evan S. Medeiros: engagement, hedging, and balancing.[30] Engagement refers to "an attempt to create a cooperative relationship through political, military, economic, or social means."[31] Balancing implies competitive or confrontational efforts to check the prevailing threat. It may involve both internal and external

The U.S. Factor and the Evolution of China–India Relations 103

Table 4.2.   The U.S. factor and the evolution of China's India perception.

	U.S. grand strategy	
	Asia-Pacific era (pre-strategic competition era)	Indo-Pacific era (strategic competition era)
India's response (India's China policy) ↓↓	Hedging	Balancing
China's India perception ↓↓	Not a threat	Not a threat?
China's India policy	Engagement	From engagement to hedging

balancing, with the former aiming to increase one's own defense capabilities and the latter aiming to "formulate alignment or alliance for its own security."[32] Hedging is an approach that combines engagement and balancing.[33] Medeiros' categorization overcomes the limitation of the traditional balance of power theory, which is dichotomized into balancing and bandwagoning, and can be applied to interpret the behavior of the dominant power (such as the U.S.) or the stronger state (such as China in the case of China–India relations).

4.3. The U.S. Factor and India's China Policy

It is generally acknowledged by the international academic circle that there was a major perception gap between China and India after the 1988 normalization. Susan L. Shirk, in 2004, termed China–India relations "a one-sided rivalry," with India viewing China as "an economic and political rival and as [a] security threat," while China was not taking India seriously "as a security threat."[34] The perception gap is mainly caused by their different strategic focuses, which originate from their different geopolitical environments. In this sense, the U.S. factor does not play a significant role in India's perceptions of China; it is China itself. Being the largest neighbor with which India still has a border dispute, China is inevitably a focal point in India's strategic calculus. Shyam Saran proclaimed that "China shares a very long border with India and is the power that has the most impact on India's strategic space."[35]

4.3.1. *India's threat perception of China*

India has always perceived the "China threat," at least in the security domain.[36] According to official documents, India's security concerns about China largely involve the border dispute, China's military modernization, and China's strategic ties with Pakistan. Even at the high points of their bilateral relations, such as 2005 and 2014, India's defense annual reports continued to highlight these concerns. The 2005 *Annual Report* stated that despite positive trends in India–China relations, India continued to monitor "China's military modernization, with sustained double digit growth in its defence budget for over a decade, as also development of infrastructure in the India–China border areas," while still being concerned about "close defence exchanges and nuclear and missile cooperation between China and Pakistan."[37] The 2015 *Annual Report* asserted India's growing concerns about "China's increasing military profile in our immediate and extended neighbourhood" and pledged to take "necessary measures to develop the requisite capabilities to counter any adverse impact on our own security."[38]

In 2009, India's concerns started to extend to China's attitude toward India's rise.[39] The Indian strategic community complained that China was the only major power that did not accept India as a global player. China's ambiguous position toward India's candidacy as a permanent member of the UN Security Council (UNSC) and its opposition to India's entry into the Nuclear Suppliers Group (NSG) were cited as strong evidence. China's growing presence in South Asia and the Indian Ocean region through the Belt and Road Initiative, including the China–Pakistan Economic Corridor, was perceived as a great challenge to India's regional primacy. In short, it reinforced the belief among Indian political leaders that China was posing a "serious threat" to India.[40]

4.3.2. *The U.S. factor and India's China policy in the 1990s*

Although the U.S. factor is not very relevant to India's perspectives on China, it does have a solid impact on India's approach to China. In the 1990s, still estranged Indo–U.S. relations restrained India from taking advantage of Sino–U.S. tensions,[41] which were represented by U.S. sanctions following China's political turmoil in 1989, intensified disputes on human rights, arms control, the Taiwan issue, and the U.S. bombing of China's embassy in Belgrade in 1999. The Clinton administration's India policy focused on non-proliferation and the Kashmir issue. It exerted persistent pressure on India's nuclear and missile programs and endeavored to cap, reduce, and eliminate India's strategic aspirations.[42] It questioned the legitimacy of Indian-administered Kashmir and supported international intervention in longstanding conflicts around the world.[43]

Obviously, U.S. pressure outweighed the "China threat" and became a bigger security concern for India in the 1990s. Simultaneously facing U.S. pressure, India and China converged to resist U.S. unipolar hegemony.[44] It was against this background that the Indian strategic community suggested that China did not pose an immediate threat to India and that India should maintain a "good working relationship" with China.[45] As a result, India adopted a hedging policy toward China. On the one hand, India engaged China by exchanging high-level visits. It also signed with China the well-known 1993 and 1996 agreements, which provided frameworks and guidelines for maintaining peace and tranquility along the LAC in the border areas. On the other hand, India exercised internal balancing. The 1998 Indian nuclear tests were designed not only to increase India's international standing but also to build up its capabilities in dealing with China and Pakistan.[46] India also started to accelerate its program for building missiles capable of reaching China.[47]

The fact that the Vajpayee government justified the tests in terms of "China threat"[48] indicated how India tried to take advantage of the problematic Sino–U.S. relations to win over U.S. support. Contrary to India's wishes, Bill Clinton not only imposed sanctions on India but also signed a joint statement with China concerning South Asia, committed to preventing a nuclear and missile race in that region and assisting India and Pakistan in resolving their longstanding differences, including the Kashmir issue.[49] Consequently, India began to soften its stance towards China, and bilateral relations were back on track by June 1999. The above interplay among India, China, and the U.S. demonstrates how the U.S. factor significantly impacted India's approach to China during the 1990s.

4.3.3. *The U.S. factor and India's China policy in the 2000s*

The U.S. has courted India as a strategic partner in balancing a rising China since the early 2000s, pledging to help India become a great power.[50] However, India responded cautiously in the 2000s and tried to hedge between China and the U.S. On the one hand, India strengthened political engagement and economic cooperation with China. The 2003 Vajpayee visit to China was deemed a big breakthrough in China–India relations. India further recognized that "the Tibet Autonomous Region is an integral part of the People's Republic of China," while China, for the first time, recognized Sikkim as a state of the Indian Union. They also initiated the mechanism of appointing special representatives for border talks. In 2005, India agreed to establish a strategic and cooperative partnership with China and signed an agreement on political parameters and guiding principles for the settlement of the China–India boundary question. In March 2008, China replaced the U.S. as India's largest trading partner.[51]

On the other hand, India pursued a strategic partnership with the U.S. Apart from the nuclear deal, which was finalized in 2008, India and the U.S. signed a ten-year defense framework agreement in 2005, aiming to expand bilateral security cooperation. They engaged more often in joint military exercises, including a major one at sea that was also attended by Japan, Australia, and Singapore in 2007. Generally, during this period, India remained cautious about joining the U.S. to balance China. In view of China's concerns, India quit the Quad 1.0 soon after it was launched in 2007. India was also lukewarm to the U.S. proposal to sign all of the four "foundational agreements." Therefore, on the balancing side of India's China policy in the 2000s, India introduced limited external balancing while still largely relying on internal balancing. India initiated programs to upgrade infrastructure and strengthen military deployment in its northern border areas.[52]

According to Ashley J. Tellis, the U.S. relationship with both Pakistan and China fueled doubts in India "about American credibility in different ways."[53] In the 2000s, intensified Sino–U.S. constructive cooperation significantly contributed to India's hedging policy toward China. Obviously, the 9/11 terrorist attacks led to a positive turning point in Sino–U.S. relations. The U.S. administration under George W. Bush, who designated China as a "strategic competitor" during his presidential campaign, began treating China as a "stakeholder" in the international system.[54] Apart from deepening cooperation on global and regional issues, China and the U.S. became economically interdependent. In the early months of Obama's first term, two proposals on China–U.S. cooperation made India uncomfortable. One was the G2 concept, which suggested that the U.S. and China were to lead jointly in addressing global challenges facing the international system.[55] The other was the 2009 Sino–U.S. joint statement, in which the U.S. and China were not only committed to

The U.S. Factor and the Evolution of China–India Relations   107

"a positive, cooperative and comprehensive China–U.S. relationship" but also promised to make joint efforts to promote peace, stability, and development in South Asia and "support the improvement and growth of relations between India and Pakistan."[56] The latter proposal, Sino–U.S. cooperation to mediate the India–Pakistan dispute, was immediately and officially rejected by India as unnecessary.[57] A warmer relationship between the U.S. and China was viewed by India "as a threat to its own rise as a global power."[58] It also undermined India's trust in the U.S. This shows the strategy of hedging can help India reduce the risk of putting all its eggs in one basket.

4.3.4. *The U.S. factor and India's China policy since 2010*

The 2010s witnessed the U.S.' strategic shift, including Obama's pivot, or rebalance, to the Asia-Pacific and Trump's Indo-Pacific strategy. The Biden administration generally inherited the Indo-Pacific strategy, confirming "extreme competition" with China and recommitting to alliances and partnerships.[59] In this process, India has been increasingly viewed as a "lynchpin" partner of the U.S.[60] India has adapted its foreign policy accordingly. S. Jaishankar, the Indian Minister of External Affairs, proclaimed that the U.S.–China dynamic "is the global backdrop for Indian policymaking."[61] Along with a continued deterioration of Sino–U.S. ties, India's China policy is shifting from hedging to balancing.

In the Obama era, the U.S. attempted to balance the rise of China by increasing military deployment in the Asia-Pacific, strengthening its alliance system, and exploring new partnerships, as well as forging China-excluded regional economic groups such as the Trans-Pacific Partnership (TPP). Meanwhile, the U.S. agreed to build "a new model" of relations with China and made progress in cooperation on issues such as climate change.[62] Against this backdrop, India continued its hedging policy toward China and established "a closer developmental relationship" with China in 2014. At the bilateral level, the Modi government encouraged Chinese investors to actively get involved in the "Make in India" campaign and infrastructure, pledging to improve India's business environment.[63] At the multilateral level, India joined hands with China to reform global governance. In 2014, BRICS (the five leading emerging economies: Brazil, Russia, India, China, and South Africa) launched two new initiatives, the New Development Bank and the Contingent Reserve Arrangement. In 2016, India joined the Asian Infrastructure Investment

Bank (AIIB) as a founding member and became the second-largest shareholder, just after China.

After designating China as a strategic competitor of the U.S. and introducing the Indo-Pacific strategy, the Trump administration not only launched a trade war but also clashed with China on multiple fronts, such as human rights and COVID-19 origin tracing. As a result, Sino–U.S. relations experienced a nosedive during Trump's term. Since Biden largely maintained Trump's policies toward China, Sino–U.S. tensions continued unabated during the Biden administration. Coincidentally, India's China policy has demonstrated more balancing than hedging. India even started to restrict its economic engagement with China, a strong pillar in their relations. Since 2020, "a host of offensive measures" have been announced to reduce India's trade and investment links with China.[64] It was not only a consequence of the latest border standoff but also a response to the U.S. decoupling from China.[65]

Moreover, India has been strengthening both internal balancing and external balancing against China since 2010. In terms of internal balancing, India stepped up its military capacity-building along the border, "including by raising an entirely new corps in the Indian Army to face China and by building new transportation infrastructure in the border regions."[66] In fact, since 2006, India has been preparing for a "two-front" war with Pakistan and China. The plan was formally articulated in the Indian Defense Minister's operational directive in 2009. The core design was "to prepare for a primary and a secondary front, and to prevent any loss of territory through deterrence and dissuasion."[67] Despite silence from political leaders, Indian military commanders have recently become more vocal and confirmed the readiness of India's armed forces for such a two-front war.[68]

In terms of external balancing, the past decade also witnessed India overcoming "the hesitations of history" and "embracing" the U.S.[69] In 2015, India joined the U.S. to "affirm" the importance of ensuring freedom of navigation and overflight in the South China Sea.[70] India has completed the signing of the foundational agreements with the U.S.—the Logistics Exchange Memorandum of Agreement (LEMOA) in 2016, the Communications Compatibility and Security Agreement (COMCASA) in 2018, and the Basic Exchange and Cooperation Agreement (BECA) in 2020—which "enable greater access to U.S. logistical facilities, high-tech communications infrastructure, and geospatial data."[71] The agreements seem to have played a role when the U.S. provided assistance to India in the latter's latest border standoff with China.[72] India's support for the reactivation of the Quad in 2017 and Biden's efforts to boost the group's regional cooperation have also indicated that it is already on board the U.S. strategy to "reconfigure the Indo-Pacific balance of power."[73]

4.4. The U.S. Factor and China's India Perception

Compared with India, China's strategic surroundings are more complex. India is only a major power in China's neighborhood. There are other "directions" in China's strategic calculus, and the East, i.e., the Asia-Pacific, has dominated as its foremost strategic focus since the end of the Cold War. Three factors contribute to China's strategic focus on the Asia-Pacific region. First, China's political and economic centers are concentrated in the eastern region, especially the coastal provinces. They provide gateways to the world, as well as being engines for China's economic growth. Second, the Asia-Pacific direction is significant to many of China's security concerns, including the risk of "Taiwan independence," territorial and maritime disputes in the South and East China seas, Japanese militarization, and stability on the Korean Peninsula. Third and foremost, the U.S. and its alliance system play a major role in the region and constitute growing strategic challenges to China's security interests.[74]

4.4.1. *China's India perception in the Asia-Pacific era*

With the Asia-Pacific region dominating China's strategic calculus, India seemed not to be on China's strategic radar before the great-power competition loomed large. China has issued 10 defense white papers since 1998, and the latest one was released in 2019.[75] Since its second defense white paper issued in 2000, the U.S. has been clearly identified as a major challenge to China's security and Asia-Pacific stability. While India has only "marginally figured" in these documents, they highlight the security threat caused by several provocative activities of the U.S., including its growing military presence and military alliances in the Asia-Pacific region, continued arms sales to Taiwan, and "meddling in South China Sea affairs," as well as the introduction of both the previous "rebalancing" strategy and the latest "Indo-Pacific" strategy.[76,77] The 1998 *Defense White Paper* underlined the threat posed by India's and Pakistan's nuclear tests to the international nuclear non-proliferation regime. The 2004 and 2019 white papers, respectively, raised concerns about potential conflicts between India and Pakistan. What has been touched upon more regarding India in the discussions are the confidence-building measures (CBMs) and military exchanges between China and India. Moreover, top Chinese leaders have consistently portrayed India as a friend and partner,[78] which sounds idealistic given India's cautious designation of the bilateral relationship.

China's positive perception of India carries both realistic and visionary meanings. In terms of the realistic meaning, it implies that China does not view India as a threat. In 1981, Deng Xiaoping said that India could not be a threat on its own, and China viewed India as a threat in the 1960s and 1970s only because India sided with the Soviet Union, China's major enemy at the time.[79] It more or less reflected the logic in China's threat calculus regarding India. It was against this backdrop that the U.S. factor began playing a role in China's perception of India after the U.S. and India clinched a nuclear deal in 2005. The Bush administration did not hide its intention to counterbalance the rise of China by assisting India in becoming a global power.[80] The Obama administration moved further to involve India in its rebalancing strategy, which was directed at China, and advance India to become "a major defence partner" of the U.S. The growing proximity between India and the U.S. did generate concerns in China, but it did not significantly alter China's perception of India during those days. There were mainly two reasons. First, China still believed that India would observe strategic autonomy. Even though India was moving away from its traditional creed of non-alignment, it would be difficult for India to forge an alliance with the U.S.[81] India's hedging policy also provided some support in this regard. Second, cooperation remained an important part of China–U.S. relations, and China advocated for a new model of major-power relationship with the U.S., observing the principles of no conflict, no confrontation, mutual respect, and win-win cooperation.[82] The U.S. was also hedging between China and India, limiting India–U.S. strategic cooperation in balancing China.

In terms of the visionary meaning, China's positive perception of India reflects its expectation for a friendly relationship with India, as this will not only help ensure a peaceful environment for China's economic development but also enable it to focus on dealing with security challenges from the east. As a result, China's India policy has long been dominated by engagement (or cooperation). Notwithstanding differing interpretations on the Indian side, China has invested heavily in befriending India. Apart from strengthening the development partnership, enhancing multilateral coordination (on issues such as climate change, global financial governance, and energy security), and exercising restraint on the border dispute, China has made obvious efforts to accommodate India's concerns. On the Kashmir issue, since the 1990s, China has gradually shifted its stance from endorsing Pakistan's position on self-determination for Kashmiris based on UN resolutions to supporting a peaceful solution through Indo–Pakistani negotiations, which conforms to India's bilateralism on this issue.[83]

On India's nuclear ambitions, China demonstrated flexibility with the 2008 NSG waiver for the U.S.–India civil nuclear deal. China had solid grounds to oppose such a specific exemption. First, it would undermine the international non-proliferation regime since India refused to sign the Nuclear Non-Proliferation Treaty (NPT) and the Comprehensive Test Ban Treaty (CTBT).[84] Second, India used the so-called "China threat" as a major justification for its 1998 nuclear tests. Third, it was widely believed that the nuclear deal would help the U.S. use India to check and balance China.[85] However, for the sake of the health of its relations with India as well as with the U.S., China chose to abstain from the final vote.[86]

On India's UNSC bid, China's public position has been generally positive, saying China "understands and supports India's aspiration to play a greater role in the United Nations including in the Security Council."[87] According to Chinese academia, the main obstacle for China in providing unambiguous support to India joining the G4 nations which includes Japan, Brazil and Germany. The G4 nations agree to support each other's bids for permanent seats on the United Nations Security Council. Candidature Beijing absolutely "opposes for historical reasons."[88] Xi has also told Modi that India, like China, is an "important pole" in the world,[89] and that India plays a significant role in shaping the security architecture of the Asia-Pacific.[90] To allay India's concerns about China's growing economic presence in South Asia, China, which shares borders with five of the eight South Asian Association for Regional Cooperation (SAARC) members, told Nepal in 2012 that "it would be better and fruitful for Nepal to maintain good relations with India."[91] In recent years, China has proposed to "explore a gradual expansion of the 'China–India Plus' cooperation to South Asia, Southeast Asia and Africa."[92] In October 2018, China and India initiated a joint training program for Afghan diplomats.

4.4.2. *China's India perception in the Indo-Pacific era*

The introduction of the U.S. Indo-Pacific strategy in 2017 represents the U.S.' strategic shift to great-power competition, and the Indo-Pacific has become "the frontline" in the U.S.' "strategic competition with China."[93] As a result, the cooperative nature of Sino–U.S. relations has been drastically eclipsed by competition and confrontation. From the Chinese perspective, the security challenges posed by the U.S. to China have intensified significantly. Under Trump, the U.S.' China policy became so extreme that it even called for a regime change in China.[94] Despite China's strong opposition, the Biden administration has continued to define Sino–U.S. relations as competitive and pledged to "prevail in strategic competition with China" in the 21st century.[95] Biden has inherited many of Trump's policies toward China, especially the Indo-Pacific strategy. Under his leadership, the Quad Summit has been convened regularly, and a rich agenda for practical cooperation has been established. He has also introduced the AUKUS, a controversial trilateral security pact between Australia, the U.K., and the U.S. Therefore, the Chinese government has publicly criticized the U.S. for using the Quad to build a "new NATO" in the Indo-Pacific region and attempting to "contain China."[96] China regards the Indo-Pacific Economic Framework (IPEF) as another U.S. attempt to isolate it in the economic domain after the failed Trans-Pacific Partnership (TPP).[97]

In the Indo-Pacific era, India's position in China's strategic calculus has begun to change in the following two aspects. First, India is no longer marginalized but has become an important factor to be taken into account. Now that the U.S. regards the Indo-Pacific as its primary theater of defense and security[98] and views "a strong India" as "a counterbalance to China,"[99] the U.S. geopolitical challenges to China are extending from the Asia-Pacific to the Bay of Bengal and the Indian subcontinent. According to the declassified *U.S. Strategic Framework for the Indo-Pacific*, the U.S. will not only accelerate India's ability to play a role in regional security by deepening defense cooperation and reactivating the Quad but also "offer support to India—through diplomatic, military and intelligence channels—to help address continental challenges such as the border dispute with China and access to water."[100] It is natural for China to adjust its strategic focus and include India in it.

Second, as India continues to align itself more closely with the U.S., from China's traditional perspective, this means that India is challenging

China not on its own. China and India are part of the U.S. Indo-Pacific strategy, with China being the target and India a partner of the U.S. In recent times, non-alignment has been replaced with "multi-alignment" and "issue-based alignment" in the mainstream narratives of India.[101] They reflect the hedging nature of India's foreign policy in a general sense. However, as discussed in the previous section, India's China policy is moving from hedging to balancing. Apart from strengthening strategic cooperation with the U.S., both bilaterally and within the Quad framework, the India–U.S. Initiative on Critical and Emerging Technologies (iCET) becomes a new pillar in the India–U.S. relationship. The iCET is expected to catalyze Indo–U.S. technology cooperation and is even regarded as important as the Indo–U.S. nuclear deal.[102] Even though the current Indo–U.S. relations do not represent a *de facto* alliance, the fact that India is actually on board of the U.S. Indo-Pacific strategy provides enough grounds for China to pay closer attention. In the ongoing Russia–Ukraine war, India did not join the U.S. in condemning Russia but instead defied Western sanctions by purchasing Russian oil at substantial discounts. The fact that India attributed its neutrality to the purpose of preventing Russia from embracing closer ties with China[103] only reinforces China's belief that India's strategic autonomy may not apply to the China-directed cooperation between India and the U.S.

Although the Chinese government insists that "China's strategic assessment of China–India relations has not changed" and that the two countries are partners rather than threats and "offer development opportunities to each other,"[104] China's perceptions of India are undergoing a kind of change. Extensive debates on how to view India have emerged in China's academic circle in recent years. Some assert that India has become the major competitor rather than a partner of China in the southwest, a strategic direction secondary to the Asia-Pacific. Even though China should avert a two-front confrontation, it should not "make excessive compromise" with disproportionate returns and fuel its competitor's larger ambitions of gaining excessive benefits.[105] Some predict that if India becomes too reliant on U.S. strategies for balancing China, it may force China to become tougher toward India because India's siding with the U.S. will undermine China's security interests.[106] Some believe that India and the U.S. are becoming allies and will form a maritime quasi-alliance.[107] China is concerned about the substance and consequences of the Indo-Pacific Maritime Domain Awareness Initiative (IPMDA), announced by the Quad. It is believed that, "Though unstated, the main target of this initiative appears to be China."[108] Some argue that India has become a defense ally of the U.S. and is attempting to take advantage of Sino–U.S. strategic competition to accelerate its rise.[109] These perceptive changes may provide some clues and explanations for China's tougher response to the border standoffs since May 2020.

4.5. Conclusion

This chapter attempts to find a variable which can better explain the evolution of China–India relations since 1988 in general and an emerging new normal, represented by the border standoffs, since May 2020 in particular. As the sole superpower following the Cold War, the U.S. has been a significant element in the respective strategic calculus of China and India and has become a core third-party factor in academic analyses of China–India relations. However, the existing studies either concentrate on the trilateral or triangular interactions among China, India, and the U.S. or explore how the intensified Indo–U.S. strategic partnership affects China–India relations. This research treats the U.S. factor as an independent variable to examine its respective impacts on China and India regarding their decision-making toward each other. It also inspects the interactions of those impacts in order to provide a better explanation and even an effective prediction of the future ups and downs of China–India relations.

This chapter finds that the U.S. factor has impacted India's policy toward China while also affecting China by influencing its perceptions of India. Owing to the different strategic surroundings of China and India, there has been an asymmetry in their mutual perceptions. India views China more through the lens of competition, while China always highlights the cooperative side of the relationship. Especially since 2000, India has regarded U.S. strategic support as leverage in dealing with China but had apprehensions about a G2 scenario, both globally and in South Asia. Therefore, India has observed a typical hedging policy toward China, its major competitor. For China, the complex evolution of Asia-Pacific geopolitics requires a stable relationship with India to avoid the dilemma of a two-front confrontation. Despite regular breakthroughs in Indo–U.S. relations, India's upholding of its strategic autonomy and the Sino–U.S. consensus on cooperation amid competition have provided some room for China to engage with and befriend India. As a result, China–India relations have achieved significant progress, especially in development cooperation, both bilaterally and multilaterally. Although frictions have emerged from time to time, they were eventually resolved or well managed, and each time the relationship was able to get back to business as usual.

Since the U.S. identified China as a strategic competitor and introduced the Indo-Pacific strategy, its "extreme competition" with China has provided India with a *de facto* strategic opportunity. India has overcome its hesitation and embraced the U.S. Indo-Pacific strategy. India's China policy is moving from hedging to balancing. Meanwhile, with the incorporation of India, the U.S. Indo-Pacific strategy is forcing China to face an emerging two-front strategic pressure. China has to consider India more carefully in its core strategic calculus, and it has started to take the possible threat from India more seriously. The asymmetry of mutual threat perceptions between China and India is rapidly decreasing. China is introducing balancing into its India policy, which has long been dominated by engagement.

China–India relations seem to be increasingly framed in the backdrop of U.S.–China strategic competition. Believing that India is siding with the U.S. to counter it, China, while still committed to engagement, may have no choice but to invest more in balancing against India to prevent the worst-case scenario: a military showdown in the border areas and a new cold war in Asia. A tougher China may reinforce India's long-standing threat perception of China and consequently lead India to focus on balancing, especially through a further tilt toward the U.S. If China and India cannot find convincing common ground to engage in an era of great-power competition, their relations will move into a state of mutual balancing.

Endnotes

1 M. Bhalla, "The China factor in India's economic diplomacy," 26 April 2021. https://www.orfonline.org/expert-speak/china-factor-india-economic-diplomacy/ (Accessed 9 January 2022).

2 S. Haidar and A. Krishnan, "Jaishankar, Wang Differ on way forward for India-China ties," *The Hindu*, 15 July 2021.

3 V. Gokhale, "The road from Galwan: The future of India-China relations," *Working Paper, Carnegie India*, p. 1, March 2021. https://carnegieendowment.org/files/Gokhale_Galwan.pdf (Accessed 9 January 2022).

4 Hu Shisheng, Wang Jue, and Liu Chuanxi, "Cong jialewan hegu chongtu kan yindu lusuo shi anquan siwei kunju (The land-locked mentality in security through the lens of the Galwan conflict)," *Yinduyang jingjiti yanjiu* (*Indian Ocean Economic and Political Review*), 4, 2 (2020).

5 S. Kalyanaraman, "The China-India-US triangle: Changing balance of power and a new cold war," Manohar Parrikar Institute for Defence Studies and Analyses, 21 September 2020. https://www.idsa.in/idsacomments/the-china-india-us-triangle-kalyanraman-210920.

6 P. Robertson, Yuan Jingdong, and H. K. Mudiyanselage, "China, India and the contest for the Indo-Pacific," *Indian Growth and Development Review*, 13(2), 289–317 (2020).

7 S. Ganguly, "Recent developments in Sino-Indian relations," *India Review*, 19(3), 301–306 (2020).

8 I. Denisov, I. Safranchuk, and D. Bochkov, "China–India relations in Eurasia: Historical legacy and the changing global context," *Human Affairs*, 30(2), 224–238 (2020). See also Wu Fuzuo, "India's pragmatic foreign policy toward China's BRI and AIIB: Struggling for relative and absolute gains," *Journal of Contemporary China*, 29(123), 354–368 (2020).

9 Zhang Jiadong and Sun Qian, "China–India relations: A premature strategic competition between the Dragon and the Elephant," *Issues and Studies*, 55(3), 1 (2019).

10 Tien-sze Fang, *Asymmetrical Threat Perceptions in India-China Relations* (New Delhi: Oxford University Press, 2014).

11 P. K. Singh, "Book review: Asymmetrical threat perceptions in India–China relations," *Journal of Defence Studies*, 9(4), 146 (2015).

12 Haiqi Zheng, "China-India relations: How different perceptions shape the future," *ISAS Insights*, 659, 2, 5, 1 April 2021. https://www.isas.nus.edu.sg/papers/china-india-relations-how-different-perceptions-shape-the-future/ (Accessed 9 January 2022).

13 Gokhale (2021), *Op. cit.*

14 Xiaoyu Pu, "Asymmetrical competitors: Status concerns and the China-India rivalry," in T. V. Paul (ed.) *The India-China Rivalry in the Globalization Era* (Washington, DC: Georgetown University Press, 2018), p. 67; also see Xiaoyu Pu, "The status dilemma in world politics: An anatomy of the China–India asymmetrical rivalry," *The Chinese Journal of International Politics*, 15(3), 227–245 (2022).

15 Zheng (2021), *Op. cit.*, p. 6.

16 Wu Lin, "India's perception of and response to China-US competition," *China International Studies*, 6, 130–155 (2020).

17 Lin Minwang, "Da bianju xia yindu waijiao zhanlue: mubiao dingwei yu tiaozheng fangxiang (India's foreign strategy in a transformed world: Objectives and trends)," *Dangdai shijie* (*Contemporary World*), 4, 24–29 (2021).

18 Hu Shisheng and Wang Jue, "The behavioral logic behind India's tough foreign policy toward China," *Contemporary International Relations*, 30(5), 37–65 (2020).

19 Zorawar Daulet Singh, "The future of India-China relationship is now all about the flux in US-China ties," *The Print*, 22 February 2021. https://theprint.in/opinion/the-future-of-india-china-relationship-is-now-all-about-the-flux-in-us-china-ties/608958/.

20 S. R. Chinoy, "India and the changing dynamics of the Indo-Pacific," *Asia Policy*, 15(4), 34 (2020).

21 Gokhale (2021), *Op. cit.*

22 J. P. Panda, "China as a revisionist power in Indo-Pacific and India's perception: A power-partner contention," *Journal of Contemporary China*, 30(127), 17 (2021).

23 S. Saran, "Changing dynamics in India-China relations," *China Report*, 53(2), 259–263 (2017).

24 K. Bajpai, "Modi's China policy and the road to confrontation," *Pacific Affairs*, 91(2), 246, 260, 248, 245 (2018).

25 Lou Chunhao, "Yindu duihua zhengce de zhuanbian yu zhongguo de zhengce fansi (The changes of India's China policy and China's response)," Xiandai guoji guanxi (*Contemporary International Relations*), 11, 26–34 (2020).

26 Gokhale (2021), *Op. cit.*

27 Please refer to World Bank Open Data. https://data.worldbank.org/?locations=CN-IN.

28 Rohan Mukherjee, "Chaos as opportunity: The United States and world order in India's grand strategy," *Contemporary Politics*, 26(4), 420–438 (2020).

29 T. Madan, "The U.S.-India relationship and China," Brookings, 23 September 2014. https://www.brookings.edu/research/the-u-s-india-relationship-and-china/.

30 E. S. Medeiros, "Strategic hedging and the future of Asia-Pacific stability," *The Washington Quarterly*, 29(1), 145–167 (Winter 2005–2006).

31 Kei Koga, "The concept of 'hedging' revisited: The case of Japan's foreign policy strategy in East Asia's power shift," *International Studies Review*, 20(4), 636 (2018).

32 *Ibid.*, p. 637.

33 Medeiros (2005–2006), *Op. cit.*

34 S. L. Shirk, "One-sided rivalry: China's perceptions and policies toward India," in F. R. Frankel and H. Harding (eds.) *The India-China Relationship: Rivalry and Engagement* (New Delhi: Oxford University Press, 2004), p. 75.

35 S. Saran, *How India Sees the World: Kautilya to the 21st Century* (New Delhi: Juggernaut, 2017), p. 106.

36 Panda (2021), *Op. cit.*
37 *Annual Report 2005–2006*, Ministry of Defense, Government of India, p. 10. https://www.mod.gov.in/documents/annual-report?page=1.
38 *Annual Report 2014–2015*, Ministry of Defense, Government of India, p. 6. https://www.mod.gov.in/sites/default/files/AR1415_0.pdf.
39 Gokhale (2021), *Op. cit.*
40 H. V. Pant, "The India–US–China triangle from New Delhi: Overcoming the 'hesitations of history,'" *India Review*, 18(4), 386–406 (2019).
41 D. Kux, *India and the United States Estranged Democracies, 1941–1991* (Washington DC: National Defense University Press, 1993).
42 C. R. Mohan, *Crossing the Rubicon: The Shaping of India's New Foreign Policy* (New Delhi: Penguin/Viking, 2003), pp. 88–89.
43 *Ibid.*, pp. 97–98.
44 C. R. Mohan, "Diplomacy for the new decade," Seminar #605, January 2010. https://www.india-seminar.com/2010/605/605_c_raja_mohan.htm.
45 J. N. Dixit, *India's Foreign Policy and its Neighbors* (New Delhi: Gyan Publishing House, 2001), p. 223, 227.
46 S. Ganguly, "India's pathway to Pokhran II: The prospects and sources of New Delhi's nuclear weapons program," *International Security*, 23(4), 148–177 (Spring 1999).
47 S. P. Cohen, *India: Emerging Power* (Washington, DC: Brookings Institution Press, 2001), p. 187.
48 A. B. Vajpayee, "Nuclear anxiety; Indian's letter to Clinton on the nuclear testing," *The New York Times*, 13 May 1998.
49 "Sino-U.S. joint statement on South Asia," 27 June 1998. http://www.china-embassy.org/eng/zmgx/zysj/kldfh/t36228.htm.
50 A. Ayres, *Our Time Has Come: How India Is Making its Place in the World* (New Delhi: Oxford University Press, 2018), p. 210.
51 S. K. Mohanty, "India-China bilateral trade relationship: Study prepared for Reserve Bank of India," July 2014. https://rbidocs.rbi.org.in/rdocs/Publications/PDFs/PRSICBT130613.pdf (Accessed 9 January 2022).
52 *Annual Report 2009–2010*, Ministry of Defense, Government of India. https://www.mod.gov.in/sites/default/files/AR910.pdf.
53 A. J. Tellis, "US-India relations: The struggle for an enduring partnership," in D. M. Malone, C. R. Mohan, and S. Raghavan (eds.) *The Oxford Handbook of Indian Foreign Policy* (New Delhi: Oxford University Press, 2015), p. 492.
54 "President Bush and President Hu of People's Republic of China participate in arrival ceremony," 20 April 2006. https://georgewbush-whitehouse.archives.gov/news/releases/2006/04/20060420.html.

55 R. C. Bush, "The United States and China: A G-2 in the Making?" Brookings, 11 October 2011. https://www.brookings.edu/articles/the-united-states-and-china-a-g-2-in-the-making/.

56 "China-US Joint Statement," 17 November 2009. https://www.fmprc.gov.cn/mfa_eng/wjb_663304/zzjg_663340/bmdyzs_664814/gjlb_664818/3432_664920/3434_664924/t629497.shtml.

57 "A third country role cannot be envisaged nor is it necessary," *Outlook*, 18 November 2009. https://www.outlookindia.com/website/story/a-third-country-role-cannot-be-envisaged-nor-is-it-necessary/262929.

58 L. Polgreen, "China gains in U.S. Eyes, and India feels slights," *The New York Times*, 23 November 2009.

59 "Biden says there will be 'extreme competition' with China, but won't take Trump approach," *CNBC*, 7 February 2021; "Interim National Security Strategic Guidance," 3 March 2021. https://www.whitehouse.gov/wp-content/uploads/2021/03/NSC-1v2.pdf.

60 M. Pubby, "US says India 'lynchpin' of rebalancing strategy," *The Indian Express*, 7 June 2012.

61 S. Jaishankar, *The India Way: Strategies for An Uncertain World* (Noida: HarperCollins Publishers, 2020), p. 6.

62 J. Calmes and S. Lee Myers, "U.S. and China move closer on North Korea, but not on cyberespionage," *The New York Times*, 8 June 2013.

63 "Full text of PM Modi's speech at the India-China business forum in Shanghai," 16 May 2015. https://www.ndtv.com/business/full-text-of-prime-minister-narendra-modis-speech-at-the-india-china-business-forum-in-shanghai-763530.

64 "India may not alter rules of engagement with AIIB," *Mint*, 29 July 2020.

65 "S. Cohen and B. Narayanan Gopalakrishnan, "US-China Decoupling and India," *The Daily Guardian*, 4 January 2021. https://thedailyguardian.com/us-china-decoupling-and-india/.

66 R. Rajagopalan, "India's strategic choices: China and the balance of power in Asia," *Paper, Carnegie India*, p. 16, 14 September 2017. https://carnegieindia.org/2017/09/14/india-s-strategic-choices-china-and-balance-of-power-in-asia-pub-73108.

67 S. Singh, "The challenge of a two-front war: India's China-Pakistan dilemma," *Issue Brief*, p. 2, 19 April 2021. https://www.stimson.org/2021/the-challenge-of-a-two-front-war-indias-china-pakistan-dilemma/.

68 *Ibid.*

69 "Full text of PM Narendra Modi's historic speech in the US Congress," *India Today*, 6 June 2016. http://indiatoday.intoday.in/story/full-text-of-pm-narendra-modis-historic-speech-in-the-us-congress/1/687644.html.

70 "US-India joint strategic vision for the Asia-Pacific and Indian Ocean Region," 25 January 2015. http://www.mea.gov.in/bilateral-documents. htm?dtl/24728/USIndia_Joint_Strategic_Vision_for_the_AsiaPacific_ and_Indian_Ocean_Region.

71 Mukherjee (2020), *Op. cit.*, p. 421.

72 "We stood with India as it faced Chinese aggression along its border," *Business Standard*, 17 December 2020.

73 C. R. Mohan, "AUKUS, the Quad, and India's strategic pivot," *Foreign Policy*, 23 September 2021.

74 Ye Hailin, "Zhongguo jueqi yu ciyao zhanlue fangxiang tiaozhan de ying- dui- yi donglang shijian hou de zhongyin guanxi weili (How should a rising China address the challenge from the secondary strategic direction? A case study on Sino-Indian relations in Post-Doklam period)," *Shijie jingji yu zhengzhi* (*World Economics and Politics*), 4, 106–128 (2018).

75 Please refer to the website of the State Council Information Office of the People's Republic of China. http://www.scio.gov.cn/zfbps/index.htm.

76 *China's Military Strategy*, 26 May 2015. http://www.scio.gov.cn/zfbps/ ndhf/2015/Document/1435159/1435159.htm.

77 J. W. Garver, "Asymmetrical Indian and Chinese threat perceptions," *The Journal of Strategic Studies*, 25(4), 109–134 (2002).

78 "Wen Jiabao addresses Delhi Institute of Technology," 12 April 2005. http://www.fmprc.gov.cn/mfa_eng/topics_665678/wzlcfly_665842/ t191619.shtml.

79 S. Swamy, *India's China Perspective* (Delhi: Konark Publishers, 2001), Appendix III, pp. 175–178.

80 The testimonies of Condoleezza Rice before the House International Relations and Senate Foreign Relations Committees can be found at http:// www.state.gov/secretary/rm/2006/64146.htm, http://www.state.gov/secretary/rm/2006/64136.htm; See also: Ayres (2018), *Op. cit.*

81 Rong Ying, "The 'Modi Doctrine' and the future of China-India relations," *China International Studies*, 1, 26–43 (2018).

82 "Xi Jinping holds talks with President Barack Obama of the US," 12 November 2014. https://www.fmprc.gov.cn/mfa_eng/topics_665678/ ytjhzzdrsrcldrfzshyjxghd/t1211022.shtml.

83 Li Li, *Security Perception and China-India Relations* (New Delhi: KW Publishers, 2009), p. 137.

84 C. Buckley, "China state paper lashes India-U.S. nuclear deal," *Reuters*, 6 September 2008.

85 Shen Dingli, "Building China-India reconciliation," *Asian Perspective*, 34(4), 139–163 (2010).

86 N. Misra, "China says it backs India's N-ambitions," *Hindustan Times*, 7 September 2008.

The U.S. Factor and the Evolution of China–India Relations   121

87   "Joint statement between the India and China during Prime Minister's visit to China," 15 May 2015. https://www.mea.gov.in/bilateral-documents.htm?dtl/25240/Joint_Statement_between_the_India_and_China_during_Prime_Ministers_visit_to_China.

88   "India's UNSC alliance with Japan biggest mistake: Chinese media," *The Economic Times*, 12 July 2018.

89   "Xi Jinping meets with Prime Minister Narendra Modi of India," 14 July 2014. http://www.fmprc.gov.cn/mfa_eng/zxxx_662805/t1175135.shtml.

90   "Chinese President Xi Jinping speaks on China-India relations," 19 September 2014. http://english.cntv.cn/2014/09/19/VIDE1411059120512826_2.shtml.

91   *The Economist*, "Yam yesterday, Yam today," 18 January 2012.

92   "President Xi Jinping and Indian Prime Minister Narendra Modi continue their meeting in Chennai," 12 October 2019. https://www.fmprc.gov.cn/mfa_eng/zxxx_662805/t1707848.shtml.

93   "Advancing U.S. engagement and countering China in the Indo-Pacific and beyond," 17 September 2020. https://2017-2021.state.gov/advancing-u.s.-engagement-and-countering-china-in-the-indo-pacific-and-beyond/index.html.

94   "Mike Pompeo urges Chinese people to change communist party," *The Wall Street Journal*, 23 July 2020.

95   "Interim National Security Strategic Guidance," p. 20, 3 March 2021. https://www.whitehouse.gov/wp-content/uploads/2021/03/NSC-1v2.pdf.

96   "Wang Yi: U.S. 'Indo-Pacific strategy' undermines peace and development prospects in East Asia," 13 October 2020. http://ch.china-embassy.gov.cn/ger/zgxw/202010/t20201015_3208143.htm; "Trump's Indo-Pacific strategy aimed to 'contain' Beijing: Chinese official," *NDTV*, 13 January 2021. https://www.ndtv.com/world-news/donald-trumps-indo-pacific-strategy-aimed-to-contain-beijing-chinese-official-zhao-lijian-2352095.

97   "U.S. 'Indo-Pacific Strategy' bound to fail: Chinese FM," *Xinhua*, 23 May 2022. https://english.news.cn/20220523/2e35f4d7edef417196ace8b8939ff24b/c.html.

98   *Indo-Pacific Strategy Report: Preparedness, Partnerships, and Promoting a Networked Region,* 1 June 2019. https://media.defense.gov/2019/Jul/01/2002152311/-1/-1/1/DEPARTMENT-OF-DEFENSE-INDO-PACIFIC-STRATEGY-REPORT-2019.PDF.

99   "US strategic framework for the Indo-Pacific," p. 2, 5 January 2021. https://trumpwhitehouse.archives.gov/wp-content/uploads/2021/01/IPS-Final-Declass.pdf.

100   *Ibid.*, p. 5.

101   P. S. Raghavan, "The making of India's foreign policy: From non-alignment to multi-alignment," *Indian Foreign Affairs Journal*, 12(4), 326–341 (2017); "India is no longer 'non-aligned', Says Foreign Secretary Vijay

Gokhale," *The Print*, 10 January 2019. https://theprint.in/diplomacy/india-is-no-longer-non-aligned-says-foreign-secretary-vijay-gokhale/176222/.

102 "iCET initiative as important as India-US nuclear deal: US-India business council president Atul Keshap," *The Print*, 1 June 2023. https://theprint.in/world/icet-initiative-as-important-as-india-us-nuclear-deal-us-india-business-council-president-atul-keshap/1606401/.

103 S. Johny, "View from India. How does India look at the Ukraine war?" *The Hindu*, 26 February 2024.

104 "Wang Yi meets with Indian external affairs minister Subrahmanyam Jaishankar," 15 July 2021. https://www.fmprc.gov.cn/mfa_eng/zxxx_662805/t1892327.shtml.

105 Ye Hailin, "Zhongguo jueqi yu ciyao zhanlue fangxiang tiaozhan de yingdui- yi donglang shijian hou de zhongyin guanxi weili (How should a rising China address the challenge from the secondary strategic direction? A case study on Sino-Indian relations in Post-Doklam period)," *Shijie jingji yu zhengzhi* (*World Economics and Politics*), 4, 106–128 (2018).

106 Xie Chao, "Zhanlue xuanbian yu zhanlue pingheng: modi zhengfu duihua waijiao zhanlue ji yanbian (Taking sides or keeping balance: Evolving China policy of Modi administration)," *Yinduyang jingjiti yanjiu* (*Indian Ocean Economic and Political Review*), 5, 53–71 (2019).

107 Xing Rong, "Zoujin mengyou: meiyin haishang anquan hezuo de weilai zouxiang tanxi (Becoming allies: The future of U.S.-India maritime security cooperation)," *Nanya yanjiu* (*South Asian Studies*), 3, 128–155 (2020).

108 Rebecca Zhang, "The Quad, China, and maritime domain awareness in the Indo-Pacific," *Australian Institute of International Affairs*, 20 June 2022. https://www.internationalaffairs.org.au/australianoutlook/the-quad-china-and-maritime-domain-awareness-in-the-indo-pacific/.

109 Lin Minwang, "Chongxin renshi zuowei meiguo mengyou de yindu (Rediscover India, an ally of the US)," *Huanqiu shibao* (*Global Times*), 3 September 2020.

© 2025 World Scientific Publishing Europe Ltd.
https://doi.org/10.1142/9781800616318_0006

Chapter 5

The Himalayan Barrier: India–China Relations since Galwan[*]

Shounak Set[†,‡] and Harsh V. Pant[†,§,¶]

†King's College London, UK
‡Defence Academy, UK
§Delhi University, India
¶Observer Research Foundation, India

The bilateral relations between India and China in the coming decades will shape the Asian landscape and, arguably, the global order as well. Similar yet distinct in several ways, China and India are inheritors of ancient civilizations, colonial depredations, significant geographic expanses, considerable demographic foundations, robust internal political systems, and expanding economies. Historically, both have been significant players in the global order; however, their rising profiles and geographic proximity complicate their contemporary relationship. Despite an initial period of bonhomie, the rivalry between China and India predates the

---

[*]This chapter was originally printed as "The Himalayan Barrier: India-China Relations since Galwan." *The China Review*, Vol. 23, No. 1 (2023): 135–159. https://www.jstor.org/stable/48717991. Reproduced with kind permission of CUHK Press.

Asian century; their concurrent rise in the post–Cold War era has only contributed to its complexity. Since the Sino–Indian border clashes of 1962, India has consistently sought to balance China; however, the precise methods and mechanisms for doing so have remained inchoate. The clashes along the Himalayan border in 2020, however, removed residual doubts in India about the confrontational dynamics of the relations—in both elite and public opinion; this is an extraordinary and irreversible shift in India's policy toward China. These events accelerated a series of steps by New Delhi, which can best be understood through the lens of internal balancing. Notably, these nascent steps are occurring in parallel with global developments such as recent policy expressions on the Indo-Pacific in varying degrees across different countries. Since the Galwan crisis, both sides have been engaged in successive rounds of mutual talks and restraint. While there have been efforts to stabilize the relations, the evolving political and economic trends since then suggest that India–China relations have now taken the form of economic and political competition, particularly in relation to the emerging Indo-Pacific order. This chapter explores the evolving trajectory of Sino–Indian relations from the perspective of India's foreign policy and national security priorities, situating it within the broader global context.

As of the time of this chapter's publication, the Indian economy has been steadily gaining momentum, with stated official aims of becoming a US$10-trillion economy by the end of this decade. In contrast, the Chinese economy has been plateauing due to a complex set of macroeconomic issues, declining demographic growth, weak post-pandemic recovery, and domestic political complexities. These trends, however, had been apparent for a while. During the pandemic, as per the International Monetary Fund's World *Economic Outlook 2020*, China (US$13.6 trillion GDP) and India (US$2.7 trillion GDP) were projected to grow by 8.2 percent and 8.8 percent, respectively, in the financial year 2021–2022,[1] thereby boosting the post-pandemic global economic recovery. The 2022 *Outlook*, however, indicated a real GDP growth of 6.8 percent for India and, correspondingly, 3.2 percent for China amid the worsening global economic climate due to the ongoing Ukraine conflict and supply chain disruptions.[2] This trend has continued and intensified as the Indian economy has accelerated steadily on the back of a robust post-pandemic recovery and the diversification of global supply chains away from China.

While the economic trajectories of India and China are a testament to the heft of these two rising Asian giants in the world order, the border clash of 2020 also pointedly reveals the fragility of Sino–Indian relations and their inherent complications. The bilateral relations between India and China in the coming decades will indubitably shape the Asian landscape and, arguably, the global order as well—one of the key underlying drivers of the evolving Indo-Pacific order. Significantly, this does not preclude convergences of interests on certain issues, such as climate change and trade agreements, in a general sense. These are shaped, in turn, by the distinctive experiences of both countries as developing and post-colonial societies. Likewise, significant interlinkages prevail between the two countries, which, despite their saliency, remain under-examined as deteriorating political relations stymie the dividends which could be expected from this bilateral interdependence. In a similar vein, India and China are two rising superpowers, sharing a contested land border, marked by historical animosity and starkly divergent perceptions of values on the global and regional order. Arguably, this setting challenges conventional notions of cooperation and conflict, which are largely derived from anachronistic and Eurocentric international relations frameworks.

Yet, despite continuing talks on the border issue that aim to stabilize the situation, growing Indian skepticism regarding broader economic agreements with China—as opposed to general trade exchanges— is evident. This can be traced to India's exit from the Regional Comprehensive Economic Partnership (RCEP) in 2019, confirmed by the nature and form of Indian economic pacts since. The Indian state has adroitly positioned itself to benefit from the U.S.' "friend-shoring" policies that envisage the diversification of global supply chains away from China and toward friendly countries, which is reflected in steady growth in India's development and export of electronics and critical industries. Significantly, the complex relationship between China and India stimulates scholars and analysts, and general agreement on the broad contours of the relationship notwithstanding, the precise drivers and dynamics of India–China relations remain elusive to analytical clarity. This chapter surveys the emerging trends at the global and regional levels and situates the evolving trajectory of Sino–Indian relations from the perspective of New Delhi's foreign policy and national security priorities. It argues that India's China policy after Galwan is subject primarily to internal balancing. This is because, external partnerships notwithstanding, the form and substance of the balancing are primarily oriented toward consolidating and advancing India's national capabilities in response to addressing the power differential between India and China, which is heavily skewed toward the latter. Nevertheless, elements of balancing notwithstanding, the precise trajectory of India–China bilateral relations depends on the evolving Asian and global geopolitics as well as prevailing domestic circumstances—including policy debates in India.

This chapter, an update and reappraisal of our earlier journal article published in 2023, is divided into five main parts, with interconnected sections in each part. The first substantial section after the introduction provides a historical background and is followed by an outline of recent trends in India–China bilateral relations. While a watertight separation between the exogenous and endogenous categories of balancing in international relations is of limited utility in the era of globalized interlinkages, the subsequent section enumerates the catalysts. The following section analyzes the Indian policy response in detail by classifying it into two broad categories of internal and external dynamics, for analytical purposes, on account of the policy specifications. This is designed to enhance rather than undermine general comprehension of the subject. The penultimate section presents an evaluation of these policies and practices, highlighting the latent variables in Indo–China bilateral relations and culminating in a discussion of the emerging policy options for India. This section provides a summary of the topic and illustrates the significance of this key bilateral relationship, its impact, and implications for the emerging world order, as well as what it means for the discipline of international relations in both theoretical and empirical terms. The chapter ends with a concluding remarks section.

5.1. Background

Being successors to ancient civilizations, cultural and commercial exchanges between India and China throughout history have been well documented.[3] After centuries of subjugation, India and China emerged as independent actors in the global arena in the late 1940s with the advent of decolonization, and bilateral relations flourished immediately thereafter. Apart from this initial period of *bonhomie* in the 1950s, rivalry between China and India predates the Asian century and can be traced most vividly to the 1962 Sino–Indian War. As India gained independence in 1947, it established itself as a democracy, and despite its partition into Pakistan and India, it inherited the historical and institutional legacy of the British

Raj.[4] This translated to an established and functioning frontier and commercial arrangements with Tibet, including a diplomatic mission in Lhasa. These arrangements were discontinued from 1952 in the wake of Chinese sensibilities and the prevailing amity in bilateral relations as Tibet was eventually incorporated into the People's Republic of China. The developments in 1950 removed the buffer of Tibet, turning China and India into immediate geographical neighbors, with telling impacts and implications for India–China bilateral relations on an enduring basis.[5]

The border between India and China is contested and ill-demarcated, which means it resembles a frontier that extends 3,488 kilometers along the Middle Himalayas (Shivalik Range) and the High Himalayas (Himadri Range), effectively making it the world's longest disputed border. Further, India is heavily invested in the security of the small Himalayan buffer states of Nepal and Bhutan, which are situated between India and China. The extreme geographic conditions contribute a distinctive dimension to the scenario. The border dispute between India and China is an integral factor in the bilateral relations, which retain their own dynamics beyond other variables such as great-power competition and economic or diplomatic convergences.[6] Additional factors such as steadily increasing regional competition and a trade imbalance (in China's favor) only contribute to the complexity. Accordingly, while this territorial dispute has been a perennial bone of contention, the rising profiles of China and India in the 21st century have only contributed to the enduring complexity; developments along the 3,488-km-long Himalayan border generate snowballing effects on peace, security, and stability in the Indo-Pacific region.[7] If successive efforts in resolving this issue have been impeded by the interlocked triangle of historical legacies, geographic intricacies, and political compulsions, then the Himalayan border clashes of 2020 mark a turning point where the hitherto established frameworks of border and conflict management, with an emphasis on conciliation and negotiation, now stand practically obsolete.

From New Delhi's perspective, this event negates the extant understanding that, despite frictions, the India–China bilateral relationship can be managed entirely through diplomatic procedures. This episode also confirms the perspective that the concurrent rise of India and China in the post–Cold War era has only contributed to the complexity of their bilateral relations, and it is set to acquire greater intensity in the coming era.[8] Since the Sino–Indian border clashes of 1962, India has consistently sought to balance China; however, the precise methods and mechanisms for doing so have remained inchoate. This is both a function and an effect of the existing power differentials between India and China, as well as the characteristic strategic ambivalence among the Indian policy elite. The border clashes of 2020, however, have removed any remaining doubts in India regarding the confrontational dynamics of the relationship—both among elites and in public opinion. These events accelerated a series of steps by New Delhi, which can best be understood through the lens of internal and external balancing. Nevertheless, these developments are similar but not identical to conventional realist injunctions and defy the existing analytical categories in practice: balancing, bandwagoning, containment, or engagement. Notably, these nascent steps are occurring in parallel with global developments such as the evolving policy frameworks in the Indo-Pacific region, to varying extents among different countries, and a growing interest in diversifying global supply chains. These take the form of economic reorientation as investments continue to flow from China to elsewhere in Asia, including India.

5.2. Mapping Bilateral Dynamics: India–China Relations Redux

Since the 1962 Sino–Indian War, India has sought to balance China by primarily prioritizing defense at the expense of offense. To this end, border issues have been extensively negotiated through special dialogues at the bilateral level, while the strategic infrastructure on the border has remained underdeveloped: partly by design and partly by default. On the security front, Indian efforts and energies were largely consumed by Pakistan; however, China's steady ascendance in the world order led to a reconfiguration of India's security landscape. Since the early 2000s, there has been a growing recognition of the widening power differential between China and India, which has driven Chinese external engagement in several dimensions.[9] Concurrently, the growth of the Indian economy and incremental additions to India's security infrastructure reduced the Pakistani threat. Likewise, Indian foreign policy actively emphasized greater politico-economic convergence with Southeast and East Asian states under the rubric of "Look East" policy and prioritized a closer overall relationship with the West, primarily the U.S. Incidentally, this gradual reorientation of Indian foreign policy was influenced by the economic and political imperatives that arose in the 1990s following the disintegration (and decline) of the Soviet Union (and Russia).

The Himalayan Barrier: India–China Relations since Galwan 129

Significantly, while the importance of China in military doctrine and exercises has progressively been accentuated over time, the overwhelming civilian control over the Indian military has resulted in the absolute marginalization of the latter in decision-making historically. Essentially, Indian policy toward China, despite its explicit strategic ramifications, is marked by an insularity from any potential military influence, much like the broader Indian strategic policymaking. In addition, it is pertinent to point out that, despite a burgeoning number of think tanks dedicated to international relations and security studies, knowledge and understanding of China remain relatively limited in India, with only a few academic departments and learned societies engaging in in-depth study of China. Existing programs of Chinese studies are predominantly under the aegis of cultural studies, with nominal engagement in studies on international relations and security. Conversely, international relations programs, devoid of language skills, are constrained by an inadequate understanding of China and exclusively rely on Western literature about China. It is important to note, however, that the hitherto dominant strand of thought in the Indian establishment, while acknowledging the rise of China, had been keen on exploring convergences between India and China as rising powers negotiating a power transition—essentially, a form of hedging.[10] This line of reasoning saw the India–China bilateral relationship through the lens of cooperation and healthy competition but eschewed confrontation.[11]

Unsurprisingly, the resulting *modus vivendi* from hedging led to exploring areas of mutual interest and potential collaboration,[12] while maintaining the status quo and ensuring peace at the border through dialogue remained the preferred option. Accordingly, elaborate frameworks to resolve differences and disputes at multiple levels were institutionalized.[13] The growth of the People's Liberation Army Navy and the "String of Pearls" approach, admittedly a natural outcome of China's expanding economy and its legitimate security concerns, reflected a fundamental transformation of the Indian Ocean region. This, along with ascending Chinese power projections, latent and overt, in multiple areas—from anti-piracy operations to anti-satellite tests—taxed India's security managers. In addition, consistent and steadfast Chinese opposition to India's membership in an expanded UN Security Council and, more particularly, the Nuclear Suppliers Group, dismayed the Indian foreign policy establishment. Likewise, stagnation in bilateral talks regarding the border and construction of dams on cross-border rivers originating in Tibet, continuing restricted market access to Indian products (especially pharmaceuticals), and increasing border incidents gradually undermined the foundations for New Delhi's hedging approach toward China. Within India, the ascendancy of the Narendra Modi–led Bharatiya Janata Party (BJP) with an outright parliamentary majority in 2014 brought fresh impetus to foreign policy, driven by Prime Minister Modi's personal initiative, unhindered legislative mandate, and the party's distinctive approach to foreign policy and national security.[14]

While these developments challenged the dominant mode of thinking that prioritized engagement with China among Indian policymakers, the initiation of the Belt and Road Initiative and particularly the China–Pakistan Economic Corridor, made this position increasingly tenuous. The Indian response was primarily driven by its concerns over the presence of Chinese projects in the areas of disputed Pakistan-administered Kashmir, which India claims sovereignty over. However, the continuity of this mode of thinking was reflected by the fact that negative developments did not preclude India from collaborating with China in creating the Asian Infrastructure Investment Bank (AIIB) and the BRICS (comprising the five leading, emerging economies: Brazil, Russia, India, China, and South Africa) Development Bank in 2015. Meanwhile, planned improvements in connectivity infrastructure along the India–China border were expedited in the latter half of the 2010s, and the pending modernization of the Indian military was authorized. Acquisitions of several forms of weapons platforms and testing of capabilities, along with the restructuring of the military and diplomatic apparatus—the latter being independent of concerns on China—were undertaken as well. Several of these developments had been in the making for years and received impetus with the arrival of Narendra Modi as Prime Minister, given his parliamentary majority and his conscious identification with the reformist constituencies within India. Nevertheless, India's foreign policy toward China continued to be subject to a hedging approach, as policies which would impose costs on Beijing were consciously avoided.

The Doklam standoff in the India–Bhutan–China trijunction during 2017 illustrated this situation—while it demonstrated greater Indian resolve, care was taken to prevent escalation; subsequent Wuhan and Mamallapuram informal summits marked Indian outreach efforts. This position would only alter with the Galwan episode, as outlined in later sections. Quite significantly, increasing border incidents since 2012 notwithstanding, Indian security concerns had hitherto continued to be primarily driven by Pakistan, which presented challenges across the spectrum—sub-conventional, conventional, and nuclear, as well as at the diplomatic level. Meanwhile, the eventual evolution of the Indo-Pacific and the Quad arrangement dovetailed with India's concerted efforts at expanding its activities in the Southeast and East Asian landscape, without committing to a binding external framework or becoming an ally of the U.S.[15] India's historical reticence toward explicit alliances stems largely from the notion that such exercises would restrict the latitude of its external choices and thus be detrimental to its interests; additionally, its position as a postcolonial state only reinforces these apprehensions. Facing the growing power differential of a potential adversary, a state in an anarchic international system has primarily three analytically distinct policy options: containment, bandwagoning, and balancing.[16]

The first option, containment, is not possible because, aside from the prohibitively expensive requirements for elaborate architecture, India considers both itself and China to be too powerful to contain or be contained. The third option, i.e., bandwagoning, would entail accepting Chinese supremacy over Indian actions, and its utility in India–China relations would be at best an academic exercise. Balancing is therefore India's preferred policy option; however, the devil lies in the detail. Balancing entails a wide variety of assumptions and probabilities, depending on the circumstances, and despite the conceptual clarity, it is far from easy to identify and ascertain the exact policies to pursue.[17] Balancing can be pursued individually and/or collectively by a state, can be "hard" or "soft" depending on the adopted mechanism, and can be either internal or external based on its focus. Each of these approaches leads to different policy pathways with associated costs, benefits, and side effects, and Indian policymakers continue to grapple with this issue. In retrospect, while balancing China is generally the preferred choice, the exact means, methods, and scope of this approach have been intensely debated and are inherently dynamic in nature. This, along with the historic and geographic aspects previously outlined, lends a distinctive dimension to India's China policy.

5.3. Immediate Catalysts and Turning Points

The frontier nature of the ill-demarcated boundary between China and India has been noted earlier; the border is essentially a notional demarcation line, officially designated as the Line of Actual Control (LAC). The

LAC is trifurcated into western, central, and eastern sectors corresponding to the Indian states of Ladakh (redesignated as a union territory), Himachal Pradesh and Uttarakhand, and Arunachal Pradesh, respectively. Incidentally, the LAC is interspersed with the borders of the adjoining Himalayan states of Nepal and Bhutan, both of which are heavily dependent on India for economic and security issues and are subject to an expanding Chinese presence. India also shares a border with China in the small Himalayan province of Sikkim, which is sandwiched between Nepal and Bhutan; however, the border there is relatively peaceful owing to mutual recognition of the same. Notably, this sector provides unique geographic advantages to India. Crucially, both civilian and military infrastructure, particularly in terms of road and connectivity, had been drastically improved on the Chinese side of the LAC. The Indian side of the LAC had relatively much poorer infrastructure and connectivity; and India had been slow to respond to these material changes but began developing its border infrastructure in 2006 and has accelerated its efforts since 2017. This, along with the qualitative and quantitative accretions of the Indian military, has had the effect of somewhat redressing the imbalance to some degree.[18] The exact extent of this is, however, open to debate.

Against this background, recurring frictions at the sub-tactical level notwithstanding, overt conflict had not occurred since the clashes at Nathu La pass in the Sikkim sector in 1967; this pattern was disrupted in 2020 as altercations escalated to kinetic engagement. On 5 May 2020, soldiers from the Indian Army (IA) and the People's Liberation Army (PLA) clashed on the northern banks of Pangong Tso, a high-altitude lake which lies across the LAC. Stemming from contending interpretations of the LAC, the standoff heightened tensions as the respective armies resorted to increased patrols and deployments. However, a severe clash on 15 June 2020 led to fatalities on both sides in the Galwan Valley of Ladakh—the first since 1975. This had the effect of dramatically accelerating the crisis, with substantial reinforcements of manpower and military hardware on both sides—a process that is still ongoing. Negotiations underway at diplomatic, political, and military levels were at an impasse; on the night of 29–30 August, the Indian Army occupied the dominating heights overlooking PLA's positions in a pre-emptive move to gain significant tactical advantage. This exercise, generally named Kailash Range Operations—involving elements of the IA as well as the Tibetan Special Frontier Force—was calibrated as a signal to demonstrate resoluteness.

Incidentally, the Galwan standoff took approximately nine months to de-escalate, with partial disengagement on both sides. An effective and complete disengagement remains elusive even today, despite a series of border talks—the 21st round of China–India border talks in February 2024 failed to reach a breakthrough, some incremental gains notwithstanding. While some disengagements were completed by both sides in September 2022, following 16 rounds of talks, disagreements on specifics and tensions abound. It is not impertinent to point out that the Galwan clash, while significant because of the disruptive outbreak of active hostility resulting in fatalities on both sides, is the latest in a long line of border incidents that have intensified since 2013. This has been a function of improved border infrastructure on the Indian side, contributing to an increased frequency of Indian patrols, with a corresponding increase in interactions between Chinese and Indian armies, and coincided with the emergence of Xi Jinping and Narendra Modi as the premiers. While disagreements and minor tussles are a regular feature given the frontier-like character of the border, a host of erstwhile border management agreements and arrangements have been rendered increasingly redundant considering these recent developments. Against this backdrop, Prime Minister Modi reached out to President Xi Jinping, a move that culminated in the informal summits at Wuhan in 2018 and Mamallapuram in 2019. The aim from the Indian side was to apprise of the limited utility of existing arrangements and look forward to initiating new mechanisms, despite a similar border standoff at Doklam on the India–Bhutan–China trijunction in 2017. Beyond border disputes, the bilateral trade imbalance (in China's favor) and U.S.–India ties were on the agenda, as reported by Indian media; and differences notwithstanding, both sides expressed intentions to work constructively and in an amicable spirit.

The Galwan incident happening barely six months after the second round summit at Mamallapuram took the Indian establishment by surprise, while the simultaneous outbreak of the COVID-19 pandemic contributed to the complexity of the situation. The way things unfolded appeared to confirm India's worst fears: China viewed India as an adversary, lending further credence to the strand of thinking within India which had advocated a stronger response to China but had historically mostly elicited indifferent reactions from established policy circles.[19] While either one of these developments, i.e., the border clashes or the pandemic, deserves to be identified as a crisis, their simultaneous convergence severely tested the mettle of the entire Indian state, with severe multiple internal and external challenges. The onset of the COVID-19 pandemic in 2020 marked a definitive watershed in the global order, as conventional assumptions became obsolete and existing arrangements and institutions faced significant strain during this period of flux; furthermore, the ongoing Galwan crisis during the pandemic tested the resolve of the Indian government, creating a range of unique challenges.

Unsurprisingly, the coincidence of the clashes with the ongoing pandemic contributed to a worsening domestic public reaction toward China (discussed in detail later). Calls for a public boycott of Chinese goods and products, although symbolic and arguably counterproductive, reflected the growing significance of evolving public opposition and potentially an audience cost that would restrict the Indian government from making concessions to China in the near future. Concurrently, while the Indian government agreed with its Chinese counterpart that the etymology of the virus should not be attributed to its country of origin, it is difficult to say whether this positivity was sustained given China's progressive intransigence regarding a UN investigation into the outbreak. Later developments, such as the Chinese refusal to recognize Indian vaccines or inflammatory social media posts from official accounts of the Communist Party of China, could have only contributed to the stiffening of the Indian stance, although this is admittedly difficult to ascertain from a research standpoint due to a lack of adequate primary sources on this issue. In essence, these developments, although very different in nature, had the singular effect of precipitating a distinct reconfiguration of India's China policy. Significantly, the centenary celebrations of the Communist Party of China were met with mixed reactions by the Indian media, while the Indian government remained muted. More importantly, the reports of expanding Chinese nuclear capabilities attracted attention in the Indian think tank community and media alike, although they elicited no official response.

Since the Galwan episode, the effect of the prevailing global situation and related developments would, in all probability, range from a moderate impact to further deterioration of bilateral ties or no substantial impact. In essence, it is certain that there have been no regional or global developments which significantly offset the prevailing frostiness in Sino–Indian relations; however, the Galwan standoff has served as a catalyst for an impending review of bilateral relations and marks a crucial watershed in their history.[20] The most telling effect of this has been the rapid decline of the existing hedging approach in relation to India–China bilateral relations among the Indian policy community and the commentariat.[21] Of no less significance is the fact that, while Chinese actions merit greater attention from the "attentive public" within India, there has been a considerable shift in public opinion against China at multiple levels. Beyond elite opinion and commentaries, mass opinion demonstrates a clear shift: a 2014 survey generated 41 percent unfavorable views of China,[22] but an August 2020 survey showed that 91 percent supported the Indian government's retaliatory economic steps against China.

5.4. India's Response and Perspective

While responding to the crisis, the Indian government undertook a series of internal and external steps. Apart from quickly mobilizing reinforcements and keeping its military services on alert to stabilize the situation without resorting to the extremes of belligerence, the Indian response took the form of actively restricting Chinese economic presence within the country. In the immediate term, the fatalities provoked domestic public outrage, calls for a boycott of Chinese products, and intense media and parliamentary attention to the issue.[23] The Indian government curtailed or imposed greater scrutiny of Chinese investments in India. In a series of sequential steps, it banned several mobile apps and social media platforms of Chinese origin, which totaled more than 200 services by November 2020 and crossed 300 by mid-2022.[24] More significantly, the Indian government restricted Chinese firms from participating in Indian infrastructure projects and barred Chinese components in electrical and power supply grids; it also prohibited Huawei and ZTE from taking part in India's 5G trials for its planned 5G network. Notably, Chinese companies have a substantial presence in the Indian telecommunication, power, and electronics sectors.

The ineluctable fact that China has been, and continues to be, India's largest trading partner and a pivotal player in the global and regional supply chain means there is only limited value to these steps. However, this also highlighted the imperative of reforms in India's domestic and regulatory frameworks to expedite economic growth and reflected a greater inclination toward imposing costs on China, even if it entailed incurring some pain. Interestingly, two-thirds of Indian respondents in a survey expressed willingness to bear economic costs arising from these steps toward China.[25] These economic measures were undertaken parallel to India's "*Atma Nirbhar Bharat*" (self-reliant India) approach, launched during the pandemic in 2020, which is meant to spur economic growth and place India as a growing player in the global economy. Beyond these external economic measures, the Indian government initiated emergency procurement of key wartime supplies, including critical ordnance from both external and indigenous sources. Intelligence and high-altitude accessories and gear were sourced from the U.S., and public acknowledgment of them was noteworthy. Probably, India also undertook high-level exchanges with the U.S., but more importantly, the Galwan incident significantly reduced India's prevailing reticence toward the Quad and the Indo-Pacific. This was evident from the subsequent statements regarding the Quad, while the pace and scope of the India–U.S. engagement, which predated the Galwan episode, were amplified. Considering this development, the slew of signed military pacts and extensive military exercises conducted with the U.S., both bilaterally and multilaterally, acquire new salience.

The Indo-Pacific, at its core, is a maritime construct, with much of the activities taking the form of naval exercises and exchanges. These cumulatively represent the trend of concerted diplomatic and military engagement by India with like-minded littoral countries of the Indian Ocean region; while these existed in other forms previously, they will arguably continue at a more intense pace for the foreseeable future. This is best demonstrated by the wide array of mutual defense and logistics-sharing agreements that India has signed with other countries in the Indo-Pacific region.[26] Far more significant and noteworthy, however, is the substantial internal restructuring across a wide spectrum of institutions and areas within India, which contributes to significant transformations in military force postures, as well as doctrinal and operational changes. Considering border management, connectivity and infrastructure along the 3,488-km India–China border have been dramatically accelerated with the view of improving border security and strategic stability. As mentioned earlier, while planned improvements can be traced back to the latter half of the 2000s, these projects have gained noteworthy momentum only since 2017 and are expected to accelerate further in the foreseeable future.

Some institutional restructuring prior to the Galwan episode is notable—since it pertains to India–China relations and the Indo-Pacific order—but after this episode, these trends have gained significant momentum. For instance, the Centre for Contemporary China Studies (CCCS), an in-house inter-departmental think tank focusing specifically on policy research pertaining to China, was established in 2018 and expanded in early 2021. Significantly, this is the first time that the Indian government has established a country-specific in-house think tank.[27] In a closed-door discussion among scholars and the CCCS leadership in late

2022, which included the first author of this chapter, the CCCS delegation affirmed that its views and outputs were regularly sought after by the apex leadership of the Indian establishment. This is in stark contrast to other think tanks and research bodies within India. The administrative organization of the Ministry of External Affairs, with its multitudes of geographic and thematic divisions, largely reflected Cold War–era geography. In early 2020, the Ministry of External Affairs restructured itself into seven new vertical structures, with one specifically dedicated to the Indian Ocean and the Indo-Pacific—the latter housed a newly created Indo-Pacific division. Bureaucratic restructurings are expressions of intent by a government and serve as a precursor to anticipated policy directions; they demand attention. Likewise, India's long-pending plans to improve tri-service coordination for joint operations have received a boost with plans for a new operational structure that will integrate the army, navy, and air force by 2024.[28]

Beyond these major reorganizations, other related developments such as the expansion and streamlining of the roles of the National Security Council Secretariat and the National Security Advisor, the creation of the Chief of Defense Staff with the Department of Military Affairs, and the ongoing theaterization of service commands would also have a bearing on India–China bilateral relations, as policy inputs and operational responses create greater synergy. With regard to security architecture, a remarkable shift was evident in terms of force postures and asset allocations, specifically directed toward China. Moreover, since then, there has been a discernible increase in budgetary and bureaucratic resources directed toward these crucial geographies and policies. In the immediate aftermath of the initial skirmishes, the rules of engagement were altered, granting greater power to local commanders and changing signaling protocols. Troops were rushed to the frontlines for both "mirror deployment" to match Chinese deployments numerically and "proactive localized preventive deployment" in the western sector to prevent further maneuvers by the PLA. Elements of armor, artillery, and air assets were also brought into action. The Indian Navy's deployment pattern was altered with forward deployment in the Indian Ocean region, while the Indian Air Force, in addition to undertaking airlift operations, moved its premium fighter jets along with radars and surface-to-air missile batteries to forward deployments on the border. These steps toward active mobilization, along with capturing the Kailash Range, were manifestations of the evolving Indian military strategy of "offensive defence" in response to China's growing hard power and assertiveness at the border.[29] Incidentally, the involvement of the Special Frontier Force, (a unit comprising Tibetan exiles in India), along with Indian Special Forces—and the public revelation of the same—was calibrated as a signaling exercise to China.

The Galwan episode marks the transformation of India's strategic posture from deterrence by denial to deterrence by punishment.[30] Accordingly, Chinese advances on the border would be met proactively by raising the costs for such exercises, as opposed to the earlier stance of addressing them reactively.[31] Further, a significant number of troops are being de-inducted from other borders and internal security duties to the India–China border, while combat formations are being reoriented specifically for high-altitude warfare roles; these changes are being undertaken on a more enduring basis rather than as a seasonal or one-time adjustment—the process continues today with restructurings and redeployments within the Indian military establishment.[32] This in itself is important to note, as it is reflective of the seriousness and intent on the Indian side. Crucially, these changes are accompanied by a greater study of China and related topics within the relevant government departments and security agencies; these changes indicate the importance devoted to China within the administrative apparatus. Of no less importance, border-guarding armed police and/or paramilitary agencies like the Indo-Tibetan Border Police and the Assam Rifles—which are by nature geared to provide wartime support to the regular army—are witnessing changes in training, roles, and deployment, specifically with China as a growing threat. Additionally, the geographic areas which have a direct connotation for India–China relations are predominantly located in remote regions characterized by persistently underdeveloped connectivity and infrastructure; these issues have gained priority on the agenda.

In addition to roads, tunnels, railways, and other facilities in the Himalayan states, the Andaman and Nicobar archipelago in the Indian Ocean, close to Myanmar, Thailand, and Indonesia, have seen rapid development of civil engineering projects and the laying of undersea cables for higher internet bandwidths. The Andaman and Nicobar archipelago hosts the only tri-service Indian command with salient military facilities, and its proximity to the Strait of Malacca renders it a critical dimension in the Indo-Pacific region and Indian naval program. Significantly, India's nuclear, outer space, and missile programs have a distinctly autonomous developmental trajectory and increasingly acknowledge the growing profile of China in research and development, particularly in the advancement of ballistic missiles with longer ranges and improved features. While the Agni series of missiles are undergoing modernization, the induction of the solid-fueled nuclear-capable Agni-V intercontinental ballistic missile deserves a special mention and elicited a sharp response from China. The domestic defense techno-industrial base in India, marked by a monopoly of public sector enterprises with mixed records of efficiency, has also been liberalized and opened to private players, while foreign acquisitions also involve a significant component of technology transfer to domestic firms. Similarly, there has been an exponential proliferation of technology start-ups catering to defense needs and strategic technologies. These steps collectively aim to augment and advance India's domestic strategic techno-industrial base and, though debated for a while, have gained notable pace since the Galwan episode. The trend now appears to be taking on an enduring form.

5.5. Summary and Evaluation

The Indian response to China primarily represents an exercise in balancing but with varying manifestations.[33] While this predates the Galwan episode, the latter has tended to reinforce this trend and indisputably marks a critical juncture.[34] The Galwan episode reveals interesting trends shaping India's strategic behavior; it not only demonstrates the efficacy of Indian policies in enhancing its internal institutions and mechanisms but also reveals the acute limitations of its capacities on certain parameters. The improvements in India's border infrastructure and logistical platforms, primarily its airlift capabilities, facilitate swift insertion of troops and military equipment at the border—a marked difference from earlier times. Yet, Indian policymakers are acutely conscious of China's overwhelming advantages in comprehensive national power, stemming primarily from its huge economic wherewithal and its edge in high-tech research.[35] Galwan is a turning point in the direction of India's policy toward China, in that it demonstrates a definitive reversal of trend, as policymakers are inclined to pursue policies which aim to impose costs on China.[36] Almost half a decade since the Galwan episode, as this chapter goes to print, the initial trends outlined in our previous work have been confirmed and indicate a new pathway for India–China relations. Since then, India has moved closer to the U.S. and prioritized the development of indigenous economic, technological, and strategic capabilities.

Such steps would invariably entail some burden on India, but this is a new reality in the contours of India–China bilateral relations. Underlying this is a national consensus on responding to China with resolve, which is shared across the political spectrum in India. Notably, Galwan has also contributed to increased attention on China in India's public discourse and greater coverage of China in the Indian media. Unsurprisingly, domestic public opinion is increasingly becoming an aspect for Indian policymakers to consider regarding India–China bilateral relations in the near future. Surveys of public opinion reveal a general support for the Indian government's policies toward China, accompanied by rising unpopularity of China and unequivocal support for robust military foundations and a nuclear arsenal. These results do not represent a deviation from Indian public opinion, but the unambiguous reference to China is a novel development. In contrast, earlier surveys had indicated a similar stance toward Pakistan rather than China. The greater attention to China from the media and parliamentary discussions on the topic and utterances by political actors further corroborate this point. The disengagement process has led to a loss of grazing pastures for cattle on the Indian side of the LAC and has generated sharp reactions in domestic politics. However, there have also been reported instances since early 2024 of Indian shepherds challenging Chinese soldiers, ostensibly backed tacitly by the Indian government.

Significantly, these trends highlight that the existence of a considerable India–China trading partnership does not necessarily accrue benefits in the security domain.[37] Rather, subsequent proactive Indian initiatives to establish semiconductor and electric vehicle battery facilities indicate India's eagerness to achieve supply chain resilience in relation to China. Crucially, this is the intersection where the efficacy of the Quad as well as Indian foreign policy will be tested. The emerging dimensions of the Quad suggest greater collaboration among its constituent states toward research and development of strategic technologies (such as 5G and artificial intelligence), and the way these materialize would impact the Indo-Pacific order. In addition, an escalation that leads to a limited conventional war between India and China could serve as a litmus test for the Quad; inadequate tangible support from Quad partners would diminish Indian enthusiasm for it, or alternatively, it could reinforce the Quad by drawing its members closer.[38] Moreover, the interaction of domestic political contexts and geopolitical imperatives in the region will also inform India–China relations. This is already evident in several Indian Ocean islands such as

Sri Lanka, the Maldives, and Mauritius, and also to a lesser extent in South Asian countries such as Bangladesh and Nepal, where public opinion and policy elites alternate between India and China (and, occasionally, other Quad partners) as their preferred external partner for cooperation.

Likewise, while developments in the India–China bilateral relations will be a crucial test for the Quad, it will also serve as a barometer for India's perennial goal of emerging as a global power. Importantly, developments in the global and regional landscape,[39] with the Indo-Pacific at their heart,[40] would unsurprisingly be a qualifying factor but not the primary driver of India–China relations. Accordingly, the U.S. and Pakistan are crucial but supplementary factors rather than drivers of this relationship. India's response to ongoing developments such as the U.S. withdrawal from Afghanistan and the AUKUS (a controversial trilateral security pact between Australia, the U.K., and the U.S.) bearing distinct but different security connotations is illustrative. India noted with concern the chaotic U.S. withdrawal from Afghanistan and cooperated closely with the U.S. for humanitarian evacuations while initiating contact with the Taliban without resorting to substantial diplomatic recognition. The fallout from Afghanistan directly impacts India by increasing terrorism in Kashmir and necessitating considerable economic and cultural investments in Afghanistan. With AUKUS, the Indian interpretation has been that it doesn't impair the Quad but has no direct relation—the former is an explicit trilateral security architecture, while the latter represents an evolving multi-domain partnership primarily driven by diplomacy and catering to the Indo-Pacific region.

This understanding was reflected in the Indian diplomatic efforts at the International Atomic Energy Agency, where a resolution on AUKUS, backed by China and Russia, was thwarted by Indian diplomats in conjunction with like-minded allies.[41] From a Chinese viewpoint, Indian actions may appear to be a function of U.S.–China relations,[42] but this does not withstand scrutiny based on empirical grounds. India had consistently balanced China since the Sino–Indian War of 1962; even the Treaty of Peace and Friendship and Cooperation between the Republic of India and the Union of Soviet Socialist Republics (1971) alleviated the Chinese threat. Incidentally, the 2008 India–U.S. Civilian Nuclear Agreement revealed the tensions surrounding the Indian position. India steadfastly refused to join any alliance treaty, and questions about whether it would become a U.S. ally sparked public debates in both the U.S. and India, but for different reasons. Crucially, the U.S. was not a factor during the India–China clash of 1967, and the Sumdorong Chu crisis (1986–1993) occurred without the presence of any extra-regional balancer, neither the Soviet Union nor the U.S. At the time, the Soviet Union was disintegrating, and India's relations with the U.S. were frosty, while a domestic economic crisis had materialized in India in the form of a severe balance of payments crisis. Nevertheless, the eight-year-long crisis demonstrated a consistent Indian position, despite difficult global and domestic environments.

This line of reasoning also has the effect of overlooking Chinese support for Pakistan, encompassing extensive strategic (including nuclear) collaboration, which has now mutated into a direct two-front military challenge for India, much to the consternation of the Indian strategic community. Likewise, earlier expressions notwithstanding, the Quad has materialized only since 2017. In addition, the Quad itself remains underdeveloped as a military arrangement,[43] leading it to be characterized as "evasive balancing."[44] Furthermore, a robust U.S.–India partnership has yet to mature. The conventional understanding of international relations would warrant an alliance with the U.S., the global hegemon directly competing with China, the challenger.[45] Despite closer relations, joining a U.S.-led alliance is unthinkable for India, and a well-regarded American observer has cautioned the U.S. against such a step.[46] Interestingly, despite starkly differing perceptions of the ongoing Ukraine conflict, India and key states of the European Union have also increased mutual exchanges and partnerships, recognizing a common challenge posed by China. This indicates the rising importance that Indian policymakers accord to China and, along with other developments, suggests that China has emerged as a key driver of Indian foreign policy. Unsurprisingly, Indian defense policy has already registered an unambiguous change regarding the recognition of China as the primary security challenge to India.

Significantly, India is the only Quad country that is not a treaty ally of the U.S. but shares a land border with China while pursuing a characteristic, doggedly independent foreign and security policy. The trajectory of India's strategic nuclear program and its recent position on Ukraine—disapproved by the West, notwithstanding—only confirm this enduring trend. These trends collectively reflect the general nature of India's response to China's ascendance and the changing patterns of India–China relations. While China's capabilities and actions complicate India's security situation, India strives to address this through internal balancing by developing its national capabilities.[47] Indian inclination toward internal balancing is derived from confidence in its own capabilities and apprehension of under-balancing arising from external alliances.[48] Beyond postcolonial sensibilities, India's reluctance to form external military alliances is influenced by strategic considerations: India, as the only Quad country sharing a land border with China, is directly competing in both the regional and global arenas. Likewise, on aggregate constitutive terms, it is the only Asian state that is a potential peer to China—current limitations (primarily economic) notwithstanding. Crucially, since the Galwan episode, India has been consistently registering a higher percentage of economic growth than China; it overtook China in terms of total population in 2023 and has demonstrated domestic political stability and economic reforms. These trends provide confidence to Indian policymakers to continue in this direction, so as to counter China without going to the extremes of belligerence while further developing India's economic and strategic foundations.

Importantly, while China's expanding nuclear and missile inventory has an impact on strategic stability and thereby affects India, Indian responses have been relatively muted since the nuclear deterrence relationship between India and China is stable and well-established on account of the "No First Use" posture of both countries.[49] Hence, barring unforeseen developments, India would continue on the path of deterrence by punishment in devising the military response to China, which is consistent with its internal balancing approach.[50] However, this would be subject to creatively responding to developments in other sectors—such as research and development in emerging technologies and targeted external partnerships—although the precise nature of the response cannot be preordained or predetermined. Any response would, in turn, depend on the continued growth of the Indian economy. A strategic policy is derived from the size and scope of the national economy, and this has consistently been a theme that underpins India's overall external engagement. Yet, the primacy of China as a crucial factor in Indian foreign policy is established, driving the Indian leadership to prioritize sustaining economic growth beyond prevailing domestic developmental imperatives. Hence, the form of growth the Indian government pursues will also arguably reflect the strategic threat from China. India's outreach to Taiwan for establishing semiconductor facilities and pursuit of tax fraud cases against Chinese multinational corporations (MNCs) operating in India are illustrative.

In sum, it is safe to infer that India's policy of hedging—much like those of other East Asian states[51]—is now a historical relic. The survey of the gamut of policies and the evolving Indian position indicates a foreign policy change of major dimension at the level of "goal change,"[52] and understanding this critical transformation is key to interpreting India–China bilateral relations. It is, however, safe to assert that India would not resort to extensive external balancing, which could culminate in uncontrolled arms races or entangling alliances; accordingly, the Indian response to the Quad and the Indo-Pacific order needs appraisal. External partnerships, such as the Quad and those in the Indo-Pacific region, individually or collectively, are vital for contributing to economic growth and sustaining beneficial ties. Essentially, Indian policymakers would resort to internal balancing and consolidating India's national capacities, without precluding the option of external engagements. As such, external partnerships would be a qualifying factor rather than a driver of India's balancing efforts. This form of balancing, because of its novelty, merits a reappraisal of traditional models of balancing, as they are largely derived from Western settings and ahistorical templates. The literature on internal balancing is underdeveloped, which in turn impedes meaningful analysis of the phenomenon.

5.6. Concluding Remarks

Although states theoretically may have multiple options, empirical realities and specific contexts limit the number of feasible options to a few; this is effectively the case with India's policy toward China. The Galwan episode represented a critical juncture in the annals of India–China bilateral relations and, in turn, the Asian security landscape. Developments on the India–China Himalayan frontier and broader India–China bilateral relations would be a crucial test for the Quad as well as Indian foreign policy. Apart from a greater demonstration of resolve, India would generally be wary of a spiraling rivalry with China—managing bilateral relations without resorting to unmitigated confrontation would be the optimal policy trajectory. This entails ensuring sustained Indian economic growth, facilitated by political and diplomatic linkages, and military modernization that encompasses transformations of doctrine and strategic force postures. Elements of these are evident in the gamut of policy trajectories undertaken since the Galwan episode; however, it is premature to draw a firm conclusion. The empirical reality of the interlinked nature of the 21st century and the complexities of the fluid post-pandemic order only contribute to the urgency of such an exercise. Pointedly, India is the only Quad country with a disputed land border with China, without a treaty alliance with the U.S., and is a rising Asian great power and a peer competitor to China. This conditions India's approach toward China, and therefore, India–China relations are subject to balancing. However, the exact manner and nature of this balancing exercise defy linear categories and conventional projections due to the peculiar historical and geopolitical context. Understanding and interpreting this is integral to ensuring peace and security in the coming decade and represents one of the key dynamics of the emerging Indo-Pacific order and the transforming global order in turn.

Endnotes

1 IMF (International Monetary Fund), *World Economic Outlook* (Washington DC: International Monetary Fund, 2020).

2 IMF, *World Economic Outlook* (Washington DC: International Monetary Fund, 2022).

3 M. Thampi (ed.) *India and China in the Colonial World* (Abingdon: Routledge with Social Science Press, 2005).

4 Z. D. Singh, *Powershift: India-China Relations in a Multipolar World* (India: Pan Macmillan, 2020).

5 R. Sikri, "The Tibet factor in India-China relations", *Journal of International Affairs*, 64(2), 55–71 (2011).

6 R. Chauhan, "Differences not disputes: India's view of the border after 1962", in K. Bajpai, S. Ho and M. C. Miller (eds.) *Routledge Handbook of China-India Relations* (Abingdon: Routledge, 2020), pp. 180–194.

7 A. Tarapore, *The Crisis after the Crisis: How Ladakh Will Shape India's Competition with China*, Lowy Institute, 6 May 2021. https://www.lowyinstitute.org/sites/default/files/TARAPORE%20Crisis%20after%20the%20 Crisis%20PDF%20FINAL%2005_05_2021%282%29.pdf.

8 V. Gokhale, "The road from Galwan: The future of India-China relations," *Working Paper*, Carnegie India, 10 March 2021.

9 "India China relations: Conflicting trends," *Indian Foreign Affairs Journal*, Debate, 9(1), 1–3.

10 Vincent Wei-cheng Wang, "'Chindia' or rivalry? Rising China, rising India, and contending perspectives on India-China relations," *Asian Perspective*, 35(3), 437–469 (2011).

11 T. Khanna, "China plus India—The power of two," *Harvard Business Review*, 85(12), 60–69.

12 J. D. Ciorciari and J. Haacke, "Hedging in international relations: An introduction," *International Relations of the Asia-Pacific*, 19(3), 367–374.

13 J. Holslag, "The persistent military security dilemma between China and India," *Journal of Strategic Studies*, 32(6), 811–840 (2009).

14 H. V. Pant, "The India-US-China triangle from New Delhi: Overcoming the 'hesitations of history,'" *India Review*, 18(4), 386–406 (2019).

15 G. J. Gilboy and E. Heginbotham, "Double trouble: A realist view of Chinese and Indian power," *The Washington Quarterly*, 36(3), 125–142 (2013).

16 S. E. Lobell, "Balance of power theory," in *International Relations* (2014). https://www.oxfordbibliographies.com/view/document/obo-9780199743292/obo-9780199743292-0083.xml.

17 D. Ahlawat and L. Hughes, "India-China stand-off in Doklam: Aligning realism with national characteristics," *The Round Table*, 107(5), 613–625 (2018).

18 F. O'Donnell and A. Bollfrass, "The Strategic Postures of China and India: A Visual Guide." Managing the Atom Project, Belfer Center, March 2020. https://www.belfercenter.org/sites/default/files/2020-03/india-china-postures/China%20India%20Postures.pdf.

19 R. Rajagopalan, *India's Strategic Choices—China and the Balance of Power in Asia*, September 2017. CEIP: Carnegie Endowment for International Peace. United States of America. Retrieved from https://coilink.org/20.500.12592/002b94 on 01 Nov 2024. COI: 20.500.12592/002b94.

20 B. Chellaney, "Why is China Making a Permanent Enemy of India?" *Nikkei Asia*, 12 May 2021. https://asia.nikkei.com/Opinion/Why-is-China-making-a-permanent-enemy-of-India.

21 H. Pant, "Lines in the hills: Indo-Chinese rivalry in the Himalayas, King's College London," 9 July 2020. https://www.kcl.ac.uk/news/lines-in-the-hills.

22 "Chapter 2: Indians view the world in Indians reflect on their country & the world," Pew Research Centre. March 2014, https://www.pewresearch.org/global/2014/03/31/chapter-2-indians-view-the-world/.

23 Yew Lun Tian and S. Miglani, "China-India border clash stokes contrasting domestic responses," *Reuters*, 23 June 2020. https://www.reuters.com/article/us-india-china-analysis-idUSKBN23U1TX.

24 "India bans 54 more Chinese app," *The Hindu*, 15 February 2022. https://www.thehindu.com/sci-tech/technology/india-bans-54-more-chinese-apps-over-security-concerns/article65052287.ece.

25 "Enemy number one," *India Today*, 17 August 2020. https://www.indiatoday.in/magazine/nation/story/20200817-enemy-number-one-1708698-2020-08-08.

26 S. Chaudhary, "India versus China India trails behind China in military power, but overshadows Beijing on another vital front," *The Eurasian Times*,

The Himalayan Barrier: India–China Relations since Galwan 147

23 October 2020. https://eurasiantimes.com/india-vs-china-india-trails-behind-china-in-military-power-but-overshadows-beijing-on-another-vital-front/.

27 N. Gokhale, "Major revamp of India's National security architecture," *BharatShakti*, 9 October 2018. https://bharatshakti.in/major-revamp-of-indias-national-security-architecture/.

28 H. V. Pant and K. Bommakanti, "India's national security: Challenges and dilemmas," *International Affairs*, 95(4), 835–857 (2019).

29 Y. Joshi and A. Mukherjee, "Offensive defense: India's strategic responses to the rise of China," in K. Bajpai, S. Ho, and M. C. Miller (eds.) *Routledge Handbook of China-India Relations* (Abingdon: Routledge, 2020), pp. 227–239.

30 Y. Joshi and A. Mukherjee, "From denial to punishment: The security dilemma and changes in India's military strategy towards China," *Asian Security*, 15(1), 25–43 (2019).

31 H. Pant, "For Beijing and New Delhi 2020 was the point of no return," *Foreign Policy*, 28 December 2020. https://foreignpolicy.com/2020/12/28/for-beijing-and-new-delhi-2020-was-the-point-of-no-return/.

32 "India shifts 50,000 additional troops to China border in historic move," *Business Standard*, 28 June 2021. https://www.business-standard.com/article/current-affairs/india-shifts-50-000-additional-troops-to-china-border-in-historic-move-121062801542_1.html.

33 S. Raghavan, "The security dilemma and India-China relations," *Asian Security*, 15(1), 60–72 (2019).

34 Gokhale (2021), *Op. cit.*

35 S. Menon, "Internal drivers of China's external behaviour," *Working Paper*, CSEP (Centre for Economic and Social Progress), 12 January 2022. https://csep.org/working-paper/internal-drivers-of-chinas-external-behaviour/.

36 H. V. Pant, "How the Galwan tragedy has clarified India's vision," *Hindustan Times*, 18 June 2020. https://www.hindustantimes.com/analysis/how-the-galwan-tragedy-has-clarified-india-s-vision/story-T9gVHpuSSwiD-n8O9wJtz4M.html.

37 S. Sitaraman, "Are India and China destined for war? Three future scenarios in hindsight," in A. L. Vuving (ed.) *Insight, Foresight: Thinking About Security in the Indo-Pacific* (Honolulu: Daniel K. Inouye Asia-Pacific Center for Security Studies, October 2020), pp. 283–306.

38 A. Tarapore, "India, China, and the Quad's defining test," 29 June 2021. https://www.aspistrategist.org.au/india-china-and-the-quads-defining-test/.

39 M. S. Pardesi, "India's China strategy under Modi continuity in the management of an asymmetric rivalry," *International Politics*, 59, 44–66 (2021).

40 A. Tarapore, *Mitigating the Risk of a China-India Conflict*, ASPI (Canberra: Australian Strategic Policy Institute, 29 June 2021).

41 R. P. Rajagopalan, "At IAEA, India supports AUKUS," *The Diplomat*, 3 October 2022.

148 *S. Set & H. V. Pant*

42 Yun Sun, "China's strategic assessment of India," War on the Rocks, 23 March 2020.

43 Captain Daniel Myers (USAF), "India and the quadrilateral forum as a means of US deterrence in the Indo-Pacific," *Journal of Indo-Pacific Affairs*, 24 November 2020. https://www.airuniversity.af.edu/JIPA/Display/Article/2425574/india-and-the-quadrilateral-forum-as-a-means-of-us-deterrence-in-the-indo-pacif/.

44 R. Rajagopalan, "Evasive balancing: India's unviable Indo-Pacific strategy," *International Affairs*, 96(1), 75–93 (2020).

45 T. Madan, *Fateful Triangle: How China Shaped US-India Relations During the Cold War* (Washington DC: Brookings Institution Press, 2020), p. 300.

46 A. Ayres, *Our Time Has Come: How India Is Making Its Place in the World* (New York: Oxford University Press, 2018).

47 S. Saran, "Letters from Peking: What Galwan valley taught us this summer," Raisina Debates, Observer Research Foundation, 21 July 2020. https://www.orfonline.org/expert-speak/letters-from-peking-what-galwan-valley-taught-us-this-summer/.

48 J. Blank, *Regional Responses to U.S.-China Competition in the Indo-Pacific: India*, RAND Corporation, Santa Monica, 2021. https://www.rand.org/pubs/research_reports/RR4412z2.html.

49 D. Das, "China's missile silos and the Sino-Indian nuclear competition," War on the Rocks, 13 October 2021. https://warontherocks.com/2021/10/chinas-missile-silos-and-the-sino-indian-nuclear-competition/.

50 N. Ronkin, "Internal balancing will determine India's relationships with the US and China," Freeman Spogli Institute for International Studies, Stanford University, 1 September 2020. https://fsi.stanford.edu/news/internal-balancing-will-determine-india%E2%80%99s-relationships-us-and-china-argues-aparc%E2%80%99s-newest.

51 Kei Koga, "The concept of 'hedging' revisited: The case of Japan's foreign policy strategy in East Asia's power shift," *International Studies Review*, 20(4), 633–660 (2018).

52 C. F. Hermann, "Changing course: When governments choose to redirect foreign policy," *International Studies Quarterly*, 34(1), 3–21 (1990).

© 2025 World Scientific Publishing Europe Ltd.
https://doi.org/10.1142/9781800616318_0007

Chapter 6

The Japan's "Free and Open Indo-Pacific" and Sino–Japanese Relations: A Chinese Perspective[*]

Guangtao Wang and Zheng Chen

Fudan University, China

This chapter examines the Chinese assessment of and responses toward Japan's "Free and Open Indo-Pacific" (FOIP) concept against the backdrop of evolving Sino–Japanese relations. Addressing both its security and economic concerns, the FOIP is Tokyo's top-level regional strategy in the context of China's rise. The development of Japan's FOIP has been fluctuating with the evolution of Sino–Japanese relations and the emergence of the Sino–United States (U.S.) strategic competition over the past decade. The complexity and fluid nature of Japan's FOIP have prompted varying assessments and policy recommendations among Chinese analysts, which can be roughly divided into three categories: the hardline approach, the hedging approach, and the docking approach. Meanwhile, remarks by Chinese officials on Japan's FOIP remain

---

[*]This chapter was originally printed as "The Japanese 'Free and Open Indo-Pacific' and Sino-Japanese Relations: A Chinese Perspective." *The China Review*, Vol. 23, No. 1 (2023): 161–186. https://www.jstor.org/stable/48717992. Reproduced with kind permission of CUHK Press.

elusive, carefully differentiating between the Indo-Pacific strategy of the U.S. and that of Japan. All of these aspects reveal the complexity and flexibility of China's policies. The COVID-19 pandemic and the recent domestic changes in Japan and the U.S. have further complicated geopolitical and geoeconomic tensions. As a consequence, the Sino–Japanese relationship has become awkward once again.

Sino-Japanese relations were locked in a spiraling diplomatic standoff when Xi Jinping and Shinzo Abe came to power in late 2012. In the following few years, the two strong statesmen launched their respective regional strategies: China's "Belt and Road" (BRI) initiative in 2013 and Japan's "Free and Open Indo-Pacific" (FOIP) strategy in 2016. Both have claimed that their initiatives are inclusive frameworks of regional cooperation. However, neither has responded positively to the other's project. From its beginning, Japan's FOIP has been widely perceived as a project to counter China's BRI.[1] Chinese antagonism toward the concept escalated after the United States (U.S.), inspired by Japan, rolled out its own Indo-Pacific strategy in 2017. Nonetheless, bilateral relations between Beijing and Tokyo gradually warmed up over the next three years, after U.S. President Donald Trump promoted an "American first" diplomacy and began an overall strategic competition with China. Amid escalating strategic rivalries between Beijing and Washington, Abe relabeled FOIP as a vision and expressed willingness to cooperate with the BRI. The Japanese official diplomatic blue book for 2019 and 2020 claimed that Japan–China relations had returned to normal and entered "a new era."[2] Unfortunately, Xi's planned official visit to Tokyo in 2020 was postponed due to the outbreak of the COVID-19 pandemic, and incidents such as the imposition of the Hong Kong national security law reversed the warming atmosphere between the two countries. Following Abe's resignation and Trump's departure from office, their successors have been actively strengthening coordination between their FOIP policies to compete with China, which rang louder alarm bells in Beijing. Sino–Japanese relations plunged back again into uncertainty.

Given that the development of Japan's FOIP has both reflected and shaped the evolution of Sino–Japanese relations, it deserves close examination. Due to its conceptual ambiguity and empirical complexity, "Indo-Pacific" has now become a catchphrase in international politics. Existing literature provides valuable insights into understanding the origins, developments, and potential tendencies of different actors' interpretations of the Indo-Pacific concept. In particular, the interactions among the rise of China, the emergence of the concept, and the contestations of regional order-building have attracted scholars' attention.[3] However, most studies are too focused on the U.S. Indo-Pacific strategy and China's response.[4] Beijing's changing attitudes and complex responses to the Indo-Pacific concept of other countries have largely been overlooked.[5] The term "Indo-Pacific" has been used by different states and international organizations to refer to divergent, sometimes conflicting, visions of the regional order. Japan, as an entrepreneur in proposing and promoting the Indo-Pacific concept, is not a passive "little brother" of Washington. The twists and turns of Japan's FOIP have generated their own momentum, which has also led to Chinese academics and government's evolving assessments and responses toward it. Examining these interactions would help us better evaluate the evolution of the Indo-Pacific strategy and its influence on China's relations with neighboring countries.

This chapter examines interactions between Japan's FOIP and Sino–Japanese relations from a Chinese perspective, focusing on Chinese analysts' diverse assessments of Japan's FOIP and nuanced responses by Chinese government officials. The first two sections present an overview of the Chinese factor in the formation and development of Japan's Indo-Pacific policies, as well as the role of Japan's FOIP in the evolution of Sino–Japanese relations in the past decade. The following two sections attempt to grasp China's assessment of and response to FOIP. As a remedy for the lack of direct evidence on the perceptions and ideas of Chinese leaders, Section 6.3 surveys debates among Chinese analysts about the nature of Japan's FOIP and what constitutes a better approach for Beijing to address this challenge. Section 6.4 examines various public comments by Chinese government officials, revealing differing rhetoric toward Japan's FOIP compared to that of their American counterparts. The concluding section offers a summary.

6.1. The Chinese Factor in the Emergence of Japan's FOIP

Abe formally introduced the concept of FOIP during a keynote address at the Sixth Tokyo International Conference on African Development

(TICAD VI) held in Nairobi in August 2016.[6] However, he had touched upon the idea of linking the two oceans together and creating a quadrilateral strategic dialogue mechanism, including the U.S., Japan, Australia, and India (the so-called "Quad") nearly a decade earlier.[7] The Indo-Pacific concept regained steam after Abe was elected as Japanese Prime Minister for the second time in 2012. As part of what he called "a diplomacy that takes a panoramic perspective of the world map," Abe proposed a "democratic security diamond" to "safeguard the maritime commons stretching from the Indian Ocean region to the western Pacific" and counterbalance Chinese "coercion." All of these practices helped to set the stage for Abe's speech in Nairobi in August 2016.

China's rise is widely regarded as a key—if not the most important—factor in the emergence of Japan's FOIP. After taking office in 2012, Abe intensified Japan's power-balancing efforts against China. The Japanese National Security Council was established in 2013, and a series of controversial new military legislation allowing the Japanese armed forces to participate in foreign conflicts was passed in 2015 under the pretext of "proactive contribution to peace." As a pivotal element in its external balancing, Tokyo managed to issue new "guidelines for Japan–U.S. defense cooperation" with Washington in 2015. Besides strengthening its own defense capabilities and the U.S.–Japan alliance, Japan also sought to develop partnerships with like-minded states, such as Australia and the Philippines, into a diplomatic and potentially military alignment. This is one of Japan's main purposes behind FOIP.

When Abe introduced FOIP in 2016, the confrontation between China and Japan showed no signs of easing. Thus, it is no surprise that most analyses at that time were inclined to explain the emergence of the concept from the perspective of balancing China.[8] Many Chinese analysts also believed that behind the expansion of Japan's geographical scope of strategic thinking was Abe's keen attempt to attract the U.S. and like-minded regional states, India and Australia in particular, to build a coalition to encircle China and counter its rise. As some Chinese analysts have suggested, Japan's FOIP was stimulated by the relative decline of U.S. power and the perceived weakening of Washington's commitment to allies in the region, as Japan now needed additional support from like-minded regional partners like India.[9] Abe went out of his way to sell FOIP to Washington. His strategy paid off, and he eventually convinced Trump to adopt the Indo- Pacific concept to replace the Obama administration's "pivot to Asia."

Besides geopolitical concerns, analysts also focused on the geoeconomic dimension of Japan's FOIP, suggesting that it is less about traditional "hard balancing" and more a part of institutional balancing and contesting dynamics in the region.[10] From this perspective, FOIP as a comprehensive regional strategy encompasses both economic and security dimensions.[11] Moreover, it is Japan's regional multilateralism project to compete with China's BRI, which embodies Beijing's counter-response to the Trans-Pacific Partnership (TPP) promoted by the Obama administration.[12] The advancement of the BRI and the expanding Chinese economic influence in Southeast Asia and Africa prompted Tokyo to take countermeasures and endorse a vision that encompassed not only the Pacific Ocean but also the Indian Ocean to include India and the east coast of Africa.[13] In this context, FOIP has emerged as a counter-project to China's BRI. While there is no necessary conflict between the two, FOIP and the BRI do present competing visions of regional order, as revealed in Tokyo's skepticism toward the BRI and, in particular, its refusal to join the Asian Infrastructure Investment Bank (AIIB). After Tokyo introduced FOIP, Chinese analysts widely interpreted it as a strategy to counter the BRI. For instance, Wu Huaizhong, a researcher at the Institute of Japanese Studies, Chinese Academy of Social Sciences (CASS), suggested that Tokyo aimed to counterbalance the BRI through FOIP, promoting Japanese firms' participation in trade, investment, and, in particular, infrastructure construction in the Indian Ocean region, which was supported by programs such as the "Asia-Africa Development Corridor Program" led by Japan and India.[14]

However, institutional contests are not necessarily zero-sum. Like other countries in the region, Japan has deep economic ties with China in terms of investment and regional supply chains. Emphasizing the economic connections between Asia and Africa, especially in the infrastructure sector, FOIP holds significant potential for competitive coexistence between China and Japan. Indeed, the dilemma Japan faces is that while it greatly benefits from economic interdependence with Beijing, it is also increasingly anxious about growing Chinese power. Amid confrontations between China and the U.S., Japan, like other regional countries, does not wish to be forced to "choose" between its security "patron" and the regional economic giant. The transition from the "Asia-Pacific" to the "Indo-Pacific" reflects the evolving Japanese regional strategy aimed at addressing security concerns without jeopardizing economic benefits.[15]

In sum, the rise of China is a key factor that prompted Tokyo to establish FOIP. The escalating competition between the U.S. and China has further complicated geopolitical and geoeconomic interactions in the region, requiring Japan to adopt a comprehensive approach to security and economics. FOIP is an attempt to help Japan combine two pillars of its regional strategy: strengthening the U.S.–Japan alliance and developing partnerships with regional like-minded countries to counter China's rise on the one hand, and expanding regional economic cooperation to safeguard a leadership role in regional affairs on the other.

6.2. FOIP and the Evolution of Sino–Japanese Relations

After its emergence, the development of Japan's FOIP has fluctuated with shifts in Sino–Japanese relations between "competitive" and "cooperative rivalry," illustrating the challenges of managing a relationship characterized by both security competition and economic interdependence (see Chapter 1). After China's national GDP surpassed Japan's in 2010, the problem of "how to accommodate two tigers on one mountain" became even more acute.[16] As bilateral relations hit a new low due to conflicts over the Diaoyu/Senkaku Islands, there was even less room for improvement in Sino–Japanese relations. As mentioned above, Abe's initial choice in dealing with the China challenge was to adopt a confrontational approach through conducting both internal and external balancing against (perceived) threats from China. For instance, Tokyo bolstered military capabilities on its southwestern islands and passed a series of security bills and policies. In the economic sphere, the Japanese government and firms strengthened their investment and development financing in Southeast Asia, intensifying economic competition with China in the region. Meanwhile, Beijing also adopted an assertive posture in defending its territory and maritime interests, sending more maritime police vessels to patrol the waters around the Diaoyu/Senkaku Islands and establishing the East China Sea Air Defense Identification Zone (ADIZ) in 2013. Both sides were also becoming increasingly vocal in their criticisms of each other regarding various topics, including historical issues and the South China Sea arbitration. It seemed that the tension between China and Japan was escalating in all directions. It was not until both Abe and Xi had consolidated their power positions that they began treating each other as

The Japan's "Free and Open Indo-Pacific" and Sino–Japanese Relations   155

long-term counterparts and, in 2017, made serious efforts to improve Sino–Japanese relations.

The arrival of U.S. President Donald Trump proved to be an important driver for Japan to repair its relations with China. The Trump administration's withdrawal from the TPP and its preference for bilateral trade negotiations dampened the prospects of U.S.–Japan joint leadership in promoting economic connectivity under FOIP. While Washington was probing the possibilities of economic decoupling with China, the escalation of the U.S.–China trade wars raised serious risks of the emergence of two competing economic blocs led by the U.S. and China, which was not in Japan's interests. Meanwhile, Tokyo itself also faced strong trade protectionist pressure from Washington, which prompted it to seek rapprochement on economic issues with Beijing.[17]

Compared to its Obama-led counterpart, the Trump administration was simply not adept at exploiting those regional countries' conflicts with China; instead, it preferred to exert pressure bilaterally, which gave China a crucial opening to circumvent its containment efforts. Thus, Beijing responded to the challenge in a more restrained manner, attempting to reassure the ASEAN states and rebuild its relations with India and Japan to prevent regional powers from joining the U.S. camp.[18] The vacuum left by the U.S. as a result of Trump's apathetic attitude toward multilateral institutions allowed Beijing the leeway to influence global governance and push forward its own multilateral projects, such as the AIIB. Cooperation from regional countries would help Beijing promote these projects and extend its international influence. For instance, the AIIB has already actively sought and expanded cooperation with the Japanese-led Asian Development Bank (ADB).

The warming of bilateral relations began with Japan's changing attitude toward the BRI. In May 2017, Toshihiro Nikai, the secretary-general of Japan's ruling Liberal Democratic Party (LDP), attended the first Belt and Road Forum in Beijing with a letter from Abe addressed to Chinese leaders. Abe also made positive comments about BRI around that time. The Chinese Premier Li Keqiang visited Tokyo in May 2018, and mutual visits between Japanese and Chinese leaders resumed. Subsequently, Abe visited China in October 2018 and December 2019. During his official visit in 2018, Abe claimed that the development of Sino–Japanese relations had evolved from "competition" to "coordination," and he stated that the bilateral relationship was now "back on a normal track." The two sides also agreed to strengthen cooperation across various fields, ranging from finance to innovation, and move "toward a new era of China–Japan relations."[19]

Shortly after his official visit, Abe stopped referring to FOIP as a *strategy* and relabeled it a *vision* during a press conference with Malaysian Prime Minister Mahathir on 6 November 2018.[20] It is widely believed that the main purpose behind Abe's recasting of FOIP as a vision was to signal his willingness to improve relations with China. As Matake Kamiya, a professor at the National Defense Academy of Japan, argues, this shift signaled Tokyo's move from a "competitive strategy" to a "coordinated strategy" toward China.[21] Several Chinese analysts share this view. For instance, Wang Wan, a scholar at CASS, suggests that this change in terminology reflects the gradual warming of Sino–Japanese relations.[22]

Other factors also prompted this change. One is the attitude of ASEAN countries. Given these states' geopolitical and economic centrality in the Indo-Pacific, FOIP is simply unworkable without their participation. To win ASEAN countries' support, Japan needs to ease their anxieties about choosing sides between great powers. Meanwhile, competition between China and Japan over infrastructure investment in Southeast Asia created space and a necessity for the two sides to coordinate with each other and avoid excessive competition that could jeopardize both sides' interests.[23] During Abe's official visit to China in 2018, the two governments signed a memorandum on cooperation in "third-party markets," primarily referring to ASEAN countries. Moreover, the recasting of FOIP from strategy to vision also has its own logic. When Abe first proposed it in 2016, FOIP appeared more like a rough exploratory concept.[24] Tokyo used an ambiguous version of the concept to gauge other states' responses and changed its strategic emphasis accordingly.[25]

Thus, Japan's FOIP has changed from a strategy to a vision and reflects the warming of the bilateral relationship. Through re-labeling FOIP as a vision, it seems that Tokyo sought to clarify that it is not a China containment strategy, but rather an inclusive framework for regional cooperation. This adjustment both reflected and promoted the warming of Japan's relations with China. The main purpose behind recasting FOIP was to signal Japan's interest in improving relations with China, an objective that Beijing also shared. It seems that while those contentious concerns—historical issues and maritime disputes—still existed between the two countries, they were swept under the carpet for the time being since both sides faced bigger challenges dealing with the U.S. on economic issues. Since then, China has responded to Japan's FOIP vision in

The Japan's "Free and Open Indo-Pacific" and Sino–Japanese Relations   157

a less confrontational manner. However, this does not mean that China has embraced Japan's FOIP wholeheartedly, and the same applies to the Japanese attitude toward China's BRI.[26]

The evolution of the bilateral relations and the accompanying geopolitical and geoeconomic concerns have been further complicated by the outbreak of the COVID-19 pandemic for both Tokyo and Beijing. Washington has taken a much tougher stance on China regarding COVID-19, economics, human rights, and high-tech developments. In September 2020, Shinzo Abe resigned as prime minister. During his tenure, Abe, as a strong leader, took a proactive stance in improving Sino–Japanese relations. Nonetheless, his successor, Yoshihide Suga, lacks strong diplomatic experience. During the first few months of his administration, Suga made no substantial moves but adopted a wait-and-see approach until the dust of the U.S. presidential election settled in January 2021. After President Joe Biden took office, the U.S. approach toward China remained aggressive, while Tokyo's role as a key ally has become more cherished. The Biden administration in Washington has repeatedly expressed its commitment to the Indo-Pacific strategy.[27] Subsequently, Tokyo's FOIP has gradually shifted back to leaning toward the U.S. The Suga and subsequent Fumio Kishida administrations have actively promoted Quad initiatives, showing great eagerness to join mechanisms such as the Five Eyes intelligence-sharing alliance and the U.S.-proposed Indo-Pacific Economic Framework (IPEF). In sum, Japan's FOIP has fluctuated significantly in recent years, from a balancing movement against China to showing gestures of cooperation with China to revealing a tendency to become subordinate to the U.S. Indo-Pacific strategy.

6.3. Discussions in Chinese Academia

How does China assess, and how will it cope with, Japan's FOIP? The following two sections examine debates among Chinese scholars and various statements by Chinese Foreign Ministry spokespersons as proxies in assessing Chinese leaders' policy orientations on this issue.[28] Chinese academics have paid close attention to FOIP in the past few years, and the growing number of research projects funded by the National Social Science Foundation of China (NSSFC) indicates the government's significant concerns on this topic.[29] The Chinese foreign policy community is not unified and coherent. The complex and fluid nature of Japan's FOIP

158   *G. Wang & Z. Chen*

and the evolution of Sino–Japanese relations have led to vibrant discussions among Chinese analysts on the nature, purposes, and impacts of Japan's FOIP in recent years, with no consensus reached on what constitutes the best policy recommendations for the government. Their debates both reflect and influence the viewpoints of the decision-making circle to some extent.

This section examines the policy analyses and debates among Chinese scholars on Japan's FOIP. It roughly divides existing discussions into three groups: the hard-line, hedging and docking approaches. It should be noted that the categorization here is tentative and that these categories are not strictly mutually exclusive. Indeed, after the emergence of Japan's FOIP, both the concept and Sino–Japanese relations have undergone significant changes, as well as those of (even the same) Chinese scholars' perceptions of FOIP and their policy recommendations.

6.3.1. *The hard-line approach*

Overall, and especially in the early stages of FOIP's development, most Chinese analysts tended to analyze it through the lens of ongoing Sino–Japanese rivalry and emerging Sino–U.S. strategic competition. They thus recommended hard-line counter-responses based on the premise that the Indo-Pacific strategy represented a new round of Tokyo's containment efforts against China. For instance, Yang Bojiang, Director of the Institute of Japanese Studies at CASS, once argued, "Japan's actual practices in implementing the Indo-Pacific Strategy, which emphasizes security concerns over [economic] ones and focuses on building the Quad coalition, have already characterized the strategy as something countering China."[30] Some other Chinese scholars even claimed that Abe's Indo-Pacific strategy distinctly targeted China, warning that its "geopolitical confrontation" thinking and "strategic competition" logic would only create strategic crises in Sino–Japanese relations.[31]

The reasons behind their assessments are easy to understand. First, after Abe proposed FOIP, comments from Japanese media and academia also highlighted its focus on "checking and balancing China." For instance, both the *Asahi Shimbun* and *Nikkei Asia* used the phrase "countering China's influences" in the headlines of their reports on Abe's 2016 proposal of FOIP in Nairobi.[32] Second, bilateral relations were at a very low point when Abe introduced FOIP. In particular, Tokyo's repeated negative comments about the BRI and AIIB on various occasions at that time incited Chinese analysts to believe that FOIP was introduced to counter the BRI. Although Japanese leaders modified their policies later and took a more cooperative stance toward the BRI, these adjustments have not removed all the suspicions of Chinese scholars. Finally, even after relabeling FOIP a "vision," Abe and his followers never ceased their efforts to attract the involvement of like-minded states in building a security coalition within FOIP framework. It was under Abe's promotion that the Trump administration formulated its own Indo-Pacific strategy. Meanwhile, Australia and India, two countries whose relations with China were under severe stress throughout this period, also unveiled their versions of an Indo-Pacific strategy. Chinese scholars suspected that FOIP would expand the geographical scope of the U.S.–Japan alliance to the Indian Ocean and further strengthen Japan's role as an indispensable ally for Washington in containing China's rise.[33] They believed that Japan was inclined to develop the Quad as an exclusive security coalition to encircle China. If FOIP had been merely a project put forward by Japan, China might have adopted a more cooperative posture toward it after Sino–Japanese relations improved. Nonetheless, as Trump put forward the U.S. version, the Indo-Pacific strategy as a whole was negatively evaluated by Chinese analysts, while the Quad further increased their anxiety over the risk of strategic encirclement.[34]

Even after Tokyo changed the terminology for FOIP from strategy to vision, many Chinese scholars chose to downplay its significance.[35] They believed that it was merely political rhetoric aimed at temporarily repairing relations between Tokyo and China. Therefore, the term "vision" (構想, *gouxiang*) was seldom adopted by them, while the use of the term "strategy" (戦略, *zhanlue*) remained mainstream in Chinese literature on Japan's FOIP.[36] Some scholars acknowledged the Japanese adjustment but warned that, in essence, the FOIP's target of containing China had never changed.[37]

In sum, the mainstream assessment of Japan's Indo-Pacific strategy among Chinese analysts is negative. They recommended remaining vigilant and adopting a hard-line approach. Their hard-line position did not ease after the modification of Japan's FOIP from a "strategy" to a "vision" and was even strengthened after the further advancement of the U.S. Indo-Pacific strategy and the convergence of Japan's FOIP with it in recent months. From their perspective, it is clear that Japan has now become one of the few Asian countries that have completely sided with the U.S. amid the Sino–U.S. strategic competition and that China should adopt a tit-for-tat strategy.[38]

6.3.2. *The hedging strategy*

However, the recovery of Sino–Japanese relations after 2017 also gave Chinese analysts some reasons for a less pessimistic assessment of Japan's FOIP, at least temporarily. A growing number of analyses recommended the more flexible approach of hedging. In international relations literature, hedging is generally considered a strategy for small- and medium-sized countries in the context of great power rivalries. According to this view, most regional countries, including Japan, have remained reluctant to take sides between the U.S. and China. In studies of the Indo-Pacific strategy, discussions on Japan's hedging against China are more common. Interestingly, as the strategic competition between the U.S. and China escalated rapidly while the value of Japan as a vital third party increased, proposals for a Chinese hedging strategy also emerged.

The idea of hedging suggests that China can coordinate and cooperate with Japan's FOIP selectively on some economic issues while remaining alert to the concept's security dimension. On this dimension, these scholars were more optimistic than those arguing for a hard-line approach. From their perspective, Japan's FOIP is more like a hedging strategy than a clear-cut China containment strategy. As it stands now, the concept lacks clarity and has visible problems in its feasibility and implementation. Japan's FOIP requires cooperation from other states or regional organizations that have differing interests and approaches. While Japan might want to turn the FOIP concept into a purely counter-China strategy, it is difficult to gain support from regional states with strong economic ties to China. Even if they agree with Japan's strategic vision, Japan and its partners, especially the U.S. and India, have different ideas about its implementation.[39]

More importantly, during the tumultuous Trump years, Washington played an unprecedentedly malicious game with China. Against this growing strategic pressure, some Chinese scholars warned that conflating the Indo-Pacific strategy of Japan and the U.S. would only further push Japan—which had the potential to take a neutral or distanced position—to the U.S. side, which is not in China's interest.[40] These analysts highlighted that U.S.–Japan relations were also strained over various issues, ranging from requests for increased payment for hosting U.S. bases in Japan to steel tariffs, the unilateral withdrawal from TPP, and other issues. Against this background, they suggested that Tokyo had become increasingly discontented with Washington's demands and, therefore, there might be a limit to its will to take a side in the Sino–U.S. contests.[41] Those scholars thus started to consider the possibilities of winning goodwill or neutralizing Tokyo in the Sino–U.S. contest.

These scholars found significant scope for cooperation on economic issues. They highlighted that the Japanese business community wanted a cooperative rapport with China and wished to secure contracts in relevant infrastructure projects around the world. Cai Liang, a research fellow at the Shanghai Institutes for International Studies, noted that while Japan's FOIP vision (notably, Cai accepted the expression "vision," 構想) contained elements deliberately designed to counter the influence of the BRI, many specific measures proposed by Japan on local economic revitalization and infrastructure development were similar to the Chinese ones. Therefore, China could treat some Japanese measures for implementing FOIP as healthy competition and should seek possibilities of cooperation with them in promoting high-quality joint construction of the BRI.[42] Lu Hao, an associate research fellow at the Institute of Japanese Studies at CASS, shared a similar view, arguing that "in the Indo-Pacific region, China's BRI as an emerging international public good can coexist with Japan's FOIP vision, and the docking of the two may create a new momentum for practical cooperation between the two countries." Meanwhile, Lu emphasized that the precondition is that Tokyo must abandon "the irrational and confrontational elements in its policy toward China."[43]

In sum, these scholars advocating a hedging approach paid more attention to the evolutionary nature of the FOIP concept, suggesting that the future direction of Japan's FOIP was still uncertain and that significant scope for cooperation with the BRI existed. They also highlighted a distinction between the economic and security dimensions of Japan's FOIP. With regard to security issues, they recognized that a strengthened U.S.–Japan alliance under FOIP would jeopardize China's security and suggested the possibility of neutralizing Tokyo. With regard to economic issues, Japan's FOIP included both competitive and cooperative strategies toward China, which would be less confrontational, allowing China to adopt more flexible policies while steadfastly defending its core interests.

6.3.3. *The docking approach*

A small number of Chinese analysts have shown even greater enthusiasm for the possibility of cooperation with Japan's FOIP between 2018 and 2020. After Abe changed his terminology from "strategy" to "vision," several analysts suggested that Japan was more willing to accommodate ideas from China and ASEAN countries and at least some room existed for closer coordination between Beijing and Tokyo on the "docking" (對接, *duijie*) between China's BRI and Japan's FOIP. According to them, docking does not mean that China should accept Japan's FOIP wholesale, nor does it mean that Beijing will come up with its own version of the Indo-Pacific strategy. Rather, focusing more on the economic areas, they suggest that China could find significant scope and opportunities for cooperation with Japan's FOIP while avoiding excessive competition, which is in no one's interest. In their eyes, although the FOIP was designed to counterbalance China's BRI initially, this containment dimension became relatively diluted as Sino–Japanese relations improved. According to them, Abe's proposal of shifting bilateral relations from "competition" to "coordination" during his 2018 visit to China signaled Tokyo's conditional willingness to collaborate with Beijing on infrastructure development through the BRI under certain conditions. This outreach indicates Tokyo's desire to engage Beijing in economic development financing. The signing of the Memorandum of Understanding on Third-Party Market Cooperation further encouraged these analysts. They believed that "docking" between the BRI and FOIP would become an opportunity for both sides to promote their interests and engage in public diplomacy.[44]

The docking approach these scholars advocated thus emphasized interfaces and coordination between the two countries in specific areas while maintaining their own autonomy. Although third-party market cooperation between China and Japan is a form of policy coordination, Chinese scholars usually perceive these as programs under the BRI framework, while their Japanese counterparts view them more as Tokyo's active attempt to integrate China within Abe's FOIP, which could help Japan implement its vision of "high-quality infrastructure investment."[45] Meanwhile, Wang Wan argued that it was the early success of the BRI initiative that had stimulated the creation of Japan's FOIP, while the latter's emphasis on "connectivity" was inspired by the BRI. Moreover, she suggested that the BRI still needs continuous improvement and refinement in its implementation. As long as those programs benefit the BRI's further development, she suggested, the Chinese side should maintain an "open and inclusive" profile when dealing with the offers of cooperation proposed by Tokyo.[46] Nonetheless, only a few people shared this view, and their voices have faded over the past months.

In sum, Chinese analysts have engaged in debates on the nature of Japan's FOIP and what constitutes China's best responses. These academic debates reflect what Beijing thinks of Japan's FOIP and how China should formulate its response. As Feng Liu and Kai He suggest, China's relations with its neighbors are shaped by "two perceptual factors: security threat and economic interest" (see Chapter 1). Other than the change in Sino–Japan relations, it must be noted that decision-makers' understanding of Japan's FOIP also depends on Chinese analysts' assessments of U.S.–Japan relations and whether the improvement of these relations constitutes a strategic interest for Tokyo. Answers to this question will affect not only Chinese scholars' perceptions but also the Chinese government's policies toward Japan's FOIP. The Indo-Pacific strategies of Japan and the U.S. have increasingly converged since the outbreak of the COVID-19 pandemic in 2020. In this context, the assessment of Chinese academics rests on the premise that FOIP is a strategy aimed at containing and even encircling China. The hard-line approach maintains its popularity, while only a few scholars still discuss the other two approaches.

6.4. The Chinese Government's Responses

So far, the Chinese government's responses to Japan's FOIP have been critical but relatively restrained. China has already actively participated in shaping the economic and security order of the Asia-Pacific region, advocating a "regional community of shared future." Nonetheless, Chinese officials are skeptical of the "Indo-Pacific" concept and refrain from using it.[47] The Chinese government has never adopted the concept of Indo-Pacific on official occasions.[48] Chinese diplomats still prefer the concept of "Asia-Pacific," and they nearly always refer to "Indo-Pacific" as "Asia-Pacific." When they must address the Indo-Pacific concept, they attach the phrase "so-called" before it.

At the beginning, Beijing questioned whether FOIP would be enduring or something short-lived, like Obama's "Pivot to Asia." For instance,

Foreign Minister Wang Yi (王毅) dismissed the "Indo-Pacific" concept as a "headline grabbing" idea that will "dissipate like *sea foam*" at a press conference on 8 March 2018.[49] Nonetheless, Beijing's tone has become even more assertive in the past few years. On 22 May 2022, on the eve of the Quad Summit in Tokyo, Wang Yi made a much more assertive remark that the Indo-Pacific Strategy "aims to contain China and attempts to make Asia-Pacific countries 'pawns' of U.S. hegemony ... It is in essence a strategy that creates divisions, incites confrontation and undermines peace. No matter how the strategy is airbrushed or disguised, it is bound to be a failed strategy."[50]

Meanwhile, senior Chinese officials have also hinted on occasion that China welcomes regional initiatives and can maintain an open position toward other regional states' visions of the Indo-Pacific. For instance, when Wang Yi was once asked by the press to comment on the "ASEAN Outlook on the Indo-Pacific," he replied that it was "an issue" involving regional cooperation and that China had always maintained an open and constructive attitude toward it. He also emphasized that existing regimes work well, and FOIP might displace ASEAN's core position in regional cooperation.[51]

As there are few better ways to explore the Chinese government's official position, we have collected and examined relevant remarks from the Chinese Foreign Ministry spokesperson since 2017.[52] From 1 January 2017 to 31 December 2023, there were 138 references to the "Indo-Pacific" (印太, *yintai*) in spokespersons' remarks during regular press conferences, of which 111 were contained in answers to journalists' questions on Indo-Pacific-related topics. Only on 27 other occasions did those spokespersons take the initiative to refer to the concept. Among the 111 Q&As, we also found a vivid pattern: those spokespersons' comments on Japan's Indo-Pacific strategy (only a small portion of the 111 remarks) were significantly different from those focused on the U.S. counterpart. For example, on 13 November 2017, in response to a request from a media reporter to comment on the Japanese side's expressed intention of seeking cooperation on FOIP with various parties, including the Chinese side, spokesperson Geng Shuang (耿爽) only responded vaguely:

> It is the shared responsibility of all regional countries to promote stability and prosperity in the Asia-Pacific. We hope that the policies and

The Japan's "Free and Open Indo-Pacific" and Sino–Japanese Relations   165

actions of relevant parties would correspond with the trend of the times that calls for peace, development, friendship and cooperation, and serve to maintain and promote regional peace, stability and prosperity.

His tone was relatively modest and neutral, and at least he did not criticize Japan's proposal. Meanwhile, Geng carefully avoided using the term "Indo-Pacific." Instead, he referred to the Asia-Pacific in his reply.[53] This is similar to Wang Yi's response to the "ASEAN Outlook on the Indo-Pacific" mentioned above.

However, while commenting on the U.S. Indo-Pacific strategy, the tone of Chinese Foreign Ministry spokespersons was significantly tougher. For example, on 3 June 2019, commenting on U.S. Acting Secretary of Defense Shanahan's speech on the U.S. Indo-Pacific strategy at the Shangri-La Dialogue two days earlier, Geng Shuang responded:

> By hyping up military undertones and confrontation, a country will only end up hurting itself [the original Chinese text is 搬起石頭砸自己的脚, *banqi shitou za ziji de jiao*, meaning lifting a rock only to drop it on one's own feet]. We hope the U.S. will consider its own interests and the common interests of regional countries and contribute to regional peace, stability and development.[54]

When commenting on the developments of Japan–U.S. relations, the spokesperson's tone was once again relatively restrained. It seems that Beijing has refrained from offending Japan. For example, on 21 September 2020, in response to an Agence France-Presse reporter's request for a comment on the phone call exchange between U.S. President Trump and Japanese Prime Minister Suga on how the two countries will pursue a free and open Indo-Pacific region, spokesperson Wang Wenbin (汪文斌) responded:

> China has no objection to the development of normal relations between other countries. In the meantime, it is our position that such exchange and cooperation should be conducive to mutual trust between regional countries and peace, stability and prosperity of the region.[55]

Besides, on 28 January 2021, when a Japanese NHK (The Japan Broadcasting Corporation) reporter requested a comment on U.S. and

166 *G. Wang & Z. Chen*

Japanese leaders' affirmation on the importance of jointly ensuring a free and open Indo-Pacific in their phone exchange, the response from spokesperson Zhao Lijian (趙立堅) was also restrained:

> We maintain that peace, development and win-win cooperation is the trend of the times and the aspiration shared by regional countries. Interactions between relevant countries should be conducive to mutual trust between regional countries, as well as peace, stability and prosperity in the region.[56]

Nonetheless, the tone of the Chinese spokesperson became stern a few months later, as it seemed that Tokyo was leaning closer to the U.S. side while Beijing faced growing pressure. For instance, on 13 June 2021, commenting on the annual Japanese *Defence White Paper*, which referred to the "importance of stability around Taiwan" for the first time, Zhao Lijian harshly criticized it:

> Enough with Japan's "lying diplomacy" and double standard! The "Indo-Pacific Strategy" aims to stoke bloc confrontation and create cliques for geopolitical game. It marks the comeback of Cold War mentality and retrogression and should be tossed into the dustbin of history.[57]

These spokespersons became even more critical of the Indo-Pacific strategy and the Biden administration's new initiative—the IPEF—in the first half of 2022. They referred to the Indo-Pacific 44 times, including taking the initiative to comment on the concept 16 times, compared to six times in the previous five years. Their criticisms peaked during the U.S.–Japan Summit and the Quad Summit in Tokyo on 22–24 May. However, most of them were directed at the U.S., while Japan was mentioned several times in discussions involving sensitive "Chinese core interests" issues such as Taiwan.

Our thorough examination of various official statements thus suggests that China does not reject the Indo-Pacific as a vision or framework for cooperation among regional countries in economic areas. Beijing opposed the U.S. Indo-Pacific strategy, but there was a certain degree of ambiguity and flexibility in its comments on Japan's FOIP. In particular, Beijing deliberately avoided using excessively strong language, except when a case is relevant to its core interests, such as Taiwan. Instead, it emphasized the need for a stable regional order. Although this modest posture is far from accommodating the BRI and FOIP visions, the different rhetoric in commenting on the Japanese and American Indo-Pacific strategies has revealed the Chinese government's complex and nuanced considerations of this issue. Although the security dimension and the Quad mechanism, in particular, have raised alarms, Beijing does not refuse to consider cooperation on economic issues. Meanwhile, China perceives the U.S. as its greatest threat and has refrained from further pushing Japan closer to the U.S. side (see Chapter 7). Nonetheless, if the Indo-Pacific strategy between Japan and the U.S. converges further, as the recent trend shows, then the Chinese government's policy of differential treatment will also change, while Sino–Japanese relations will enter a new stage of intense confrontation.[58]

6.5. Conclusion

This chapter examines Chinese responses to Japan's FOIP in the context of the evolution of Sino–Japanese relations. It finds that assessments of Japan's FOIP among the Chinese policy and scholarly communities are quite diverse and complex, and that these judgments and recommendations are heavily influenced by the evolution of the Sino–Japan–U.S. triangle relations. Chinese scholars have shown different assessments of Japan's FOIP, and there has been no consensus on what constitutes the best policy recommendation for the government. Meanwhile, comments from Chinese government officials regarding FOIP remain elusive, as they carefully and intentionally make a distinction between the Indo-Pacific strategy of Washington and that of Tokyo. These discussions provide a useful window into Beijing's complex concerns about mitigating possible security risks while continuing to seek cooperation with regional countries and extend its international influence.

The complex challenges imposed by the FOIP framework require China to take a comprehensive approach, considering both security and economic factors. In its rise, China had to navigate complicated relations with the hegemon, other great powers, and weaker/smaller neighboring countries, which encompasses complex strategic calculations. While Washington has become more inclined to balancing and containing China, its allies and partners in the region still have significant incentives to adopt strategic reconciliation. The divergence between the U.S. and its allies leaves China significant space to take a reassurance/wedge approach, delivering benevolent messages to create a cooperative incentive for those countries.[59] Beijing has thus adopted a mixed strategy, vacillating between, and simultaneously using, cooperative reassurance measures and competitive coercive tactics.

Beijing's cautious and sometimes dismissive response to Japan's FOIP since 2017 has included both optimistic and pessimistic assessments, taking into account both security and economic issues. From a geoeconomic perspective, although there is certainly competition between China and Japan in the fields of infrastructure investment and development financing, the two share some common goals and interests in regional trade cooperation. For instance, excessive competition between China and Japan in Southeast Asia has led both sides to recognize the great costs and risks involved, motivating them to sign the memorandum of cooperation in third-party markets in 2018. From a geopolitical perspective, however, the reversal of the power balance between China and Japan, as well as the escalating rivalry between China and the U.S., only make the competition between the BRI and FOIP much more like a zero-sum game. China values its relationship with Japan amid emerging Sino–U.S. strategic competition and has thus chosen to adopt a low-key approach, avoiding overt confrontation. However, at heart, relations between Japan and China are fragile due to territorial disputes, historical problems, and ideological differences.[60] The year 2022 marks the 50th anniversary of the normalization of diplomatic relations between China and Japan. However, the ongoing Russia–Ukraine conflict has provided Tokyo with a reason to strengthen its military forces and alliances with Washington, which has alarmed Beijing. At the end of 2022, the Japanese government released three documents on national security. The documents, including the *National Security Strategy*, lay out policies such as increasing defense spending to two percent of the national GDP and acquiring counterstrike capabilities to target enemy missile launch sites. In 2023, the Japanese government's decision to release wastewater from the damaged Fukushima Daiichi nuclear power plant into the Pacific Ocean and the subsequent Chinese reactions further exacerbated Sino–Japanese relations. Meanwhile, concerns surrounding mutual visa policies after the end of the COVID-19 pandemic became new obstacles to Sino–Japanese relations. On a visit to India on 20 March 2023, Prime Minister Kishida launched a revamped FOIP plan that includes a massive new infrastructure and economic assistance program for countries in the Global South. The plan, which did not mention China by name, was widely seen as a bid to counter Beijing's BRI. If Washington can induce Japan to join its

The Japan's "Free and Open Indo-Pacific" and Sino–Japanese Relations 169

intensifying containment efforts against China, it is quite certain that Japan will lean closer to the U.S. side, while Beijing's confrontational response to Japan's FOIP will only return and grow even stronger.

Acknowledgment

This chapter was originally presented as an article at an online workshop, "Discerning China's Bilateral Relations in the Indo Pacific," hosted by the Center for Governance and Public Policy at Griffith University in October 2021. We would like to thank Yinan He, two anonymous reviewers, and participants of the workshop for their helpful comments and suggestions. This work was supported by the National Social Science Fund of China (No. 21AZD093).

Endnotes

1. Ken Masujima, "Development and strategic competition in Asia: Toward polarization?" *International Relations of the Asia-Pacific*, 21(1), 91–120 (2021); Kei Koga, "Japan's 'Indo-Pacific' question: Countering China or shaping a new regional order?" *International Affairs*, 96(1), 49–73 (2020).

2. See Japanese Ministry of Foreign Affairs (MOFA), Diplomatic Bluebook 2019. https://www.mofa.go.jp/files/000527162.pdf; Japanese Ministry of Foreign Affairs (MOFA), Diplomatic Bluebook 2020. https://www.mofa.go.jp/files/100116875.pdf.

3. Tomohiko Satake and Ryo Sahashi, "The rise of China and Japan's 'vision' for free and open Indo-Pacific," *Journal of Contemporary China*, 30(127), 18–35 (2021); R. Rajagopalan, "Evasive balancing: India's unviable Indo-Pacific strategy," *International Affairs*, 96(1), 75–93 (2020); R. Mukherjee, "Looking West, acting East: India's Indo-Pacific strategy," *Southeast Asian Affairs*, 43–52 (2019); Kei Koga, "Japan's 'free and open Indo-Pacific' strategy: Tokyo's tactical hedging and the implications for ASEAN," *Contemporary Southeast Asia*, 41(2), 286–313 (2019); Haruyuki Suzuki, *Japan's Leadership Role in a Multipolar Indo-Pacific*, Center for Strategic and International Studies (CSIS), 2020, pp. 1–13; H. D. P. Envall, "The Pacific Islands in Japan's 'free and open Indo-Pacific': From 'slow and steady' to strategic," *Security Challenges*, 16(1), 65–77 (2020); F. Heiduk and G. Wacker, *From Asia-Pacific to Indo-Pacific: Significance, Implementation and Challenges*, German Institute for International and Security Affairs, July 2020. https://www.swp-berlin.org/publications/products/research_papers/2020RP09_IndoPacific.pdf; C. Paskal, *Indo-Pacific*

Strategies, Perceptions and Partnerships: The View from Seven Countries, Chatham House, The Royal Institute of International Affairs, March 2021. https://www.chathamhouse.org/sites/default/files/2021-03/2021-03-22-indo-pacific-strategies-paskal.pdf.

4 As in the case of Chinese academia, we collect and examine articles on the Indo-Pacific strategy published from the year 2017 to 2023 from the CNKI's China Academic Journals Full-text Database using *Yintai zhanlve* (印太戰略, Indo-Pacific Strategy) as keywords. Although Abe was the first leader who promoted the Indo-Pacific concept, in 2017, only two articles on the Indo-Pacific were published on CSSCI (Chinese Social Sciences Citation Index) journals, one on Japan and the other on the U.S. Only after the Trump administration adopted the concept did "Indo-Pacific" quickly become one of the hottest topics in Chinese international studies. The number of articles increased to 33 in 2018, with seven on Japan and 20 on the U.S. Moreover, most Chinese studies on Japan's FOIP also went to great lengths in discussing U.S. factors.

5 Kai He and Mingjiang Li, "Understanding the dynamics of the Indo-Pacific: US-China strategic competition, regional actors, and beyond," *International Affairs*, 96(1), 1–7 (2020); Feng Liu, "The recalibration of Chinese assertiveness: China's responses to the Indo-Pacific challenge," *International Affairs*, 96(1), 9–27 (January 2020); Weixing Hu, "The United States, China, and the Indo-Pacific strategy: The rise and return of strategic competition," *The China Review*, 20(3), 127–142 (2020); Weixing Hu and Weizhan Meng, "The US Indo-Pacific strategy and China's response," *The China Review*, 20(3), 143–176 (2020); Bo Ma, "China's fragmented approach toward the Indo-Pacific strategy: One concept, many lenses," *The China Review*, 20(3), 177–204 (2020); Xiaodi Ye, "Explaining China's hedging to United States' Indo-Pacific strategy," *The China Review*, 20(3), 205–237 (2020); Chunman Zhang, "The power of a niche strategy and China's preemptive and adaptive response to the US Indo-Pacific strategy," *The China Review*, 20(3), 239–259 (2020).

6 Shinzo Abe, "Address by Prime Minister Shinzo Abe at the Opening Session of the Sixth Tokyo International Conference on African Development (TICAD VI), MOFA," 27 August 2016. https://www.mofa.go.jp/afr/af2/page4e_000496.html.

7 Shinzo Abe, "Confluence of the two seas," Speech, MOFA, 22 August 2007. https://www.mofa.go.jp/region/asia-paci/pmv0708/speech-2.html.

8 Hiroshi Nakanishi, "Nihon Gaiko ni okeru Jiyu de Hirakareta Indo Taiheiyo ("Free and open Indo-Pacific" in Japanese diplomacy)," *Gaiko* (*Diplomacy*), 52, 12–19 (2018).

9 Huaizhong Wu, "Anbei zhengfu yintai zhanlve yu zhongguo de yingdui (Japan's Indo-Pacific strategy and China's response)," *Xiandai guoji guanxi* (*Contemporary International Relations*), 1, 18 (2018).

10 For institutional balancing, see Kai He, "Contested regional orders and institutional balancing in the Asia Pacific," *International Politics*, 52(2), 209 (2015).

11 S. Katada, "Indo taiheiyo koso to do chiiki no Keizai renkei (Indo-Pacific initiative and economic connectivity of the region)," *Kokusaimondai (International Affairs)*, 687, 26 (2019).

12 Indeed, the emergence of BRI, to a great extent, is Beijing's counter-response to the Trans-Pacific Partnership (TPP) project promoted by the former Obama administration.

13 Xue Gong, "China's economic statecraft: The Belt and Road in Southeast Asia and the impact on the Indo-Pacific," *Security Challenges*, 16(3), 39–46 (2020); B. J. Cannon, "Grand strategies in contested zones: Japan's Indo-Pacific, China's BRI and Eastern Africa," *Rising Powers Quarterly*, 3(2), 195–221 (2018).

14 Wu (2018), *Op. cit.*, p. 18.

15 Mie Oba, "Regional economic institutions and Japan's leadership: The promotion of institutional hedging," in *Shaping the Rules-Based Order in the Reiwa Era (Strategic Japan 2020)*, CSIS (Center of Strategic and International Studies), 2020.

16 M. Yahuda, *Sino-Japanese Relations After the Cold War: Two Tigers Sharing a Mountain* (London: Routledge, 2013).

17 Nicholas Szechenyi and Yuichi Hosoya, "Working toward a free and open Indo-Pacific," Alliance Policy Coordination Brief, Carnegie Endowment for International Peace, 10 October 2019. https://carnegieendowment.org/2019/10/10/working-toward-free-and-open-indo-pacific-pub-80023.

18 Liu, "The recalibration of Chinese assertiveness." This is a consensus among Chinese and Japanese analysts but there is also a subtle difference: Chinese analysts tend to emphasize that Trump's unilateral diplomacy made trouble for the US-Japan alliance. Huaizhong Wu, "Telangpu chongji xiade riben zhanlveyinying yu zhongriguanxi (Japan's strategic response to "the Trump shock" and Sino-Japanese relations)," *Riben xuekan (Japanese Studies)*, 2, 1–33 (2017).

19 Ministry of Foreign Affairs (MOFA), "Japan-China Relations: Prime Minister Abe Visits China," 26 October 2018. https://www.mofa.go.jp/a_o/c_m1/cn/page3e_000958.html.

20 Yuichi Hosoya, "FOIP 2.0: The evolution of Japan's free and open Indo-Pacific strategy," *Asia Pacific Review*, 26(1), 25 (2019).

21 Matake Kamiya, "Kyoso senryaku tame no kyoryoku senryaku: Nihon no jiyu de hirakareta indo- taiheiyo senryaku (kouso) no fukugoteki kouzo, Cooperation strategy for competitive strategy: The complex structure of Japan's Free and Open Indo-Pacific strategy (concept)," *Anzenhosho kenkyu (Security Studies)*, 1(2), 47–64 (2019).

22 Professor Wang is the wife of former Chinese Ambassador to Japan, Cheng Yonghua. Wan Wang, "Anbei zhizheng houqi de yintai gouxiang yu zhongri disanfang shichang hezuo (The Indo-Pacific vision in the late Abe administration and China-Japan third-party market cooperation)," *Zhongguo guoji zhanlve pinglun* (*China International Strategy Review*), 1, 97 (2020).

23 J. C. Liao and S. N. Katada, "Geoeconomics, easy money, and political opportunism: The perils under China and Japan's high-speed rail competition," *Contemporary Politics*, 27(1), 1–22 (2021).

24 Mie Oba, "Nihon no indo-taiheiyo koso (Indo-Pacific: From Japan's perspective)," *Kokusai anzenhosho* (*International Security*), 46(3), 12–32 (2018).

25 Koga (2019), *Op. cit.*, pp. 288–289.

26 Yoshihide Soeya, "Indo-Pacific: From strategy to vision," *CSCAP Regional Security Outlook 2020,* Council for Security Cooperation in the Asia Pacific, 2019, pp. 16–18. http://www.cscap.org/uploads/Regional%20Security%20 Outlook%202020.pdf.

27 US Department of State, "Secretary Blinken's call with Quad Ministers, Office of the Spokesperson," 18 February 2021. https://www.state.gov/ secretary-blinkens-call-with-quad-ministers.

28 On the significance of studying the views of Chinese scholars, and the possibility of using it as a proxy in understanding Chinese foreign policy and assessing China's foreign policy orientations, see Huiyun Feng and Kai He, "Why do Chinese IR scholars matter?" in Huiyun Feng, Kai He and Xuetong Yan (eds.) *Chinese Scholars and Foreign Policy: Debating International Relations* (New York: Routledge, 2019), pp. 3–20.

29 From 2018 to 2023 the fund supported 30 projects with "Indo-Pacific" in its title, compared with only 11 "Asia-Pacific" projects.

30 Bojiang Yang and Xiaolei Zhang, "Riben canyu yidaiyilu hezuo: zhuanbiandongyin yu qianjingfenxi (Japan's participation in Belt and Road Initiative: Its transformation motivation and prospect)," *Dongbeiyaxuekan* (*Journal of Northeast Asia Studies*), 3, 10 (2018).

31 Dexing Song and Zhao Huang, "Riben yintai zhanlve de shengcheng jili jiqi zhanlvexiaoneng tanxi (An analysis of the formation mechanism and strategic efficiency of Japan's 'Indo-Pacific' strategy)," *Shijie jingji yu zhengzhi* (*World Economics and Politics*), 11, 54 (2019).

32 *Asahi Shimbun*, "Afurika shien ryo yori shitsu: shushoenzetsu chugoku ni taiko TICAD (Prime Minister's speech: To counter China, aid to Africa should focus more on quality than quantity)," 28 August 2016; *Nikkei Asia*, "Japan's Abe seeks to counter China's influence in Africa," 28 August 2016. https://asia.nikkei.com/Economy/Japan-s-Abe-seeks-to-counter-China-s-influence-in-Africa.

33 Zhen Yang, Yi Ding and Liang Cai, "Yintaizhanlve kuangjiaxia de meiri haiquanhezuo (US-Japan maritime power cooperation under the framework of Indo-Pacific strategy)," *Guoji guanxi yanjiu* (*Journal of International Relations*), 6, 117 (2020).

34 For instance, Yongtao Gui, "Riben yu zhongmei zhanlvejingzheng: maoyizhan, Kejizhan ji yintaizhanlve (Japan and the U.S.-China strategic competition: Trade war, technology war, and the Indo-Pacific strategy)," *Guojiluntan* (*International Forum*), 3, 3–18 (2020); Ming Liu, Yong Chen and Biquan Shu, "Yintaizhanlve: yi meiriyinao de zhanlveluoji, liyi yu celvexuanze wei fenxishijiao (Indo-Pacific strategy: Analysis from the lens of strategic logic, interest, and tactic of the US, India, Japan and Australia)," *Dongbei ya luntan* (Northeast Asia Forum), 2, 3–21 (2021); Hu and Meng (2020), *Op. cit.*

35 Li Xue, "Riben Yintaizhanlve de jige weidu (Dimensions of Japan's Indo-Pacific strategy)," *Shijie zhishi* (*World Affairs*), 1, 31 (2020).

36 For instance, Zhenyu Wang, "Duichong yu zhiheng: riben yintaizhanlve de diyuanzhengzhi luoji yu zhiyueyinsu (Hedge and balance: The geopolitical logic and restrictive factors of Japan's "Indo-Pacific strategy")," *Ribenyanjiu* (*Japan Studies*), 1, 30–39 (2021); Xiaoxu Meng, "Ruanzhiheng: riben yintaizhanlve xiade xiaoguowaijiao (Soft balancing: Japan's diplomacy towards small powers under the Indo-Pacific strategy)," *Riben xuekan* (*Japanese Studies*), 6, 46–80 (2020).

37 Xiaoxu Meng, "Riben yintaigouxiang jiqi zhixugoujian (Japan's Indo-Pacific and the building of order)," *Riben xuekan* (*Japanese Studies*), 6, 48 (2019).

38 Feng Zhu, "Diyuanzhanlve yu daguoguanxi: zhongriguanxi jibenzoushi de zaifenxi (Geostrategy and great power relations: A reanalysis of the basic trend of Sino Japanese relations)," *Riben xuekan* (*Japanese Studies*), 1, 1–21 (2022).

39 Mong Cheung, "Anbei zhixia de riben duihua zhengce: cong zhanlve zhiheng dao zhanshu bixian (Japan's China policy under Abe administration: From strategic balancing to tactical hedging)," *Guoji an'quan yanjiu* (*Journal of International Security Studies*), 39(2), 92–95 (2021); Hongyu Liu and Bing Wu, "Liangmian xiazhu: Xin xingshi xia riben duihua zhengce de bianhua (Hedging strategy: Japan's changing policy towards China in the new situation)," *Zhanlve juece yanjiu* (*Journal of Strategy and Decision-Making*), 1,ꞏ 43–62 (2019); Xiaqin Bao and Bei Huang, "Riben nanhai zhengce zhong de duichong zhanlve jiqi pinggu: yi anbei neige de duihua zhengce wei shijiao (Assessing the hedging strategy in Japan's South China Sea policy: A perspective of the Abe administration's China policy)," *Riben xuekan* (*Japanese Studies*), 3, 42–64 (2017); Guangtao Wang and Jiaru Yu, "Shenfen kunjing yu duichong de kuozhan: zhongmei zhanlve jingzheng xia

riben duihua zhengce de xin dongxiang (The dilemma of identity and the extension of hedging: The new trend of Japan's China policy under the strategic competition between China and the US)," *Bianjie yu haiyang yanjiu* (*Journal of Boundary and Ocean Studies*), 6(4), 73–90 (2021).

40 Gui (2020), *Op. cit.*

41 Lan Gao and Lijuan Zhao, "Zhongmei jiafeng zhong de riben disanfang liliang waijiao zhengce fenxi (An analysis of Japan's foreign policy as a "third-party power" between China and the United States)," *Riben xuekan* (*Japanese Studies*), 6, 22–45 (2020).

42 Liang Cai, "Duo weidu duichong yu jianrongxing jingzheng: yintai gouxiang xia riben de duihua zhanlve pouxi (The multidimensional hedging and compatibility competition: An analysis of Japan's strategy towards China under the "Indo-Pacific vision")," *Riben xuekan* (*Japanese Studies*), 2, 22 (2021).

43 Hao Lu, "Riben waijiao yu yintai gouxiang: jiyu guoji gonggong chanpin jiaodu de fenxi (Japan's diplomacy and Indo-Pacific vision: An analysis from the perspective of international public goods)," *Riben xuekan* (*Japanese Studies*), 6, 22 (2019).

44 Yi Sun, "Jingzheng zhe de hezuo: zhongri jiaqiang jingji waijiao hezuo de yuanyin yu keneng (Cooperation between competitors: The reasons and possibility for China and Japan to cooperate in economic diplomacy)," *Riben xuekan* (*Japanese Studies*), 4, 44–65 (2019); Lili Gong, "Zhongri disanfang shichang hezuo: jiyu, tiaozhan yu yingdui fanglve (Sino-Japan cooperation on third-party market development: Chances, challenges and strategies)," *Xiandai riben jingji* (*Contemporary Economy of Japan*), 5, 44–54 (2019); Jingchao Wang, "Zhongri disanfang shichang hezuo: riben de kaoliang yu zuli (Third-party market cooperation between China and Japan: Strategic considerations and resistances in Japan)," *Guojiwentiyanjiu* (*International Studies*), 3, 81–93 (2019).

45 Yan Zhu, "Disanfang shichang hezuo: zhongri de renzhi chayi jiqi yingxiang (Third-party market cooperation: Cognitive differences between China and Japan and its impact)," *Zhongguo guoji zhanlve pinglun* (*China International Strategy Review*), 1, 115 (2020).

46 Wang (2020), *Op. cit.*, pp. 108–109.

47 There are few explicit arguments for Beijing to have its own counter version of the Indo-Pacific strategy. See D. Scott, "China's Indo-Pacific strategy: The problems of success," *The Journal of Territorial and Maritime Studies*, 6(2), 94–113 (2019); Tengfei Ge, "Yintai diqu anquan zhixu fenzheng yu zhongguo de diqu zhixu yuanjing (Disputes on Indo-Pacific regional security order and China's vision)," *Waijiaopinglun* (*Foreign Affairs Review*), 3, 73–100 (2021).

48 Gong (2020), *Op. cit.*, p. 43.

The Japan's "Free and Open Indo-Pacific" and Sino–Japanese Relations   175

49 Ministry of Foreign Affairs of the People's Republic of China (MFA), 9 March 2018. https://www.mfa.gov.cn/ce/ceom//eng/zgyw/t1540928.htm.
50 Wang Yi: The U.S. Indo-Pacific strategy is bound to be a failed strategy. MFA. https://www.fmprc.gov.cn/mfa_eng/zxxx_662805/202205/t20220523_10691136.html.
51 Ma (2020), *Op. cit.*, p. 181.
52 Regular Press Conferences, MFA. https://www.fmprc.gov.cn/mfa_eng/xwfw_665399/s2510_665401/2511_665403/.
53 Foreign Ministry Spokesperson Geng Shuang's Regular Press Conference on 13 November 2017, MFA. https://www.fmprc.gov.cn/mfa_eng/xwfw_665399/s2510_665401/t1510216.shtml.
54 Foreign Ministry Spokesperson Geng Shuang's Regular Press Conference on 3 June 2019, MFA. https://www.mfa.gov.cn/ce/cedk/eng/fyrth/t1669120.htm.
55 Foreign Ministry Spokesperson Wang Wenbin's Regular Press Conference on 21 September 2020, MFA. https://www.fmprc.gov.cn/mfa_eng/xwfw_665399/s2510_665401/2511_665403/202009/t20200921_693391.html.
56 MFA. https://www.fmprc.gov.cn/nanhai/eng/fyrbt_1/t1849185.htm.
57 Foreign Ministry Spokesperson Zhao Lijian's Regular Press Conference on 13 July 2021, MFA. https://www.fmprc.gov.cn/mfa_eng/xwfw_665399/s2510_665401/2511_665403/202107/t20210713_9170784.html.
58 Cai (2021), *Op. cit.*, p. 21.
59 See Ye (2020), *Op. cit.*
60 Rumi Aoyama, *Op. cit.*

© 2025 World Scientific Publishing Europe Ltd.
https://doi.org/10.1142/9781800616318_0008

Chapter 7

Stability and Fragility in Japan–China Relations: China's Pivotal Power and Japan's Strategic Leverage[*]

Rumi Aoyama

Waseda University, Japan

Japan's foreign policy toward China has generally been successful in handling the delicate balance between the United States (U.S.) and China. Yet, closer analysis shows that Japan's China policy is no weaker than Australia's on issues such as the South China Sea, human rights, and policies on Taiwan. This therefore raises two questions. First, why haven't relations between Japan and China soured as much as those between China and other countries that have challenged China's core interests? And second, why is the Japan–China relationship a stable but fragile one? By modifying the standard strategic triangle model, this chapter argues that China is pivotal in determining the balance of power in the strategic triangle made up of the U.S., Japan, and China. At the same time, the asymmetry of threat perceptions—Japan perceives China as its most significant security concern, while China perceives its

---

[*]This chapter was originally printed as "Stability and Fragility in Japan-China Relations: China's Pivotal Power and Japan's Strategic Leverage." *The China Review*, Vol. 23, No. 1 (2023): 187–211. https://www.jstor.org/stable/48717993. Reproduced with kind permission of CUHK Press.

greatest security threat as emanating from the U.S.—gives Japan strategic leverage over China. As a result of China's strategic policies and these asymmetric threat perceptions, relations between Japan and China are ostensibly stable but substantially fragile.

Relations between Japan and China since the late 1990s have often been described as embodying "cold politics and hot economics," which might be characterized as a relationship of "cooperative rivalry" (see Introduction). The bilateral relations hit one of their lowest points in 2012, when Japan decided to normalize the status of a chain of disputed islands in the East China Sea, known as the Senkaku Islands in Japan and the Diaoyu Islands in China. The frosty political relationship only began to thaw in 2014, when the two countries' top leaders met on the sidelines of the Asia-Pacific Economic Cooperation (APEC) Summit in Beijing. In contrast, the economic relationship between the two countries (see Figure 7.1) has been extremely vibrant, despite the ebb and flow of their political ties. Hence, the bilateral relationship between Japan and China can be described as both stable and fragile at the same time. That is, neither country has taken coercive measures such as economic sanctions or the mobilization of a national campaign against the other, and economic relations and people-to-people contacts between the two countries

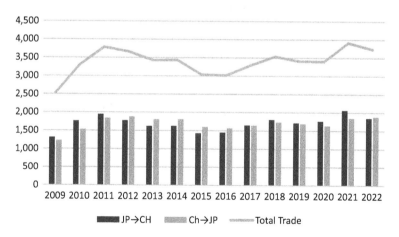

Figure 7.1. Japan–China trade, 2009–2022 (unit: billion US$).
Source: Japan External Trade Organization.

continue to be stable. However, bilateral relations are fraught with tensions due to deep-rooted security mistrust, accompanied by occasional diplomatic protests, and the possibility of disruptions in economic exchanges and people-to-people contacts is ever present.

Japan's foreign policy toward China has generally been successful in handling the delicate balance between the United States (U.S.) and China. Some argue that Japan's reluctance to adopt an overly assertive approach toward China has contributed to the relatively stable economic relationship. In this sense, U.S. President Joe Biden's containment policy *vis-à-vis* China places Japan in a difficult position. Yet, closer analysis shows that Japan's China policy is no weaker than that of other Western countries on issues such as the South China Sea, human rights, and policies on Taiwan. Indeed, since 2010, Japan has consistently challenged China's core interests by holding military exercises in the South China Sea or taking the lead in issuing international statements condemning China's Hong Kong policy.

This therefore raises two questions. First, why haven't relations between Japan and China soured as much as those between China and other countries that have challenged China's core interests? And second, why is the Japan–China relationship a stable but fragile one? By modifying the standard strategic triangle model, this chapter argues that China is pivotal in determining the balance of power in the strategic triangle made up of the U.S., Japan, and China. At the same time, the asymmetry of threat perceptions—Japan perceives China as its most significant security concern, while China perceives its greatest security threat as emanating from the U.S.—gives Japan strategic leverage over China. As a result of China's strategic policies and these asymmetric threat perceptions, relations between Japan and China are ostensibly stable but substantially fragile.

The chapter proceeds as follows. Section 7.1 explains the challenges presented by the strategic triangle theory with regard to explaining Japan's strategic leverage when it comes to relations between China, the U.S., and Japan. Section 7.2 looks into the asymmetric threat perceptions in Japan–China relations. Sections 7.3 and 7.4 examine Japan's policy toward China and China's policy toward Japan, respectively. Section 7.5 explains the nature of the stability and fragility in Japan–China relations brought about by the two countries' asymmetric threat perceptions. Section 7.6 offers some concluding remarks.

7.1. The Conundrum of Japan–China Relations

A number of studies suggest that one explanation for the "cold politics and hot economics" phenomenon lies in Japan's "non-provocative" foreign policy stance toward China. The prevailing view is that Japan is adopting a hedging policy toward China: on the one hand, Japan is strengthening its military alliance with the U.S., while on the other, it is striving to maintain good relations with China for the sake of its economic interests.

Some scholars further argue that the vision of a "Free and Open Indo-Pacific" (FOIP), promoted by both the U.S. and Japanese governments, is not necessarily designed to contain the rise of China.[1] According to this view, the Biden administration's China policy of enhancing military deterrence and promoting the economic decoupling of strategic assets poses a significant challenge to Japan. Other scholars, in contrast—approaching the subject mainly from the perspective of realist theory—contend that Japan is trying to balance against the rise of China.[2] For example, John Mearsheimer, a leading skeptic of China's "peaceful rise," has long argued that Japan will ultimately join U.S. efforts to contain China.[3]

Yet, these two explanations—that Japan's policy toward China is one of either hedging or balancing—do not fully explain the current politically tense but stable relationship between the two countries.

The relationship between Japan and China has never been solely a two-state relationship. Japan, China, and the U.S. are all engaged in a strategic triangle according to the following criteria, as defined by Lowell Dittmer: (a) the bilateral relationship among any two of these actors is contingent on their relationship with the third; and (b) each actor actively

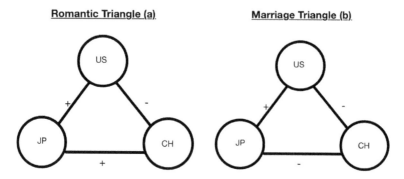

Figure 7.2. Lowell Dittmer's strategic triangle model.

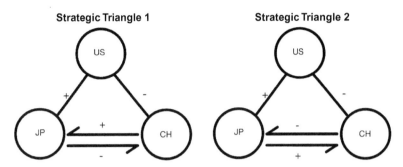

Figure 7.3. The strategic triangle model accounting for Japan challenging China's interests.

seeks to engage one or the other or both to forestall its defection or hostile collusion and advance its own interests.[4]

Hence, from the perspective of the strategic triangle theory,[5] the hedging explanation is based on the premise that Japan, China, and the U.S. are engaged in a "romantic triangle,"[6] in which Japan is actively befriending both the U.S. and China while the U.S. and China confront each other (Figure 7.2(a)). However, this view ignores the fact that Japan is challenging China's core interests—hence the fragility of the bilateral relationship.

The balancing explanation, on the other hand, is based on the premise that Japan, China, and the U.S. are engaged in a "marriage triangle," in which the U.S. and Japan are united in confronting China (Figure 7.2(b)). In this scenario, Japan has the leverage to pivot the triangle. However, this emphasis on Japan and the U.S. standing together against China does not provide a sound rationale for the stability of their bilateral relations either.

The strategic triangle theory does not accurately explain the current relationship between the U.S., Japan, and China because it assumes that when two states are in a bilateral relationship together, they will hold the same attitude toward each other, either friendly or hostile. But this is not the case with regard to relations between these three countries (see Figure 7.3).

Since the late 1990s, the bilateral alliance between Japan and the U.S. has formed the cornerstone of Japan's defense strategy and U.S. security policy in the Asia-Pacific region (+).[7] As discussed below, Japan has long regarded China as its most significant security threat. Indeed, as far as Japan is concerned, the thaw in relations with China has not brought about any change in China's coercive behavior *vis-à-vis* the Senkaku/Diaoyu Islands.

Against this backdrop, Japan's strategic choice has been simply to strengthen its ties with the U.S. and other like-minded countries—even though it had serious concerns about the U.S.' commitment to defend it under the Trump administration (2016–2020). At the same time, since the announcement of President Barack Obama's new Asia policy in 2012, with its strategic "pivot to Asia," bilateral relations between China and the U.S. have been in decline and moving toward confrontation (−).

When it comes to relations between Japan and China, however, friendship and hostility are not mutual. There are two possible triangular models to show the relationship between the U.S., Japan, and China: in one, Japan adopts a hostile policy toward China, while China is friendly to Japan (Strategic Triangle 1 in Figure 7.3); in the other, Japan adopts a friendly attitude toward China, while China is hostile to Japan (Strategic Triangle 2 in Figure 7.3).

The scenario illustrated by Triangle 1 is consistent with how Japan–China relations have been since the 2000s. Because of the power asymmetry between Japan and China, Japan considers China to be its number one security threat, while China's most significant security concern is the U.S. Due to this asymmetric threat perception, China is likely to take a friendly stance toward Japan, while Japan adopts a hostile attitude toward China.

What we see with this strategic triangle is the decisive influence that China's own policy has on its overall nature. We see the same thing even in other multilateral relationships. Take the example of the U.S., Australia, and China. It may be true that, from China's perspective, Australia has adopted a more hostile policy towards China (see Chapter 8), but it is China's hostile policy toward Australia that has turned this strategic triangle into a "marriage triangle." Conversely, China's accommodating attitude toward Japan has made the U.S.–Japan–China strategic triangle ostensibly a "romantic triangle."

It is also worth noting that the asymmetric threat perception between Japan and China in Strategic Triangle 1 gives Japan a lot of room for policy maneuvering. The relationship between Japan and China appears to be stable on the surface, as China continues to benefit on Japan despite the latter's hostility to China. However, this stability is undoubtedly very fragile, as the negative elements (Japan's China policy) offsets the positives (China's Japan policy), essentially canceling each other out.

7.2. Asymmetric Threat Perceptions between Japan and China

Since the mid-1990s, political distrust between Japan and China has increased, security tensions have worsened, and both countries currently view each other as a significant security threat. Nevertheless, the two countries' perceptions of threat are not symmetrical.

7.2.1. *Japan's biggest security concern: China*

Japan's concerns over China's military expansion have increased sharply in recent years, especially since the 2010 collision between a Chinese trawler and a Japanese Coast Guard vessel in the East China Sea close to the Senkaku/Diaoyu Islands (which are claimed by both countries). The second crisis occurred in September 2012 when Japan moved to formally incorporate the disputed islands within its national territory, despite China's objections. As far as Japan is concerned, China's assertive move since 2010 represent a coordinated move orchestrated from the highest political levels to challenge and change the status quo in the disputed waters.[8] In a further step, in November 2013, China established an Air Defense Identification Zone (ADIZ) in the East China Sea that overlaps with Japan's administrative control area. This has further sounded the alarm about China's aggressive intentions *vis-à-vis* Japanese territory.

Consequently, in 2023, for the first time in 11 years, the Japanese government increased its defense budget to 4.68 trillion yen (US$51.7 billion), an increase of 0.8 percent on the previous year. According to Japan's Ministry of Defense, the increased expenditure was to be used to "strengthen the defense of its territories, territorial waters and airspace as China's intrusions into Japan's territorial waters and violations of its airspace have increased."[9]

Repeated Chinese incursions into the waters around the Senkaku/Diaoyu Islands since 2012 have further cemented the perception that China is Japan's greatest security concern. In the Japanese government's *2018 National Defense Program Guidelines*, for the first time, China's increased military power was addressed as an issue of greater concern than nuclear-armed North Korea. In the *2020 Defense White Paper*, two years later, China was mentioned 994 times.[10] In addition, a draft cybersecurity strategy adopted by the Japanese government on 27 September 2021 identified, for the first time, China (along with Russia and North Korea) as presenting a threat to Japan's cybersecurity and accused the Chinese of stealing information from military and high-tech companies.[11]

The academic community widely shares these official security concerns. In September 2018, the Sasakawa Peace Foundation released a report entitled *Proposals for Achieving Positive Pacifism I: Strengthening the Defense System to Protect Japan*. According to this report, Japan's security legislation passed in 2015 represents a significant step forward in enabling Japan to effectively defend its territory and engage in active regional security cooperation by eliminating "excessive legal restrictions,"[12] although it also emphasizes that current legislation remains inadequate. In order to cope with China's gray zone operations (i.e., non-military actions which seek to gain advantage without provoking a conventional military response) around the Senkaku/Diaoyu Islands and the expansion of the People's Liberation Army and Navy (PLAN) as well as the Chinese Coast Guard Bureau, further legislative changes are needed.

The PHP Institute, a policy think tank, published a report in October 2018 entitled *Crisis and Revival of the Liberal International Order*. Akihiko Tanaka, president of the National Graduate Institute for Policy Studies, explicitly noted in the report that "an authoritarian China that beefs up its military power poses a threat to Japan, and a China that exports its model to the world poses a threat to liberal democracies."[13] It appears, therefore, that ideological differences have become a substantial obstacle to cooperation between the two countries. Ryoichi Oriki, another scholar involved in the research project, who is also a special advisor to the National Security Secretariat (NSS) of Japan, argues that Japan's security environment has deteriorated dramatically since 2010 because the Korean Peninsula, Taiwan, the South China Sea, and the Senkaku/Diaoyu Islands are no longer isolated, instead becoming interrelated security issues.[14]

In December 2018, the Nakasone Peace Institute also published a China-related report to commemorate its 30th anniversary. Shinichi Kitaoka, the president of the Japan International Cooperation Agency, opened the report by stating that Japan's "greatest diplomatic and security concern is China's expansion" because the country's disrespect for the rule of law threatens a free and open international order.[15] He went on to suggest that the improvement in relations between Japan and China is only temporary and that, in order to maintain stable ties with China, Japan needs to strengthen its defense capability. In his view, "China's criticism of Japan's defense build-up should not be of much concern" because "Japan's military might no longer poses a threat to China."[16] The project's security team recommended that Japan acquire the capability to strike on enemy territory when under attack, enhance its security cooperation with other "Quad" nations (officially, the Quadrilateral Security Dialogue, an informal security alliance between Japan, India, Australia, and the U.S.), and establish an Organization for Maritime Security in East Asia (OMSEA) that would include China.

All three China-related reports, released virtually simultaneously by major think tanks, reflect Japan's strong security concerns about China's military build-up. Hence, in contrast to government documents that refer to China as a security "concern," Japanese scholars have been outspoken about seeing China as a security threat. This perception of the China threat revolves around both ideology and security. Nonetheless, despite the variation in perception, these prominent think tanks largely support the government's stance by advocating a strengthening of Japan's security defenses, calling for cooperation with like-minded countries, and urging further legislative reforms of security policy so as to remove legal restrictions on future action.

Of course, there is no shortage of voices in Japan that oppose the enhancement of Japan's military capability through legal reforms. However, in the face of China's continued intrusions into the disputed waters around the Senkaku/Diaoyu Islands, such voices seem increasingly unrealistic and out of step with the mainstream.

7.2.2. *China's security concerns vis-à-vis Japan*

Increasingly in recent years, China has been expressing its concerns about Japan's growing military might. In particular, China's criticisms of Japan's domestic legal security-related reforms and the strengthening of its military power have become quite specific and explicit following Japan's annexation of the Senkaku/Diaoyu Islands in 2012.

China's 2015 military white paper, *China's Military Strategy*, notes that China faces "multiple and complex security threats."[17] Among these, special mention is made of the U.S.' rebalancing strategy in the region, "the interventions of external states" in maritime disputes, the challenges to China's sovereignty by "some neighboring countries," and the sea surveillance and reconnaissance against China by "a tiny" number of countries.

In the same context, Japan is criticized for "sparing no effort to dodge the post-war mechanism" and for "overhauling its military and security policies."

China's 2019 military white paper, *China's National Defense in the New Era*, continues along the same basic lines as the 2015 version. It criticizes the U.S. for strengthening its security alliances in the region and deploying the Terminal High Altitude Area Defense (THAAD) system in South Korea. Australia's move to strengthen its security ties with the U.S. and enlarge its security role in the Asia-Pacific region has also raised concerns in China. Regarding Japan, the 2019 white paper points out that Japan's military endeavors are becoming more outward-looking and working to "circumvent the postwar mechanism."[18]

The perception of Japan as an outward-looking military power trying to break away from the post-war system, as expressed in the 2015 and 2019 white papers, comes in stark contrast to the opinions of previous policy papers. Up until 2010, China's biennial defense white papers consistently spoke highly of the military cooperation between Japan and China. Despite China's concerns about strengthening Japanese–American military relations, missile defense cooperation between Japan and the U.S., or Japan's moves to introduce constitutional amendments, China did not continually criticize Japan in the past. For example, the 2002, 2008, and 2010 white papers—published when Japan and China were still in a warm embrace—did not specifically mention Japan's military posture.

China's current security concerns *vis-à-vis* Japan mainly revolve around the following four issues: (1) Japan's evolution into an outward-looking major military power[19]; (2) the integration of Japan's military forces with those of the U.S.; (3) Japan's activities in the South China Sea; and (4) its relations with Taiwan.

Turning to the first of these, in China's eyes, the six pacifist principles adopted by Japan after the Second World War effectively set a ceiling on its military development and prevented it from becoming a major military power. These were: the Three Principles on Arms Exports[20]; the Three Non-Nuclear Principles; the Basic Policy for National Defense; the right to exercise collective self-defense; the adoption of a defense-only military policy; and the country's pacifist constitution.[21]

Under the second Abe administration (2012–2020), the restrictions on arms exports were relaxed in April 2014. The new law of Three Principles on the Transfer of Defense Equipment and Technology allows for the transfer of defense equipment as long as the receiving country is not a party to any conflict and the transfer does not violate UN Security Council resolutions. This relaxation has paved the way for international joint development and the provision of military equipment to other countries.

The *Basic Policy for National Defense* was renamed the *National Strategy Paper* in 2013. The first *National Strategy Paper*, approved by the government in December 2013, sets out a new principle of "positive pacifism." In a similar vein, two new pieces of security-related legislation were passed by the government in 2015—Legislation for the Development of Peace and Security Laws and the International Peace Support Law— which allow Japan's Self-Defense Forces (SDF) to exercise the right to collective self-defense in the event of an "existential threat" to Japan.

In sum, alongside the discussion around revising Japan's post-war constitution, China regards the recent series of Japanese actions as signaling a transition to normal military power.[22]

China's second security concern relates to Japan's plans to integrate its military forces with those of the U.S. and the possible formation of an "Asian NATO." Japan and the U.S. updated the Guidelines for Japan–U.S. Defense Cooperation in 2015, for the first time in 18 years. In addition, Japan has made efforts to promote security cooperation with Western democracies and Southeast and South Asian countries. Multinational security dialogues between Japan, Australia and India; Japan, the U.S. and Australia; and Japan, Vietnam and the Philippines have also been established under Japan's leadership.

China views these security dialogues as a U.S.–Japanese initiative to build an Asian version of NATO to contain China within its first island chain.[23] The *PLA Daily* (the official newspaper of the People's Liberation Army) has also expressed concern that Japan's position in the U.S.–Japan security alliance is transitioning from providing logistical support to a more central role of containing China.[24] In addition, China is carefully watching to see whether Japan will host the U.S.' new intermediate-range missiles or join the "Five Eyes" intelligence alliance (which currently comprises Australia, Canada, New Zealand, the United Kingdom, and the U.S.).

Third, China is deeply concerned by the joint military exercises Japan has been conducting with countries such as the Philippines, Australia, and the U.S. in the South China Sea. As China sees it, such moves represent an attempt by Japan to become a military power, promote constitutional reform, and constrain China.[25]

Finally, with regard to Japan's policy *vis-à-vis* Taiwan, some scholars in China have long argued that Japan's maritime security strategy is aimed at bringing Taiwan under its control and preventing Chinese unification.[26]

188 R. Aoyama

Others were generally optimistic that closer ties between Japan and Taiwan would mostly center on economic relations, with no significant change on the political front.[27] Since about 2014, however, the mood among Chinese scholars has changed considerably. An article published in 2014 in *World Affairs* (a magazine affiliated with the Chinese Foreign Ministry) sounded the alarm about the possibility of Japan producing its own version of the Taiwan Relations Act.[28] It has now become mainstream to criticize Japan's double-standard stance of maintaining good relations with both China and Taiwan and to call for vigilance over Japan's moves to strengthen its ties with Taiwan.[29]

Ever since Japan moved to claim the disputed Senkaku/Diaoyu Islands in 2012, China's security concerns over Japan's increasing military power have intensified. China is particularly wary of the Biden administration—and the potential establishment of an Asian NATO—as well as the lively development of various alliances, such as the Quad and AUKUS (Australia, the United Kingdom, and the U.S.), and especially Japan's growing military role in them.

Consequently, China feels that it is encircled by NATO's eastward expansion and the U.S.' network of security alliances in Asia. Against this backdrop, the security concern presented by Japan arises mainly from its security relations with the U.S. This is why one Chinese Foreign Ministry spokesman publicly criticized Japan for "willingly being directed by the United States and acting as a strategic vassal of the United States."[30]

7.3. A Free and Open Indo-Pacific

In August 2016, Japan's Prime Minister Shinzo Abe proposed the strategy of FOIP at the Sixth Tokyo International Conference on African Development (TICADVI). This initiative calls for a free and open maritime order based on the rule of law in the Indo-Pacific region, which connects Asia and Africa through the Pacific and Indian oceans. During his visit to Japan in November 2017, American President Donald Trump expressed support for Japan's Indo-Pacific initiative, paving the way for close cooperation on FOIP between the two countries.

At its core, the FOIP initiative is a balancing strategy against China which is based on the "Democratic Security Diamond (DSD)" concept announced by Prime Minister Abe in December 2012.[31] The key premise behind the DSD is to counter China's coercive actions in the East and

South China Seas by establishing a diamond-shaped security arrangement with Australia, India, and Hawaii (as well as cooperating closely with the U.K. and France) so as to prevent the South China Sea from turning into China's "Lake Beijing."

The Abe administration pursued two major foreign strategies.[32] One of these was its ambition to achieve a strategic balance with China on a global scale, while the other was the promotion of a liberal economic order in Asia. It is clear that the FOIP initiative plays a significant role in fulfilling both security objectives.

As Japan's security concerns *vis-à-vis* China continue to grow, it is no longer worried about being drawn into a U.S.-led war. Rather, anxieties have grown over whether the U.S. will actually commit to Japan's defense. Former Japanese Defense Minister Itsunori Onodera explicitly stated that "it is no longer a question of being entrapped in a war of the United States, but a new security phase for Japan in which Japan promotes U.S. cooperation to defend its territory."[33]

Driven by the fear of being abandoned, Japan is adopting multiple hedging strategies. For example, the government is pursuing legal reforms, enhancing its military capabilities, and strengthening its security alliance with the U.S. At the same time, Japan is promoting its security cooperation with countries that "share its values" across a wide geographic range, from Southeast and South Asia to the Pacific Islands, the Middle East, Africa, and Latin America. As a priority, Tokyo is targeting the Quad nations, New Zealand, Canada, the U.K., and France. At the same time, a new alliance called the "Quad+" is taking shape, with countries such as France and the U.K. joining the Quad military exercises and Germany, the U.K., and France sending warships to the South China Sea.

Norms, rules, and global standards are the substantive concepts which underpin Japan's economic policy toward China. Japan has been playing a leading role in promoting the conclusion of two major free trade agreements (FTAs) in the region: the Comprehensive and Progressive Agreement for Trans-Pacific Partnership (CPTPP) and the Regional Comprehensive Economic Partnership (RCEP). While the CPTPP is not specifically designed to exclude China, Japan is betting that without China as a member, the CPTPP could develop into a political vehicle for regional collaboration. As Japan's current prime minister, Fumio Kishida, once made clear in an interview, "the CPTPP is not a mere economic agreement, but an agreement with strategic value."[34] In the view of Japan, the CPTPP will eventually take on major political significance in the future through regular summit meetings.

Economic security is becoming more and more important to Japan's national security strategy. Securing resources and energy, enhancing food security, and diversifying and strengthening the supply chain with like-minded countries are among Japan's top priorities. With "building strategic independence and indispensability" positioned as a core objective of the economic security strategy, Japan's economic dependence on China for its strategic assets may be significantly reduced.

Promoting cooperation in cyberspace and space exploration, developing cutting-edge technologies, and strengthening data security are also vital aspects of Japan's national security strategy. To prevent defense and cutting-edge technology data from leaking overseas, Japan is drafting a series of cybersecurity laws that will impose stricter screening measures on international students and researchers. Recognizing the importance of establishing a mechanism whereby information is only shared among countries that adhere to international standards, Japan believes it can help bring the U.S. and Europe closer together.

As Japan's foreign policy centers on balancing against China, this means that Japan is increasingly challenging China's "core national interests" in the South China Sea and Taiwan. In fact, the East and South China Seas have become twin concepts in Japan's security thinking. Admiral Katsutoshi Kawano, a former top uniformed officer in the SDF, believes that "China is now trying to dominate the waters within the first island chain. Since Hong Kong, Taiwan, and the Senkaku/Diaoyu Islands are obstacles, China's policies on these three issues are interlinked."[35] As the rhetoric claiming that "Taiwan is the most dangerous place on earth" becomes more intense, former Prime Minister Abe declared that "Taiwan's emergency is Japan's emergency."[36]

As part of its strategy to counter China's coercive actions in the East China Sea, Japan has rejected most of China's maritime claims in the South China Sea, arguing that China's claims to historical rights are illegal and calling on China to comply with the 2016 arbitral ruling of the international tribunal in the Hague, which declared large areas of the sea to be neutral international waters or the exclusive economic zones of other countries.[37] In a further move, Japan sent a submarine to the South China Sea in 2018.

Cooperation between Japan and Taiwan is also expanding. In February 2021, the Foreign Affairs sub-committee of the ruling Liberal

Democratic Party (LDP) set up two new project teams: the Taiwan Project Team and the Human Rights Diplomacy Project Team. The purpose of the former is to discuss security, economic relations, and cultural exchange between Japan and Taiwan, while the latter focuses on China's crackdown on the Uyghurs in Xinjiang and the situation in Hong Kong. The ruling parties in each country—the LDP in Japan and the Democratic Progressive Party (DPP) in Taiwan—launched dialogues on the two countries' defense and foreign policy (party-to-party talks equivalent to formal 2+2 talks), with the first meeting held on 28 August 2021. Tokyo also joined the Global Cooperation and Training Framework (GCTF) a month later, which is a platform established by the U.S. and Taiwan in 2015 to "expand Taiwan's international engagement."

The present situation is such that security and democratic values have become a quintessential source of confrontation between Japan and China. With over 30,000 Japanese companies operating in China, Japan needs to maintain political harmony to ensure that its economic interests in China are not affected. In this regard, Japan has been treading a cautious path, avoiding specific mentions of China when discussing its foreign policy. However, as support for protecting fundamental democratic values and the rule of law grows among politicians and the public, Japan's balancing strategy toward China—or at best, its policy of "confrontation for cooperation"—is unlikely to change.

7.4. China's Belt and Road

The Belt and Road Initiative (BRI) is a signature foreign policy initiative launched by the Xi Jinping administration in 2013. It is a strategy to connect China with vast regions of Asia, Europe, Africa, the Arab world, and the Pacific island countries via land and sea. President Xi proposed the Silk Road Economic Belt Initiative (the land element) in Kazakhstan in September 2013 and the Maritime Silk Road Initiative in Indonesia in October 2013.

Since taking office in 2013, Xi Jinping has intensified China's strategic competition on every front. With China and the U.S. competing for global security, economic, technological, and ideological dominance, Asia has become the key battleground for this contest. In October 2013, President Xi hosted a two-day foreign affairs meeting that emphasized the importance of improving relations with neighboring countries.[38]

Thus, Japan, as an important neighboring country, has become an essential partner in promoting the BRI. Despite Japan's nationalization of the Senkaku/Diaoyu Islands, China softened its critical attitude, and the bilateral political relationship began to thaw at the end of 2014.[39]

At the 19th National Congress of the Communist Party of China (CPC) in October 2017, Xi Jinping mapped out China's grand goals in the run-up to the centenary of the founding of the People's Republic of China in 2049. Covering 15 years from 2020 to 2035, the first stage aims to achieve shared wealth throughout the nation by significantly narrowing the urban–rural gap in living standards. Over the longer term, the country aspires to become a global leader in terms of national strength and international influence as it approaches the mid-21st century. "Made in China 2025" and the 14th Five-Year Plan both play an essential role in ushering in the new era.

China is increasingly adopting a confrontational stance *vis-à-vis* the U.S. as a result of its perception of the changing international order. The prevailing view in China is that the future global order is moving toward a bipolar system dominated by the U.S. and China. Yan Xuetong, a well-known international relations scholar, argues that in 10 years' time, we will live in a world where these two superpowers constantly compete with each other because the gross domestic product (GDP) of any other country will be less than one-half or one-quarter of that of the U.S. or China, respectively.[40] As a result, many in China now believe that China's rising national power makes strategic competition and a major confrontation with the U.S. at some point inevitable.

Consequently, China's foreign policy and its stance toward the U.S. have become increasingly assertive. A few days after the beginning of the transition process to the new Biden administration was announced, Fu Ying, vice-chair of the Foreign Affairs Committee of China's National People's Congress, wrote an article in *The New York Times*. In the article, she called on the two countries to develop a relationship of "coopetition" (i.e., cooperation and competition). Although this sounds like a positive concept, if we examine internal Chinese reports, it becomes clear that the relationship between China and the U.S. is largely confrontational, that the idea of "competition" equates to "struggle," and that China intends to fight hard against the U.S. while hoping to avoid severing the bilateral relationship.

Stability and Fragility in Japan–China Relations 193

President Xi Jinping has been emphasizing "struggle" on every front in recent years. In a speech at the Party School of the CPC in September 2019, he referred to "struggle" 58 times.[41] With the combination of "cooperation and competition" being advocated as a major feature of Xi's diplomatic thinking, this spirit of struggle has also been incorporated into China's stance on foreign affairs.

China is confident in its future economic growth and believes that time is on its side. In November 2020, the Fifth Plenary Session of the 19th CPC Central Committee set the goal of reaching the level of a moderately developed country in terms of GDP per capita by 2035—15 years ahead of Deng Xiaoping's original timetable. Nevertheless, in the short term, China still faces the risk of being "strangled" by the U.S. in the fields of science and technology. To get itself out of this predicament, the Chinese government has emphasized the importance of economic security and, particularly, the "self-reliance and self-sufficiency" of Chinese science and technology. In the meantime, strengthening economic links with global markets remains an essential element of China's national vision—what is known as the "Dual Circulation" strategy. Establishing stable global supply and value chains, promoting FTAs, and creating digital economy zones through financial cooperation and e-commerce are key objectives of this strategy.

In this context, the strategic importance of the Asia-Pacific region to China's foreign policy has further increased. In China's eyes, the Asia-Pacific will play an increasingly important role as an engine of world economic growth, meaning that the competition for supremacy in this region will become more intense in the future. Furthermore, it is widely believed in China that the Asia-Pacific will become a third free trade area—alongside the Americas/Europe and Central Asia—in the wake of the U.S. and China's strategic rivalry and the COVID-19 pandemic. This is why China pushed to establish the APEC organization and is currently applying to join the CPTPP.

China is making every effort to improve its political and economic ties with other countries in the Asia-Pacific. However, there is a wide divergence of opinion within China concerning relations with Japan. While the vast majority of scholars believe that these should be stabilized, some believe that China should not invest significant diplomatic resources toward improving Japan–China relations. Surrounded by such intense disagreement, Beijing focuses primarily on making sure its relations with Tokyo do not deteriorate (see Chapter 6).

7.5. Relations between Japan and China: Stable but Fragile

In reality, both China and Japan have tried to warm up their political relations since the sudden chill brought about by the Senkaku/Diaoyu Islands dispute in 2012. In November of that year, the first China–Japan summit meeting since the start of the second Abe administration was held on the sidelines of the APEC Summit in Beijing. Premier Li Keqiang later visited Japan in May 2018, and Prime Minister Abe's visit to China in October of the same year further accelerated the thawing of relations between the two countries. They pledged to cooperate on a wide range of issues, including macroeconomics and finance, energy saving and the environment, aging populations, tourism, and disaster prevention.[42]

Perhaps the most symbolic development was the announcement by Prime Minister Abe of Japan's participation in the BRI. As part of Prime Minister Abe's visit to China in October 2018, the two countries signed 52 memoranda of understanding (MOUs) on economic cooperation with the private sector in third countries involved in the BRI. Although Japan's participation is conditional, both governments have spoken glowingly of Japan's involvement and described their bilateral relationship as transitioning "from competition to cooperation."[43] Nonetheless, even as progress was being made to improve their relations, Japan strongly denounced China's "unilateral action to change the status quo in the East China Sea and the South China Sea."[44]

The improvements in Japan–China relations have come about mainly due to a change in China's policy stance. China's official view of Japan since the 1990s has been that "Japan is experiencing an upsurge of nationalism and is flooded with right-wing ideas." However, an abrupt change of tack on China's part was witnessed after President Xi assumed office in March 2013. In order to boost bilateral ties, China adopted a low-key attitude *vis-à-vis* Japan's proactivity, such as the strengthening of its security ties with the U.S. or the conducting of joint military exercises in the South China Sea.[45]

Given that stability in relations with China has also been a key priority of the Abe administration, bilateral relations appear to be stable. However, they remain extremely fragile because neither China nor Japan have actually changed any of their security policies or behaviors. Indeed, despite the improvement in political relations, the thaw has failed to ease confrontation at the security level. And even though China's and Japan's top leaders have reached agreements on several crucial confidence-building measures (CBMs), such as an Air–Sea Contact Mechanism and a hotline between their respective defense agencies, none of these have yet materialized.

China's assertive actions in the waters around the Senkaku/Diaoyu Islands—particularly its gray zone operations—represent a major security concern for Japan and have prompted its military build-up and balancing policy *vis-à-vis* China. From Japan's perspective, China's military expansion is carried out through joint operations among its army, navy, and coast guard, whereby "China's Coast Guard Bureau and maritime militia operate at the forefront, with China's Navy in the back, forcing foreign countries to negotiate on China's terms."[46] Consequently, in the eyes of Japan, this is the same salami-slicing strategy under the "People's Liberation Army–law enforcement–military cooperation defense system"[47] that China already utilizes in the South China Sea.

Since the early 2000s, gray zone operations have emerged as a security topic that is as hotly debated in China as it is elsewhere. Academic works on gray zone strategy by Chinese authors often quote the definition provided by the U.S. Special Operations Command (SOCOM), namely, that it involves "competitive interactions among and within state and non-state actors that fall between the traditional war and peace duality."[48]

However, China's interest in gray zone operations has rarely focused on Japan. Instead, it has paid far closer attention to the U.S.' development of its gray zone operations. It is widely believed that the U.S. is enhancing its irregular warfare capabilities—such as intelligence warfare, psychological warfare, and asymmetric means—to ensure its strategic primacy.[49] In China's view, the U.S. has a long history of employing such strategies to achieve its ideological, political, and military ends, including the CIA's involvement in training and militarily supporting Tibetan guerrillas during the Cold War, the CIA's alleged involvement in the assassination of Cuba's leader Fidel Castro, the raid on Osama bin Laden in Abbottabad in Pakistan, and U.S. support for the so-called "color revolutions" in Central Asia.[50]

China is likewise vigilant about the cooperation between the U.S. Coast Guard and the maritime forces of the Quad nations and other Asian countries. Unsurprisingly, therefore, the U.S.' gray zone operations in the South China Sea represent another significant security concern for China, and it views the U.S.' Freedom of Navigation Program (FONOP) as a "political and military provocation that threatens China's sovereignty and security."[51]

Against such a backdrop, numerous policy recommendations on new CBMs with the U.S. have been put forward to prevent an emergency situation from arising. With regard to Japan–China relations, however, the issue of gray zone operations has been left unaddressed, and Japan's security concerns have generally been ignored by China. Instead, frustration is building on both sides because the thaw in relations has not brought about the changes hoped for: no change in Japan's policy regarding the South China Sea and Taiwan, and no change in China's assertive policy toward the Senkaku/Diaoyu Islands.

7.6. Conclusion

Japan, China, and the U.S. are engaged in a strategic triangle, with Japan and the U.S. working together to contain a rising China. Due to the asymmetrical threat perceptions that exist between Japan and China, China tends to accept Japan's assertive stance concerning its core national interests, which gives Japan strategic leverage over China.

Contrary to the common understanding of the strategic triangle theory, which posits that a pivot policy exists only in the "marriage triangle," this chapter finds that pivot policies are also possible in the two strategic triangle models presented in Figure 7.3. In the case of Strategic Triangle 1, Japan has pivotal power, whereas in the case of Strategic Triangle 2, China has the leverage to tilt the triangle toward something approximating either a "marriage triangle" or a "romantic triangle."

Japan's strategic position in relation to China's foreign policy strategy has led China to value its relationship with Japan and therefore to adopt a low-key approach, avoiding overt confrontation. However, at their heart, relations between Japan and China are fragile and always susceptible to change. China's asymmetric threat perceptions have led it to ignore Japan's security concerns, thus hindering the establishment of an effective mechanism to prevent contingencies from arising. Consequently, the chances of building confidence between the two countries in the near future remain slim.

It is also important to note that Japan–China relations are at a turning point toward a "marriage triangle." With Japan's involvement in the establishment of FOIP and the Indo-Pacific Economic Framework (IPEF), the Chinese government has begun to take note of Japan's active initiatives in forming a containment network around China. This sense of threat perception has undermined the foundation of the current "romantic triangle" between the U.S., Japan, and China.

Endnotes

1. Satake Tomohiko and Sahashi Ryo, "The rise of China and Japan's 'vision' for free and open Indo-Pacific," *The Journal of Contemporary China*, 30(127), 18–35 (2021).
2. J. Hornung, "Japan's pushback of China," *The Washington Quarterly*, 38(1), 167–183 (2015); B. E. M. Grønning, "Japan's shifting military priorities: Counterbalancing China's rise," *Asian Security*, 10(1), 1–21 (2014).
3. J. Mearsheimer, "The rise of China will not be peaceful at all," *The Australian*, 18 November 2005. https://www.mearsheimer.com/wp-content/uploads/2019/06/The-Australian-November-18-2005.pdf.
4. L. Dittmer, "The Sino-Japanese-Russian triangle," *Chinese Journal of Political Science*, 10(1), 1–21 (2005).
5. Ming Zhang and Ronald N. Montaperto, *A Triad of Another Kind: The United States, China, and Japan* (New York: St. Martin's Press, 1999).
6. Lowell Dittmer, "The strategic triangle: An elementary game-theoretical analysis," *World Politics*, 33(4), 485–515 (1981).
7. Rumi Aoyama, "Diplomatic history of Japan-China relations: Navigating between power balance, economic interests and domestic politics," in *Strategic Japan 2021* (Center for Strategic and International Studies (CSIS)).
8. Ryoko Nakano, "The Sino-Japanese territorial dispute and threat perception in power transition," *Pacific Review*, 29(2), 165–186 (2016).
9. Defense Ministry of Japan, *Defense of Japan: 2013*. https://dl.ndl.go.jp/pid/8672143/1/24?tocOpened=1.
10. Defense Ministry of Japan, *Defense of Japan: 2020*. https://www.mod.go.jp/en/publ/w_paper/wp2020/DOJ2020_Digest_EN.pdf.
11. "Chū-Ro ya Kitachōsen wo 'Kyōi' Nintei Jiki Saibā Sekyuritī Senryaku Hōsin (China, Russia, and North Korea identified as 'threats' in 'next cyber security strategy' policy)," *The Asahi Shimbun*, 27 September 2021.
12. "Sekkyokuteki Heiwa Shugi Jitugen no tame no TeigenI: Waga Kuni wo Mamorinuku Bouei Taisei no Kyōka (Proposals for achieving positive Pacifism I: Strengthening the defense system to protect Japan)," Sasakawa Peace Foundation, September 2018.
13. Akihiko Tanaka, "Taisen go no Rekishi Isō to Bei-chū Sinreisen—Reisen go Chitsujo no Dōyō de Arawa ni natta Chūgoku no Kyōi (Historical phases after World War II and the new cold war between the US and China: China's threat revealed in the turmoil of the post-cold war order)," *Voice*, 6, 57 (2019).
14. *Ibid.*, p. 57.
15. Shinichi Kitaoka, "Atarashii Kaikoku Shinshu: Jiritsu to Chōsen (Reopening of our country and initiative spirit: Independence and challenge)," *30th Anniversary Policy Papers*, Nakasone Peace Institute, December 2018.

16 *Ibid.*
17 *China's Military Strategy 2015*. http://www.china.org.cn/china/2015-05/26/content_35661433.htm.
18 *China's National Defense in the New Era* (2019). https://english.www.gov.cn/archive/whitepaper/201907/24/content_WS5d3941ddc6d08408f502283d.html.
19 "Rimei junshi yitihua jiasu tuijin (Japanese-Milanese military integration accelerates)," *PLA Daily*, 11 January 2018. http://www.81.cn/jfjbmap/content/2018-01/11/content_196745.htm.
20 Three Principles on Arms Exports was declared in April 1967 by Prime Minister Eisaku Sato. It prohibits Japan from exporting arms to (1) Communist bloc countries, (2) countries subject to arms embargoes under UN resolutions, and (3) countries that are or may be parties to international conflicts.
21 "Riben junshi zhengchanghua de liudaokan (Six hurdles to Japan's "military normalization")," *PLA Daily*, 20 December 2013. http://japan.people.com.cn/BIG5/n/2013/1220/c35469-23895561.html.
22 "Riben juli zhuiqiu junshi kuozhang (Japan's intensive pursuit of "military expansion")," *PLA Daily*, 18 April 2019. http://www.81.cn/jwgz/2019-04/18/content_9481332.htm.
23 "Riben da da nanhai pai de kaolaing (Japan's calculation of playing the "South China Sea Card")," *Liaowang Zazhi* (Outlook), 24 (2015).
24 *PLA Daily* (2018), *Op. cit.*
25 "Guize yu zhixu jianshe: nanhai xingshi yanbian de xin geju (Rules and order building: New patterns in the evolution of the South China Sea)." http://www.nanhai.org.cn/review_c/305.html.
26 Qianli Ma, "Riben xin haiyang anquan zhanlue zhong de duitai zhengce (Japan's counter-Taiwan policy in the new maritime security strategy)," *Taipingyang xuebao* (*Pacific Journal*), 91–98 (April 2012).
27 Chen Youjun, "Riben duitai zhengce de tiaozheng jiqi dongyin (Adjustment of Japan's policy toward Taiwan and its motivation)," *Xiandai Taiwan yanjiu* (*Modern Taiwan Studies*), (2), 38–44 (2013).
28 Wanhong Wu, "Riben ban Taiwan guanxi fa chunchunyudong (The Japanese version of the "Taiwan relations act": Waiting for a chance to launch)," *Shijie zhishi* (*World Affairs*), (11), 72 (2014).
29 Huang Dahui and Jin Xiaofeng, "Zhengzhi youqing hua yu lengzhan hou Riben zhengjie qintai shili de yanbian (Political right-leaning and the evolution of pro-Taiwan forces in Japanese politics after the cold war)," *Waijiao pinglun* (*Foreign Affairs Review*), (3), 50–76 (2017).
30 Foreign Ministry Spokesperson's Regular Press Conference. https://www.fmprc.gov.cn/web/fyrbt_673021/t1861952.shtml.

31 "Jiyū de Hirakareta Indo Taiheiyō: Tanjō Hiwa (Free and open Indo-Pacific: The secret story)," *NHK*, 30 June 2021.

32 Nobukatsu Kanehara, "Abe Chōki Seiken no Rekishi teki Isan: Jiyū Shugi teki na Kokusai Chitsujo no Rīdāshippu (The historical legacy of Abe's long-term: Leadership of the liberal international order)," *Gaiko* (September/October 2020), 13.

33 Itsunori Onodera, "Niti-bei 'Ittaika' de Towareru Nihon no Yakuwari (Japan's role challenged by Japan-US "integration")," *Gaiko*, May/June 2020.

34 Fumio Kishida, "Kantō Intabyū Kishida Fumio: 'Henka no Toshi' wo tenbō suru (Interview with Fumio Kishida: Looking ahead to the "year of change," *Gaiko*, 41 (January 2017).

35 Katsutoshi Kawano, "From the dispatch of marine sweepers to the Aegis Ashore: Japan's security environment and the Japan-US alliance from the perspective of the SDF," *Gaiko*, 63, 8–9 (September/October, 2020).

36 "Abe says Taiwan emergency is Japan emargency," *Jiji Press*, 2 December 2021. https://www.nippon.com/en/news/yjj2021120100874/.

37 "Update: Who's taking sides on China's maritime claims?" In *Asia Maritime Transparency Initiative*, Center for Strategic and International Studies (CSIS), 30 September 2021. https://amti.csis.org/whos-taking-sides-on-chinas-maritime-claims/.

38 "Xi Jinping zai zhoubian waijiao gongzuo zuotanhuishang fabiao zhongyao jianghua qiangdiao: wei woguo fazhan zhengqu lianghao zhoubian huanjing (Xi Jinping delivered an important speech at a work forum on peripheral diplomacy: Striving for a favorable peripheral environment for China's development)," *People's Daily*, 26 October 2013.

39 Rumi Aoyama, "China, Japan and economic integration in Asia: Asymmetric threat perception and FTAs," in Chien-wen Kou, Chiung-Chiu Huang, Brain Job (eds.) *The Strategic Options of Middle Powers in the Asia-Pacific* (New York, NY: Routledge, 2022), pp. 215–232.

40 "Yan Xuetong: weilai shinian guojizhengzhi de geju bianhua (Xuetong Yan: The changing landscape of international politics in the next decade)," *Pengpai xinwen* (*The Paper*), 14 December 2020. https://www.thepaper.cn/newsDetail_forward_10384350.

41 For details on Xi Jinping's speech at the Central Party School, see http://www.xinhuanet.com/politics/xxjxs/2019-09/04/c_1124960210.htm.

42 Japan Ministry of Foreign Affairs, "Premier of the state council of China Li Keqiang visits Japan: Japan-China summit meeting and banquet," 9 May 2018. https://www.mofa.go.jp/a_o/c_m1/cn/page3e_000857.html.

43 "Nicchū Sin Jidai e 3 Gensoku Shunō Kaidan 'Kyōsō kara kyōchō' (Three principles for a new era, Japan-China summit "from competition to cooperation")," *Nikkei*, 26 October 2018.

44 Japan Ministry of Foreign Affairs, *Diplomatic Bluebook 2020*. https://www.mofa.go.jp/policy/other/bluebook/2022/pdf/en_index.html.

45 Rumi Aoyama, "Japan-China ties are tightening," *East Asia Forum*, 24 May 2018. https://www.eastasiaforum.org/2018/05/24/japan-china-ties-are-tightening/.

46 A. S. Erickson and R. D. Martinson (eds.) *China's Maritime Gray Zone Operations* (Annapolis, MD: Naval Institute Press, 2019).

47 M. B. Petersen, "The Chinese maritime gray zone: Definitions, dangers, and the complications of rights protection operations," in A. S. Erickson and R. D. Martinson (eds.) *China's Maritime Gray Zone Operations* (Annapolis, MD: Naval Institute Press, 2019).

48 United States Special Operations Command, "The gray zone," *White Paper*, 9 September 2015. https://www.soc.mil/swcs/ProjectGray/Gray%20Zones%20-%20USSOCOM%20White%20Paper%209%20Sep%202015.pdf.

49 "Mei feizhenggui zhanzheng lilun de weixian zhaunxing (The U.S. dangerous transition to 'irregular warfare' doctrine)," *PLA Daily*, 12 December 2017. http://www.81.cn/jfjbmap/content/2020-12/03/content_277306.htm.

50 "Meijun lianhe tezhong zuozhan silingbu te zai na? (What is the "special" of the United States military special operations command?)," *PLA Daily*, 12 September 2017. http://military.people.com.cn/n1/2017/0921/c1011-29549158.html.

51 Mei Liu, "Haishang junshi huodong de jieding yu meiguo nanhai huise didai xingdong (The definition of maritime military activities and US "gray area operations" in the South China Sea)," *Guoji anquan yanjiu* (*Journal of International Security Studies*), (3), 102–131 (2021).

© 2025 World Scientific Publishing Europe Ltd.
https://doi.org/10.1142/9781800616318_0009

Chapter 8

China–Australia Relations and China's Policy Choices toward Australia: A Chinese Perspective[*]

Fangyin Zhou

Guangdong University of Foreign Studies, China

Since 2016, Australia's attitude toward China has taken a turn for the worse, resulting in a significant decline in Sino–Australian relations. Chinese scholars initially analyzed the change in Australia's attitude toward China mainly from the perspective of the U.S.–Australia alliance and the China–U.S.–Australia triangle, viewing U.S. influence as the key reason for the change in Australia's policy toward China. Later, Chinese scholars have become increasingly aware of the significant autonomy in Australia's China policy and the inadequacy of viewing it from the U.S. perspective. On the one hand, Australia's unique threat and interest perceptions have shaped the characteristics of its China policy; on the other hand, how to effectively balance security and economic interests is a long-standing dilemma faced by Australia in the strategic

---

[*] This chapter was originally printed as "China-Australia Relations and China's Policy Choices toward Australia: A Chinese Perspective." *The China Review*, Vol. 23, No. 1 (2023): 213–42. https://www.jstor.org/stable/48717994. Reproduced with kind permission of CUHK Press.

competition between China and the U.S. The Australian government has shown a degree of policy flexibility in its approach. The limited coercive economic measures taken by China against Australia have sent clear policy signals to Australia and have become a factor influencing its policy toward China. In the coming years, it will be difficult to achieve substantial improvements in China–Australia relations; however, both sides' strategies are likely to be more calm and pragmatic, and China–Australia relations can be expected to remain basically stable, especially to reduce the interference of political and security factors in bilateral economic cooperation, enabling both countries to better realize their respective intentions and needs.

Since 2016, there has been a significant decline in Australia's relations with China. Under the Turnbull and Morrison governments, Australia was viewed by China as a prominent United States (U.S.) ally in its opposition to China. Australia is an important ally of the U.S. in the Asia-Pacific region and the only country among U.S. allies that is also a member of AUKUS, the Quadrilateral Security Dialogue, and the Five Eyes countries, which are currently multilateral alliances or mechanisms with prominent anti-China overtones. On the other hand, Australia considers itself a middle power, and its economic and trade relations with China have been quite close. Australia's high dependence on China for trade, combined with China's perception that it does not pose a serious threat to Australia, has caused many Chinese people to wonder: why is Australia so anti-China, how far will Australia's anti-China policy continue, and under what conditions might Australia's policy toward China change? Analyzing the Chinese side's perception of the above questions can help us understand China's diplomatic thinking and analyze and predict the development of its policy toward Australia.

8.1. Australia: An Anti-China Vanguard in China's Eyes

Following the end of the Cold War, especially after 2000, China–Australia relations developed quite well, with their economic and trade ties becoming increasingly close. In 2005, China replaced the U.S. as Australia's largest source of imports, and in 2007 it became Australia's largest trading partner for the first time, a position it has maintained since 2009. China–Australia relations were upgraded to a comprehensive strategic partnership in November 2014.[1] In March 2015, Australia applied to join the Asian Infrastructure Investment Bank (AIIB), initiated by China as a founding member, and in June 2015, China and Australia signed a high-level free trade agreement that came into effect in December of the same year. These events reflect the well-developed bilateral relationship. However, the Sino–Australian relationship has changed since then.

Since 2016, there has been a marked increase in negative events in the China–Australia relationship. The Australian government publicly supported the Philippines in taking the South China Sea dispute to international arbitration and criticized China's defense of its sovereignty in the South China Sea as detrimental to regional peace and stability.[2] Australia has continued to take an antagonistic stance against China after the issuance of the South China Sea arbitral award. On 23 July 2020, the Australian mission at the UN submitted a *note verbale* to the Secretary-General of the United Nations, rejecting China's arguments against the The United Nations Convention on the Law of the Sea (UNCLOS) ruling and affirming its final and binding nature.[3] The *note verbale* adopted a rather fierce tone on the South China Sea issue, largely abandoning Australia's relatively neutral position on the maritime dispute prior to the South China Sea arbitration.[4] Australia's policy stance on the South China Sea has caused strong resentment in China.

Australia's continued unfriendly posture has reinforced the impression of its anti-China attitude on the Chinese side. On 13 March 2017 in Singapore, then Australian Foreign Minister Julie Bishop said that the U.S. must play a greater role in the Indo-Pacific region. She implied that China is not a democracy and is not fit to be a regional leader.[5] In June 2017, Australian Prime Minister Malcolm Turnbull claimed at the Shangri-La Dialogue that China sought to implement a modern version of the Monroe Doctrine in Asia and impose coercive diplomacy on some of its neighboring countries.[6] In the same month, in an Australian television interview, Bishop said that China's "unilateralist" behavior in the South China Sea "is in direct disregard to the international rules based order."[7] Australia actively supports the US Indo-Pacific strategy, with over 60 mentions of "Indo-Pacific" in its 2017 *Foreign Policy White Paper*, which has clear implications for China.[8] In December 2017, Turnbull publicly declared that "the Australian people stand up," accusing China of using its influence to interfere in Australian politics and emphasizing the need for Australians to defend their sovereignty.[9] In June 2018, the Australian Parliament passed the National Security Legislation Amendment (Espionage and Foreign Interference) Bill 2018 and the Foreign Influence Transparency Scheme Bill 2018, addressing the national security concern of "opposing foreign interference" at the legislative level.[10] The Australian government has repeatedly vetoed major investment projects proposed by Chinese companies in Australia, and it has banned Huawei and ZTE from participating in the construction of Australia's 5G network on security grounds. In September 2021, the U.S., the United Kingdom (U.K.), and Australia formed the AUKUS trilateral security partnership, which has strong military implications for China. The establishment of AUKUS and Australia's role in it show that Australia is more firmly aligned with the U.S. in its anti-China policy.[11]

Australia's stance on the Hong Kong issue, the Xinjiang issue, and the origin tracing of COVID-19 has also upset China. During the "legislative amendment" incident in Hong Kong in 2019, Australian Foreign Minister Marise Payne made high-profile statements about her support for "Hong Kong independence" and Hongkonger's right to free speech.[12] On 23 April 2020, Australian Prime Minister Scott Morrison attempted to push through an international investigation into the COVID-19 pandemic, a move that had implications for China. He said he had called the leaders of France, Germany, and the U.S. and planned to lobby the U.K. and Canada for international support from "like-minded" countries.[13] China was angered by this approach. A few days later, China's ambassador to Australia, Cheng Jingye (成競業), warned the Morrison government that its pursuit of an independent inquiry into the coronavirus pandemic origin could spark a Chinese consumer boycott of students and tourists visiting Australia, as well as sales of popular agricultural exports like beef and wine.[14] On 21 March 2021, the Australian and New Zealand foreign ministries issued a joint statement reiterating their concerns about human rights abuses against ethnic Uighurs and other Muslim minorities in Xinjiang.[15] Issues concerning the South China Sea, Hong Kong, Xinjiang, and the origin tracing of the COVID-19 pandemic are all matters of great concern to the Chinese government. Australia's explicitly China-specific positions and policy actions on a range of issues highly concerning to China have undoubtedly created a very negative perception of Australia in China, further locking China–Australia relations on a vicious path of deterioration and making it challenging to achieve stabilization or improvement.

8.2. Chinese Scholars' Understanding of the Motivation of Australia's Policy toward China

The deterioration of China–Australia relations since 2016 is not due to territorial conflicts or conflicting economic interests between the two countries, nor historical feuds or other structural conflicts. This is obviously different from the deterioration in relations between China and Japan, the Philippines, Vietnam, and the U.S. after 2012. China, in general, did not initiate tough measures or exert much policy pressure on Australia until 2020, except for anti-dumping and countervailing measures with some retaliatory implications against a few Australian exports (whose total economic value is relatively low), and as a result, trade between China and Australia maintained a rapid upward trend between 2015 and 2019.[16] Thus, Australia's approach is not a reaction to Chinese pressure. Moreover, Australia's approach, which has exacerbated Sino–Australian relations, fails to offer clear security or economic benefits, but rather hurts its economic interests to a certain extent and increases the uncertainty of its external security environment.

As early as 2017, Australian scholar Hugh White argued that the Australian Prime Minister threatened China with Cold War–style containment: "no regional leader—not even Japan's bellicose PM Shinzo Abe—has ever gone this far before."[17] Australia is taking more prominent anti-China actions than those of the Philippines and Vietnam, both of which have intense maritime rights disputes with China. Australia is also at the forefront among U.S. allies in banning the use of Huawei's 5G devices, when it could have adopted a wait-and-see approach, following other countries. Australia's outburst has puzzled many Chinese scholars, so much so that one scholar voiced the sentiment, "Why should Australia force itself to the forefront of confrontation?"[18] The following sections explore the prevailing views among Chinese scholars regarding the motivation of Australia's policy toward China.

8.2.1. *Australia's policy toward China: The first group of views*

The first group of views argues that in the China–U.S.–Australia triangle, the strategic competition between China and the U.S. is intensifying. This constrains the space for Australian policy toward China due to the close alliance between the U.S. and Australia, coupled with the significant asymmetry in U.S.–Australian power.

Within this analytical framework, there are two distinct understandings. The first understanding holds that the dominant role of the U.S. in the U.S.–Australia alliance is the main reason for Australia's anti-China policy. This was the dominant view among Chinese scholars studying Australia until 2019. Liu Changming and Sun Tong believe that the special U.S.–Australia relationship has played a direct role in promoting Australia's open involvement in the South China Sea dispute.[19] According to Yu Lei, Australia faces extremely strong exogenous dynamics encompassing military, political, and economic pressures from the U.S. in following it and helping it maintain the hegemonic system.[20] In Zhang Qi's view, the power gap between China and the U.S. in the Asia-Pacific region has narrowed further, forcing Australia to "choose sides" between the two. Based on strategic interests and political identity, Australia is likely to align with the U.S. for security and political reasons, which will continue the downward spiral of China–Australia relations in the future.[21] According to Zhang Guoxi and Xie Tao, anti-China activities in Australia are, to some extent, a product of Australia's foreign policy dilemma of balancing economic and security interests to continue its dependence on the U.S.–Australia alliance. The intertwining of anxiety in the face of China's rise and fear of being "abandoned" by a powerful U.S. ally has largely shaped Australia's anti-China sentiment.[22] Hu Bo argues that, even though Australia is extremely reluctant to sever ties with its largest economic partner (China) it is difficult to refuse and does not want to resist the demands of its biggest ally, the U.S.[23]

The underlying logic of this understanding of the decline in China–Australia relations is that Australia faces strong pressure from the U.S., as the latter actively pressures its allies to adopt anti-China policies in order to encircle China internationally against the backdrop of intensified strategic competition between China and the U.S. The asymmetry of power between Australia and the U.S., as well as the fact that Australia has attached great importance to its alliance with the U.S. for decades, has made Australia's policy toward China bound by the U.S. strategy toward China. This is both the result of realist politics and the influence of Australia's long-established mindset of dependence on the U.S.

Such an interpretation is consistent with the basic logic of realist international relations theory, but it faces insurmountable problems: although the U.S. has significantly increased its strategic pressure against China since the Obama administration launched its Asia-Pacific rebalancing strategy in 2011, Sino-Australian relations continued to improve between 2011 and 2015, as typified by the elevation of the relationship to a comprehensive strategic partnership, the signing of a high-level free trade agreement between China and Australia, and Australia's application to join the AIIB despite U.S. opposition.[24] This suggests that although Australia attaches great importance to its alliance with the U.S., its foreign policy remains highly independent and does not simply follow the U.S. position on China.[25] The question arises as to why U.S. pressure did not play a significant role in 2011–2015 but has been able to play a much greater role since 2016.

This view also faces other explanatory difficulties. First, the U.S. has a number of allies in the Asia-Pacific region, such as Japan, South Korea, the Philippines, and Thailand, all of which have asymmetrical relationships with the U.S. If the alliance with the U.S. has significant traction, why are these nations not generally as prominent in their anti-China efforts as Australia, particularly given that countries such as Japan and the Philippines have substantial conflicts with China over the Diaoyu/Senkaku Islands and the South China Sea?[26]

Second, can credible evidence be found to suggest that Australia's policy changes were influenced by U.S. pressure? Specifically, this requires evidence in two areas: evidence that the U.S. exerts enormous policy pressure on Australia, and evidence that Australia's unfriendly policy toward China is the result of such pressure. In particular, there is a significant difference between U.S. pressure on Australia during the periods of 2011–2015 and 2016–2020. Third, with similar U.S. attempts to push New Zealand into adopting an anti-China policy (including the request that New Zealand not use Huawei's 5G facilities), why has New Zealand, a much weaker country, been able to withstand U.S. pressure for a longer period than Australia, which has yielded to U.S. pressure and complied with its demands?

Fourth, 2018–2019 marked a critical period for the Trump administration to launch a trade war with China, which was probably the most significant U.S. policy toward China at the time, and at the beginning of the trade war in March 2018, then Australian Foreign Minister Bishop, who had previously been far from friendly toward China, advocated resolving the U.S.' trade dispute with China through the World Trade Organization (WTO).[27] When asked about U.S. tariffs on 6 November 2018, Australian Trade Minister Simon Birmingham stated that Australia's position has been clear: it does not approve or support the U.S.' actions of increasing tariffs unilaterally on Chinese goods.[28] On 4 August 2019, Birmingham stated that "the unilateral tariff actions is something that we have not welcomed, and may well be [a breach of WTO rules]."[29] These views, expressed by Australian officials, clearly ran counter to the wishes of the Trump administration. Pressure from the U.S. hardly explains the above policy stance of Australia.

208   F. Zhou

Due to the above-mentioned difficulties in the first explanation, some scholars propose a second explanation within the same analytical framework of the China–U.S.–Australia triangle. This explanation analyzes the motivation for Australia's policy toward China in the context of the internal management of the U.S.–Australia alliance while acknowledging the intensified China–U.S. strategic competition and the asymmetry in the alliance. The difference between this explanation and the first one is that the former focuses on Australia's policy choices within the constraints of the "U.S.-led-Australia-subordination" alliance relationship.

Xu Shanpin and Zhang Tao argue that Australia faces an alliance dilemma in its own relations with the U.S.—it fears "abandonment" if it highlights strategic autonomy but also dreads "entrapment" if it further consolidates its alliance with the U.S. Against the backdrop of China's rapid rise and intensified strategic competition with the U.S., Australia fears that U.S. strategic contraction could increase the risk of "abandonment." Therefore, Australia's priority is to reduce this risk, for which it has adopted a policy of limited upgrading of the Australia–U.S. alliance.[30] Chen Hong believes that, amid a highly uncertain global landscape, Australia's active cooperation and support for the U.S. against China can highlight Australia's strategic value to the U.S. and increase the "certainty" of the Australia–U.S. relationship.[31]

This explanation focuses more on Australia's policy autonomy in the asymmetric alliance with the U.S., arguing that Australia made the choice to actively cooperate with the U.S. based on its own assessment of national interest. This explanation seems to be more logically plausible than the first one. While acknowledging the intentional or unintentional policy pressure exerted by the U.S. on Australia, it reasonably adds the factor of Australia's policy autonomy, which makes the explanation richer and more realistic.

The challenge faced by this explanation is whether other allies within the U.S.-led alliance, all of which have asymmetrical power relationships with the U.S. (to a greater or lesser extent), need to reduce the risk of "abandonment" through a limited upgrading of their alliance with the U.S. in the context of a limited U.S. strategic contraction.[32] In other words, did the risk of Australia being "abandoned" by the U.S. really change in 2016 and has it significantly increased since then? Why hasn't New Zealand, a fellow Oceania country, taken a similar path as Australia, and why isn't it worried about the risk of "abandonment"? Moreover, what does "abandonment" mean in the context of the U.S.–Australia alliance? In the sense of classical alliance theory, "abandonment" occurs when an ally fails to provide support to its partner, thus leaving it at risk of being isolated in the event of a crisis or conflict.[33] In this sense, "abandonment" means that the U.S. fails to fulfill its security commitments to protect Australia in the face of an attack from another country. Is Australia, a country considered to have a very secure territory, really worried about this prospect?

A poll conducted by the Lowy Institute in Australia found that the main perceived possible threats to Australia's vital interests from 2017 to 2019 were climate change, international terrorism, North Korea's nuclear program, cyberattacks from other countries, and a severe global economic downturn.[34] The top five threats identified in the 2020 poll were: drought and water shortages, COVID-19 and other potential epidemics, a severe global economic downturn, environmental disasters such as bushfires and floods, and climate change.[35] If these represent the major threats facing Australia, then strengthening the alliance with the U.S. does not appear to be the most effective way to mitigate them. The issue of "abandonment" in its traditional sense seems to have little to do with these threats.

Moreover, why was Australia not very concerned about the risk of abandonment before 2016? Against the backdrop of a degree of strategic contraction by the U.S. Obama administration, Australia strengthened its cooperation with China during 2010–2015. According to a 2019 Lowy Institute poll, 69 percent of Australians believe that "Australia's alliance with the U.S. makes it more likely Australia will be drawn into a war in Asia that would not be in Australia's interests."[36] From this perspective, it seems that Australia is not only facing the problem of being "abandoned" by the U.S. but also the increasing possibility of being "entrapped" by it.

8.2.2. *Australia's policy toward China: The second group of views*

The second category of views discusses the changes in Australia's policy toward China at the bilateral level of China–Australia relations, especially focusing on how Australia can better achieve its security and economic interests simultaneously in the context of China's rise. From this perspective, there are two noteworthy aspects of the China–Australia relationship.

First, Australia's unique threat perceptions and interests have shaped its policy toward China. Australia's national situation is somewhat unique in international society. Australia is a middle power with interests different from those of major powers and small states. Australia has certain international ambitions but is fully aware of the limitations of its capacity in international society. Australia also has certain unique advantages in terms of its vast size, rich resources, and long-term economic prosperity. Its geography is unique in that it remains one of the safest countries in the world, with a low risk of direct military threat, even against the backdrop of a profound transformation of the international system.[37] At the same time, Australia is a typical country of immigration, characterized by a highly open society and an economy that is highly dependent on an open and stable international order for its prosperity. In the absence of imminent economic and security threats for a long period, a high degree of concern for the stability and direction of the international order, the transformation of the international system, and the uncertainty that accompanies it is an ongoing driver in Australia's foreign policy. For Australia, maintaining the stability of a free, open, rule-based international order is of fundamental importance. Compared to most other countries, Australia has shown exceptional sensitivity to this.[38]

With China overtaking Japan to become the world's second-largest economy in 2010, Australia has expressed extraordinary concern about China's rising power. At the same time, Australia believes that China's Belt and Road Initiative, its behavior in the South China Sea, and its rapid modernization of its military forces all reflect, to some extent, shifts in China's strategic intentions.[39] Australia believes that China's attitude toward the South China Sea arbitration and its so-called "militarization" of the region reflect its future approach to international order and rules. The July 2016 South China Sea arbitration, and the West's subsequent failure to pressure China into accepting it, led to an important change in Australia's perception of China's approach to the international order,[40] and it was against this backdrop that Australian Prime Minister Turnbull claimed in June 2017 that China sought to implement the Monroe Doctrine in Asia, which undoubtedly surprised China.

Scholars generally acknowledge that the rise of China and the relative change in the power balance between China and the U.S. do not mean that Australia must identify China as a threat; after all, this transformation has been unfolding since 2008. Xu Shaomin argues that the important change in Australia's policy toward China around 2016 was due to a significant change in Australia's threat perception of China based on several factors: first, the growing trend toward the permanence of the Chinese model, which is increasingly unlikely to resemble Western democracies; second,

China's military modernization, "assertive" diplomacy, and active policy in the South China Sea are "threatening" the regional balance of power and the rules-based international order that Australia depends on for its survival; third, China's increasing influence in the Pacific Island region; and fourth, China's "sharp power" offensive, which takes advantage of the openness of Australian society.[41]

Such an analysis differs from those that focus on the U.S.–Australia alliance, as it argues that around 2016, Australia's perception of China's strategic intentions, threats from China, and the relationship between China and the international order underwent a turning point due to the cumulative effect of multiple factors, which drove the directional change in Australia's policy toward China.

Another notable aspect is how Australia strategically balances its security and economic interests and what practical effects its approach has had. As the strategic competition between China and the U.S. intensifies, Australia faces the question of how to choose between China and the U.S. while balancing its security and economic interests effectively. On the one hand, Australia has a long-standing and stable alliance with the U.S., which has long been the bedrock of its security relationship. In the view of Australian scholars, alliances are not merely expedient but are based on shared values, institutions, and processes. The U.S. will remain Australia's first preference in an extreme scenario where a military force is used against Australia.[42] On the other hand, Australia has strong economic ties with China, which has been its largest trading partner since 2009. Despite the rather tense Sino–Australian relations in 2020, China's share of Australia's goods and services exports remained high at 36.4 percent, more than the combined total of Japan, the U.S., South Korea, the U.K., India, and Singapore, which were ranked second to seventh, respectively.[43] As strategic competition between China and the U.S. intensifies and Australia's position in the U.S. Asia-Pacific/Indo-Pacific strategy becomes more prominent, it is becoming increasingly difficult for Australia to balance its economic prosperity with its security ties.

Faced with the obvious mismatch between the regional economic structure and security structure, especially given the fact that the main economic and security partners of many countries in the region are China and the U.S., which are in strategic competition, most Asia-Pacific nations opt for a hedging strategy against China in order to better balance their economic and security interests. According to Wang Lianhe, "Australia is well positioned to use its good relationship with China to seek greater voice and autonomy in the U.S.–Australia alliance; it can also use its strategic and geopolitical advantages to reap greater benefits from its economic ties with China."[44] In other words, Australia could play the China card against the U.S. and the U.S. card against China as a way to expand its policy space and further its interests. However, the hedging strategy would likely result in certain negative impacts on Australia's relationship with China. Wei Zongyou believes that, under the influence of Australia's hedging strategy against China, China–Australia economic cooperation will likely continue to strengthen, although political and security mutual trust may become constrained.[45]

In fact, Australia's policy toward China since 2016 has largely gone beyond a hedging policy and veered closer toward a policy of balancing. This raises the question: in the changing international environment, is Australia's policy approach in line with its national interests? On the surface, it is true that Australia's strengthening of the U.S.–Australia alliance has, to some extent, worsened its relationship with China, but the question is whether Australia's China–related economic interests have been significantly harmed by this policy. Looking at the data on Australia–China economic relations, Australia's exports to China have shown a consistent upward trend, at least between 2016 and 2019. Australia's exports of goods and services to China rose from AU\$95.68 billion in 2016 to AU\$168.573 billion in 2019, an increase of 76.2 percent over four years. Australia's trade surplus in goods and services with China increased from AU\$33.36 billion to AU\$85.81 billion over the same period, a four-year increase of 157.2 percent.[46]

In terms of policy outcomes, Australia's unfriendly behavior toward China, while causing some deterioration in Sino–Australian relations, did not have a significant economic cost to Australia over a not-so-short period of time. Against the backdrop of a global economic recession and significant declines in international trade due to the COVID-19 pandemic in 2020, Australia's total exports of goods and services to the rest of the world fell by 11.5 percent, while its exports to China fell by only 5.8 percent and maintained a surplus of AU\$72.68 billion.[47] If such a dynamic can continue, then strategically, Australia's approach remains effective in achieving its economic and security interests. The basic logic behind this is that adopting a certain degree of moderately unfriendly policy toward China—if it does not entail a significant economic cost and Australia's relationship with the U.S. is strengthened as a result—is actually an approach that can achieve both economic and security interests. From this perspective, Australia appears to be making a rational policy choice. The future validity of such a strategy relies on the premise that the economic costs of continuing Australia's unfriendly policy toward China will not increase significantly.

A prominent feature of the U.S.–China strategic competition during and after the Trump administration is that the U.S. is willing to take actions that impose certain, and sometimes significant, costs on itself in order to curb the rise of Chinese influence, as long as those actions impose greater costs on China. In other words, as China's power continues to rise, the U.S. has become more concerned with relative gains in its China policy,[48] rather than solely pursuing absolute gains. As a key ally highly compatible with U.S. policy toward China, Australia may also weigh its relative benefits when dealing with China and be willing to suffer limited losses in absolute benefits. One manifestation of this is that China has intensified its economic pressure on Australia to some extent since 2020; however, Australia has not made any significant adjustments to its China policy in response and even further solidified the AUKUS trilateral security partnership with the U.S. and the U.K. in September 2021. The establishment of the AUKUS not only has practical implications in the security arena but also serves as a signal from Australia to China of its firmness in supporting U.S. policy toward China and the immutability of its policy direction.

8.2.3. *Domestic political factors in Australia*

In addition to these two main viewpoints, some Chinese scholars also emphasized domestic political factors in Australia, an approach based partly on the understanding that although China's power is rising rapidly and the strategic competition between China and the U.S. is intensifying, Australia is generally considered a very safe country with no significant material interests at odds with China. Since 2016, Australia has been willing to strengthen its alliance with the U.S. at the expense of Sino–Australian relations to some extent, in line with the U.S. strategy toward China. Australia has also demonstrated a strong policy initiative in advancing the Indo-Pacific strategy, which carries clear China-specific overtones.[49] Therefore, Australia's policy changes have been driven by strong domestic political factors.

Ning Tuanhui considers party politics to be an important factor in influencing Australia's policy shift toward China. The differing traditions and preferences of the Liberal–National coalition and Labor Party regarding foreign policy, along with the games and compromises between the two major parties, and the internal factional struggles within these parties, have collectively shaped Australia's policy toward China. In addition, minor parties outside of the mainstream have also exerted some influence on it.[50] For example, whether Australia should participate in China's Belt and Road Initiative is not only an issue of rational choice from the perspective of national interests but also a hot topic of policy debates and among mutual accusations between the Liberal–National coalition and the Labor Party. In the ever-changing internal and external environments, the different positions taken by political parties influence voter attitudes toward them, which is a complex interactive process. It should be noted, however, that while there are some differences in the policy orientations of Australia's two major parties toward China, significant policy consensus also exists,[51] and it would be inappropriate to exaggerate these differences, much less to attribute Australia's current China policy primarily to the domestic political considerations of the Liberal–National coalition.

Another view in the domestic political interpretation is that Australia's military and defense establishment has become significantly more influential in shaping Australia's policy toward China, thereby marginalizing the role of the Australian foreign services, which has had a perverse effect on the policy.[52] For example, in 2018, without naming specific countries, Australian Security Intelligence Organization Director-General Duncan Lewis stated that foreign interference was occurring "at unprecedented scale" in Australia.[53] The rise of security and intelligence influence over foreign policy has implications for how Australia approaches its policy toward China. But this should be seen more as a result of the decline in China–Australia relations than as the cause of the decline. Rather than the security and intelligence complex controlling Australia's foreign policy, the logic of emphasizing geopolitical competition and national security priorities currently dominates Australian diplomatic thinking.[54]

From a domestic political perspective, identity politics is an important factor contributing to Australia's negative perceptions of China, exacerbating its fears and anxieties about China's growing political and economic influence.[55] Many Chinese scholars have noted the importance of this factor in Australia's foreign policy.[56] However, its interpretation also faces certain challenges: (1) Australia has long embraced a Western identity, but Sino–Australian relations improved from 2010 to 2015 and deteriorated significantly from 2016 to 2021. Are Australia's actions to improve and subsequently worsen Sino–Australian relations both in line with its Western identity? (2) Does Western identity have such a strong influence on Australia's foreign policy? In contrast, New Zealand, which also has a Western identity, has a significantly more moderate policy toward China. If Australia's approach aims solely to show that it is on the side of the West, then there is no need to be so "aggressive" in its China policy, and it could have taken more symbolic measures. This would have been enough to make its position clear and would not have substantially harmed Sino–Australian relations. In general, Australia's Western identity acts as a driving factor in Australia's policy toward China; however, it is not the fundamental reason for the recent changes in this policy.

Scholars' views have debated various perspectives on the main factors affecting the current Australian policy toward China; by synthesizing their analyses, we can better understand the mechanisms through which different factors come into play. In the introductory chapter of this volume, Feng Liu and Kai He propose an "interest–threat nexus" model, arguing that China's bilateral relationships are a function of convergent or divergent threat perceptions and economic interests between China and other states (see Chapter 1). The analysis in this chapter shows that the influencing factors and the way they work in China–Australia relations are more complex than in the situation discussed by Liu and He. One reason for this is that while Liu and He attempt to explore general patterns in China's relations with the U.S., Japan, Australia, and India, this chapter attempts to analyze changes in Australia's specific policies toward China. These are two different directions of explanation. Although Liu and He's attempts to distill the general pattern can achieve a certain degree of formal concurrence, many rich details and interpretive subtleties are inevitably overlooked.

The U.S.–Australia asymmetric alliance has been a fundamental factor influencing Australia's policy toward China, although its impact varies in magnitude across different international contexts. The apparent intensification of strategic competition between China and the U.S. since 2018 has increased the influence of the U.S.–Australia alliance on Australia's policy toward China. However, Sino–Australian relations began to deteriorate significantly in 2016, reflecting the independent influence of Australia's perception factors on China. This indicates that Australia's policy toward China is highly autonomous, and we cannot analyze it too much from the perspective of strategic competition between China and the U.S. Even within the area of security, Australia still shows a relatively high degree of policy autonomy, which is clearly reflected in its initiative

216 *F. Zhou*

to promote the formation of trilateral security cooperation among the U.S., the U.K., and Australia.[57] In contrast, while the influence of domestic politics on Australia's China policy is auxiliary, it does play a role in the specific formulation and implementation process of that policy.

8.3. China's Policy toward Australia under the Asymmetric Perception

There is an obvious gap between China's perception of Australia and Australia's perception of China. From China's perspective, China and Australia have neither historical grudges nor fundamental conflicts of interests, their economic interests are highly complementary, China does not pose a pragmatic threat to Australian homeland security, there is ample room for cooperation between the two countries, and their relationship could have been further strengthened. From Australia's perspective, China's rising power and its changing strategic intentions have already had a strong impact on Australia's national interests.[58] In this context, Australia increasingly sees China as a strategic threat at global and regional levels, despite its close ties with the Chinese economy.

The perception gap between Australia and China is based in part on the power asymmetry that exists between the two sides. Brantly Womack argues that asymmetry is a widespread phenomenon in international relations. As the two sides interact over time, the asymmetric relationship may habituate into a mutually acceptable pattern of interaction. Asymmetries of concern exist between states possessing asymmetrical power. In the long-term interaction between powerful state A and relatively weak state B, state A cares more about whether state B's attitude is "friendly" or "unfriendly" and less about many of state B's specific interests and psychological concerns. In contrast, state B is prone to being overly concerned about state A.[59] Asymmetrical concerns seem to exist in the China–Australia relationship. One manifestation of this is that when the relations are relatively friendly, Chinese people generally pay little attention to them; however, as relations deteriorate, a rather irritated mood arises in Chinese media and society, which generally see it as a result of Australia adopting an "unfriendly" attitude toward China, often without delving into the specific motives behind each of Australia's policy actions.

Shortly after Australia published its 2017 *Foreign Policy White Paper*, the Chinese newspaper *Global Times* published an editorial commenting on Australia's policy toward China, saying, "China and Australia are not supposed to be geo-linked, but Australia has been pushing hard to get into disputes around China" and it "call [s] for the U.S. to come over more often to balance China, urging neighboring countries to be tough on China, while until today, China has done nothing wrong to Australia." According to the article, many of Australia's actions are really confusing: "Its attitude toward China is very much like 'pick up the bowl and eat the meat, put down the chopsticks and curse.'"[60] This editorial typifies how many Chinese people perceived Australia's policy toward China at that time, the main aspects of which were as follows: first, there was no structural conflict of interests between China and Australia; second, China had not taken any initiative to harm Sino–Australian relations; third, it is incomprehensible for Australia to adopt unfriendly policies toward China while deriving important benefits from the Chinese market. On this basis, many Chinese people have developed a labeled perception that Australia's policy toward China is malicious and that Australia is an anti-China vanguard.

In contrast, Australia has shown a high degree of sensitivity to changes in China's power and foreign policies. In past polls, Australians were among the first in the world to believe that China would overtake the U.S. as the leading global economy. According to a Lowy Institute poll as early as 2010, 55 percent of Australians considered China to be the world's leading economic power. By comparison, only 32 percent said that the U.S. was the world's leading economic power in the same year.[61] Previously, international polls conducted by the Pew Research Center in 2008 and 2009 on similar issues showed that Australia held the most optimistic estimate of China's economic power of all countries surveyed, including China. In a 2008 survey, 40 percent of Australians believed China to be the world's leading economic power, the highest percentage among countries surveyed. By comparison, only 37 percent of Australians considered the U.S. to be the world's leading economic power.[62] And the fact is that China was only the world's third-largest economy in 2008, with its GDP less than a third of that of the U.S.

The presence of asymmetric concerns has created misperception in both China and Australia, manifesting itself in the fact that China is highly concerned about the U.S.' every move but not deeply enough about Australia's. As a result, China's understanding of Australia's policy motives tends to be simplistic. Consequently, it would be easy for China to believe that Australia has a tendency to be unfriendly toward it due to

U.S. influences or changes in Australia's domestic politics, ignoring the relative complexity of Australia's policy toward it. For example, it is seldom noted that Australia did not clearly side with the Trump administration in the U.S.–China trade war, yet Turnbull's labeling statement, "The Australian people stand up," has become quite popular among the Chinese.

Australia, on the other hand, is very sensitive to changes in China, especially China's South China Sea policy, Belt and Road initiative, cooperation with Pacific Island countries, and expanding investment in Australia. Australia tends to believe that there are complex strategic motives behind China's economic cooperation behavior, such as deliberately challenging the existing international order or testing the waters in this regard.

At the policy level, there are some noteworthy aspects of China–Australia relations. First, the relations have continued to deteriorate since 2016 and until the Albanese government came into power in May 2022, while their economic ties have remained very strong. In this regard, one question that arises is whether the two sides will continue to maintain close economic ties if the relations fail to improve. This chapter's view is that there is little room for further decline in China–Australia relations. The factors driving Australia to adopt policies that are not conducive to preventing the deteriorating bilateral relations over the past few years include the rise of China's power, the intensified strategic competition between China and the U.S., the development of China's relations with Pacific Island countries, the unsettled situation in the South China Sea, political changes in Hong Kong, the COVID-19 pandemic, and inconsistencies on human rights and values between China and Australia. Therefore, as long as these factors do not change significantly, there is limited room for further decline in China–Australia relations in the future. In any case, China does not constitute an important and imminent pragmatic security threat to Australia, and there has been no historical hatred between the two sides. Australia will keep its policy toward China in check. While China is unhappy with Australia's unfriendly practices, it has no intention of engaging in a major confrontation with Australia. Maintaining strong economic and trade ties serves the interests of both parties. Although China–Australia economic and trade relations may be adversely affected by the decline of bilateral relations, China's position as Australia's largest trading partner and largest export market will not change.

Australia is trying to promote diversification of its trading partners, whereas China is trying to reduce its dependence on Australia in areas such as iron ore and coal imports. China and Australia will make some efforts in this regard, but it will be difficult for Australia to find alternative buyers of its voluminous natural resources outside of China, and it would not be economically wise for Australia, as a country that maintains a massive trade surplus with China, to actively reduce its share on the Chinese market. From this perspective, Australia's attempts to promote diversification of trading partners will not have a fundamental impact on China–Australia trade relations. The economic ties between the two will become more resilient if Sino–Australian relations show signs of stability or improvement. Following the lifting of China's anti-dumping and countervailing measures on Australian barley in August 2023, China quickly re-emerged as Australia's largest export market for barley, and in December 2023, 90 percent of Australian barley exports were shipped to China. This striking change demonstrates the immense appeal of the Chinese market and the irreplaceable position it holds for some Australian products.[63]

Second, China has taken successive measures such as increased product inspections and the imposition of anti-dumping duties on Australian products, such as beef, wine, coal, and barley, since 2017, which is seen by the Australian media as economic coercion. Related questions are: how far will China continue to extend its economic pressure on Australia? Will China significantly intensify these measures? And under what circumstances might China reduce this economic pressure on Australia?

The measures taken by China against some of Australia's exports have served several purposes: first, they signal to the Australian government that China is dissatisfied with Australia's disrespect for its important interests, a message made undoubtedly clear to the Australian side. Second, to a limited extent, it has caused Australia to pay an economic price for its actions. In the case of barley, for example, from November to December 2018, the Chinese Ministry of Commerce launched an investigation into whether Australian barley had been dumped on the Chinese market and benefited from subsidies. On 18 May 2020, the Ministry of Commerce ruled that there was dumping and subsidization of Australian barley, and decided to impose anti-dumping and countervailing duties on the above-mentioned products from then onward, with an anti-dumping rate of 73.6 percent, a countervailing duty rate of 6.9 percent, and a levy period of five years.[64] As a result, Australian barley exports to China experienced a significant short-term decline. The average monthly value of

Australian barley exports to China from January to May 2020 was AU$88.08 million, and from June to September 2020, it fell sharply to AU$13.698 million.[65] In terms of a single product, the policy impact of China's measures is not insignificant. However, in the overall context of Australia's trade with China, the cost of China's economic measures to Australia has not yet been significant.[66] In 2020, Australia's total merchandise exports to China amounted to A$364.6 billion,[67] with barley accounting for a very small portion of the total. As a result, despite the economic measures taken by China, the trade volume between Australia and China has remained at a very high level.

The limited coercive economic measures taken by China mainly serve as a signal to Australia regarding its attitude and policy response and to make Australia pay a certain economic price, thus making Australia realize that it could put the Sino–Australian relationship in greater danger if it goes further down the anti-China path. It is more of a warning than a punishment. China's economic measures will also have a negative impact on China–Australia relations, but they partially achieve one of China's goals: preventing Australia from excessively adopting an unfriendly policy toward China and making its policy behavior relatively cautious and pragmatic. Through its economic measures against Australia, China is also trying to signal to other U.S. allies the importance of exercising basic prudence and restraint in adopting unfriendly policies toward it.

Australia has long attached great importance to its alliance with the U.S., and the intensifying strategic competition between China and the U.S. generates important constraints for Australia's handling of its relations with China. Under this premise, there is limited room for China to maneuver its policy toward Australia. China would like to maintain basic stability and reduce trouble in Sino–Australian relations; however, achieving this goal is very difficult given the current international context. If China significantly increases its economic coercion on Australia, considering that Australia is a middle power with a developed economy, strong social capacity, and support from the U.S., such coercion would hardly push Australia's policy toward China in a direction conducive to improving relations but could instead push Australia into becoming more anti-China. Moreover, a policy of intense pressure on Australia could have unfavorable consequences for China internationally, creating confusion in the international community's expectations of the direction of China's foreign policy, which could be used by the U.S. in a broader international mobilization against China. In addition, China is dependent on Australia for iron ore, coal, and various other products. Restricting imports of these crucial fossil energy sources and ores would entail significant economic costs for China and would not be in China's own interests.

On the other hand, Australia's anti-China policy in recent years has been the result of many factors. Especially at present, the general perception of Australian society toward China is quite negative. China and Australia have big differences on a number of issues that are highly sensitive for China: the South China Sea, Hong Kong, and Xinjiang. Therefore, China has little room for a policy of appeasement toward Australia; even if it adopts such a policy, it would be difficult to produce a significant policy effect.

Combining these two aspects, it is unlikely that China will either significantly increase its policy pressure on Australia in the next few years or adopt a more substantial policy of appeasement. It is more likely that China will continue to maintain limited pressure on Australia while demonstrating a relatively flexible policy stance. On the other hand, it is not in Australia's economic interests to cause a sharp decline in Sino–Australian relations, and it may also increase Australia's security risks, so Australia will be careful to exercise proportionality in its approach to China. From a strategic point of view, against the backdrop of intense U.S.–China strategic competition and the difficulty for China and Australia to find room for cooperation in the security field, what the two countries can do is reduce irritating statements on core interests and principles between each other, lower the tone of antagonistic discourse, and promote practical cooperation in the economic field in a relatively flexible manner, so as to minimize political-security interference in the non-sensitive economic cooperation.

8.4. Conclusion

From the beginning of 2016 to May 2022, China–Australia relations experienced a downward spiral. Chinese scholars mainly hold the following interpretations of the changes in Australia's policy toward China: the first group of views originates from the China–U.S.–Australia triangle, arguing that the intensified strategic competition between China and the U.S., along with the close alliance between the U.S. and Australia, have jointly shaped Australia's policy toward China. Within this category of views, the main difference lies in whether there is more emphasis on the dominant role of the U.S. in the U.S.–Australia alliance or on Australia's policy autonomy in the alliance. The second category of views discusses the changes in Australia's policy toward China at the bilateral level between China and Australia, focusing especially on how Australia views the impact on its interests in the context of China's rise and how it balances its security and economic interests. In addition, some scholars also emphasize the role of domestic political factors in Australia. Overall, Chinese scholars possess a rather in-depth understanding of China–Australia relations and hold a relatively diverse range of views. These views have influenced the Chinese government's policy thinking on Australia in a variety of ways, such as academic views expressed publicly in articles, recommendations in policy reports, and viewpoints shared during internal discussions, and have particularly helped enrich the policy community's understanding of China–Australia relations.

China has made some policy responses to Australia's unfriendly policy toward China but has generally tried to stabilize Sino–Australian relations. The purpose of China's economic pressure on Australia is to prevent it from going too far in its anti-China policy, without expecting a significant change of direction, let alone a significant warming of Sino–Australian relations. China's approach has provoked some negative reactions from Australia; however, it has still partially achieved its policy objectives.

In May 2022, after the new Albanese administration took office in Australia, China–Australia relations showed a trend of stabilization and limited improvement. Its most important symbol was Albanese's visit to China in November 2023, the first visit to China since 2016 by an Australian prime minister. Prior to this, China gradually lifted import restrictions on Australian timber, beef, barley, and other goods destined for China, and Australian coal began returning to the Chinese market. On the one hand, the Albanese government's policy stance toward China shows strong continuity, particularly in maintaining and consolidating the U.S.–Australia alliance, its position on the South China Sea, and its cooperation with the U.S. Indo-Pacific strategy.[68] At the same time, in the absence of structural changes in China–Australia relations, the Albanese government has adopted a more flexible policy stance toward easing tensions in Sino–Australia relations.[69] China has shown a welcoming attitude toward Australia's policy changes from the perspective of responding to the strategic competition between China and the U.S. and reducing its international pressure. In the process of stabilization and limited improvement of bilateral relations, both China and Australia have adopted a calm, pragmatic, and cautious approach. Neither side has high expectations for how much bilateral relations will improve, and they have taken a measured, step-by-step approach to improving relations, keeping a low profile regarding disagreements on important issues. This approach in itself reflects the multifaceted difficulties and some of the structural obstacles to improving China–Australia relations.

Both China and Australia clearly recognize the practical value of improved relations. For China, in addition to the economic value of China–Australia cooperation, the improvement in relations can help decrease Australia's anti-China efforts in the international arena; it can show the international community that U.S. allies are not so firm and consistent in cooperating with the U.S. in opposing China, potentially having a demonstrative effect in the international arena and reducing strategic pressure on China from a U.S. encirclement strategy.

From Australia's side, the basic stability of China–Australia relations will help in balancing security and economic interests while ensuring that its security cooperation with the U.S. does not significantly harm economic and trade relations with its largest economic partner. This economic interest is particularly important against the backdrop of the sluggish recovery of the world economy after the pandemic and the not-so-optimistic economic situation in Australia. Second, Australia's unsuccessful efforts over the past few years to find alternative international buyers for its barley, iron ore, and other products suggest that it faces significant practical difficulties in diversifying its export markets and that its heavy dependence on the Chinese market will likely persist for a long time. China will remain Australia's top trading partner, its largest export market, and the primary source of its trade surplus for the foreseeable future. In addition, easing tensions between the two will improve Australia's security environment, reduce the risk of political altercations causing a downward spiral in relations, and help mitigate, to some extent, the negative impacts of U.S.–China strategic competition.

On the other hand, there is relatively limited room for improvement in Sino–Australian relations in both the current and future periods, and against the backdrop of the Russia–Ukraine conflict, Australia's perceptions of China could be influenced by the close Sino–Russian relationship, potentially intensifying negatively.[70] It is difficult to see a significant and substantial improvement in China–Australia relations, especially in the security area. Given this premise, improvements in China–Australia relations are more likely to occur in areas such as economic cooperation and addressing climate change, where the two countries share clearer common interests. In the economic sphere, an important manifestation of improved relations would be for both sides to take steps to prevent political factors from becoming very damaging to the economic relationship, rather than to elevate economic cooperation to a much higher level.

Although there have been some positive signs of improvement in China–Australia relations since May 2022, we cannot be too optimistic about the future of their relationship. The continued improvement faces many obstacles, including U.S.–China strategic competition, constraints imposed by the U.S.–Australia alliance on Australia's foreign and security policies, domestic opposition faced by the Albanese government, China's concerns about another shift in Australia's policies in the future, and the difficulty of significantly easing the antagonism of civil society on both sides in the short term. From this perspective, the fact that China–Australia relations have been able to maintain the current relatively stable situation and that economic cooperation between the two has been able to remain free from significant interference on political grounds is already a very good result that can be achieved in bilateral relations.

Endnotes

1 Xi Jinping, "Address to the Parliament of Australia," Parliament of Australia, 17 November 2014. https://parlinfo.aph.gov.au/parlInfo/search/display/display.w3p;query=Id%3A%22chamber%2Fhansardr%2F35c9c2cf-9347-4a82-be89-20df5f76529b%2F0005%22;src1=sm1.

2 Shannon Tiezzi, "Australia's foreign Minister gets chilly welcome in China," *The Diplomat*, 19 February 2016. https://thediplomat.com/2016/02/australias-foreign-minister-gets-chilly-welcome-in-china/.

3 United Nations *Note Verbale* No 20/026, United Nations. https://www.un.org/depts/los/clcs_new/submissions_files/mys_12_12_2019/2020_07_23_AUS_NV_UN_001_OLA-2020-00373.pdf.

4 C. Thayer, "Australia abandons its neutrality on the South China Sea maritime disputes," *The Diplomat*, 27 July 2020. https://thediplomat.com/2020/07/australia-abandons-its-neutrality-on-the-south-china-sea-maritime-disputes/.

5 J. Bishop, "Change and uncertainty in the Indo-Pacific: Strategic challenges and opportunities," Minister for Foreign affairs, the Hon Julie Bishop MP, 13 March 2017. https://www.foreignminister.gov.au/minister/julie-bishop/speech/change-and-uncertainty-indo-pacific-strategic-challenges-and-opportunities.

6 M. Turnbull, "Keynote Address at the 16th IISS Asia Security Summit, Shangri-La Dialogue," 3 June 2017. https://malcolmturnbull.com.au/media/keynote-address-at-the-16th-iiss-asia-security-summit-shangri-la-dialogue.

7 J. Bishop, "Sky news first edition, interview with Kieran Gilbert," Transcript, Minister for Foreign Affairs, the Hon Julie Bishop MP, 5 June 2017. https://www.foreignminister.gov.au/minister/julie-bishop/transcript-eoe/sky-news-first-edition-interview-kieran-gilbert-5.

8 Department of Foreign Affairs and Trade (Australia), 2017 *Foreign Policy White Paper*, Canberra. https://www.dfat.gov.au/sites/default/files/2017-foreign-policy-white-paper.pdf.

9 "'The Australian people stand up': PM defiant over Chinese political interference," *SBS News*, 9 December 2017. https://www.sbs.com.au/news/the-australian-people-stand-up-pm-defiant-over-chinese-political-interference.

10 G. Hutchens, "Sweeping foreign interference and spying laws pass senate," *The Guardian*, 28 June 2018. https://www.theguardian.com/australia-news/2018/jun/29/sweeping-foreign-interference-and-spying-laws-pass-senate (Accessed 10 September 2021).

11 The White House, "Joint leaders statement on AUKUS," 15 September 2021. https://www.whitehouse.gov/briefing-room/statements-releases/2021/09/15/joint-leaders-statement-on-aukus/.

12 W. Ziebell, "Australia says diplomats should not undermine rights, after HK protest," *Reuters*, 27 July 2019. https://www.reuters.com/article/us-hongkong-extraditions-australia-idUSKCN1UM03M.

13 CBC, "Australia to pursue coronavirus investigation at World Health Assembly," 23 April 2020. https://www.cbc.ca/news/world/australia-who-coronavirus-pandemic-investigation-1.5542172.

14 A. Tillett, "China consumer backlash looms over Morrison's coronavirus probe," *Financial Review*, 26 April 2020. https://www.afr.com/politics/federal/china-consumer-backlash-looms-over-morrison-s-coronavirus-probe-20200423-p54mpl.

15 Minister for Foreign Affairs (Australia), "Joint statement on human rights abuses in Xinjiang," 23 March 2021. https://www.foreignminister.gov.au/minister/marise-payne/media-release/joint-statement-human-rights-abuses-xinjiang.

16 Total trade in goods and services between Australia and China rose from AU$86.74 billion in 2015 to AU$168.57 billion in 2019, a five-year increase of 94.3 percent. Calculations based on data from the Australian Department of Foreign Affairs and Trade. https://dfat.gov.au/trade/resources/trade-statistics/Pages/trade-time-series-data.aspx.

17 H. White, "Malcolm Turnbull condemns China but has no alternative plan," *Financial Review*, 4 June 2017. http://www.afr.com/opinion/col-

umnists/malcolm-turnbull-condemns-china-but-has-no-alternative-plan-20170604-gwk1un.

18 Hu Bo, "Ao hebi ba ziji bi dao duikang qianyan? (Why should Australia force itself to the forefront of confrontation?)," *Huanqiu shibao* (*Global Times*), 7 July 2021, p. 14.

19 Liu Changming and Sun Tong, "Nanhai zhengduan zhong de aodaliya: zhengce, dongyin yu quxiang (Australia's South China Sea policy, driving forces and tendency)," *Guoji Guancha* (*International Review*), 2, 143–156 (2018).

20 Yu Lei, "Ao mei tongmeng xia aodaliya duichong celue de jiangou yu yingxing: jiyu quanli jiagou lilun (The constructs and effects of Australia's hedging strategy under the Australia-US alliance: Based on power architecture theory)," *Tongyi zhanxian xue yanjiu* (*Journal of United Front Science*), 6, 94–105 (2020).

21 Zhang Qi, "Fenqi tuxian de zhongao guanxi jiang chixu xiahua (Divergent China-Australia relations to continue decline)," *Guoji zhengzhi kexue* (*Quarterly Journal of International Politics*), 3(2), 158–160 (2018).

22 Zhang Guoxi and Xie Tao, "Aodaliya jinqi fanhua fengbo jiqi yingxiang tanxi (Exploring recent Anti-China activities in Australia and their impact)," *Xiandai guoji guanxi* (*Contemporary International Relations*), 3, 26–34 (2018).

23 Hu Bo (2021), *Op. cit.*

24 Australia chose to announce its application to join the AIIB after the UK, New Zealand, France, Germany, and Italy to avoid accusations from the US, but this still displeased the US and Australia knows it well. See S. H. Rimmer, "Why Australia took so long to join the AIIB," *The Interpreter*, 30 March 2015. https://www.lowyinstitute.org/the-interpreter/why-australia-took-so-long-join-aiib.

25 Zhou Fangyin, "Tixi zhuanxing beijing xia de weixie renzhi yu aodaliya duihua zhengce bianhua (Threat cognition in the context of transformation of the international system and the change of Australian policy towards China)," *Shijie jingji yu zhengzhi* (*World Economics and Politics*), 1, 22–59 (2020).

26 The dispute between China and the Philippines over the South China Sea has heated up significantly since the second half of 2023, but at least during Duterte's administration from June 2016 to June 2022, Sino-Philippine relations were generally stable, and the Philippines did not take a drastic approach to challenging China over the South China Sea, suggesting that the Philippines' policy toward China can be largely independent of the influence of the Philippine-U.S. alliance, even in the context of the long-running Sino-Philippine dispute over the South China Sea, and the strong Philippine reliance on the U.S. in the security arena.

27 J. Bishop, "Interview with Kieran Gilbert, Sky News," Transcript, Minister for foreign affairs, the Hon Julie Bishop MP, 5 March 2018. https://www.foreignminister.gov.au/minister/julie-bishop/transcript-eoe/interview-kieran-gilbert-sky-news-1.

28 S. Birmingham, "Interview on RN breakfast with Fran Kelly," Transcript, Minister for Trade, Tourism and Investment, Minister for Finance, Senator the Hon Simon Birmingham, 6 November 2018. https://www.trademinister.gov.au/minister/simon-birmingham/transcript/interview-rn-breakfast-fran-kelly-1.

29 S. Birmingham, "Interview on Sky News live with Speers on Sunday," Transcript, Minister for Trade, Tourism and Investment, Minister for Finance, Senator the Hon Simon Birmingham, 4 August 2019. https://www.senatorbirmingham.com.au/interview-on-sky-news-live-with-speers-on-sunday/.

30 Xu Shanpin and Zhang Tao, "Lianmeng kunjing, lixing xuanze yu ao mei tongmeng de youxian shengji (Alliance dilemma, rational choice and the limited upgrading of Australia-US alliance)," *Guoji anquan yanjiu* (*Journal of International Security Studies*), 39(2), 107–131 (2021).

31 Chen Hong, "Shoushuliangduan de aodaliya duihua zhengce (The wavering Australia policy toward China)," *Shijie zhishi* (*World Affairs*), 17, 62–63 (2020).

32 Zhou Fangyin, "Youxian zhanlue shousuo xia de tongmeng guanxi guanli: aobama zhengfu yu telangpu zhengfu de zhengce xuanze (Managing alliances under limited strategic contraction: Policy choices of the Obama and Trump administrations)," *Guoji zhengzhi kexue* (*Quarterly Journal of International Politics*), 4(2), 1–34 (2019).

33 G. H. Snyder, "The security dilemma in alliance politics," *World Politics*, 36(4), 461–495 (1984).

34 A. Oliver, "Understanding Australian attitudes to the world," *Lowy Institute Poll 2017* (Sydney: Lowy Institute for International Policy, 2017), p. 11; A. Oliver, "Understanding Australian attitudes to the world," *Lowy Institute Poll 2018* (Sydney: Lowy Institute for International Policy), 2018, p. 8; N. Kassam, "Understanding Australian attitudes to the world," *Lowy Institute Poll 2019* (Sydney: Lowy Institute for International Policy, 2019), pp. 12–13.

35 N. Kassam, "Understanding Australian attitudes to the world," Lowy Institute Poll 2020 (Sydney: Lowy Institute for International Policy, 2020), pp. 16–17.

36 Kassam (2019), *Op. cit.*, p. 10.

37 Department of Foreign Affairs and Trade (Australia), *2017 Foreign Policy White Paper*, p. 6.

38 Zhou (2020), *Op. cit.*

39 N. Bisley and B. Schreer, "Australia and the rules-based order in Asia," *Asian Survey*, 58(2), 302–319 (2018); R. Medcalf, "Australia and China: Understanding the reality check," *Australia Journal of International Affairs*, 73(2), 109–118 (2019).

40 Zhou (2020), *Op. cit.*

41 Xu Shaomin, "Guojia liyi, weixie renzhi yu aodaliya duihua zhengce de chongzhi (National interests, threat perception and Australia's China "reset")," *Waijiao pinglun (Foreign Affairs Review)*, 5, 52–86 (2020); Medcalf (2019), *Op. cit.*; M. Wesley, "Oceania: Cold war versus the Blue Pacific," in A. J. Tellis *et al.* (eds.) *Strategic Asia 2020: U.S.-China Competition for Global Influence*, The National Bureau of Asian Research, p. 204, March 2020.

42 R. Huisken, "How to think about Australia's relationship with China," *Australian Journal of International Affairs*, 71(6), 563–567 (2017).

43 Department of Foreign Affairs and Trade (Australian Government). https://dfat.gov.au/trade/resources/trade-statistics/Pages/trade-time-series-data.aspx.

44 Wang Lianhe, "Zhanlue liangnan yu liyi junzhan: zhongguo jueqi beijing xia de aodaliya zhanlue jiexi (Strategic dilemma and equal share: Australia's Asia-Pacific strategy in the context of China's rise)," *Guoji guancha (International Review)*, 4, 98–112 (2016).

45 Wei Zongyou, "Aodaliya de duihua duichong zhanlue (Australia's hedging strategy on China)," *Guoji wenti yanjiu (International Studies)*, 4, 54–67 (2015).

46 Calculations based on data from the Australian Department of Foreign Affairs and Trade, see Department of Foreign Affairs and Trade of Australian Government. https://dfat.gov.au/trade/resources/trade-statistics/Pages/trade-time-series-data.aspx.

47 *Ibid.*

48 For discussions of relative gains, see J. Grieco, "Anarchy and the limits of cooperation: A realist critique of the newest liberal institutionalism," *International Organization*, 42(3), 485–507 (1988); R. Powell, "Absolute and relative gains in international relations theory," *American Political Science Review*, 85(4), 1303–1320 (1991); D. Snidal, "Relative gains and the pattern of international cooperation," *American Political Science Review*, 85(3), 701–726 (1991).

49 Xu Shaomin, "Aodaliya 'yintai' zhanlueguan: neihan, dongyin he qianjing (Australian views of the "Indo-Pacific": Implications, drivers and prospects)" *Dangdai yatai (Journal of Contemporary Asia-Pacific Studies)*, 3, 115–156 (2018).

50 Ning Tuanhui, "Zhengdang zhengzhi yu aodaliya duihua zhengce de zhuanbian (Party politics and the transformation of Australia's policy towards

China)," *Guoji zhengzhi kexue* (*Quarterly Journal of International Politics*), 6(3), 95–124 (2021).

51 Xu (2020), *Op. cit.*

52 D. Brophy, "Australia's China debate in 2018," in J. Golley *et al.* (eds.) *China Story Yearbook: Power* (Canberra: Australian National University Press, 2018), p. 156; J. Menadue, "Contracting out our foreign and defence policies," *John Menadue's Public Policy Journal*, 4 January 2018. https://johnmenadue.com/john-menadue-militarysecurity-takeover-of-australias-foreign-policy/.

53 T. F. Chan, "Australia's intelligence chief warns of 'unprecedented' foreign interference with more spies now than during the cold war," *Insider*, 25 May 2018. https://www.businessinsider.com/australian-intelligence-head-sounds-alarm-over-unprecedented-foreign-interference-2018-5.

54 Xu (2020), *Op. cit.*

55 Chengxin Pan, "The Indo-Pacific and geopolitical anxieties about China's rise in the Asian regional order," *Australian Journal of International Affairs*, 68(4), 453–469 (2014); Chengxin Pan, "Identity politics and the poverty of diplomacy: China in Australia's 2017 foreign policy white paper," *Security Challenge*, 14(1), 13–20 (2018).

56 Wang Lei, "Aodaliya dui mei lianmeng zhong de shenfen zhengzhi: lishixing fenxi (1942–2016) (The impact of identity politics in Australia's alliance with United States on its Asia policy: A diachronic analysis, 1942–2016)" *Jiangnan shehui xueyuan xuebao* (*Journal of Jiangnan Social University*), 18(4), 40–45 (2016); Xu Shanpin and Wang Shucheng, "Guojia shenfen shijiao xia aodaliya de waijiao zhengce xuanze (Australia's foreign policy: From a perspective of national identity)," *Yinduyang jingjiti yanjiu* (*Indian Ocean Economic and Political Review*), 3, 67–84 (2018); Xu (2020), *Op. cit.*

57 Chinese scholars have a clear perception of this initiative shown by Australia, see Xu Shaomin and Li Qi, "Aodaliya zhanlue shiye xia de AUKUS xuanze (An examination of Australia's strategy for AUKUS)," *Zhanlue Juece Yanjiu* (*Journal of Strategy and Decision-Making*), 2, 81–104 (2023).

58 Medcalf (2019), *Op. cit.*; M. Varrall, "Australia's response to China in the Pacific: From alert to alarmed," in G. Smith and T. Wesley-Smith (eds.) *The China Alternative: Changing Regional Order in the Pacific Islands* (Canberra: Australian National University Press, 2021), pp. 107–141.

59 B. Womack, *Asymmetry and International Relationships* (Cambridge: Cambridge University Press, 2016), pp. 47–53.

60 "Sheping: Aodaliya duanqiwan chirou, fangxia kuaizi maniang (Editorial: Australia picks up bowl to eat meat, puts down chopsticks to curse)," *Huanqiu shibao* (*Global Times*), 23 November 2017, Huanqiu Net. https://opinion.huanqiu.com/article/9CaKrnK5OTB.

61 F. Hanson, "Australia and the world: Public opinion and foreign policy," *Lowy Institute Poll 2010* (Sydney: Lowy Institute for International Policy, 2010), p. 9.

62 The Pew Global Attitudes Project, p. 25, 12 June 2008. https://www.pewresearch.org/global/2008/06/12/chapter-1-views-on-economic-issues/ (Accessed 13 September 2021).

63 M. Condon, "Grains industry expresses risk to barley trade as China takes lion's share of Australian exports," *ABC News*, February 14, 2024. https://www.abc.net.au/news/2024-02-14/grains-industry-risk-to-barley-trade-as-china-takes-lions-share/103460760.

64 Ministry of Commerce of the People's Republic of China, "Shangwubu gongbu dui yuanchan yu aodaliya de jinkou xiaomai fanqingxiao diaocha he fanbutie diaocha de zuizhong chaiding (The Ministry of Commerce announced the final decision on the anti-dumping investigation and countervailing investigation of imported barley originating from Australia)," 18 May 2020. http://www.mofcom.gov.cn/article/ae/ai/202005/20200502965864.shtml.

65 Australian Bureau of Statistics. https://stat.data.abs.gov.au/#.

66 J. Laurenceson, "Australia's luck in handling Chinese trade coercion," *East Asia Forum*, 18 August 2021. https://www.eastasiaforum.org/2021/08/18/australias-luck-in-handling-chinese-trade-coercion/.

67 https://www.dfat.gov.au/trade/trade-and-investment-data-information-and-publications/trade-statistics/trade-time-series-data.

68 L. Hunt, "Albanese to maintain Australia's strong stance on China," *VOA*, 5 June 2022. https://www.voanews.com/a/albanese-to-maintain-australia-s-strong-stance-on-china-/6603936.html; "'We need to stay the course': Australia's stance on China remains unchanged, Anthony Albanese says," *SBS News*, 5 August 2022. https://www.sbs.com.au/news/article/we-need-to-stay-the-course-australias-stance-on-china-remains-unchanged-anthony-albanese-says/nqo742lz3.

69 "How Albanese came to terms with China," *Financial Review,* 15 November 2022. https://www.afr.com/politics/federal/how-albanese-came-to-terms-with-china-20221114-p5bxyu.

70 A poll released by the Lowy Institute in Australia in June 2022 showed that, more than six in ten Australians (65 percent) say China's foreign policy poses a critical threat to Australia's vital interests, three-quarters of Australians (75 percent) say it is very or somewhat likely that China will become a military threat to Australia in the next 20 years, an increase of 29 points since 2018. The 2022 poll shows that Australians' negative perceptions of China in the security area are further reinforced. See N. Kassam, "Understanding Australian attitudes to the world," *Lowy Institute Poll 2022* (Sydney: Lowy Institute for International Policy, 2022), pp. 9–10, 18. See also Bates Gill' chapter in this issue for more information on Australia's perception of China's intentions, and threat perceptions: Chapter 9.

© 2025 World Scientific Publishing Europe Ltd.
https://doi.org/10.1142/9781800616318_0010

Chapter 9

Explaining the Troubled Australia–China Relationship: A Perspective from Australia[*]

Bates Gill

The National Bureau of Asian Research, United States

Macquarie University, Australia

Across a range of indicators, relations between Australia and the People's Republic of China (PRC) have sunk to their lowest level since establishing diplomatic relations in 1972. What explains this dramatic shift in Australia–China ties, and what are the prospects for the relationship going forward? Applying a basic neoclassical realist framework, this chapter argues that Australia's more cautious, distrustful, and defensive policies toward China arise from changes in the international power structure—especially the PRC's emergence as a stronger and more influential actor—and how those changes are in turn interpreted through Australian domestic norms, worldviews, processes, and incentives. The chapter explores and explains these developments through a discussion of the overarching geostrategic and normative precepts which have consistently shaped Australia's past, present, and future approach to the world, including its approach to relations with China; the application of

---

[*]This chapter was originally printed as "Explaining the Troubled Australia-China Relationship: A Perspective from Australia." *The China Review*, Vol. 23, No. 1 (2023): 243–275. https://www.jstor.org/stable/48717995. Reproduced with kind permission of CUHK Press.

232   B. Gill

a neoclassical realist framework for understanding changes in Australian policies toward China; an in-depth look at three key intervening domestic variables which shape Australia's increasingly tough approach to China; and an overview of key Australian policy outcomes *vis-à-vis* China. Based on this analysis, the chapter finds that Australia–China relations are likely to face a prolonged period of tension and distrust.

Across a range of indicators in diplomatic, political, economic, and security ties, relations between Australia and the People's Republic of China (PRC or China) have sunk to their lowest level since they established diplomatic relations in 1972. Their relationship is increasingly characterized by "bounded engagement": a mix of interactions primarily in the economic sphere, paired with greater suspicions, limited official contacts, and punitive measures across other aspects of bilateral ties.[1] As argued in the opening chapter of this book by Liu and He, Australia–China relations have transitioned from "cooperative partnership" to "competitive rivalry" (see Chapter 1).

What explains this dramatic shift in Australia–China ties and what are the prospects for the relationship going forward? This chapter applies a basic neoclassical realist framework to show that Australia's more cautious, distrustful, and defensive policies toward China arise from changes in the international power structure—especially the PRC's emergence as a stronger and more influential actor—and how those changes are in turn interpreted through Australian domestic norms, worldviews, processes, and incentives. On the basis of this analysis, this chapter finds that Australia–China relations are likely to face a prolonged period of tension and distrust.

The chapter explores and explains these developments for Australia–China relations across the following four dimensions:

- the overarching geostrategic and normative precepts which have consistently shaped Australia's past, present, and future approach to the world, including its approach to relations with China;
- a neoclassical realist framework for understanding the changes in Australian policies toward China;
- a set of three key intervening domestic variables which shape Australia's increasingly tough approach to China; and
- the key Australian policy outcomes *vis-à-vis* China.

Explaining the Troubled Australia–China Relationship 233

The chapter concludes with a brief section outlining the key challenges in Australia–China relations now and in the coming five to ten years.

Before proceeding, it may be useful to draw some overall comparisons and contrasts between this chapter and the preceding one by Fangyin Zhou (see Chapter 8). Interestingly, while we adopt different analytical approaches, our findings and conclusions do not fundamentally differ. We point to many of the same key underlying factors that can help explain Australia's approach to China. These include Australia's close relationship with the United States (U.S.), Australia's particular geostrategic and geoeconomic circumstances, the role of Australian domestic political actors, norms, and identity politics, and Australia's changing security perceptions in the face of an increasingly asymmetrical relationship with China. We also agree on the range of precipitating actions by both China and Australia during 2015–2021, which have further contributed to the worsening relationship. Where our differences may lie is in the emphasis this chapter places on longer-term, consistent geopolitical, and normative precepts in Australia and how, with those in mind, Australians have reacted with increasing sensitivity and concern to China's growing power. In the end, we reach a similar conclusion: owing to a range of factors, such as those identified above, Australia and China should not expect to see much improvement in their relationship in the years ahead.

9.1. Consistent Geostrategic and Normative Precepts

Geopolitics—the mix of geography, history, demography, and politics and how they affect relations with other countries—is a good place to start for understanding Australia's past, present, and future approach to the world, particularly its approach to relations with China.

Australia is a comparatively remote, continent-sized island nation with a relatively small population of about 26 million people, predominantly concentrated in major coastal cities. Rich in highly valued natural resources, Australia is a Group of 20 (G20) country with the world's 12th-largest economy when measured by nominal GDP. Among the G20 countries, Australia has the second-largest GDP per capita (after the U.S.) and ranks 11th in the world by that indicator.[2] Australia's economic success and prosperity rely on unimpeded international flows of trade, investment, and information.

Geographically situated in the Indo-Pacific, Australia has, for historical reasons, been closely linked—normatively, ethnically, and politically—with Europe and with the United Kingdom (U.K.) in particular. Importantly, Australia's parliamentary democracy, rule of law, and market-based economic principles draw directly from British traditions. Owing to its lengthy history of shared experiences, interests, and values with the U.S.—including as former British colonies which began as settler nations and through fighting side-by-side in every major conflict in which either one or the other has been engaged since World War I—Australia also has a strong strategic affinity with the U.S., especially since the end of World War II.

Owing to its relative geographic isolation and small population, Australia has traditionally relied on "great and powerful friends"—as famously stated by former Australian Prime Minister Robert Menzies—to help provide for its security. For most of Australia's history since the beginning of European settlement in the late 18th century, that role was filled by the U.K. Since World War II, and especially with the signing of the Australia, New Zealand, and United States Security Treaty (ANZUS), in 1951, the U.S. has been that security partner.

Australia's geopolitics since European settlement have served the country's foreign relations fairly well. As a comparatively distant and geographically vast island, supported by powerful allies, Australia has never known foreign invasion or occupation since the late 18th century. Despite its remoteness, it has achieved a broadly prosperous, democratic, peaceful, and—over the past several decades—multicultural society.

As Australian scholars such as Mark Beeson, Jinghan Zeng, and Michael Wesley make clear, Australia's geostrategic environment results in a predominantly realist understanding of its place in the world. This Australian approach is characterized by features such as "perennial anxiety" and preoccupation with its peculiar geopolitical position, "systemic pessimism" toward major shifts in geostrategic power, and a resultant "strategic dependence" on a powerful friend, which is a "hard-wired" and "non-negotiable" core element of its strategic policy.[3] This dominant *weltanschauung* runs deeply in Australia and profoundly shapes how its decision-makers think about relations with China.[4]

But there are other important aspects of Australian worldviews which modulate a strictly realistic approach. For example, an Australia that is able to "punch above its weight" has also actively pursued an independent "middle power" diplomatic strategy, which has elements of liberal

Explaining the Troubled Australia–China Relationship 235

internationalism: the belief that diplomacy, multilateralism, and strong international institutions can provide an added layer of protection for a liberal international order, preserve state sovereignty and policy independence (especially for weaker states), and embed stronger powers in a system of norms and rules conducive to Australian interests in stability and predictability. Hence, these factors underpin Australia's traditionally strong support for the United Nations and its important contributions to the development of regional institutions such as the Asia-Pacific Economic Cooperation (APEC) forum and the Association of Southeast Asian Nations (ASEAN) Regional Forum (ARF).

It is also important to acknowledge the strong ideational streak within Australian political circles, which shapes the country's perceptions and incentives regarding the international system. Australia's traditional identity as part of the "Anglosphere," as a democracy, and as a defender of liberal values is more than rhetorical. It actually reinforces the country's overwhelming proclivity to strategically partner with "like-minded" partners, especially the U.S. It helps explain the ready ease with which Australia takes part in the "Five Eyes" intelligence-sharing pact with Canada, New Zealand, the U.K., and the U.S., the instinctive embrace of the Australia–United Kingdom–United States (AUKUS) relationship, and Australia's increasing enthusiasm for the Quadrilateral Security Dialogue (or Quad) among four major Indo-Pacific democracies (Australia, India, Japan, and the U.S.) in support of a "free and open Indo-Pacific."[5] The fact that Australia is an electoral democracy also means that its political leaders will be closely attuned to public opinion, which can also be a mediating factor in the deliberation and execution of foreign policy.

9.2. A Framework for Assessing Australia–China Relations

While Australian realism best explains the country's strategic outlook overall, important domestic perceptions and incentives in relation to the international system—such as leaders' perceptions of the international offense–defense balance, liberal internationalist tendencies, domestic politics, ideational factors, and public attitudes—can play an intervening role in shaping the country's foreign policy outcomes. Thus, applying a neoclassical realist framework—whereby responses to the changing external or systemic environment are deliberated and implemented based

236   *B. Gill*

on internal processes—helps us understand the ongoing shifts and increasing difficulties in the Sino–Australian relationship.[6] In the words of Randall Schweller:

> Neoclassical realism does not reject systemic theory but instead combines it with domestic-level theorizing, exploring the internal processes by which states arrive at policies and decide on actions in response to pressures and opportunities in their external environment.[7]

Applying a basic neoclassical realist framework for understanding and explaining Australian foreign policy decision-making, we can see how Australia's approach to China has changed over time to the point that the PRC's rise and growing power would increasingly be seen as a challenge to Australian interests and values.

For understandable economic self-interest reasons, Australia embraced the benefits of exporting much of its abundant endowment of ores, energy, and agriculture to the Asian economic miracle, beginning with Japan's revival in the 1960s, followed by that of the "four tigers" (Hong Kong, Singapore, South Korea, and Taiwan) in the 1970s and 1980s, and the spectacular rise of China beginning in the 1990s.[8] Around 2008–2009, China overtook Japan as Australia's number one export destination, a position that Japan had held since the mid-1960s, when it overtook the U.K. China today is by far Australia's largest trading partner. As of mid-2020, two-way trade with China accounted for nearly 29 percent of all Australian trade, dwarfing that with its second-largest trading partner, the U.S., which accounted for just over 9 percent.[9] As an export destination, China looms even larger for Australia: some 35–40 percent of Australian exports by value go to China; this was true even in 2020 and 2021, amid the COVID-19 pandemic and punitive Chinese trade measures against Australia, largely owing to surging iron ore prices during this period.[10]

Formally establishing a "comprehensive strategic partnership" in 2014 and launching the China–Australia Free Trade Agreement in 2015 were the crowning achievements of this deepening economic relationship. The benefit to Australia's national interest is clear: prior to the COVID-19-induced recession which hit Australia in 2020, the country had enjoyed nearly 29 years of economic growth without a recession, a record among the world's advanced economies.[11]

Canberra's generally positive approach to China in the past was grounded in the widespread appreciation within Australia that the shifting international balance of economic power brought substantial benefits to the country. But in addition, taking economic advantage of the ongoing changes in the international system was further reinforced at home by perceptions that China's growing power could be peacefully integrated into a web of norms and rules aligned with Australian interests in stability and predictability. For example, Canberra's decision to join the China-led Asian Infrastructure Investment Bank (AIIB), despite Washington's protests, was based partly on the belief that "being in the tent" was a way to ensure the institution played by accepted rules and could further socialize Beijing to accept longstanding international norms. Meanwhile, though ideational concerns about China's authoritarian nature persisted among Australian foreign policy elites, they remained largely beneath the surface and did not significantly intervene to affect Canberra's policies toward the PRC.

However, as China's economic success has increasingly transformed into strategic and military power, it was only a matter of time before Australia's consistent underlying worldviews of "perennial anxiety" and "systemic pessimism" came to the fore. As the Australian Department of Defense Strategic Update 2020 states, "Australia's region, the Indo-Pacific, is in the midst of the most consequential strategic realignment since World War II." As a result, it continues, "[s]trategic competition, primarily between the United States and China, will be the principal driver of strategic dynamics in the Indo-Pacific", and "[t]hough still remote, the prospect of high intensity military conflict in the Indo-Pacific is less remote than in the past."[12] In the midst of this changing strategic dynamic, it should surprise no one that Australia will align with the U.S., despite its economic relationship with China.

As the international power structure changed, so too did domestic perceptions in Australia about the vulnerability of the liberal international order and China's role within it. China, like other major powers, increasingly chafes at the strictures of some norms and institutions that run counter to its interests, refuse to grant the level of respect Beijing believes it deserves, or do not properly reflect its growing influence in world affairs. Across many dimensions of regional and global affairs, the PRC seeks changes to how the international system should work as Xi Jinping has promoted a far more active effort to build up China's "international narrative [or discourse] power" (國際話語權 *guoji huayu quan*), "tell China's story well and spread China's voice" (講好中國故事，傳播好中國聲音 *jianghao Zhongguo gushi chuanbo hao Zhongguo shengyin*), and put forward a "Chinese solution" (中國方案 *Zhongguo fangan*) for the reform of the international system, offering Chinese ideas to address 21st-century global problems, and even proposing that aspects of China's social, economic, and political development model could be adopted by other countries.[13]

Australian leaders find this discomfiting and are concerned that China will work to undermine aspects of the liberal rules-based order—such as free markets, freedom of navigation and overflight, international law of the sea, respect for human rights, press freedoms, an open internet, and peaceful settlement of disputes—on which Australian national interests and values have relied in the past.

Importantly, Australian foreign policy elites increasingly perceive changes in the international system through the lens of ideational politics, which have become a larger factor in how Australians approach their relationship with the PRC—or, more to the point, with the country's ruling regime, the Chinese Communist Party (CCP or Party). There was no doubt some expectation in Australia that, with "reform and opening," the PRC's sociopolitical system would evolve in a more open and just direction. In many respects, that expectation has been borne out, certainly in comparison to the excesses of the Maoist period. However, during the Xi Jinping era, Australians increasingly see a China as more authoritarian, less open, and less just. To the degree that China's foreign policy seeks, in the words of Jessica Chen Weiss, to "make the world safe for autocracy,"[14] generate legitimacy and even approbation for one-party rule, and denigrate (or possibly interfere with) democratic systems of government, Australian foreign policy elites will respond negatively in their policy approaches toward China.

9.3. Three Key Intervening Variables

The following section applies the neoclassical realist framework to examine three key internal variables which help explain the increasingly cautious, distrustful, and defensive Australian policies toward China, especially since 2016. These are: views of the changing regional security environment; concerns over domestic political interference; and shifting public opinion.

9.3.1. *Changing regional security environment*

Australian political leaders and other foreign policy elites have become increasingly concerned about the ongoing shift in the regional balance of power. These concerns are driven first and foremost by the PRC's dramatic and continuing emergence as a more powerful and capable military player, especially in the Indo-Pacific region but also further afield, which in turn has a profound effect on Australia's strategic environment and national interests.

China is easily the largest military spender in the region, with an annual military budget in 2020 three times that of the region's next closest spender, India; when measured over the period 2011–2020, China spent four times as much as India on its military. Indeed, China's military spending in 2020 was larger than the combined amounts of the next nine defense budgets in Asia (see Figure 9.1). Globally, China has the world's second-largest military budget; the U.S. has the largest at US$778.2 billion, which is about three times the size of China's.[15]

With over 350 ships and submarines (including 130 major surface combatants, 60 submarines, and soon-to-be three aircraft carriers), China's navy is the world's largest.[16] China also fields the largest air force in Asia

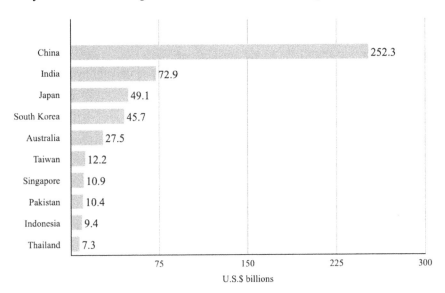

Figure 9.1. Top 10 military spenders in Asia, 2020.

Note: Figures expressed in current U.S. dollars for 2020.
Source: Stockholm International Peace Research Institute (SIPRI) Military Expenditure Database.

and the third largest worldwide, with 2,500 aircraft (of which about 2,000 are combat aircraft).[17] In addition, the People's Liberation Army (PLA) deploys over 1,250 land-based ballistic and cruise missiles. It has also made significant strides in expanding and improving its nuclear forces; according to the Federation of American Scientists, China surpassed France in 2020 to become the world's third-largest nuclear arsenal.[18]

In addition to building up its military hardware, the PLA is also undergoing a major reform and reorganization program, starting in early 2016, to streamline the Chinese military and transform it into a more modern and technologically sophisticated fighting force capable of conducting joint operations against advanced adversaries and projecting power further from PRC shores. Xi Jinping has set a timeline for the PLA that aims to achieve a "fully modernized" force by 2035 and a "world class military" in time for the PRC's 100th anniversary in 2049.[19]

For Australian leaders and strategic planners, these developments pose numerous challenges.[20] First, the PLA is placing significant resources into the development and deployment of stand-off, precision-strike weapons (such as land-, air-, and sea-based missiles), as well as at-sea and land-based air defenses, all enabled by more technologically advanced space and cyber capabilities. This gives China a range of more lethal options to deter and attack opposition naval and air forces. Australia's far smaller naval and air forces on their own will increasingly be outgunned in comparison to the PLA, particularly at sea.

Second, responding to what it sees as its principal threats and missions in the near to medium term, the PLA has focused on developing and deploying capabilities that can concentrate firepower on a range of increasingly contested spaces around China's periphery, especially its so-called "near seas" (近海, *jinhai*), also often referred to as the "first island chain."[21] Within this maritime expanse, which encompasses the Japan Sea, the East China Sea, the Taiwan Strait, and the South China Sea, China has several ongoing and highly contentious sovereignty and territorial disputes with its neighbors. Many of these neighbors are either allies or close security partners with the U.S., such as Japan, the Philippines, and Taiwan.

Third, the PLA is increasingly capable of projecting power and maintaining a more regular military presence beyond the first island chain, including a growing presence in the Indian Ocean, the western Pacific Ocean, and in and around the straits and archipelagos which form the northern approaches to the Australian continent. The PLA Navy, the PLA Air Force, and the PLA Rocket Force, all with support from the PLA

Strategic Support Force, regularly carry out routine patrols, surveillance missions, and other exercises in these areas. The PLA Rocket Force also operates medium- and long-range ballistic and cruise missiles, such as the DF-21 (with a range of 1,500 kilometers), the DF-26 (4,000 kilometers), and DH-10 (1,500 kilometers), capable of attacking targets on land and at sea, including those well beyond the first island chain. The PLA does not yet have a large-scale expeditionary force but has demonstrated an ability to mount and sustain armed forces for longer periods farther from its shores through such activities as anti-piracy task forces in the Gulf of Aden, United Nations peacekeeping deployments, and the establishment of its first overseas military base in Djibouti.[22]

These changes in the regional security environment have contributed to shifts in Australian thinking about China and the potential threats it may pose to Australian interests. At a basic level, China is increasingly seen as more of a "security threat" than as an "economic partner" (see Figure 9.2). The crossover in sentiments, as shown in Figure 9.2, around 2020 symbolizes an important milestone in Australian strategic thinking, even though China remains the dominant trading partner for Australia. The weightiness

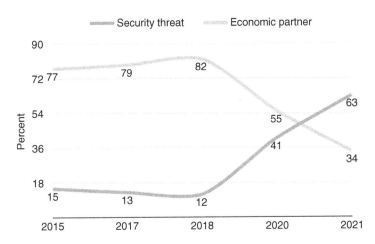

Figure 9.2. Is China more a security threat or economic partner?

Note: Percentage of respondents agreeing with one or the other proposition. The question asked was: "In your own view, is China more of an economic partner or more of a security threat to Australia?" From 2015–2018, the question was phrased: "Is China more of an economic partner or more of a military threat?"

Source: The Lowy Institute. See: https://poll.lowyinstitute.org/charts/china-economic-partner-or-security-threat/.

242   *B. Gill*

of concerns regarding China as a security threat was reflected in responses to another poll question. When asked to rank the threat posed by Australia–China relations to Australian vital interests, 56 percent of respondents said this was a "critical threat," 40 percent found it "an important but not critical threat" and only 3 percent felt they were not an important threat at all.[23] These developments provide further evidence in support of Liu and He's argument, at the outset of this special issue, that Australia–China relations have shifted from a "cooperative partnership" to a "competitive rivalry" (see Chapter 1).

9.3.2. *Domestic political interference*

Beginning in 2015 and 2016, a range of public revelations and allegations emerged concerning Party and PRC government efforts to cultivate and influence elite and societal views in Australia about China and the Chinese Communist Party. Concerns also began to mount and became more public about investments by PRC entities in Australian critical infrastructure, as well as ongoing espionage and state-backed cyber intrusion activities emanating from China.

Many of these developments became headline news and the subjects of high-profile investigative journalism, best-selling books, and defamation lawsuits.[24] As noted specialist on China and the media Wanning Sun argues, the hard-hitting and influential *Four Corners* investigation into PRC influence activities, which aired in June 2017—and which has since come under some criticism for its coverage—nevertheless "has significantly shaped the ways in which China has been reported [in Australia] in subsequent years."[25]

Among the most explosive revelations and concerns are:

- the acquisition of a 99-year lease in 2015 by a PRC company to operate the Australian port of Darwin; other high-profile bids by PRC companies for Australian infrastructure and large-scale agricultural operations were rejected by Australian authorities;
- acceptance by Federal Member of Parliament Sam Dastyari of personal cash support and travel funding from PRC-based companies and Party organizations, while also controversially voicing support for certain PRC government policies (while he had not acted illegally, Dastyari eventually resigned in 2016, and his case came to symbolize broader concerns over PRC political influence activities);

Explaining the Troubled Australia–China Relationship   243

- acceptance by Australia's major political parties of millions of dollars in donations from PRC nationals and wealthy Australians with close political and economic connections to the PRC[26];
- extensive ownership of Chinese-language media in Australia by PRC state-owned media companies[27];
- reports in 2016 that Australian government and business cyber networks had been hacked and infiltrated by PRC-based entities, including Austrade, the Bureau of Meteorology, the Defence Science Technology Group, and NewSat Ltd.[28];
- attempts by PRC government representatives to silence critics in Australia and pressure local governments to adopt PRC-friendly postures;
- efforts by PRC government officials to monitor the activities of Chinese students attending Australian universities and cultivate PRC-friendly Chinese diaspora groups in the country.

In addition, the PRC embassy in Canberra sent an unprecedented message to Australian officials in late 2020 by intentionally releasing a 14-point set of grievances to local media outlets. Saying the Australian government would need to address and resolve these grievances in order to stop "poisoning bilateral relations," the embassy's list included: the denial of certain PRC investments in Australia, such as banning Huawei from involvement in the country's fifth-generation (5G) network; funding certain "anti-China" think tanks, such as the Australian Strategic Policy Institute; raiding the offices and homes of PRC journalists working in Australia; issuing critical statements about PRC policy toward Hong Kong, the South China Sea, Taiwan, and Xinjiang; targeting China with foreign interference legislation; allowing allegations against China for cyberattacks; and calling for an independent, international body to investigate the source of the COVID-19 pandemic. A facsimile of the complete list, reproduced in the *Sydney Morning Herald*, is shown in Figure 9.3.[29]

Such demands only further underscored the image of PRC officials conducting "wolf warrior diplomacy" (戰狼外交, *zhanlang waijiao*) in a ham-fisted effort to influence Australian policy toward China.

These and related developments had a direct effect on the Australian public and its politicians. While not citing China specifically, polling by the Lowy Institute finds that Australians' concerns about "cyberattacks from other countries" and "foreign interference in Australian politics" are considered among the most critical threats to Australia's vital interests.

244 *B. Gill*

- Foreign investment decisions, with acquisitions blocked on opaque national security grounds in contravention of ChAFTA / since 2018, more than 10 Chinese investment projects have been rejected by Australia citing ambiguous and unfounded "national security concerns "and putting restrictions in areas like infrastructure, agriculture and animal husbandry.
- The decision banning Huawei Technologies and ZTE from the 5G network, over unfounded national security concerns, doing the bidding of the US by lobbying other countries.
- Foreign interference legislation, viewed as targeting China and in the absence of any evidence.
- Politicization and stigmatization of the normal exchanges and cooperation between China and Australia and creating barriers and imposing restrictions, including the revoke of visas for Chinese scholars.
- Call for an international independent inquiry into the COVID -19 virus, acted as a political manipulation echoing the US attack on China.
- The incessant wanton interference in China's Xinjiang, Hong Kong, and Taiwan affairs; spearheading the crusade against China in certain multilateral forums.
- The first non-littoral country to make a statement on the South China Sea to the United Nations.
- Siding with the US' anti-China campaign and spreading disinformation imported from the US around China's efforts of containing COVID-19.
- The latest legislation to scrutinize agreements with a foreign government targeting towards China and aiming to torpedo the Victorian participation in B & R.
- Provided funding to anti-China think tank for spreading untrue reports, peddling lies around Xinjiang and so-called China infiltration aimed at manipulating public opinion against China.
- The early dawn search and reckless seizure of Chinese jounalists' homes and properties without any charges and giving any explanations.
- Thinly veiled allegations against China on cyber attacks without any evidence.
- Outrageous condemnation of the governing party of China by MPs and racist attacks against Chinese or Asian people.
- An unfriendly or antagonistic report on China by media, poisoning the atmosphere of bilateral relations.

Figure 9.3. "14 grievances" in the dossier provided by the PRC embassy in Australia to Australian media outlets, November 2020.

Source: *Sydney Morning Herald*, 18 November 2020.

Between 2014 and 2021, the percentage of Australians who considered cyberattacks a critical threat rose from 51 to 62, while those expressing concern about foreign interference went from 41 to 49 percent between 2018 and 2021.[30]

9.3.3. *Public attitudes*

Australian public views toward China have deteriorated considerably in recent years, especially since 2018. Broadly, Australians have less and

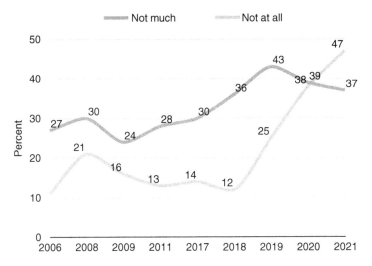

Figure 9.4. Australians' trust of China to act responsibly in the world, 2006–2021.

Note: Percentage of respondents replying either "not much" or "not at all." The question asked was: "How much do you trust [China] to act responsibly in the world?" Possible responses were: not at all; not very much; somewhat; a great deal; and don't know.

Source: The Lowy Institute. See: https://poll.lowyinstitute.org/charts/trust-in-global-powers.

less confidence in how China and its leaders approach the world. Remarkably, since 2018, the percentage of Australians surveyed who express no trust at all in China to act responsibly in the world has quadrupled, from 12 to 47 percent. That figure, when combined with the 37 percent who express "not much" trust in Beijing's approach to the world, means a vast majority of Australians—84 percent—are distrustful of China's role on the global stage (see Figure 9.4).

In addition, this distrust extends to Xi Jinping himself. The percentage of people expressing "no confidence at all" in Xi Jinping to do the right thing in world affairs more than tripled between 2016 and 2021, from 16 to 53; a total of 78 percent of Australians had either "not too much confidence" or "no confidence at all" in Xi's approach to world affairs (see Figure 9.5). These data on Australians' degree of trust in China and Xi Jinping are consistent with other major polls. For example, in 2020, the Pew Research Centre found that 81 percent of Australians had either a "somewhat unfavorable" or "very unfavorable" opinion of China, while 79 percent expressed a lack of confidence in Xi Jinping to do the right thing in world affairs; in 2021, the number of unfavorable views toward China dropped slightly to 78 percent.[31]

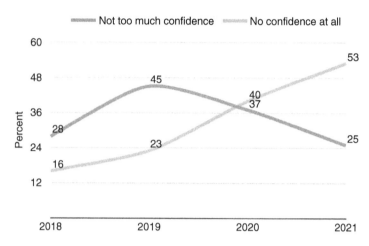

Figure 9.5. Australians' confidence in Xi Jinping to do the right thing in world affairs.

Note: Percentage of respondents replying either "not too much confidence" or "no confidence at all." The question asked was: "Tell me how much confidence you have in [Xi Jinping] to do the right thing regarding world affairs?" Possible responses were: no confidence at all; not too much confidence; some confidence; a lot of confidence; and don't know.

Source: The Lowy Institute. See: https://poll.lowyinstitute.org/charts/confidence-in-world-leaders/.

These trends in Australian attitudes are perhaps best captured by the Lowy Institute's "feelings thermometer," a gauge of sentiments that has been in place since 2007. Respondents are asked to rate their feelings toward other countries, with 100 indicating "very warm and favorable" and zero indicating "very cold and unfavorable." When this question first appeared in Lowy polling in 2007, China was rated relatively favorably. In 2007, for example, it rated just below Japan, about on par with such countries as India and the U.S., and above South Korea and Iran. However, with time, Australians' sentiments toward China have chilled, especially since 2018. The rating for 2021—at 32—was the lowest to date, placing China well below other places such as Japan (73), the European Union, Taiwan, Thailand and the U.S. (62), India (56), Myanmar and Russia (41), and Iran (34) (see Figures 9.6 and 9.7).

Starting from around 2016–2017, Australian comparative attitudes toward the U.S. and China also began to swing increasingly in favor of the former. When asked in 2020 which relationship—with the U.S. or with China—is more important to Australia, 55 percent of respondents said the U.S., a 15-point difference from those who identified relations with China

Explaining the Troubled Australia–China Relationship   247

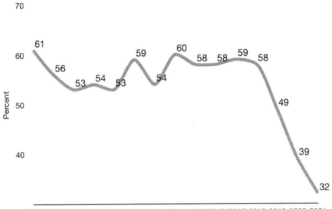

Figure 9.6. "Feelings Thermometer": Australian feelings of "Warmth" toward China, 2007–2021.

Note: On a scale of 0 (coldest) to 100 (warmest). The question asked was: "Please rate your feelings towards some countries and territories, with one hundred meaning a very warm, favorable feeling, zero meaning a very cold, unfavorable feeling, and fifty meaning not particularly warm or cold. You can use any number from zero to one hundred: the higher the number the more favorable your feelings are toward that country or territory. If you have no opinion or have never heard of that country or territory, please say so."
Source: The Lowy Institute. See: https://poll.lowyinstitute.org/charts/feelings-towards-other-nations/.

as more important. Responses from only three or four years earlier were about evenly divided (see Figure 9.8).

For the Australian public, the most important drivers behind this substantial downward shift in attitudes appear to be Beijing's actions at home and abroad, including those directly targeting Australians. These actions include:

- China's campaign to build and arm artificial island islands in the disputed waters of the South China Sea (especially from 2013 to 2015) and subsequent refusal to recognize the finding of the Arbitral Tribunal which, in accordance with the United Nations Convention on the Law of the Sea, invalidated the PRC's "nine-dashed line" as the basis for its claims in this vast waterway;
- the launching in 2014 of a renewed "Strike Hard Campaign Against Violent Terrorism" (嚴厲打擊暴力恐怖活動專項行動, *yanli daji*

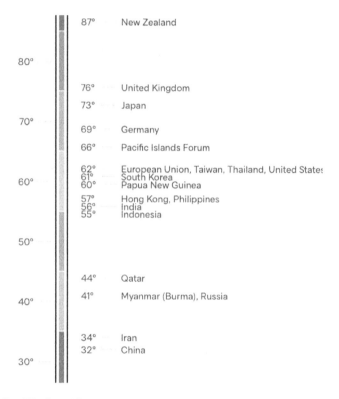

Figure 9.7. "Feelings Thermometer," 2021.

Source: The Lowy Institute. See: https://poll.lowyinstitute.org/charts/feelings-towards-other-nations/.

baoli kongbu huodong zhuanxiang xingdong) with Xinjiang as the "main battleground," the subsequent large-scale internment since 2017 of an estimated one million or more Uyghurs and other Muslim minorities in hundreds of detention centers for the purposes of training and patriotic education, and related destruction of Islamic religious sites[32];
- the crackdown against protestors in Hong Kong, including the "Umbrella Movement" in 2014 and massive street demonstrations in 2020–2021, which called for a more democratic local electoral process, the imposition of much stricter security and election laws in territory, the ongoing erosion of the "high degree of autonomy" promised to the people of Hong Kong as part of the reversion agreement

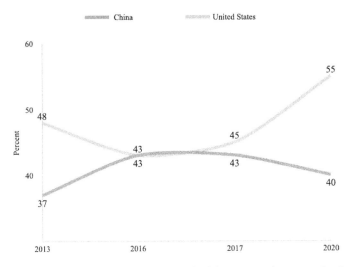

Figure 9.8. Are relations with China or the United States more important for Australia?

Note: The question asked was: "Now about Australia's relationships with China and the United States. And which relationship do you think is more important to Australia?"

Source: The Lowy Institute. See: https://poll.lowyinstitute.org/charts/relations-with-superpowers-us-and-china.

between the PRC and the U.K. in 1997, and the apparent abandonment of the "one country, two systems" model which formerly characterized relations between Beijing and Hong Kong[33];
- other domestic sociopolitical developments in China characterized by increasing intolerance for dissent, greater censorship and surveillance, and a more pervasive role of the Chinese Communist Party in social, economic, and intellectual life;
- the imposition in 2020 of tariffs and restrictive regulatory barriers on a range of Australian exports, including beef, barley, coal, timber, wine, and other products, as well as the issuance of official warnings against travel to Australia, in apparent retaliation for Canberra's call for an independent international investigation into the origins of the COVID-19 pandemic; and
- the harrassment of Australian journalists in China, including the detention (in August 2020) and charging (in February 2021) of an Australian national and journalist, Cheng Lei, accused of divulging state secrets[34]; from August 2020 to August 2024, there was no representative of any major Australian media outlet based in the PRC.

In addition to these developments, the outbreak of widespread human-to-human transmission of COVID-19 in Wuhan, China, and its subsequent global spread was a crucial factor in generating more negative public sentiments toward China in Australia. When asked how well or how badly China handled the COVID-19 pandemic, 69 percent of Australians in 2020 replied either "very badly" or "fairly badly," a number which improved to 52 percent in 2021.[35] Moreover, a large majority of Australians—68 percent—said they have less favorable views toward China's system of government as a result of its handling of the outbreak; only 5 percent said they had a more favorable view.[36] These polling numbers are consistent with the analysis by China expert Wanning Sun on Australian media coverage of China and COVID-19. She found that, "[a]cross the board, there is a high level of unfavorable reporting about China in relation to COVID-19," serving as "a continuation and embodiment of the 'China threat' and 'Chinese influence' discourses that have now dominated the Australian media for a number of years."[37]

Moreover, China's policy stance in the wake of Russia's invasion of Ukraine in February 2022 would further undermine Australian confidence in Beijing. By remaining largely diplomatically supportive of Moscow—or even trying to portray a policy of "neutrality"—China's positions are seen as contrary to international norms at best and a deeply cynical power calculation at worst. In public, the Australian government has adopted a slightly more measured tone. For example, in her speech to the United Nations General Assembly in September 2022, Australian Foreign Minister Penny Wong criticized Russia for its "illegal, immoral invasion of Ukraine" and called on China to show greater leadership: "it is especially important for countries that play leading roles in international fora, and countries with influence on Russia, to exert their influence to end this war. In this, the world looks to China, a great power, a Permanent Member of the Security Council, with a 'no limits partnership' with Russia."[38]

Public sentiments toward China in Australia are unlikely to change anytime soon and may worsen before they get better. Overall, only about 4 percent of Australians feel that Australia is more to blame for the current difficulties in relations with China. The vast majority in Australia feels either that China is more to blame (56 percent) or that both sides share equally in the blame (38 percent).[39]

9.4. Policy Changes

Using a neoclassical realist framework, we can see how changes in the international distribution of power, mediated by perceptions and incentives among Australian foreign policy elites, initially led to a positive trend in Australia–China relations—roughly between the mid-1990s and the mid-2010s—but have since led to a tougher foreign policy line toward China. With this background in mind, we can turn to outcomes: some of the specific Australian policies toward China, which took a decidedly harder turn beginning around 2016.

9.4.1. *Bolstering defense*

Based on their views of the changing regional security environment, especially China's growing military capabilities, Australian leaders and strategic planners have shifted the country's defense strategy since the mid-2010s. These efforts are intended to more openly acknowledge and confront the military and security challenges emanating from China.

Guaranteeing access to sea lanes in Australia's immediate vicinity and ensuring that the neighboring region to its north remains independent, stable, and generally friendly to Australia are critical national interests. Hence, Australian defense planners watch China's increasing presence and capabilities in these areas with intense scrutiny.[40] Moreover, as a treaty ally of the U.S., a security partner with many countries involved in disputes with China, and with an enormous national interest in the continued peace and stability of the Indo-Pacific region, Australia is compelled to contribute where it can, including through military means, to meet its defense and security commitments and defend its national interests. Prudent planning dictates that Australian armed forces be prepared for a future in which the PLA will be able to impose higher costs on them, especially in areas that may involve U.S. and allied intervention close to the PRC mainland, in and around the first island chain.

In response to these developments and potential threats, the Australian Defence Force—like many other militaries across the region which share similar concerns about China's capabilities and intentions—has increasingly shifted its procurement priorities to make significant new investments in longer-range, precision strike cruise missiles (such as anti-ship missiles) as well as more advanced submarines, surface warships, anti-submarine warfare capabilities, and fourth- and fifth-generation combat aircraft. By 2019, as part of a deepening defense relationship with the U.S.,[41] Australia became the world's second-largest arms importer on the back of its acquisition of a range of advanced U.S. weapons, including EA-18G Growler electronic warfare aircraft, E-7A Wedgetail airborne early warning and control aircraft, C-27J battlefield airlift aircraft, MH-60R Seahawk antisurface and antisubmarine helicopters, and 72 F-35 fighter aircraft.[42] In addition, Canberra decided in 2016 to develop and produce, in cooperation with France, up to 12 new diesel-powered submarines to replace its aging fleet of *Collins*-class boats.

Stepping up the momentum in 2020, Australian leaders announced a major new procurement plan, developed in cooperation with U.S. defense contractors, to give even greater priority to acquiring a range of long-range, precision-strike weapons, with a focus on anti-ship missiles (such as Tomahawk missiles) and including hypersonic missiles.[43] Further, in one of the country's most important strategic decisions in decades, in 2021, Australia partnered with the U.S. and the U.K. to establish a long-term defense and military-technical pact. AUKUS, the acronym by which the partnership is known, will initially have as its centerpiece the provision of nuclear-propelled attack submarines to Australia.[44]

But while the 2021 submarine deal garnered enormous attention, related announcements between the U.S. and Australia also signaled their intent to deepen defense-industrial research and production cooperation, increase the rotations of U.S. submarines, surface combatants, aircraft, and military personnel through Australian territory, and build a greater capacity in Australia to maintain, repair, and overhaul forward-deployed U.S. weapons, as well as store pre-positioned U.S. military equipment, ammunition, and other *matériel*.[45]

These developments mark a significant new phase in Australian strategic thinking and defense planning. These plans, if realized, will cost hundreds of billions of dollars and also represent a major commitment on the part of the U.S. and Australia to further deepen and sustain an already robust security partnership. These strategic choices flow directly from Australian leaders' assessments of the changing regional security environment, especially with regard to China's growing military capabilities and strategic ambitions.

9.4.2. Countering foreign interference

The Australian government has taken a number of measures in recent years to curb unwelcome foreign influence and other forms of what former Prime Minister Malcolm Turnbull called "covert, coercive or corrupt" activities which cross the line between "legitimate influence" and "unacceptable interference."[46] In late 2017, declaring in Chinese that "Australia has stood up" (澳大利亞人站起來了, *Aodaliya ren zhanqilai le*), Turnbull proposed a slate of new foreign interference legislation, which was eventually passed into law. Among other elements, this legislation restricts foreign political donations at the federal level and also introduces a transparency scheme which requires individuals and entities to publicly register certain activities (such as lobbying, communications work, and payments) if they are undertaken on behalf of foreign principals (such as governments, political organizations, government entities, and government-related individuals).

The Australia's Foreign Relations (State and Territory Arrangements) Act 2020 marked another move to regulate Australians' engagement with foreign entities and limit their potentially negative effects.[47] The law requires Australian state governments, local governments, and public universities and their staff to notify the federal government of any agreements or other formal relationships they may have with foreign entities. Under the law, the Minister for Foreign Affairs has sole discretion to decide whether such arrangements can continue. It was under this law that the Australian federal government decided in 2021 to abrogate the agreement reached between the government of the state of Victoria and the PRC National Development and Reform Commission to cooperate under the auspices of the Silk Road Economic Belt and the 21st Century Maritime Silk Road Initiative (also known as the Belt and Road Initiative, or BRI).

The Australian government also strengthened its scrutiny of foreign investments, especially those in critical infrastructure.[48] Some experts claimed that the measures to tighten oversight of foreign investments were intended to make investments from China more difficult.[49] In a major decision taken in August 2018—but which had been signaled for more than a year—Canberra decided to ban any company "subject to extrajudicial directions from a foreign government" from participating in the country's rollout of 5G broadband communication networks. This decision, while not expressly disclosing names, effectively barred China's Huawei and ZTE from involvement in this important element of Australia's critical infrastructure.[50]

These moves drew a clearer line between acceptable and unacceptable forms of engagement with China. Less clear is whether unwelcome PRC influence has been substantially affected. In 2019 and again in 2020, Australian government and intelligence officials accused PRC state actors of conducting cyberattacks against Australian entities, including the national Parliament, the country's three major political parties, hospitals, and utilities, and being involved in the global Microsoft Exchange hack in 2021.[51]

9.5. Key Challenges Ahead

Across nearly all aspects of Australia–China ties, the relationship is deeply troubled, and prospects for improvement are poor in the near to medium term. Political and diplomatic relations improved slightly, as China allowed for the resumption of high-level contacts in 2023. The Sino–Australian "strategic partnership," announced in 2013, has remained in place, but will not fully recover given the difficulties in the relationship over the past 5–10 years. The centerpiece of the agreement, an annual head-of-government summit between the Australian Prime Minister and the PRC Premier, was suspended by Beijing between 2017 and 2023 owing to its dissatisfaction with the direction of Canberra's China policy.

On the economic front, the bilateral trade relationship continues apace, and the China–Australia Free Trade Agreement is still in effect. However, the two sides are nevertheless attempting, with varying degrees of success, to reduce their dependencies on one another. PRC trade restrictions on Australian exports remain in place, and Chinese investment in Australia continues to plummet. In 2020, PRC investment in Australia, at AU\$2.5 billion, was down from AU\$3.4 billion in 2019, its lowest level since 2007; this continues a trend of steadily declining Chinese investment each year since 2016 (when it stood at AU\$15 billion). This downward trajectory is likely to continue as Chinese investment shifts to smaller, less sensitive deals in Australia, Beijing's overseas direct investment strategy shifts to prioritize domestic demand, and the Australia–China political relationship remains strained.[52]

Moreover, if China's longer-term economic strategies announced at the 2021 National People's Congress succeed, it could have significant implications for the Australia–China economic relationship.[53] For example, if China continues to slow its capital-intensive development model and expand its consumption-led and green-growth plans, this would negatively affect traditional Australian exports of iron ore and coal. Other Australian export sectors could benefit if China successfully transitions to a per capita high-income country, such as education, tourism, high-end agricultural products, and lifestyle brands. But these sectors are now in damage control mode owing to the strained political relationship and the effects of the COVID-19 pandemic and may take years to recover, if ever.

From an Australian perspective, China will also remain a security challenge across multiple levels and issues. At one level, these concerns arise from the steadily intensifying strategic competition between China, on the one hand, and Australia's closest and most important strategic partner and ally, the U.S., on the other. Australian leaders understand the strategic importance of the U.S.–Australia relationship and the benefits it derives from it. In all likelihood, Australian leaders will continue to deepen ties with the U.S. Moreover, as a treaty ally and close security partner, Australia will also continue to work with Washington in order to deter and counter threats China may pose to their collective interests. At another level, Australians are increasingly recognizing that China can pose direct threats to Australia, whether through increasingly sophisticated cyberattacks, espionage, information and influence campaigns, punitive economic measures, or military force. As long as that remains the case, Australians and their leaders will remain wary of China's ambitions and intentions and will prepare accordingly.

However, despite these difficulties, there are some developments which open the door to stabilizing the Australia–China relationship. Most important in this regard was the change in government in Canberra in May 2022. With the new Labor government in place, there appears to be some possibility of resetting the bilateral relationship. Ministerial-level communications were restarted after a three-year hiatus, with the Australian defense and foreign affairs ministers meeting their counterparts shortly after taking office.[54] The new government also pledged to use a different "tone" in its relations with China.[55] That in turn may lessen what some saw as unfounded "threat inflation," both on the part of the previous Liberal-National coalition governments led by Prime Ministers Abbott, Turnbull, and Morrison and on the part of the Australian media.[56]

In another potentially positive development, the National Foundation for Australia–China Relations, formally established by the Australian government in 2020, aims to "strengthen understanding and engagement between Australia and China." In its first two years, with grants totaling over AU$8 million, the foundation supported a range of cooperative and exchange efforts between the two countries, including in areas such as health, elder care, astrophysics, environmentally friendly energy sources, youth dialogues, sports, arts, and culture.[57]

In addition, it is possible that other pressing challenges will demand the attention of the Australian populace and its leaders, such as climate change, global economic inequality and regional instabilities, pandemics, and the proliferation of weapons of mass destruction. Indeed, fully addressing these kinds of threats to humankind will not be possible without far greater international cooperation, including with China. Importantly, polling in Australia suggests a strong reluctance to engage China in conflict, even as those surveyed find much to dislike about the PRC and its leaders.[58]

However, for the foreseeable future, Australian leaders and citizens will remain uncomfortable and critical of the Leninist, authoritarian, one-party nature of the PRC governance system. Australian leaders and citizens will remain committed to maintaining an open, liberal, rules-based system conducive to Australia's values and interests and will seek to oppose efforts by China or other nations to undermine it. A majority of Australians will continue to see more challenges than opportunities in the way China conducts itself at home, in the region, and across the globe. Reflective of these views, as of early 2024, the Labor government had not fundamentally altered the overall strategic approach toward China.

As such, as a nation fundamentally realist in its outlook and one which sees itself as a beneficiary and defender of liberal values, there should be little surprise that Australia seeks to counterbalance against such challenges and concerns emanating from China. While this probably does not mean conflict, its likelihood has increased. Looking ahead, Sino–Australian relations will remain troubled.

Endnotes

1 B. Gill, "Bounded engagement: Charting a new era in Australia-China relations," in *Disruptive Asia*, Vol. 3 (Melbourne: Asia Society Australia, 2019), pp. 3–6. https://disruptiveasia.asiasociety.org/volumes/volume-3.
2 International Monetary Fund, "GDP per capita, current prices (2021)." https://www.imf.org/external/datamapper/NGDPDPC@WEO/OEMDC/ADVEC/WEOWORLD.

3 M. Beeson and Jinghan Zeng, "Realistic relations? How the evolving bilateral relationship is understood in China and Australia," *Pacific Focus,* 32(2), 159–181 (2017); M. Wesley, "The rich tradition of Australian realism," *Australian Journal of Politics & History*, 55(3), 324–334 (2009).

4 Beeson and Zeng (2017), *Op. cit.*, pp. 164–167.

5 Prime Minister of Australia, "Quad leaders' summit communique," 24 September 2021. https://www.pm.gov.au/media/quad-leaders-summit-communique.

6 G. Rose, "Neoclassical realism and theories of foreign policy," *World Politics*, 51(1), 146 (1998). See also N. M. Ripsman, J. W. Taliaferro and S. E. Lobell, *Neoclassical Realist Theory of International Politics* (New York: Oxford University Press, 2016).

7 R. Schweller, "Opposite but compatible nationalisms: A neoclassical realist approach to the future of US-China relations," *The Chinese Journal of International Politics,* 11(1), 28 (2018).

8 Reserve Bank of Australia, "Box A: Growth of Australia's major trading partners," Statement of Monetary Policy, May 2014. https://www.rba.gov.au/publications/smp/2014/may/box-a.html.

9 Department of Foreign Affairs and Trade (Australia), "Trade and Investment at a Glance 2021." https://www.dfat.gov.au/sites/default/files/trade-and-investment-glance-2021.pdf.

10 *Ibid.*; B. McKee, "Australian exports to China set new records in first half of 2021," *Sky News,* 15 July 2021. https://www.skynews.com.au/world-news/china/australian-exports-to-china-set-new-records-in-first-half-of-2021/news-story/28be306f765a69fc42dbd20c13d7d80d.

11 "Australia in first recession in nearly 30 years," BBC, 2 September 2020. https://www.bbc.com/news/business-53994318.

12 Department of Defence (Australia), *2020 Defence Strategic Update Factsheet*, 1 July 2020. https://www1.defence.gov.au/about/publications/2020-defence-strategic-update.

13 The English translation "China solution" for *Zhongguo fangan* is used in "Speech by H. E. Xi Jinping President of the People's Republic of China at the Körber Foundation," Berlin, Germany, 28 March 2014. https://www.fmprc.gov.cn/mfa_eng/wjdt_665385/zyjh_665391/t1148640.shtml and in Xi Jinping, "Stay true to our original aspiration and continue marching forward," Speech to commemorate the 95th anniversary of the CCP, 1 July 2016, in Xi Jinping, *The Governance of China II* (Beijing: Foreign Languages Press, 2017), p. 17. The English translation has also appeared as "Chinese input" and "Chinese approach" in other official publications.

14 J. C. Weiss, "A world safe for autocracy?: China's rise and the future of global politics," *Foreign Affairs,* 98(4), 92–102 (2019).

15 Data on PRC and regional military spending is from Stockholm International Peace Research Institute (SIPRI) Military Expenditure Database. https://www.sipri.org/databases/milex.

16 Office of the Secretary of Defense (United States), Military and Security Developments Involving the People's Republic of China 2020 (Washington, DC: United States Department of Defense, 2020), p. ii; M. P. Funaiole, J. S. Bermudez Jr. and B. Hart, *China's Third Aircraft Carrier Takes Shape*, Center for Strategic and International Studies, 15 June 2021. https://www.csis.org/analysis/chinas-third-aircraft-carrier-takes-shape.

17 Office of the Secretary of Defense (2020), *Op. cit.*, p. viii.

18 H. M. Kristensen and M. Korda, "Status of world nuclear forces," Federation of American Scientists. https://fas.org/issues/nuclear-weapons/status-world-nuclear-forces/.

19 Xi Jinping, Secure a Decisive Victory in Building a Moderately Prosperous Society in All Respects and Strive for the Great Success of Socialism with Chinese Characteristics for a New Era, Report delivered at the 19th National Congress of the Chinese Communist Party, 18 October 2017. http://www.xinhuanet.com/english/special/2017-11/03/c_136725942.htm.

20 B. Gill, A. Ni and D. Blasko, "The ambitious reform plans of the People's liberation army: Progress, prospects and implications for Australia," *Australian Journal of Defence and Strategic Studies*, 2(1), 5–26 (2020).

21 A. S. Erickson, "China's near-seas challenge," *The National Interest*, 129, 60–66 (2014). The "first island chain" refers to the line of islands extending from the Kuril Islands in the north and circling south to the Japanese islands, Taiwan, the Philippines, Borneo, and the northern parts of the Indonesian archipelago. The "second island chain" extends roughly from the Japanese home islands to the Mariana Islands, which include the U.S. territory of Guam, and continues south to Papua New Guinea.

22 K. Allen, P. C. Saunders and J. Chen, *China's Military Diplomacy, 2003–2016: Trends and Implications,* China Strategic Perspectives 11 (Washington, D.C.: National Defense University Press, 2017). On China's first overseas base, see J.-P. Cabestan, "China's military base in Djibouti: A microcosm of China's growing competition with the United States and new bipolarity," *Journal of Contemporary China*, 29(125), 731–747 (2019). On the PRC's expanding "interest frontiers" (*liyi bianjiang*) and how China's armed forces and other security actors are tasked to protect them, see A. Ghiselli, *Protecting China's Interests Overseas: Securitization and Foreign Policy* (New York: Oxford University Press, 2021).

23 "Relations in the Indo-Pacific: Threats to Australia's vital interests," *Lowy Institute Poll 2021*. https://poll.lowyinstitute.org/charts/threats-australias-vital-interests.

24 For details, see B. Gill and L. Jakobson, *China Matters: Getting it Right for Australia* (Melbourne: Latrobe University Press and Black Inc., 2017), especially Chapter 4; C. Hamilton, *Silent Invasion: China's Influence in Australia* (Richmond: Hardie Grant Books, 2018); P. Hartcher, *Red Zone: China's*

Challenge and Australia's Future (Melbourne: Black Inc., 2021). See also the Australian Broadcasting Commission (ABC) investigative program *Four Corners* and its episodes on "Power and Influence," 5 June 2017. https://www.abc.net.au/4corners/power-and-influence-promo/8579844 (currently unavailable online) and "Interference," 8 April 2019. https://www.abc.net.au/4corners/interference/10982212.

25 Wanning Sun, "The virus of fear and anxiety: China, COVID-19, and the Australian media," *Global Media and China*, 6(1), 27 (2021).

26 C. Uhlmann, A. Greene and S. Anderson, "Chinese donors to Australian parties: Who gave how much?" *ABC News*, 21 September 2016. See also records of annual donor returns with the Australian Electoral Commission for 2012–2013, 2013–2014, and 2014–2015. https://transparency.aec.gov.au.

27 Wanning Sun, *Chinese-Language Media in Australia: Developments, Challenges, and Opportunities*, Australia-China Relations Institute, 8 September 2016. https://www.australiachinarelations.org/content/chinese-language-media-australia-developments-challenges-and-opportunities-2.

28 L. Besser, J. Sturmer and B. Sveen, "Government computer networks breached in cyber attacks as experts warn of espionage threat," *ABC News Four Corners*, 29 August 2016. https://www.abc.net.au/news/2016-08-29/chinese-hackers-behind-defence-austrade-security-breaches/7790166.

29 J. Kearsley, E. Bagshaw and A. Galloway, "'If you make China the enemy, China will be the enemy': Beijing's fresh threat to Australia," *Sydney Morning Herald*, 18 November 2020. https://www.smh.com.au/world/asia/if-you-make-china-the-enemy-china-will-be-the-enemy-beijing-s-fresh-threat-to-australia-20201118-p56fqs.html.

30 "Relations in the Indo-Pacific: Threats to Australia's vital interests," *Lowy Institute Poll*. https://poll.lowyinstitute.org/charts/threats-australias-vital-interests.

31 L. Silver, K. Devlin and C. Huang, *Large Majorities Say China Does Not Respect the Personal Freedoms of Its People*, Pew Research Center, 30 June 2021. https://www.pewresearch.org/global/2021/06/30/large-majorities-say-china-does-not-respect-the-personal-freedoms-of-its-people/; L. Silver, K. Devlin and C. Huang, *Unfavorable Views of China Reach Historic Highs in Many Countries*, Pew Research Center, 6 October 2020. https://www.pewresearch.org/global/2020/10/06/unfavorable-views-of-china-reach-historic-highs-in-many-countries/.

32 "Gonganbu kaizhan yanli daji baoli kongbu huodong zhuanxiang xingdong (Ministry of public security launches strike hard campaign against violent terrorist activities) *Xinhua*, 25 May 2014. http://www.gov.cn/xinwen/2014-05/25/content_2686705.htm; A. Ramzy and C. Buckley, "'Absolutely no mercy': Leaked files expose how China organized mass detentions of Muslims," *The New York Times*, 16 November 2019. https://

www.nytimes.com/interactive/2019/11/16/world/asia/china-xinjiang-documents.html; C. Buckley and A. Ramzy, "China is erasing mosques and precious shrines in Xinjiang," *The New York Times,* 25 September 2020. https://www.nytimes.com/interactive/2020/09/25/world/asia/xinjiang-china-religious-site.html. See also the detailed personal account of Anar Sabit in Raffi Khatchadourian, "Surviving the crackdown in Xinjiang," *The New Yorker,* 5 April 2021. https://www.newyorker.com/magazine/2021/04/12/surviving-the-crackdown-in-xinjiang.

33 "English translation of the law of the People's Republic of China on safeguarding national security in the Hong Kong Special Administrative Region," *Xinhua Net,* 1 July 2020. http://www.xinhuanet.com/english/2020-07/01/c_139178753.htm; "Hong Kong security law: What is it and is it worrying?" *BBC,* 30 June 2020. https://www.bbc.com/news/world-asia-china-52765838.

34 See the accounts of Australian journalists in B. Birtles, *The Truth about China: Propaganda, Patriotism, and the Search for Answers* (Crows Nest: Allen & Unwin, 2021); M. Smith, *The Last Correspondent: Dispatches from the Frontline of Xi's China* (Sydney: Ultimo Press, 2021).

35 "United States: Global responses to Covid-19," *Lowy Institute Poll.* https://poll.lowyinstitute.org/charts/global-responses-to-covid-19.

36 "China: China's system of government," *Lowy Institute Poll.* https://poll.lowyinstitute.org/charts/chinas-system-of-government.

37 Sun (2021), *Op. cit.,* pp. 24, 35.

38 Minister for Foreign Affairs Senator the Hon Penny Wong, "National statement to the UN General Assembly, New York," 23 September 2022. https://www.foreignminister.gov.au/minister/penny-wong/speech/national-statement-un-general-assembly-new-york; see also Minister for Foreign Affairs Senator the Hon Penny Wong, Press Conference, New York, 24 September 2022. https://www.foreignminister.gov.au/minister/penny-wong/transcript/press-conference-new-york-0.

39 "China: Tensions in the Australia-China relationship," *Lowy Institute Poll.* https://poll.lowyinstitute.org/charts/tensions-australia-china-relationship.

40 M. Varrall, *Lowy Institute Poll.* Australia's response to China in the Pacific: From alert to alarmed," in G. Smith and T. Wesley-Smith (eds.) *The China Alternative: Changing Regional Order in the Pacific Islands* (Canberra: Australian National University Press, 2021), pp. 107–141.

41 B. Gill and T. Switzer, "The new special relationship: The U.S.-Australia alliance deepens," *Foreign Affairs,* 19 February 2015. https://www.foreignaffairs.com/articles/australia/2015-02-19/new-special-relationship.

42 A. Greene, "Australia now world's second-biggest weapons importer behind only Saudi Arabia: Analysts," *ABC News,* 30 September 2019. https://www.abc.net.au/news/2019-09-30/australia-worlds-second-biggest-weapons-importer-behind-saudi/11558762.

43 Department of Defence (Australia), *2020 Force Structure Plan*, Canberra (July 2020). https://www1.defence.gov.au/sites/default/files/2020-11/2020_Force_Structure_Plan.pdf.
44 The White House, "Joint leaders statement on AUKUS," 15 September 2021. https://www.whitehouse.gov/briefing-room/statements-releases/2021/09/15/joint-leaders-statement-on-aukus/.
45 United States Department of State, "Joint statement on Australia-U.S. Ministerial Consultations (AUSMIN) 2021," 16 September 2021. https://www.state.gov/joint-statement-on-australia-u-s-ministerial-consultations-ausmin-2021/.
46 M. Turnbull, "Speech introducing the National Security Legislation Amendment (Espionage and Foreign Interference) Bill 2017," 7 December 2017. www.malcolmturnbull.com.au/media/speech-introducing-the-national-security-legislation-amendment-espionage-an.
47 *Australian Foreign Relations (State and Territory Arrangements) Act 2020*, Parliament of the Commonwealth of Australia. https://parlinfo.aph.gov.au/parlInfo/download/legislation/bills/r6596_aspassed/toc_pdf/20119b01.pdf; fileType=application%2Fpdf.
48 *Security of Critical Infrastructure Act 2018*. Federal Register of Legislation. https://www.legislation.gov.au/Details/C2021C00113.
49 D. Mercer and J. Hayes, "Foreign investment clampdown prompts claims of Chinese buyers being 'frozen out,'" *ABC News*, 14 December 2020. https://www.abc.net.au/news/rural/2020-12-14/china-investment-freeze-foreign-relations/12967554.
50 M. Slezak and A. Bogle, "Huawei banned from 5G mobile infrastructure roll-out in Australia," *ABC News*, 23 August 2018. https://www.abc.net.au/news/2018-08-23/huawei-banned-from-providing-5g-mobile-technology-australia/10155438; G. Wyeth, "Why did Australia block Huawei, ZTE from 5G roll out?" *The Diplomat*, 28 August 2018. https://thediplomat.com/2018/08/why-did-australia-block-huawei-zte-from-5g-roll-out/.
51 C. Packham, "Exclusive: Australia concluded China was behind hack on parliament, political parties—sources," *Reuters*, 16 September 2019. https://www.reuters.com/article/us-australia-china-cyber-exclusive-idUSKBN-1W00VF; G. Hitch and A. Probyn, "China believed to be behind major cyber attack on Australian governments and businesses," *ABC News*, 19 June 2020. https://www.abc.net.au/news/2020-06-19/foreign-cyber-hack-targets-australian-government-and-business/12372470; J. Evans, "Home Affairs Minister vows to continue to hold China accountable for cyber attacks," *ABC News*, 21 July 2021. https://www.abc.net.au/news/2021-07-20/china-hack-microsoft-international-blame/100306254.
52 D. Ferguson, H. Z. Dent, S. Qian, H. Hendrischke and Wei Li, *Demystifying Chinese Investment in Australia* (Sydney: KPMG/University of Sydney, July

2021). https://assets.kpmg/content/dam/kpmg/au/pdf/2021/demystifying-chinese-investment-in-australia-july-2021.pdf.

53 State Council of the People's Republic of China, "Full text: Report of the Work of the Government," 13 March 2021. http://english.www.gov.cn/premier/news/202103/13/content_WS604b9030c6d0719374afac02.html.

54 E. Connors and M. Smith, Marles, "Wei break Australia-China meeting drought," *Australian Financial Review*, 12 June 2022. https://www.afr.com/world/asia/china-bites-back-after-us-smears-talks-of-war-in-taiwan-20220612-p5at3u; C. Barrett, "Wong meets Wang as ministers attempt to stabilise China-Australia relations," *Sydney Morning Herald*, 8 July 2022. https://www.smh.com.au/world/asia/wong-meets-wang-as-ministers-attempt-to-stabilise-china-australia-relations-20220708-p5b0a8.html.

55 D. Hurst, "Thaw or cold war: Will labor succeed in unfreezing Australia-China relations?" *The Guardian*, 17 June 2022. https://www.theguardian.com/world/2022/jun/18/thaw-or-cold-war-will-labor-succeed-in-unfreezing-australia-china-relations.

56 See, for example, Sun (2021), *op. cit.*; B. Scott, "Smart China choices," *The Interpreter*, 1 October 2020. https://www.lowyinstitute.org/the-interpreter/smart-china-choices.

57 See the Foundation Website. https://www.australiachinafoundation.org.au.

58 For example, see "Relations in the Indo-Pacific: Potential military conflict between China and the United States," *Lowy Institute Poll 2021*. https://poll.lowyinstitute.org/charts/military-conflict-between-china-and-united-states.

© 2025 World Scientific Publishing Europe Ltd.
https://doi.org/10.1142/9781800616318_0011

Chapter 10

Reinforcing Wedging: Assessing China's Southeast Asia Policy in the Context of Indo-Pacific Strategy[*]

Ruonan Liu

University of International Business and Economics, China

From the Asian financial crisis in 1997 to 2010, China's self-restraint and strategic reassurance toward ASEAN countries created a favorable regional environment for its rise. After 2010, the South China Sea disputes and Sino–U.S. strategic competition intensified. During this period, China simultaneously pursued a wedging strategy which aimed to prevent Southeast Asia from completely leaning toward the United States (U.S.). Since the Trump administration launched the Indo-Pacific strategy, Sino–U.S. relations have transitioned from competitive to confrontational, significantly increasing the importance of Southeast Asia as a buffer between China and the U.S. At the same time, intensified economic dependence on China by ASEAN countries and the uncertainty surrounding the U.S.' strategic attention to the region have increased the costs and risks of alienating China. Both China and ASEAN countries cannot afford any further deterioration in their relations. In the context

---

[*] This chapter was originally printed as "Reinforcing Wedging: Assessing China's Southeast Asia Policy in the Context of Indo-Pacific Strategy." *The China Review*, Vol. 23, no. 1 (2023): 277–306. https://www.jstor.org/stable/48717996. Reproduced with kind permission of CUHK Press.

of the Indo-Pacific strategy, the primary goal of China's Southeast Asia policy is to reduce ASEAN countries' willingness and ability to rely on external powers to exert pressure on them while strengthening the region's function as a bridge to the global industrial chain and undermining the legitimacy of the Indo-Pacific strategy by advocating for ASEAN-led multilateralism. China's Southeast Asia policy effectiveness depends on Beijing's ability to alleviate the internal dilemma within its policy goals, which have been intensified by the U.S.' Indo-Pacific strategy. Currently, this strategy has gained some support in Southeast Asia and weakened the regional countries' domestic support for pro-China policy. Future challenges in China's relations with ASEAN countries do not depend exclusively on the dynamics of Sino–U.S. relations, given that domestic political changes in key regional countries are also closely tied to China's relations with the region.

The Southeast Asia region has always been of strategic importance to China's neighboring diplomacy. Engaging ASEAN-centered institutions was once the primary channel for China to integrate into the region after the end of the Cold War.[1] Between the 1997 Asian Financial Crisis and 2010, China's self-restraint and strategic reassurance contributed to its acceptance as a member of the regional community. Since 2013, the Belt and Road Initiative (BRI) has led to closer economic ties between China and ASEAN. By 2020, China had been ASEAN's largest trading partner for over a decade and one of its top investors.[2] At the same time, China has significantly strengthened its security presence in the South China Sea, leading to an often intense relationship with the Philippines and Vietnam. China's artificial island-building has also attracted great concern from the United States (U.S.) and some of its allies. On the other hand, China continues to consolidate its leading position in continental Southeast Asia by actively establishing governance mechanisms and launching development projects.

As Chinese influence continues to grow, the perception that China has become, or will soon become, a dominant power in Southeast Asia has taken shape. Recent surveys conducted by the ISEAS – Yusof Ishak Institute reveal that there is widespread concern among Southeast Asian elites about the rise of China and the decline of the U.S.[3] Sebastian Strangio notes that nowhere is the rise of China's economic and military power so directly and clearly felt as in Southeast Asia, where China is rapidly reshaping the region from the Mekong River Basin to the South China Sea.[4] Moreover, Graham Allison makes it clear that the balance of power between the U.S. and China is tipping in China's favor and that the relationship between Southeast Asia and China in the future will resemble that between Latin America and the U.S.[5] All of these judgments seem to conclude that Southeast Asia has become a Chinese sphere of influence. Such arguments might have some merit if China's relations with Southeast Asian countries were viewed superficially. It is true that China is already the most important economic engine in the region and has gained considerable advantage over Southeast Asian countries in terms of military power in the South China Sea.

However, placing China's relations with Southeast Asia within the context of its overall foreign relations reveals a more complex situation. After the end of World War II, maritime Southeast Asia remained on the periphery of the U.S.-led liberal order; and to this day, all national security establishments in Southeast Asia except in Cambodia, Laos, and Myanmar have close ties with the U.S.[6] The U.S. remains the primary balancer of the regional security order and is this recognized by most regional countries. Despite China's rapidly growing influence, it is still far from being a legitimate dominant power. Therefore, China is partly dealing with the U.S.-led security order in its relations with Southeast Asia.[7] China's Southeast Asia strategy is linked to its relationship with the U.S., which is uneasy because of China's power and legitimacy disadvantages. This means that China faces the challenge of how to drive a wedge between the established power and its neighbors as it rises.

This challenge has become even more acute with the launch of the Indo-Pacific strategy. This strategy, first introduced by the Trump administration and continued under the Biden administration, has been perceived by Beijing as a hegemonic effort to "contain China" and "provoke tensions and mess up the Asia Pacific region."[8] Japan, Australia, and some other countries have responded positively and cooperated with the U.S. to adopt a more active policy in Southeast Asia. India and ASEAN have also partially embraced the Indo-Pacific strategy, but expressed reservations about confronting China. Applying the "interest–threat nexus" model of bilateral relations developed by Feng Liu and Kai He, we find that the bilateral relationships between China and most ASEAN states can be defined as cooperative partnerships, characterized by a high level of economic interdependence and a low level of security competition (see Chapter 1). Only a few ASEAN states perceive China as a cooperative rival because of maritime disputes in the South China Sea. Against the backdrop of intensifying geopolitical competition in the Indo-Pacific region, China has been making greater efforts to stabilize its relationships with Southeast Asian states, thereby attempting to avoid a counter-China coalition in the region.

This chapter focuses on how China's Southeast Asia policy will evolve in the face of intensifying Sino–U.S. competition that has shown no sign of easing. Specifically, how does the Indo-Pacific strategy pose difficulties for China's reassurances to Southeast Asia? What does China's Southeast Asia policy seek to achieve under these circumstances? What reassurance policies has China adopted to this end, and how effective have they been? The rest of the chapter is organized as follows. Section 10.1 examines the role that Southeast Asian countries play in the U.S. Indo-Pacific strategy; it then discusses how the recent development in relations between the U.S. and Southeast Asia intensifies China's external pressure. Section 10.2 explores the objectives China seeks to achieve through its wedging strategy and how it is implemented in the context of the Indo-Pacific strategy. Section 10.3 analyzes the responses of Southeast Asian countries to China's wedging strategy, examining both the effectiveness of this strategy and the challenges China faces.

10.1. The Impact of the Indo-Pacific Strategy on China–Southeast Asia Relations

In November 2017, President Trump proposed a "Free and Open Indo-Pacific" at the APEC Summit in Vietnam, and in December, the new "National Security Strategy" (NSS) placed the Indo-Pacific first in the section on regional strategy. In 2018, U.S. policy reports under the Indo-Pacific framework and speeches by senior officials at various occasions continued to refine and clarify the objectives, scope, and means of the Indo-Pacific strategy. In June 2019, the *Indo-Pacific Strategy Report* was published by the U.S. Department of Defense, marking the formal transformation of the Indo-Pacific from a vision to a national strategy. Since Biden came to office in early 2021, he has not abandoned the Indo-Pacific Strategy but has upgraded it in some respects, including reengaging regional allies and partners and adding a new economic pillar, the Indo-Pacific Economic Framework (IPEF). The continuities and changes of the U.S. Indo-Pacific strategy pose challenges to China's efforts in stabilizing its relationships with Southeast Asian countries.

10.1.1. *The role of Southeast Asia in the U.S. Indo-Pacific strategy*

The strategic importance of Southeast Asia in the Indo-Pacific strategy was vague at the beginning and only became clearer after 2018. At the start of the Trump administration in 2016, the U.S. did not pay enough attention to Southeast Asia. The 2017 NSS only mentioned Southeast Asia in the discussion of the Indo-Pacific, which included the importance of allies and partners in security and economics, as well as the centrality of ASEAN and APEC in the regional architecture.[9] In comparison to its 2015 version, the 2017 NSS was longer but devoted less ink to Southeast Asia. It is apparent that the Trump administration had not developed a strategic vision of Southeast Asia's role in U.S. foreign policy during this period.[10]

In 2018, as the Indo-Pacific strategy was put into action, the role of Southeast Asia became clearer through the surrounding discourse. At the East Asia Summit, then Vice-President of the U.S., Michael Pence, stated that "ASEAN is at the heart of our Indo-Pacific strategy" and expressed support for the South China Sea Code of Conduct (COC) in the context of China's "militarization and expansion," but also suggested that the U.S. did not wish for the code to prevent countries from building partnerships.[11] Since then, the U.S.' intention of bringing Southeast Asian countries together to counterbalance China's rise through the Indo-Pacific strategy has become explicit.

In June 2019, the U.S. Department of Defense's *Indo-Pacific Strategy Report* clearly articulated the role of Southeast Asian countries in the Indo-Pacific strategic framework. In addition to giving importance to its allies, the U.S. stated that Singapore is a trusted and capable partner in the region. It highlighted the impressive economic performances and key strategic locations of Vietnam, Indonesia, and Malaysia.[12] In November 2019, the U.S. Department of State released *A Free and Open Indo-Pacific: Advancing a Shared Vision*, in which Southeast Asian countries were ranked after Japan, South Korea, and India and ahead of the Pacific Islands. The report further divides Southeast Asia into maritime and continental components, emphasizing the need to continue consolidating security relations with the former and taking measures to help the latter defend their independence and autonomy.[13]

Compared with the Trump administration, the Biden administration has paid more attention and devoted more resources to attracting Southeast Asian countries. When virtually attending the annual U.S.–ASEAN

Summit in October 2021, President Biden emphasized "the importance the United States places on our relationship with ASEAN."[14] In May 2022, a U.S.–ASEAN Special Summit was convened in Washington, D.C., as an effort to demonstrate U.S. commitment to ASEAN centrality and attempt to induce these countries to support U.S. regional initiatives under the Indo-Pacific strategy.[15] However, following the outbreak of Russia's war on Ukraine, Southeast Asian states have serious concerns about the economic impact of this conflict and the subsequent sanctions on Russia, on the one hand, and the consistency of U.S. commitment to the region, on the other hand. As some have nicely observed, this conflict reinforces "long-standing concerns in Asia that despite America's intention to 're-pivot' to the region, it will periodically be distracted by events in Europe or the Middle East."[16]

Overall, the strategic need to contain China has increased the importance of the Indo-Pacific region to the U.S., as it increasingly measures the value of Southeast Asia in the broader context of its comprehensive and sustainable strategic competition with China. Within the framework of the Indo-Pacific strategy, the continuity of the U.S. Southeast Asia policy is reflected in the importance given to like-minded allies and partner countries. Furthermore, the U.S. Southeast Asia policy has become more flexible, emphasizing bilateral cooperation with those willing to support its leadership, highlighting a coordinated economic strategy with security, maintaining symbolic support for multilateralism, and moderately using value-oriented diplomacy to manage bilateral relations.

10.1.2. New challenges in China–Southeast Asia relations

In the 2017 NSS, China was explicitly labeled as a revisionist state and strategic competitor; the report noted that China wants to replace the U.S. in the Indo-Pacific region and shape the regional order according to its own interests. The language used in the NSS in framing China's strategic desires and the subsequent National Defense Strategy (NDS) in 2018 signaled the beginning of a shift in U.S. policy toward the comprehensive containment of China. China's strong response to the change in U.S. policy was evident in 2018, when it reciprocated three rounds of tariff increases initiated by the U.S., and four dialogues between the two were put on hold. Since the outbreak of the COVID-19 pandemic, mutual accusations have further exacerbated the animosity between the two, with competition in the economic, security, and technological spheres spilling over into ideology and civil society. After President Joe Biden came into office, the U.S. continued to pass domestic legislation and coordinated with its allies to target China, which demonstrates that a long-term, comprehensive competitive strategy against China is irreversible. As clearly stated in the 2022 NSS under the Biden administration, the U.S. regards Russia as "an immediate threat" after its invasion of Ukraine but China as "America's most consequential geopolitical challenge."[17]

The major geopolitical competition is taking place in China's neighboring region. Under the Indo-Pacific strategy, the U.S., Japan, Australia, and India formed the Quadrilateral Security Dialogue (Quad), thereby encircling China from the east, south, and southeast. The only region in the Indo-Pacific that overlaps with China's neighboring region and has not fully come onboard the U.S. Indo-Pacific camp is Southeast Asia. The region consists of small- and medium-sized states that are highly diverse and have close and complex historical and economic ties with China. Facing encirclement from the Quad, ASEAN's strategic importance has significantly increased for China as a buffer between itself and the U.S. However, changes in the domestic and foreign policies of ASEAN countries at this time have brought new challenges to China's Southeast Asia policy in three ways.

The first challenge is that some ASEAN countries show considerable interest in the Indo-Pacific strategy. The possible emergence of quasi-pillar states in Southeast Asia will worsen China's security. After Duterte, Former President of the Philippines, shelved the South China Sea arbitration ruling in 2017, Vietnam and Singapore repaired their relationships with China as well. However, friction between China and other claimants in the South China Sea disputes persists. Against this backdrop, Vietnam could be considered a potential quasi-pillar of the Indo-Pacific strategy since it holds a positive view of the Indo-Pacific concept. Former President of Vietnam Tran Dai Quang used the concept of "Indo-Asia-Pacific" during his visit to India, and Vietnam's 2019 *Defense White Paper* mentions its readiness to participate in the security and defense mechanisms of the Indo-Pacific region.[18] Vietnam is highly placed in the U.S. Indo-Pacific strategy, and the U.S.–Vietnam security relationship was significantly strengthened during the Trump administration. In March 2020, Vietnam was also invited to participate in a Quad Plus video conference on the fight against the pandemic. Vietnam has responded positively to the Indo-Pacific strategy due to the high compatibility between some key tenets of this strategy and its national interests.[19] Vietnam's complete embrace of the U.S. Indo-Pacific strategy would be an unacceptable prospect for China; hence, diplomatic efforts have been directed at engaging Vietnam. Since 2019, Chinese and Vietnamese top officials have maintained close communication to ensure that Vietnam's China policy remains stable ahead of its ASEAN presidency and the 13th Communist Party Congress.

Other than Vietnam, Indonesia is also proactive in advocating for the Indo-Pacific concept; while hesitant to fully embrace the U.S. Indo-Pacific strategy, it hopes that China will accept the ASEAN Outlook on the Indo-Pacific (AOIP). Indonesia has taken a leading role in pushing ASEAN to take an active part in the discourse about the new concept and has lobbied other ASEAN countries intensively for their support for Jakarta's draft of the AOIP, which was finally published in 2019. From Indonesia's perspective, the AOIP demonstrates its middle-power approach to the evolving Indo-Pacific geopolitical dynamic, and support for the AOIP is a form of reassurance from great powers in the Indo-Pacific era.[20] Although recognizing that the AOIP differs from the U.S. Indo-Pacific strategy by emphasizing ASEAN centrality in an open and inclusive Southeast Asia, China remains skeptical and resistant to using the term "Indo-Pacific." Out of the desire to reassure ASEAN, particularly Indonesia, China has stated its partial endorsement of the AOIP. For example, Foreign Affairs Minister of China Wang Yi stated in the press conference following a China–ASEAN ministers meeting that, "many of these principles and ideas are consistent with those of the Chinese side."[21] In his speech at the ASEAN–China Special Summit 2021, President Xi Jinping mentioned that China seeks "cooperation between the Belt and Road Initiative and the ASEAN Outlook on the Indo-Pacific."[22] However, since the Biden administration introduced the IPEF, Chinese officials have tried to persuade ASEAN countries to distance themselves from this new economic initiative, even though seven ASEAN states have joined in the first round of negotiations of the IPEF.[23]

The second challenge stems from the danger of U.S.' economic decoupling from China. Trade has long been the indispensable anchor of stable Sino–U.S. relations. However, since Trump came into office, U.S. economic engagement with China has been overshadowed by economic competition. It has been the U.S. bipartisan consensus that China's free riding on globalization endows it with the ability to undermine or even challenge U.S. primacy in military superiority and high-tech industries. Medeiros called this securitization of bilateral economic relations the new most worrisome driver of Sino–U.S. competition.[24] Trump stated that the

U.S.' support of China's entry into the WTO was a mistake and launched an intensive and costly trade war against China by imposing sanctions on Chinese enterprises. The Biden administration has inherited these measures but is placing more emphasis on coordination with allies and partners, organizing a democratic supply chain alliance, and trying to build a China-free tech chain with Indo-Pacific allies such as Japan, Australia, and South Korea. Although China's dependence on foreign trade has been declining since 2008, it remains one of the main sources of growth. Since China's inner consumption-driven economy is not yet fully developed, once the developed economies of Europe and the Indo-Pacific detach from China in terms of trade, a domestic economic crisis will follow. Even if decoupling only occurs in high-tech industries, it will bring serious losses to China.

To respond, in April 2020, China introduced the concept of a "double-cycle economy" based on internal circulation and sought to create a wedge between the U.S. and Europe by persuading the latter to remain open to Chinese enterprises and commodities. Foreign Minister Wang Yi chose Europe for his first stop in "face-to-face" diplomacy after the pandemic subsided, advocating that "neither of them [China or Europe] should allow the so-called 'decoupling' to interfere with the normal operation of the global industrial and supply chains."[25] To avoid being marginalized or even excluded from the global manufacturing supply chain, reinforcing economic relations with ASEAN has become increasingly indispensable for China. China must continue upholding ASEAN as the first runner in East Asia's economic integration to hedge against possible decoupling from the West.[26]

The third challenge arises from within ASEAN countries, where friendly policies toward China will generate greater domestic pressure. China's image in Southeast Asia has not improved proportionally with its rise. In 2019, the Pew Research Centre surveyed six major Asia-Pacific countries on their perceptions of China and the U.S. The survey results showed that despite the decline in perceptions of goodwill during the Trump administration, a higher percentage of people maintained a positive attitude toward the U.S. than China, with the Philippines at 80 versus 42 percent and Indonesia at 42 percent versus 36 percent.[27] In a recent study, Indonesian diplomats' and foreign policy scholars' perceptions of China show that the tendency to perceive it as a threat is more prevalent than the tendency to see it as offering opportunities for mutual gain.[28] The situation has not changed since the outbreak of the COVID-19 pandemic. The 2022 survey by the

ISEAS – Yusof Ishak Institute shows that the percentage of respondents who believe China is a "revisionist power" trying to turn Southeast Asia into its sphere of influence is as high as 41.7 percent.[29]

Although the spread of the pandemic from China to Southeast Asia is the direct cause of this result, the underlying reason is still the continued expansion of China's economic activities and security presence. Three factors notably contribute to the less favorable perception of China. First, the expanded scope and increased frequency of Chinese naval and maritime administrative activities in the waters near neighboring countries in recent years have exacerbated the latters' insecurity. Second, the expansion of economic activities beyond trade, particularly infrastructure investments, has raised fiscal, environmental, and social concerns. Third, the English-language news media, which has great power in swaying discourse and narratives, has largely focused its coverage on the frictions between China and Southeast Asian countries. Many of them use terms such as "bullying," "coercion," and "intimidation" to describe what China does to Southeast Asian countries, echoing the language used by U.S. officials. It is a similar story whenever English-language media cover the BRI. They portray China as the creator of debt traps and environmental problems and rarely offer any positive comments. China's unfavorable image in Southeast Asia had resulted in hardline policies toward it to gain broader domestic support, while leaders seeking friendly relations with China face greater political pressure from the public, opposition parties, or even their own party members. Pursuing a bandwagoning policy in such a domestic political environment is almost impossible (except in Cambodia and Laos). This is especially true for issues that garner a strong public response, such as the acceptance of China's COVID-19 vaccine. For example, Vietnam's low level of trust in China's vaccine was evident as it was the last ASEAN country to approve Chinese vaccines. Similarly, the Philippines former President Duterte's pro-Chinese policies faced huge pressure from both the military and the public, resulting in the complete restoration of the Philippines–United States Visiting Forces Agreement in the final year of his term.[30]

10.2. China's Wedging Strategy toward U.S.–ASEAN Partnership

After the launch of the Indo-Pacific strategy, as mentioned above, China faced multiple new challenges. On top of those challenges, the strategic importance of Southeast Asia as a buffer presents a pressing need for China to reverse the region's "close but not intimate" attitude toward itself. To this end, China has taken both rewarding and coercive measures to wedge ASEAN countries and the U.S., including increasing economic concessions or tolerating losses, expressing procedural adaptability on sensitive issues such as security, and providing public goods in need. Meanwhile, a combination of diplomatic and political means has been set in motion at the bilateral level to prevent key states from embracing the Indo-Pacific strategy. However, China has been increasingly resorting to coercive measures, such as ceasing political contact, imposing informal economic sanctions, and cutting tourism, if the reward policy fails to prevent ASEAN countries from crossing the red line China has drawn.[31]

10.2.1. *Defining the wedging strategy*

The wedging strategy has gained attention in conjunction with alliance studies. Wedging refers to a state's attempt to prevent, break up, or weaken a threatening or blocking alliance at an acceptable cost.[32] Wigell notes that wedging is a policy of dividing a target country or coalition, thereby weakening its counterbalancing power.[33] The wedging strategy applies not only to great powers but also to small powers. Small states adopt a wedging strategy to improve their bargaining position in a situation where great powers are competing for influence.[34] Many studies identify two ways to implement a wedging strategy: reward and coercion.[35] Taffer notes that there are three kinds of wedging: demonstrative, conditional, and coercive wedging.[36] Conditional wedging, according to Taffer, is a combination of reward-based and coercive-based wedging.

More important than the method of wedging is under what circumstances a specific method of wedging can succeed. In other words, the goal of wedging is more likely to be achieved under certain conditions. Crawford states that whether the wedging strategy succeeds or fails depends on its goals and tools. To induce target states to become or remain neutral, selective accommodation is effective; this is especially the case when the economic relationships of the targets are under the control of the dividers.[37] Yasuhiro Izumikawa offers a different insight by noting that the level of threat determines the effectiveness of reward-based wedging. Under a low-level threat, a divider's reward-based wedging is likely to succeed; however, it may resort to coercive measures if it perceives a grave threat as a result of the target's alignment with its primary enemy.[38]

Dian and Kireeva argue that instead of relying on pure reward or coercion, a wedging strategy comprising a mix of positive economic and political incentives and limited coercion can succeed in producing dis-alignment in the opposing camp.[39]

The wedging strategy is not entirely new in China's neighborhood diplomacy. Surrounded by so many neighbors in its immediate regions, Beijing always worries about the possibility of being contained by a counter-China coalition led by the U.S. Since the early 1990s, maintaining a relatively benign regional environment for its internal development has consistently been a goal of China's neighborhood diplomacy. To achieve this goal, Beijing primarily adopts reassurance policies toward its neighbors by maintaining restraint in territorial disputes, engaging in ASEAN-centered regional institutions, and promoting economic integration with other regional actors.[40] In recent years, however, China's reassurances have increasingly become selective and conditional, usually combined with coercive measures targeting specific countries.[41] Therefore, a wedging method that uses both reassurance and coercion more accurately describes China's mixed strategies toward ASEAN states. In one respect, China has sometimes put a wedge among ASEAN countries, a move which has been widely known as "divide and rule." The other aspect of wedging targets ASEAN countries as a whole, aiming to alienate them from the U.S. Since the Indo-Pacific strategy increases the prospect of a tighter alignment between the U.S. and ASEAN countries, China's necessity for a wedging strategy surges as a result of increasing external pressure. China simultaneously intensifies its new charm offensive and non-military coercion with the advance of a comprehensive, long-term, and global Sino–U.S. competition.[42]

10.2.2. *Objectives of wedging*

Beijing's judgment of trends in Sino–U.S. relations, especially the perceived changes in relative strengths and U.S. intentions, is a major influential factor in its neighborhood strategy. In the context of a hardening policy by the U.S. toward China, the importance and urgency of driving a wedge between neighboring countries and the U.S. come to the fore. In such circumstances, if China perceives a significant power gap with the U.S., it is more likely to reward and reassure its neighbors to ensure a peaceful environment for domestic development. Otherwise, China will adopt a strategy that combines rewards and coercion. The two working conferences of the Communist Party of China's (CPC's) Central Committee on neighborhood security both reflected the linkage between neighborhood diplomacy and top leaders' perceptions of Sino–U.S. relations. The 2001 meeting was held after U.S. President George W. Bush's identification of China as a strategic competitor,[43] while the 2013 meeting took place against the backdrop of the U.S.' "pivot to Asia" and China's policy shift toward "striving for achievement" after the 18th National Congress.[44] China's relationship with the U.S. has always been a central theme in its neighborhood policy, and it has not changed with the emergence of the U.S. Indo-Pacific strategy.

China's policy toward ASEAN countries takes into account its own domestic economic development and the overall external pressure as its starting point and is adjusted according to the dynamics of Sino–U.S. relations. The goals of China's wedging policy can be divided into three progressive levels: first, to ensure that the region remains open and neutral in terms of both security and economy, so that not many neighbors, if any, will join a counter-China coalition led by the U.S.; second, to ensure ASEAN continues to serve as a bridge for China's integration into the regional international community; and third, to encourage more countries to welcome China's leading role (at least in some areas) within the regional order. It is observed that the extent to which each goal is pursued varies at different stages of China's rise. In the mid-to-late 1990s, Chinese leaders, recognizing the disparity in power with the U.S., chose to focus on domestic development, while adopting a defensive posture externally.[45] Hence, China's wedging strategies were geared toward achieving the first policy goal and setting the stage for the second.

After 2010, like previous rising powers with considerable economic capacity, China's judgment of the power parity between itself and the U.S. started to change due to the 2008 financial crisis. As a result, China sought to strengthen its security presence in East Asia. The South China Sea has become a central flashpoint in China's relationship with ASEAN countries. Moreover, China had not anticipated the U.S. and Vietnam expressing their concerns about its behavior in the South China Sea at the ASEAN Regional Forum around 2010. At almost the same time, a debate emerged internationally about whether China viewed the South China Sea as a core interest. Since then, China has frequently expressed its opposition to the involvement of external powers in South China Sea disputes at diplomatic occasions, denying the legitimacy of the U.S. involvement by referring to it as a non-claimant state, a non-regional state, and a violation of the principle of non-interference. In addition to the U.S., the non-disputing states targeted by China also include U.S. allies such as Japan, Australia, the United Kingdom, and France.

The goals of China's Southeast Asia policy have not changed much since the U.S. presented its Indo-Pacific strategy. From China's perspective, the Indo-Pacific strategy stirs up Cold War–like confrontation and stokes geopolitical competition, aiming to maintain the hegemony of the U.S.[46] The Indo-Pacific strategy is likely to target the BRI and create a wedge between China and its neighboring countries.[47] It indeed increases the strategic significance of ASEAN for China. However, ASEAN countries are unlikely to support a strategy that antagonizes China, and the solidarity of the Quad remains to be seen. Hence, there is still a strategic space for China to weaken and wedge the Indo-Pacific strategy in terms of geopolitics, economy, and values.

To this end, China hopes to achieve three goals through its interactions with ASEAN. The first is to ensure that ASEAN countries remain neutral amid Sino–U.S. competition. ASEAN has accepted and redefined the concept of the Indo-Pacific out of concern that it might become irrelevant with the advance of the Indo-Pacific era. However, ASEAN's strong desire to avoid taking sides still allows China considerable leeway to wedge ASEAN countries, and the U.S., China, and ASEAN share some similarities in the vision of regional order, which includes inclusiveness of regional architecture and limited great power competition. ASEAN countries worry that the Indo-Pacific strategy will challenge these aspirations, while the U.S. expects ASEAN countries to adopt a more explicit and unified China policy and wants them to be more operational in terms of collective security, neither of which is unlikely to be achieved.[48] China exploits ASEAN countries' reservations toward the security aspect of the U.S.' Indo-Pacific strategy and seeks to expand common understandings with ASEAN on regional security issues.

Second, China—against the backdrop of the U.S.' economic sanctions and decoupling—places great strategic importance in securing Southeast Asia as a trade transit point to avoid being excluded from the global production network. The U.S. encourages its allies and partners to reduce their dependence on China as part of the Indo-Pacific strategy. One of China's responses is to enhance economic integration with ASEAN countries. That's part of the reason why China is keen to join the Regional Comprehensive Economic Partnership (RCEP) and urges other members, including ASEAN countries, to ratify the trade deal as soon as possible after negotiations conclude.[49] By joining the RCEP, Chinese firms can shift their operations abroad to avoid U.S. trade tariffs. Also, the trade of intermediate goods, which dominates China–ASEAN trade, can be further promoted. In fact, China has called on ASEAN to reject protectionism and unilateralism since the beginning of the Sino–U.S. trade conflict.[50] Furthermore, trade between the two sides has grown rapidly in recent years. Since 2020, ASEAN has been China's largest trading partner for three consecutive years. These trends further reinforce that ASEAN serves as China's bridge to global manufacturing networks amid trade tensions with the U.S.

Third, China needs to weaken the legitimacy of U.S. efforts to mobilize its allies, including the Quad, by supporting and emphasizing ASEAN centrality, reinforcing multilateralism, and advocating the legitimate advantages of regional inclusiveness. Since U.S. President Biden came into office, trust in the U.S. has been restored, and cooperation within the Quad has been upgraded. The European Union (EU) has also issued an Indo-Pacific Cooperation Strategy report that echoes the Quad.[51] As such, China has been experiencing a significant increase in pressure from the U.S. and its allies, leading to Chinese state media publishing lengthy articles pointing out the "seven sins" of the U.S. and its allies.[52] During his visit to Indonesia in early 2021, Foreign Minister Wang Yi stated, "We are against closed-group politics in the name of multilateralism, oppose imposing rules made by a handful of countries to the international community."[53] When attending the ASEAN series in 2021, Wang Yi said that China opposes treating ASEAN as a mere figurehead and other forms of pseudo-multilateralism, and it also resists bloc confrontation on the pretext of multilateralism in the region in particular.[54] The comments are aimed at seeking the goodwill of ASEAN, but more importantly, they criticize the Quad without explicitly naming it. In response to the U.S. Indo-Pacific strategy, China has expressed that ASEAN is its preferred approach to multilateralism and cooperation in the region. Similar statements by China have been made in other contexts, such as its preference for the UN regarding global political order and the WHO on the issue of fighting the pandemic.

10.2.3. *Measures for wedging*

China's "smile diplomacy," or charm offensive, includes security assurance and economic attraction. Historically, security reassurance has been the most important, and the 2002 Declaration of the Conduct of Parties in the South China Sea (DOC) laid the foundation for the rapid development of China–ASEAN relations thereafter. Since then, security reassurance accompanied by economic attraction has frequently been used to describe China's Southeast Asia policy in the 2000s.[55] However, the escalation of the South China Sea disputes has led to ASEAN countries warmly welcoming the U.S. pivot, which increases China's anxiety about a worsening strategic environment in its periphery.[56] As a result, China has been increasing efforts on reward measures, such as enhancing mutual assurance, making ambitious economic cooperation plans, and supplying much-needed public goods. At the same time, more coercive measures have been used when reward measures have been ineffective.

First, China reassures ASEAN countries by accelerating the COC negotiations and seeks assurance from ASEAN countries when the U.S. military presence is reinforced. The South China Sea disputes are always at the core of China–ASEAN security relations. To mitigate the potential of ASEAN countries' alignment with the U.S. and its allies, China and ASEAN formally started consultations on the COC in 2013. Although China was dissatisfied with ASEAN's prior consultation, it still respected this multilateral approach rather than insisting on bilateral negotiations. China's desire to accelerate COC consultations grew stronger after ASEAN's statement on the South China Sea arbitration in July 2016.[57] The consultations were put on hold due to the outbreak of the pandemic and resumed in June 2021; all parties agreeing to resume the second reading of the Single Draft COC Negotiating Text as soon as possible.[58]

COC is not only the most viable mechanism to realize Southeast Asian countries' shared interests regarding South China Sea disputes but also meets China's demand to reduce ASEAN claimants' need to involve the U.S. in the disputes.[59] Usually, China actively moves forward with the COC when tensions heighten and ASEAN claimants urgently look to U.S. involvement or international law, as they did in 2013 and 2016. However, negotiation and coercion are not mutually exclusive. During the negotiations, China has consolidated its *de facto* control over the South China Sea and sometimes adopted non-military coercive measures, such as diplomatic sanctions, economic sanctions, and gray zone coercion.[60] In short, China's policy on the South China Sea is determined by its overall strategic goals and how the region fits into this larger picture, which refers to the stability of the neighborhood environment and Sino–U.S. relations.[61] Moreover, the COC serves as a multilateral policy tool for China to drive a wedge between ASEAN claimants and the U.S. China will stick to its claim to sovereignty but will not rule out bilateral negotiations or even compromise on the allocation of interests or crisis management with the intention of wedging ASEAN claimants while advancing its overall strategic goals. Besides COC consultations, China's very recent attempt to assure ASEAN countries is multilaterally reflected in its partial acceptance of the AOIP, noting that it reaffirms the principles of the AOIP in the Joint Statement of the ASEAN–China Special Summit commemorating the 30th anniversary of their dialogue relations. At the same time, China has also persuaded ASEAN to distance itself from the U.S. version of the Indo-Pacific strategy by clarifying that the AOIP "is ASEAN's independent initiative, being open and inclusive ... and is not aimed at creating new mechanisms or replacing existing ones."[62]

With the advance of strengthened cooperation between the U.S. and ASEAN countries, China is eager to seek assurance from the latter that there will always be leeway to wedge in the U.S.–ASEAN partnership. For example, in July 2020, Former United States Secretary of State Mike Pompeo stated that Beijing's claims across most of the South China Sea are unlawful.[63] It was the first time that the U.S. explicitly rejected China's maritime claims in the South China Sea. Shortly after Pompeo's remark, Chinese President Xi called on the Thailand and Singapore prime ministers to obtain reassurances. Foreign Minister Wang Yi also received a similar promise from his Philippine counterpart through a virtual meeting.[64] Another example is the establishment of AUKUS, a new enhanced trilateral security partnership between Australia, the U.K., and the U.S. Some ASEAN countries, especially Indonesia and Malaysia, have expressed their critical attitudes toward the creation of AUKUS. To ensure ASEAN countries' neutrality, China's Ministry of Foreign Affairs convened the five ambassadors of ASEAN countries immediately after the establishment of AUKUS and confirmed their concerns over the emergence of the new military pact.[65]

Second, China continues to provide economic rewards to expand common interests as much as possible, and, to a certain degree, it has been willing to endure economic losses in some cases. Closer economic and trade relations are the primary motivation for ASEAN countries to maintain a friendship with China. When developing economic and trade relations, China strives as much as possible to tailor its economic and trade policies to the macro and long-term development needs of Southeast Asia. For example, the BRI dovetails with bilateral and domestic development plans, such as the "Two Corridors and One Economic Belt" between China and Vietnam, the "Eastern Economic Corridor" of Thailand, and the "Global Maritime Axis" of Indonesia. When the domestic politics of host countries hinder the progress of projects financed by China, it generally adopts a persuasive, coordinated, and adaptive attitude without exerting excessive political pressure. For instance, China and Malaysia signed a supplementary agreement on the East Coast Rail Link, reducing the construction costs and paving the way for its resumption.[66] Myanmar's Letpadaung copper mine has experienced setbacks and adjustments as well. China has shown that project agreements can be adjusted to ease the domestic pressure faced by local governments, and it has maintained an open attitude toward criticism from international society.

At the same time, as a wedging strategy tool, China's economic rewards have been partially driven by its security interests. China tends to offer more economic incentives to administrations that acquiesce to or recognize its leading position, such as the Duterte and Najib administrations. Meanwhile, informal economic sanctions were employed for explicit attempts to balance against China with external powers or to constrain China by international norms. For instance, the Aquino III administration in the Philippines suffered economic sanctions and political disengagement from China.

Third, China provides regional public goods that Southeast Asian countries need. Previously, China had provided assistance to Southeast Asia during the Asian financial crisis, the Indian Ocean tsunami, and the 2008 global economic crisis.[67] Such moves have helped China build its image as a responsible power in Southeast Asia. Since the outbreak of the COVID-19 pandemic, China has been actively providing medical assistance to Southeast Asian countries through Chinese embassies and the ASEAN Secretariat; China's aid consists of masks and equipment, as well as dispatching medical experts. On the condition of a positive response from Southeast Asian countries, vaccine cooperation has been carried out, including trials, sales, donations, and local production. In August 2020, Sinovac Biotech collaborated with Indonesia on Phase III vaccine clinical trials, and President of Indonesia Joko Widodo was the first Southeast Asian leader to receive the Chinese vaccine. China also regards ASEAN as its primary partner in cooperation to combat the pandemic. At a special China–ASEAN foreign ministers' meeting in Chongqing, many Southeast Asian countries raised challenges related to vaccine shortages and economic recovery, to which China responded positively. Singapore's Foreign Minister Vivian Balakrishnan commented that helping each other build trust in times of need bodes well for future relations.[68]

China's role as a provider of public goods has also intensified in non-traditional security domains, including, maritime cooperation, disaster management, and environmental cooperation.[69] After a severe drought hit the entire Mekong River basin in 2019, China decided to share year-round hydrological data with the Mekong River Commission (MRC), fulfilling a long-standing call from downstream countries. Previously, China had also taken measures such as sharing some hydrological data and emergency water releases. An Pich Hatda, the MRC Secretariat Chief Executive Officer, called the China–MRC agreement "a landmark in the history of China–MRC cooperation."[70] Although sharing data alone still falls short of the expectations of downstream countries that hope China will join the MRC, it at least reflects substantial progress in the governance of the transboundary river.

10.3. The Effectiveness and Dilemmas of China's Wedging Strategy

After years of economic incentives combined with reassurances, China has established a solid and significant influence in Southeast Asia. Most ASEAN countries recognize China's economic success and great power status, and regard stability in their relations with China and maintaining a balance between China and the U.S. as their fundamental interests. Hence, ASEAN countries hope to exercise restraint rather than containment on China. Under the shadow of the Indo-Pacific strategy, ASEAN countries' economic ties with China have become closer, and China continues to hold on to its position as the top trading partner of all ASEAN countries, with the exception of Brunei and Laos.

On security, China holds an absolute advantage, and the gap in military capacity between China and its neighbors seems to have widened. In this context, for ASEAN countries, the cost of alienating from China has increased. From this perspective, the first-level goal of China's policy for its Southeast Asian neighbors—to not align with external powers to contain China—has been partially achieved, but not entirely due to the effectiveness of wedging. However, the highest goal of wedging, which is to win over more ASEAN countries to become followers of China's policy stance, has clearly not been achieved. China has fewer followers in terms of security. Cambodia might be seen as a client state of China, but it is unlikely to support China again at the cost of ASEAN solidarity, as it did in 2012. Similarly, in order to dispel any notion of becoming a client, Prime Minister Hun Sen denied reports of a secret agreement granting China access to the Ream Naval Base. Even in the economic realm, China is not yet a fully recognized leader, for the BRI remains controversial and bilateral trade is sometimes used as a political tool.

The effectiveness of wedging is essentially limited by the contradictory nature of China's two strategic goals: buying time to increase strength before matching the U.S. in terms of power, and asserting its leading position in the region. In history, rising powers usually cannot resist the temptation to become dominant powers in their neighborhoods, and China is no exception. Unlike other rising powers, the rival China faces in the region is a mature global hegemon with an absolute advantage in both capacity and prestige. Although the U.S. occasionally neglects Southeast Asia, regional allies and partners ensure that the U.S.-led order remains vibrant. Thus, China needs to balance between accommodating ASEAN countries to ensure that it continues to serve as a buffer and project its regional leadership in the region. The tension between these two goals is the core dilemma of China's policy toward Southeast Asia. The U.S. Indo-Pacific strategy has not led to a substantial change in China's relationship with Southeast Asia. Instead, changes began quietly a decade ago with the advance of the U.S. Rebalance to Asia and the Pacific under the Obama administration.[71] However, the shift in U.S. policy toward China, as illustrated by the Indo-Pacific strategy, has significantly exacerbated the contradiction between China's two objectives. Specifically, this contradiction manifests itself in four ways.

First, China's economic "punishment" jeopardizes the effectiveness of economic rewards. As mentioned above, China's economic incentives for Southeast Asia are increasingly tied to security. China has drawn red lines in relation to the behavior of some Southeast Asian countries since 2010 and imposed economic penalties for crossing them, such as directly or openly provoking China with the help of the U.S. or international norms, as in the cases of the Philippines in 2012, Vietnam in 2014, and Australia in 2020. Whether the economic penalties are effective is not easy to judge; however, they clearly run counter to China's goal of gaining the goodwill of ASEAN countries through economic attraction. The latter fear losing the ability to say "no" to China and to defend their interests in the event of a security conflict with China.[72]

Second, China faces a contradiction between the increasing need to anticipate ASEAN countries' domestic political trends and the principle of non-interference. In most Southeast Asian states, the leaders and ruling elites play a dominant role in foreign policymaking. Therefore, domestic power transitions may result in dramatic changes to a country's China policy in general and its willingness to adopt a cooperative stance toward Chinese-led regional initiatives in particular.[73] In this regard, the dramatic shift in Philippine policy toward China from the Aquino III administration to the Duterte administration provides a telling case.[74] In the context of the Indo-Pacific strategy, China's desire for predictable foreign policies of ASEAN countries becomes more intense. On the one hand, China supports efforts to consolidate the positions of leaders who show deference and prevent the sustainability of their policies from being overturned by leadership changes. On the other hand, China maintains contact with opposition parties and social groups in order to forecast possible political changes. The objectives are to prevent disputes in the South China Sea from escalating and to reduce political risks to Chinese investments. In recent years, China has become more active in engaging with domestic political actors in its neighboring countries. However, China's "creative involvement" may also be perceived as an effort to influence domestic affairs.[75] For example, the links between Chinese embassies and overseas Chinese communities have been regarded by some local media as having a political purpose. China's growing "united front" activities among ethnic Chinese communities have already concerned intelligence officials in Southeast Asia.[76]

The third is the contradiction between striving for the support of key countries and upholding the centrality of ASEAN as a whole. ASEAN countries do not share the same position on some regional issues. China seeks to ensure that it has firm followers within ASEAN while being supportive of ASEAN centrality, thereby strengthening the collective buffer role of ASEAN and allowing China to take the moral high ground. However, given the louder voices of ASEAN's older members, such as Indonesia and Singapore, ASEAN will not accept the pro-China positions that Cambodia and Laos may propose. That said, China is not the only one facing such a dilemma. The U.S. also seeks loyal followers within ASEAN. Both China and the U.S. support ASEAN-led regional multilateralism by paying diplomatic lip service while investing more resources in countries that share common interests at the bilateral level.

Fourth, the contradiction manifests as a strategic dilemma between the need to hedge against the risk of short-term policy fluctuations and a durable and stable strategy. Compared with the U.S., the durability and stability of Southeast Asian policies are China's comparative advantages.

China seldom neglects the region as the U.S. did during the Bush and Trump administrations. In contrast to the Biden administration's inaction, China initiated its diplomatic offensive in Southeast Asia once the pandemic had subsided. However, under the shadow of the U.S. Indo-Pacific strategy, Southeast Asian countries' interactions with the Quad and the possibility of domestic political changes have increased the uncertainty and unpredictability of their China policies. In response, China needs to adopt more stopgap measures, such as economic sanctions or bilateral talks on disputes which may undermine its long-term regional strategy.

China's wedging strategy focuses on creating common interests rather than reducing conflicts of interest. The ineffectiveness of addressing the latter does not necessarily lead to a deterioration in China's relations with ASEAN countries. Although ASEAN countries' intentions to constrain China's influence have become stronger, the cost of alienating or angering China is too high given its geographical proximity, the disparity in military power, and the uncertainty of the U.S.' commitment. With the combination of China's show of muscle during and after the arbitration and the U.S. response falling short of expectations, ASEAN countries appear to have no choice but to move closer to China. This has been the case for the Philippines, Vietnam, and Singapore since the second half of 2016. This does not mean that ASEAN countries will simply become followers of China's policies (with the exception of Cambodia and Laos); rather, at least in the face of Sino–U.S. competition, it becomes almost impossible for them to side completely with the U.S.

If ASEAN countries continue to move closer to the U.S. in terms of security, China will reinforce negative interdependencies in ways that increase the cost of confronting it, such as economic sanctions and ceasing political or social contacts. Therefore, the Indo-Pacific strategy will not sway ASEAN countries completely to the U.S. side. China's wedging strategy does play a part in preventing this shift, but more importantly, it is due to ASEAN countries' fear of confrontation with a powerful neighbor. Amid heightened tensions between China and the U.S., regional states have become more sensitive to rising security risks and a shrinking room for maneuvering. As Singapore's Prime Minister Lee Hsien Loong has repeatedly stated in recent years, it would be very costly for regional middle and small states to take sides in the Sino–U.S. rivalry.[77] At the same time, China cannot afford to lose Southeast Asia as a buffer zone either. The negative interdependence of the two sides will be an indispensable stabilizer in current and future China–ASEAN relations.

10.4. Conclusion

Since the introduction of the Indo-Pacific strategy, the geopolitical competition between China and the U.S. has significantly intensified. The U.S. has chosen Japan, Australia, and India as pillar states in China's neighborhood. The status of the Southeast Asian region, although not yet a firm follower of the U.S. Indo-Pacific strategy, has risen in China's strategic priority. This poses at least three challenges for China: ASEAN's desire for China to accept its outlook on the Indo-Pacific, the emergence of quasi-pillar states within the Indo-Pacific strategy, and the weakening domestic political will in favor of friendship with China. To alleviate these pressures, China has addressed the challenges through bilateral economic concessions, multilateral security coordination with reservations, and the provision of public goods. The central aim is to prevent Southeast Asia from embracing the U.S. Indo-Pacific strategy and to continue to act as a strategic buffer zone. The closer relationship between China and Southeast Asian countries, compared to what they had established before the Indo-Pacific strategy, cannot be entirely attributed to the effects of China's reassurances. The reinforcement of negative interdependence plays a critical role in stabilizing their relationship, and neither China nor Southeast Asia can afford to alienate or antagonize each other.

The "close-but-not affinity" between China and Southeast Asia will continue in the future. The geographic proximity, power disparity, and economic interdependence that have led to this status will persist. For China, a neutral Southeast Asia serves as a geopolitical buffer against pressure from the U.S. and its allies, and predictable relations with China are crucial to Southeast Asian countries' security and prosperity. After all, domestic politics, the relative decline in power, and a history of interaction with Southeast Asia can hardly instill confidence that the U.S. will definitely fulfill its commitment. Therefore, in contrast to Japan and Australia—the two most reliable U.S. allies in the region—most ASEAN states will not openly support the U.S.' attempt to organize a counter-China coalition. However, they will still want to maintain a hedging stance and preserve some leeway. Whether Southeast Asia's attitude toward China can change from "no clear opposition" to support will depend on whether China can win the trust of Southeast Asian governments and people. China needs to do more to address the relative gains and reduce the pushback between the two sides' relations while enlarging common interests. In addition, the positions of key countries have a demonstration and driving effect, such as the Philippines and Vietnam, which are claimants in the South China Sea, and Indonesia, the only recognized middle power in the region—these should be the main targets of China's reassurance efforts.

Acknowledgment

The author would like to express sincere gratitude to two anonymous reviewers, Mingjiang Li, and other participants of the workshop "Discerning China's Bilateral Relations in the Indo Pacific," hosted by the Center for Governance and Public Policy at Griffith University in October 2021, for their helpful comments. This research is supported by the National Social Science Fund of China (no. 20CGJ032).

Endnotes

1 A. I. Johnston and P. Evans, "China's engagement with multilateral security institutions," in A. I. Johnston and R. Ross (eds.), *Engaging China: The Management of an Emerging Power*, (London: Routledge, 1999), pp. 235–272; D. Shambaugh, "China engages Asia: Reshaping the regional order," *International Security*, 29(3), 64–99 (2005); Feng Liu, "China's security strategy towards East Asia," *Chinese Journal of International Politics*, 9(2), 151–179 (2016).

2 ASEAN Stats Data Portal. https://data.aseanstats.org/trade-annually, https://data.aseanstats.org/fdi-by-hosts-and-sources.

3 S. Seah, Hoang Thi Ha, M. Martinus and Pham Thi Phuong Thao, *The State of Southeast Asia: 2021 Survey Report* (Singapore: ISEAS-Yusof Ishak Institute, 2022). https://www.iseas.edu.sg/wp-content/uploads/2021/01/The-State-of-SEA-2021-v2.pdf; S. Seah, Joanne Lin, S. Suvannaphakdy, M. Martinus, Pham Thi Phuong Thao, Farah Nadine Seth and Hoang Thi Ha, *The State of Southeast Asia: 2022 Survey Report* (Singapore: ISEAS-Yusof Ishak Institute, 2022). https://www.iseas.edu.sg/wp-content/uploads/2022/02/The-State-of-SEA-2022_FA_Digital_FINAL.pdf.

4 S. Strangio, *In the Dragon's Shadow: Southeast Asia in the Chinese Century* (New Heaven: Yale University Press, 2020), p. 3.

5 G. Allison, "The new sphere of influence: Sharing the globe with other great powers," *Foreign Affairs*, 99(2), 36–37 (2020).

6 D. Shambaugh, *Where Great Powers Meet: America and China in Southeast Asia* (Oxford: Oxford University Press, 2021).

7 E. Goh, "Hierarchy and the role of the United States in the East Asian Security order," *International Relations of the Asia-Pacific*, 8(3), 353–377 (2008); Xuefeng Sun, "Rethinking East Asian regional order and China's rise," *Japanese Journal of Political Science*, 14(1), 9–30 (2013).

8 Wang Yi, "The U.S. Indo-Pacific strategy is bound to be a failed strategy," 22 May 2022. https://www.fmprc.gov.cn/mfa_eng/wjb_663304/zzjg_663340/yzs_663350/xwlb_663352/202205/t20220523_10691136.html. For Chinese perceptions and responses on the Indo-Pacific strategy, see Feng Liu, "The recalibrating of Chinese assertiveness: China's responses to the Indo–Pacific challenge," *International Affairs*, 96(1), 9–27 (2020); Weixing Hu, "The United States, China, and the Indo-Pacific strategy: The rise and return of strategic competition," *The China Review*, 20(3), 127–142 (2020); Weixing Hu and Weizhan Meng, "The US Indo-Pacific strategy and China's response," *The China Review*, 20(3), 143–176 (2020).

9 The White House, *National Security Strategy of the United States of America*, 18 December 2017. https://www.whitehouse.gov/wp-content/uploads/2017/12/NSS-Final-12-18-2017-0905.pdf.

10 R. Dossani and S. W. Harold, *U.S. Policy in Asia: Prospects for the Future* Santa Monica: Rand Corporation, 2018), p. 84.

11 "Remarks by Vice President Pence at the 6th U.S.-ASEAN summit," U.S. Mission to ASEAN, 16 November 2018. https://asean.usmission.gov/remarks-by-vice-president-pence-at-the-6th-u-s-asean-summit/.

12 "Department of Defense (U.S.), *Indo-Pacific Strategy Report: Preparedness, Partnerships, and Promoting a Networked Region*, 1 June 2019. https://media.defense.gov/2019/Jul/01/2002152311/-1/-1/1/DEPARTMENT-OF-DEFENSE-INDO-PACIFIC-STRATEGY-REPORT-2019.

13 Department of State (U.S.), *A Free and Open Indo-Pacific: Advancing a Shared Vision*, 3 November 2019. https://www.state.gov/a-free-and-open-indo-pacific-advancing-a-shared-vision/.

14 The White House, "Remarks by President Biden at the annual U.S.-ASEAN summit," October 26, 2021. https://www.whitehouse.gov/briefing-room/speeches-remarks/2021/10/26/remarks-by-president-biden-at-the-annual-u-s-asean-summit/.

15 A. Gallagher, *U.S.-ASEAN Summit Focused on Building Ties, Not Countering China*, The United States Institute of Peace, 12 May 2022. https://www.usip.org/publications/2022/05/us-asean-summit-focused-building-ties-not-countering-china.

16 I. Storey and W. Choong, "Russia's invasion of Ukraine: Southeast Asian responses and why the conflict matters to the region," ISEAS Perspective, 24(9), March 2022, p. 7. https://www.iseas.edu.sg/wp-content/uploads/2022/02/ISEAS_Perspective_2022_24.pdf.

17 The White House, *National Security Strategy*, October 2022, p. 8, 11. https://www.whitehouse.gov/wp-content/uploads/2022/10/Biden-Harris-Administrations-National-Security-Strategy-10.2022.pdf.

18 The Socialist Republic of Vietnam, "Viet Nam National Defense WHITE PAPER 2019," Online Newspaper of the Government, 20 December 2019. http://news.chinhphu.vn/Home/Viet-Nam-National-Defense-WHITE-PAPER-2019/201912/38323.vgp.

19 Nguyen Cong Tung, "Uneasy embrace: Vietnam's responses to the U.S. free and open Indo-Pacific strategy amid U.S.-China rivalry," *The Pacific Review*, 35(4), 884–914 (2021).

20 D. F. Anwar, "Indonesia and the ASEAN outlook on the Indo-Pacific," *International Affairs*, 96(1), 111–129 (2020).

21 Ministry of Foreign Affairs of People's Republic of China, "Wang Yi talks about Indo-Pacific concept," 31 July 2019. https://www.fmprc.gov.cn/mfa_eng/zxxx_662805/t1685652.shtml.

22 Xi Jinping, "For a shared future and our common home," Speech at the Special Summit to Commemorate The 30th Anniversary of China-ASEAN Dialogue Relations, 22 November 2021. https://www.fmprc.gov.cn/mfa_eng/topics_665678/kjgzbdfyyq/202111/t20211122_10451280.html.

23 Ministry of Foreign Affairs of the People's Republic of China, "Director-General of the Department of Asian Affairs of the Foreign Ministry Liu Jinsong meets with Vietnamese Ambassador to China Pham Sao Mai," 25 June 2022. https://www.fmprc.gov.cn/mfa_eng/wjbxw/202206/t20220627_10710374.html.

24 E. S. Medeiros, "The changing fundamentals of U.S.-China relations," *The Washington Quarterly*, 42(3), 93–119 (2019), p. 99.

25 "Decoupling existing cooperation between countries doomed to Boomerang: Chinese FM," *Xinhua Net*, 25 August 2020. http://www.xinhuanet.com/english/2020-08/25/c_139315986.htm.

26 Xue Gong, "Weathering the storm? RCEP, Chinese regionalism, and great power competition," in Tiang Boon Hoo and Jared Morgan Mckinney (eds.) *Chinese Regionalism in Asia: Beyond the Belt and Road Initiative* (London: Routledge, 2022), pp. 44–56.

27 Pew Research Center, "People in Asia-Pacific regard the U.S. more favorably than China, but Trump gets negative marks," 25 February 2020. https://www.pewresearch.org/fact-tank/2020/02/25/people-in-asia-pacific-regard-the-u-s-more-favorably-than-china-but-trump-gets-negative-marks/.

28 A. E. Yeremia, "'Indonesian diplomats' and foreign policy scholars' perceptions and their implications on Indonesian foreign ministry bureaucratic responses to a rising China," *The Pacific Review*, 35(3), 529–556 (2020).

29 Seah *et al.* (2022), *Op. cit.*, p. 34.

30 Branda Tan, "Friend or foe: Explaining the Duterte administration's China policy in the South China Sea," *Cornell International Affairs Review*, 14(2), 4–47 (2021).

31 A. Korolev, "Shrinking room for hedging: System-unit dynamics and behavior of smaller powers," *International Relations of the Asia-Pacific*, 19(3), 419–452 (2019).

32 T. W. Crawford, "Preventing enemy coalitions: How wedge strategies shape power politics," *International Security*, 35(4), 155–189 (2011); T. W. Crawford, *The Power to Divide: Wedge Strategies in Great Power Competition* (New York, NY: Cornell University Press, 2021).

33 M. Wigell, "Hybrid interference as a wedge strategy: A theory of external interference in liberal democracy," *International Affairs*, 95(2), 255–275 (2019).

34 H. Ebert and D. Flemes, "Regional powers and contested leadership, hedging and wedging: Strategies to contest Russia's leadership in Post-Soviet Eurasia," in H. Ebert and D. Flemes (eds.), *Regional Powers and Contested Leadership*, (Cham: Palgrave Macmillan, 2018), p. 321.

35 Yasuhiro Izumikawa, "To coerce or reward? Theorizing wedge strategies in alliance politics," *Security Studies*, 22(3), 498–531 (2013); Yuxing Huang, "An interdependence theory of wedge strategies," *Chinese Journal of International Politics*, 13(2), 253–286 (2020).

36 A. D. Taffer, "Threat and opportunity: Chinese wedging in the Senkaku/ Diaoyu dispute," *Asian Security*, 16(2), 157–178 (2020).

37 Crawford (2011), *Op. cit.*

38 Yasuhiro Izumikawa, "To coerce or reward? Theorizing wedge strategies in alliance politics," *Security Studies*, 22(3), 498–531 (2013).

39 M. Dian and A. Kireeva, "Wedge strategies in Russia-Japan relations," *The Pacific Review*, 35(5), 853–883 (2021).

40 Xuefeng Sun, "Why does China reassure South East Asia?" *Pacific Focus*, 24(3), 298–316 (2009).

41 Feng Liu, "China's security strategy towards East Asia," *The Chinese Journal of International Politics*, 9(2), 151–179 (2016); Feng Zhang and Barry Buzan, "The relevance of deep pluralism for China's foreign policy," *The Chinese Journal of International Politics*, 15(3), 246–271 (2022).

42 Minghao Zhao, "Is a new cold war inevitable? Chinese perspectives on US–China strategic competition," *The Chinese Journal of International Politics*, 12(3), 371–394 (2019), p. 372; Jue Zhang and Jin Xu, "China-US strategic competition and the descent of a porous curtain," *Chinese Journal of International Politics*, 14(3), 321–352 (2021).

43 R. Baum, "From strategic partners to strategic competitors: George W. Bush and the politics of U.S. China policy," *Journal of East Asia Studies*, 1(2), 191–220 (2001).

44 Xuetong Yan, "From keeping a low profile to striving for achievement," *The Chinese Journal of International Politics*, 7(2), 153–184 (2014).

45 Yan (2014), *Op. cit.*

46 "U.S. Indo-Pacific strategy undermines peace, development prospect in East Asia:Wang Yi," *Xinhua Net*, 13 October 2020. http://www.xinhuanet.com/english/2020-10/13/c_139437326.htm.

47 "Vice Foreign Minister Le Yucheng's exclusive interview with the *Financial Times*," *China Daily*, 26 September 2018. https://www.chinadaily.com.cn/a/201809/26/WS5bab2f67a310c4cc775e8304.html; Ministry of Foreign Affairs of the People's Republic of China, "Foreign Ministry Spokesperson Hua Chunying's remarks on 5 August 2019." https://www.fmprc.gov.cn/mfa_eng/xwfw_665399/s2510_665401/t1686226.shtml.

48 See Seng Tan, "Consigned to hedge: Southeast Asia and America's free and open Indo-Pacific's strategy," *International Affairs*, 96(1), 131–148 (2020).

49 Ministry of Foreign Affairs of the People's Republic of China, "Wang Yi meets with ASEAN Secretary-General Dato Lim Jock Hoi," 7 June 2021. https://www.fmprc.gov.cn/mfa_eng/zxxx_662805/t1882093.shtml.

50 "Full text of Chinese Vice Premier Hu Chunhua's speech at opening ceremony of World Economic Forum on ASEAN," *Xinhua Net*, 13 September 2018. http://www.xinhuanet.com/english/2018-09/13/c_137463760.htm.

51 The European Union, *EU Strategy for Cooperation in the Indo-Pacific*, February 2022. https://www.eeas.europa.eu/sites/default/files/eu-indo-pacific_factsheet_2022-02_0.pdf.

52 "Recounting 'seven sins' of the US' alliance system," *Xinhua Net*, 24 August 2021. http://www.news.cn/english/2021-08/24/c_1310145214.htm.

53 Ministry of Foreign Affairs of the People's Republic of China, "Wang Yi: 'Four adherences' and 'three oppositions' are needed for genuine multilateralism," 13 January 2021. https://www.fmprc.gov.cn/mfa_eng/zxxx_662805/t1846417.shtml.

54 Ministry of Foreign Affairs of the People's Republic of China, "Wang Yi: China opposes treating ASEAN as a mere figurehead and starting all over again," 5 August 2021. https://www.fmprc.gov.cn/mfa_eng/zxxx_662805/t1897492.shtml.

55 Sun (2009), *Op. cit.*; Feng Liu, "China's security strategy towards East Asia," *Chinese Journal of International Politics*, 9(2), 151–179 (2016).

56 Liu (2020), *Op. cit.*

57 Tan Hui Yee, "China calls for fast-track talks on code of conduct," *The Straits Times*, 26 July 2016. https://www.straitstimes.com/asia/china-calls-for-fast-track-talks-on-code-of-conduct.

58 Ministry of Foreign Affairs of the People's Republic of China, "The 19th senior officials' meeting on the implementation of the declaration on the

conduct of parties in the South China Sea held in Chongqing," 7 June 2021. https://www.fmprc.gov.cn/mfa_eng/wjbxw/t1882173.shtml.

59 Le Hu, "Examining ASEAN's effectiveness in managing South China Sea disputes," *The Pacific Review*, 36(1), 119–147 (2023).

60 Ketian Zhang, "Cautious bully, reputation, resolve, and Beijing's use of coercion in the South China Sea," *International Security*, 44(1), 117–159 (2019).

61 Zhou Fangyin, "Between assertiveness and self-restraint: Understanding China's South China Sea policy," *International Affairs*, 92(4), 869–890 (2016).

62 Ministry of Foreign Affairs of the People's Republic of China, "Joint statement of the ASEAN-China special summit to commemorate the 30 anniversary of ASEAN-China dialogue relations: Comprehensive strategic partnership for peace, security, prosperity and sustainable development," 22 November 2021. https://www.fmprc.gov.cn/mfa_eng/zxxx_662805/202111/t20211122_10451478.html.

63 M. R. Pompeo, "U.S. position on maritime claims in the South China Sea," Press Statement of U.S. Department of State, 13 July 2020. https://2017-2021.state.gov/u-s-position-on-maritime-claims-in-the-south-china-sea/index.html.

64 Hu (2023), *Op. cit.*

65 Ministry of Foreign Affairs of the People's Republic of China, "Director-General of the Department of Asian Affairs of the Foreign Ministry Liu Jinsong holds talks with ambassadors of some ASEAN countries to China about trilateral military cooperation between the United States, the United Kingdom and Australia," 23 September 2021. https://www.fmprc.gov.cn/mfa_eng/wjbxw/t1909571.shtml.

66 Malaysia Prime Minister's Office, "Press statement by YAB Prime Minister Tun Dr. Mahathir Bin Mohamad on East Coast Rail Link (ECRL) Project," 15 April 2019. https://www.pmo.gov.my/wp-content/uploads/2019/04/Press-Statement-by-PM-on-ECRL_15April2019.pdf.

67 Wang Lina and Zhai Kun, "China's policy shifts on Southeast Asia: To build a 'community of common destiny,'" *China Quarterly of International Strategic Studies*, 2(1), 81–100 (2016).

68 E. Law, ASEAN, "China foreign ministers discuss Covid-19, South China Sea and Myanmar," *The Straits Times*, 9 June 2021. https://www.straitstimes.com/asia/east-asia/asean-china-foreign-ministers-meet-discuss-trade-covid-19-myanmar.

69 Lina Gong and Mingjiang Li, "China–Southeast Asian nontraditional security engagement: A soft power mode in Beijing's regional diplomacy?" *The China Review*, 21(4), 1–9 (2021); Ying Hui Lee and Jane Chan, "China-ASEAN nontraditional maritime security cooperation," *The China Review*, 21(4), 11–37 (2021).

70 Mekong River Commission, "China to provide the Mekong River Commission with year-round water data," 22 October 2020. https://www.mrcmekong.org/news-and-events/news/china-to-provide-the-mekong-river-commission-with-year-round-water-data/.

71 P. Harris and P. Trubowitz, "The politics of power projection: The pivot to Asia, its failure, and the future of American primacy," *Chinese Journal of International Politics*, 14(2), 187–217 (2021).

72 Huong Le Thu, "China's dual strategy of coercion and inducement towards ASEAN," *The Pacific Review*, 32(1), 20–36 (2019).

73 A. M. Murphy, "Great power rivalries, domestic politics and Southeast Asian foreign policy: Exploring the linkages," *Asian Security*, 13(3), 165–182 (2017); Shaofeng Chen, "Regional responses to China's Maritime Silk Road Initiative in Southeast Asia," *Journal of Contemporary China*, 27(111), 344–361 (2018); L. S. Skalnes, "Layering and displacement in development finance: The Asian Infrastructure Investment Bank and the Belt and Road Initiative," *Chinese Journal of International Politics*, 14(2), 257–288 (2021); Zhaohui Wang and Yuheng Fu, "Local politics and fluctuating engagement with China: Analysing the Belt and Road Initiative in Maritime Southeast Asia," *Chinese Journal of International Politics*, 15(2), 163–182 (2022).

74 R. J. Heydarian, "Tragedy of small power politics: Duterte and the shifting sands of Philippine foreign policy," *Asian Security*, 13(3), 220–236 (2017).

75 "Creative involvement" is a term coined by Yizhou Wang to describe Chinese more active engagement stance, as a departure from, or complement to, its traditional non-interference policy. See Yizhou Wang, *Creative Involvement: The Evolution of China's Global Role* (London: Routledge, 2017).

76 D. Shambaugh, "U.S.-China rivalry in Southeast Asia," *International Security*, 42(2), 85–127 (2018), p. 115.

77 Lee Hsien Loong, "The endangered Asian century: America, China, and the perils of confrontation," *Foreign Affairs*, 99(4), 52–64 (2020); Prime Minister's Office Singapore, "PM Lee Hsien Loong at the Aspen Security Forum," 3 August 2021. https://www.pmo.gov.sg/Newsroom/PM-Lee-Hsien-Loong-at-the-Aspen-Security-Forum; Prime Minister's Office Singapore, "National day message 2022," 8 August 2022. https://www.pmo.gov.sg/Newsroom/National-Day-Message-2022.

© 2025 World Scientific Publishing Europe Ltd.
https://doi.org/10.1142/9781800616318_0012

Chapter 11

Herding Cats: Coordination Challenges in ASEAN's Approach to China[*]

Ja Ian Chong

National University of Singapore, Singapore

ASEAN–China relations do not fit neatly within the rubric of bilateral ties, unlike those of the dyadic interactions examined in this collection. ASEAN is a disparate collection of states that sometimes work with each other based on some mutual understanding about consensus, non-intervention, and autonomy, claims about centrality notwithstanding. Domestically, ASEAN members also need to navigate various political cleavages and latent anti-colonial, even anti-Chinese, sentiments that can emerge when interacting with China. Any position or arrangement that the grouping undertakes with respect to China, particularly the Chinese state, must first overcome these coordination problems. One way is through the presence of a common focal point among ASEAN members, which can be difficult to realize. ASEAN's unwieldy policy-making process, born from an initial desire to deescalate tensions and avoid conflict among members, can prevent the group and its members from being forced to take positions by major powers, including the People's Republic of China (PRC). This is exemplified by ASEAN's repeated claims of wanting to avoid choosing between the United States (U.S.)

---

[*] This chapter was originally printed as "Herding Cats: Coordination Challenges in ASEAN's Approach to China." *The China Review*, Vol. 23, No. 1 (2023): 307–339. https://www.jstor.org/stable/48717997. Reproduced with kind permission of CUHK Press.

and PRC to sidestep difficult decisions that may invite major power blowback. Yet, this slow and halting approach also stymies ASEAN's ability to take the initiative and establish conditions that enable meaningful autonomy amid intensifying U.S.–PRC competition. This chapter explains why this phenomenon persists despite the growing risks it poses to ASEAN and its relations with the PRC.

Discussing ASEAN bilateral relations seems like a misnomer. ASEAN, or the Association of Southeast Asian Nations, is a regional organization consisting of 10 states covering all of mainland and most of maritime Southeast Asia. Timor Leste is not currently a member, but it may be on track to join ASEAN having received observer status in November 2022.[1] Member states consist of high-income countries such as Singapore and energy-exporting Brunei, middle-income countries including Indonesia, the Philippines, Malaysia, Thailand, and Vietnam, and low-income states such as Cambodia, Myanmar, and Laos. Atop significant ethnic, religious, cultural, and linguistic diversity, Southeast Asia includes regime types ranging from democratizing polities and Leninist states to absolute monarchies, soft authoritarian states, and military juntas. Holding the group together is a set of general principles known as the "ASEAN way," based on consensus decision-making, mutual non-interference, and respect for autonomy, grounded in several broadly worded documents.[2]

ASEAN's pluralism and amorphousness permit significant flexibility but also create coordination challenges for the grouping, not least when managing their complex and multifaceted relationship with the People's Republic of China (PRC). ASEAN members often claim that their considerations originate from the fact that they "do not wish to choose sides" between the United States (U.S.) and the PRC and an insistence on "ASEAN centrality."[3] Rather than following any coherent approach, clearly established procedures, or collective "hedging," ASEAN members appear to adjust their behaviors in directions they deem most individually beneficial at any given moment.[4] I contend that ASEAN's positions on China-related issues often exhibit the quality of a collection of states operating with limited coordination, despite their statements about unity and unanimity. ASEAN member states tend to overcome coordination challenges in engaging China when issues are less contentious and have focal points that establish clear pathways for cooperation.

This chapter reviews the modes of ASEAN's efforts at cooperation and highlights key features of intra-ASEAN ties. I consider the role of coordination challenges in shaping ASEAN behavior and the conditions under which these challenges are either overcome or overwhelm efforts by member states to work together. This approach enables me to develop a conceptual framework for testing, as well as isolating specific behaviors and conditions when examining ASEAN–PRC relations. I then apply and test my explanations for intra-ASEAN cooperation on several key instances of ASEAN–PRC interactions: managing differences over the South China Sea (SCS), trade liberalization, and responding to Vietnam's invasion and the occupation of Cambodia. Comparisons of key elements in ASEAN–PRC ties, both historically and in the contemporary period, enable this study to emphasize the contours of this relationship in ways that support the extraction of broader theoretical and policy implications.

Notably, unlike other actors discussed in this volume, ASEAN is not a state. Its ability to exercise agency as a unit remains a matter of debate. Such conditions make treatments of ASEAN–PRC relations as bilateral and dyadic more challenging. If ASEAN is treated as a collection of states, then its relationship with the PRC is multilateral. Multilateral ties have more complicated dynamics than bilateral or dyadic ones by virtue of the simple fact that they involve more actors and potential veto players. Even if treated as a unit, ASEAN is an organization that consists of states, which means that it sits at a different level of analysis compared to the other units considered in this special feature. ASEAN–PRC interactions would therefore involve an international organization and a state, rather than being state-to-state relations.

11.1. Hedging or Haphazardness

A popular descriptor of ASEAN policy toward Beijing—and Washington—is that the organization is "hedging" between the two major powers. Derived from the practice of taking countervailing investment or betting positions to mitigate uncertainty and loss, "hedging" suggests deliberate and coherent strategic actions.[5] In international relations, this entails adopting policies that are similarly designed to purposefully mitigate risks.[6] In the context of ASEAN, this has come to mean concurrent cooperation with both the U.S. and PRC while leaving room for the option of siding with one major power should ties with the other deteriorate.[7] "Hedging" suggests coherent, strategic action, including the ability to appropriately adjust one's behavior in a timely fashion when circumstances dictate. Effective risk mitigation is particularly important for weaker actors, and "hedging" offers a potential strategy for achieving this.

ASEAN's current behavior toward the U.S. and PRC, however, suggests a certain haphazardness that contrasts with considered and concerted action. The group's desire to "not choose sides" while insisting on "centrality," for instance, does not suggest a clear direction or effort to work together collectively.[8] The multiple dialogues and minilaterals, in which ASEAN takes great interest, provide some basis for cooperation, including with non-member states; however, they seem to prioritize individual acts of engagement over broader objectives.[9] This organic approach to regional cooperation can also be seen in ASEAN's most recent Outlook on the Indo-Pacific.[10] Importantly, the conditions or even considerations that may frame how countervailing "hedging" investments might operate are at best unclear. ASEAN responses to increased assertiveness or isolation by either the U.S. or the PRC, or both major powers, appear to be neither well-thought-out nor extensively discussed among its member states, if at all.

Rather than hedging, ASEAN appears ambivalent on key collective issues that affect the entire group. On the SCS, some member states differ on how strongly they wish to stake their claims and interests. Some mainland Southeast Asian states seem ready to back off, while their maritime counterparts generally prefer a somewhat stronger stance; however, all are reluctant to upset Beijing.[11] Likewise, ASEAN members move back and forth over how active they wish the U.S. to be in the region and how much they are willing to accept PRC dominance. Some ASEAN members act as if they could strike some lasting deal with Beijing and Washington, while others appear to think they can significantly influence the roles of the U.S. and China in the region.[12]

A similarly mixed approach seems to apply to more formal pathways to cooperation. Several supposedly key ASEAN-related mechanisms, such as the ASEAN Regional Forum and ASEAN High Council, seem to be in suspended animation, even in the face of crises such as the Rohingya genocide, the 2021 Myanmar coup, and the COVID-19 pandemic.[13] In trade, some ASEAN members appear willing to join exclusive extra-regional groupings, such as the Comprehensive and Progressive Trans-Pacific Partnership (CPTPP) and the Indo-Pacific Economic Framework for Prosperity (IPEF), while others seem to prefer more limited bilateral free trade agreements (FTA). In addition, they all seem to favor comprehensive, region-wide arrangements such as the ASEAN–China Free Trade Area (ACFTA) and the Regional Comprehensive Economic Partnership (RCEP).[14] ASEAN states can appear to want everything, even if this comes at the expense of a more coherent regional voice or greater effectiveness at collective bargaining.

A closer look at individual members' actions on key issues further points to multiple policy directions that do not apparently settle on any common position on PRC ties. Indonesia seems to be seeking to shape regional dynamics, advancing its position as a "maritime fulcrum," and promoting the ASEAN Outlook on the Indo-Pacific, while occasionally challenging PRC claims as it maintains some distance from the U.S.[15] The Philippines and Malaysia aim to maintain their SCS claims but vacillate on how much resolve they demonstrate often across different administrations as well as within government terms.[16] Singapore continues to prioritize its longstanding approach of emphasizing U.S. relations for security purposes while simultaneously investing in the PRC for economic gains, whereas Thailand and Brunei seem to largely look toward Beijing for economic collaboration.[17] Vietnam appears to be attempting to expand its strategic options while maintaining an economic relationship with China, unlike Cambodia and Laos, which are leaning toward Beijing.[18] Myanmar's ties with the PRC have fluctuated over time, but its foreign policy has been in disarray since the February 2021 coup and subsequent civil war; however, the military junta seeks Beijing's support—with at best varying levels of success.[19]

Where ASEAN falls in terms of the "interest–threat nexus" developed by Liu and He is consequently more difficult to ascertain (see Chapter 1). Individual member states have distinct interests, and only some of these converge concurrently with each other and the PRC. ASEAN members may have interests that either converge with those of other members but not with the PRC, or with the PRC but not with fellow member states. Likewise, different ASEAN states differ in how they identify their relations with the PRC. Some are obviously more enthusiastic about Beijing, while others appear more distant or see the PRC as a threat due to unresolved disputes or historical frictions, even if they are open to cooperation at present. Conceptions of interest, identity, and threat, of course, also often change over time and can take on different levels of salience depending on the issue at hand or contingent factors such as leadership changes or exogenous shocks. A cooperative moment may be upset with, say, the sudden discovery of vessels in disputed waters triggering a protest or nationalist sentiment.[20]

Given the discrepancies between the claimed ASEAN position toward the PRC and the behavior of both the grouping as well as individual members, this chapter examines the drivers behind ASEAN actions and explores their implications. I focus more on what ASEAN member states are doing than on more familiar perspectives that privilege ASEAN statements and their supposed meanings. To the extent that I uncover the mechanisms and motivations behind the actions of ASEAN members as they attempt to coordinate and cooperate, I can shed light on where ASEAN tends to fall short in fulfilling its stated intentions and where it does not. Such an approach highlights the contours of the ASEAN–PRC relationship and draws attention to the tensions between speech acts and other forms of behavior, as well as their consequences. This can also help inform more realistic expectations about ASEAN, whether in terms of its ties with Beijing or other issues.

11.2. Getting to Coordination

Behind ASEAN's seemingly confounding positions, there appear to be several overlapping coordination problems. As Kai He pointed out, loose, convention-based organizations, like ASEAN, can address non-traditional security issues by reducing uncertainty and providing focal points for cooperation but are less effective when faced with uneven distributions of costs and gains.[21] Since the topics framing ASEAN–PRC ties are more constrained than those affecting the full range of issues in ASEAN, I propose an extension and modification of He's model for ASEAN cooperation that focuses on "stag hunt" and "battle of the sexes" coordination games, as seen in Figure 11.1. The fact that there are 10 ASEAN members makes these issues more complex than standard two-actor models; however, the underlying logic remains the same. Moreover, ASEAN members tend to be more sensitive to absolute gains rather than relative ones *vis-à-vis* each other when it comes to interactions with the PRC since one actor having better bilateral ties with Beijing does not affect another's relations.

Stag hunt dynamics tend to apply to intra-ASEAN coordination over traditional security domains in the setting of ASEAN–PRC relations.[22] On issues such as managing—not resolving—territorial disputes with Beijing, for example, ASEAN states have low conflicts of interest since their main disputes tend to be with the PRC rather than among themselves. Resolving

(a) Stag hunt game under high uncertainty and low conflict of interest

		Hunter 1	
		Stag	Rabbit
Hunter 2	Stag	10, 10	0, 8
	Rabbit	8, 0	7, 7

(b) Battle of the sexes game under low uncertainty and low conflict of interest

		Spouse 1	
		Boxing	Opera
Spouse 2	Boxing	1, 2	0, 0
	Opera	0, 0	2, 1

(c) Chicken game under low uncertainty and high conflict of interest

		Driver 1	
		Stay	Swerve
Driver 2	Stay	1, 2	0, 0
	Swerve	0, 0	2, 1

Figure 11.1.   (a-c) Three coordination games.

Note: Pure Nash equilibria underlined.
Source: gamethoery.net and adapted from Kai He, "A Strategic Functional Theory of Institutions and Rethinking Asian Regionalism: When Do Institutions Matter?" *Asian Survey*, Vol. 54, No. 6 (2014), pp. 1184–1208.

disputes increasingly adopts a "chicken game" dynamic, in which greater pressure to demonstrate resolve raises the risk of catastrophic confrontation.[23] However, there is high uncertainty over whether other ASEAN members will take a common position given the unequal distribution of

300   *J. I. Chong*

gains and costs. Knowing whether other actors will maintain a common position is difficult, and there is a similar chance that other actors might not cooperate. Such conditions make self-interested ASEAN members just as susceptible to chasing after the proverbial hare as to working together to hunt the proverbial stag.

Complicating matters is the possibility of side payments from Beijing. That the PRC can entice mainland Southeast Asian states to forego common positions on the SCS just as they prompt maritime Southeast Asian states to give in on issues facing the management of the Mekong increases uncertainty. All ASEAN members could gain from a common position; however, mainland states gain less on SCS issues, while maritime states gain less on riparian ones.[24] Cognizance of this reality fosters greater mutual suspicion within ASEAN, making coordination on traditional security issues more difficult. These dynamics repeating across 10 actors make the situation more trying.

The battle of the sexes dynamics tend to apply more to the other key area of ASEAN–PRC interactions, namely economics. Here, there is low uncertainty, low conflicts of interest, and fewer acute differences in the distribution of gains and costs.[25] All actors understand that they are overall better off with cooperation over trade or investment deals. The more inclusive the agreement, the more they stand to gain, even if unevenly. Under such circumstances, ASEAN states may disagree on the specific arrangements to be made with the PRC since each government wishes to maximize its own gains. However, each ASEAN member state also recognizes that it stands to be better off by cooperating with each other, even compromising, and reaching a deal with Beijing rather than being left out or blocking an agreement. Such considerations likely form the basis for the conclusions of ACFTA and RCEP, which are built on other bilateral and multilateral deals.

The existence of a focal point can help ameliorate some of the obstacles to intra-ASEAN coordination when managing relations with Beijing, especially where multiple equilibria exist. Should ASEAN members have some shared pre-existing beliefs or views on an issue or process, it can further reduce transaction costs and help ASEAN develop and maintain a coherent position. Perhaps the best example of this involves trade, given the general view across ASEAN member states that trade liberalization and integration remains positive for all.[26] In this respect, ASEAN members seem willing to lean toward reducing and even removing tariffs when negotiating with the PRC, often differing only on pace and scope but not

Herding Cats: Coordination Challenges in ASEAN's Approach to China 301

on fundamental principles. Focal points do not eliminate the distinction between more challenging stag hunt situations and relatively more straightforward battle of the sexes circumstances, but they do make coordination easier in both instances.

Most international organizations face questions of coordination; however, ASEAN's decision-making procedures and institutional characteristics amplify these effects. The restricted capacity of ASEAN's underfunded and understaffed secretariat, along with a lack of monitoring and enforcement mechanisms, places substantial limits on its ability to reduce uncertainty.[27] The premium on consensus decision-making means that each ASEAN member holds veto power over any issue, including those regarding PRC relations. This creates incentives to frame intra-ASEAN agreements based on the lowest common denominator.[28] Insisting solely on "centrality," being in the "driver's seat," or referring to an "epicentrum"—sometimes regardless of substantive content—can result in directions that lack clarity on how to navigate an issue.[29] These characteristics reduce ASEAN's capacity to decrease transaction costs in ways that could help member states overcome coordination problems more easily.

The nature of ASEAN's membership presents further restrictions on the group's capacity to reduce transaction costs and ease coordination challenges. ASEAN comprises members with a variety of income levels and regime types, in addition to distinctions between maritime and mainland states. It includes low-income countries such as Cambodia, Laos, and Myanmar, of which Laos remains a Stalinist regime, while Cambodia is an electoral authoritarian state and Myanmar is mired in anarchy following the February 2021 coup.[30] Indonesia and Malaysia are democratizing, while the Philippines and Thailand are competitive authoritarian states; however, Vietnam remains a Stalinist state, although all are middle-income countries.[31] The high-income member Brunei is an absolute monarchy, while Singapore is another electoral authoritarian regime.[32] Mainland states tend to care less about issues such as the law of the sea, even as maritime states pay less attention to issues such as sharing riparian resources.

Given the multidimensional diversity among ASEAN members and the group's own institutional constraints, the group has perhaps less ability to deal with coordination problems than other regional organizations. The ASEAN expansion in the 1990s exacerbated these conditions by increasing the number of veto players and the range of divergent preferences they represent without directly addressing these issues.[33] Contemporaneous democratization among older ASEAN members, along with the Asian Financial Crisis and the end of the Cold War, led to the collapse of the old conservative, anti-communist, developmentalist paradigm that had previously served as a focal point.[34] Faced with an actor like the PRC, which is willing to exploit differences among members when expedient, intra-ASEAN differences can become serious impediments to the development of an effective ASEAN response to Beijing's more assertive actions.[35] Such challenges are likely to expand given the new pressures that result from intensifying U.S.–China competition.

Efforts by Beijing to employ wedge strategies, as detailed in an earlier contribution to this volume, exacerbate coordination problems among ASEAN members. ASEAN's norms of mutual respect, consensus decision-making, and a desire to seek cooperation with all sides tend to work best when unchallenged. Heightened rivalries between the PRC and key regional players such as the U.S., Japan, India, and Australia, discussed in the introduction by Liu and He, reduce ASEAN's ability to bridge differences and pull member states in different directions, depending on their existing interests (see Chapter 1). Greater competitiveness incentivizes Beijing to drive a wedge between ASEAN and its competitors, as argued by Ruonan Liu in the previous chapter, and within ASEAN in an attempt to prevent the group from becoming an impediment to its goals (see Chapter 10). Such dynamics exacerbate existing divisions within ASEAN and further degrade its ability to coordinate, as seen in periodic mutual recriminations among its members in recent years and its stasis over the Myanmar civil war.[36] Despite verbal support for ASEAN's "Five Point Consensus" for handling the Myanmar crisis, for instance, Beijing along with Moscow allegedly supply arms to the junta, according to the United Nations Special Rapporteur for Myanmar.[37]

I turn to three cases of ASEAN–China interactions to highlight how the dynamics identified above operate, especially how the presence or absence of clear focal points affects intra-ASEAN coordination. The first is ASEAN–PRC efforts to manage disputes over the SCS that directly involve Beijing, Hanoi, Manila, Putrajaya, and Bandar Seri Begawan but also indirectly Jakarta and Singapore. The second examines the trade liberalization that took the form of ACFTA and RCEP. A third, more historical, case focuses on ASEAN–PRC cooperation in response to the 1979–1989 Vietnamese invasion and occupation of Cambodia. The first two cases provide examples of the stag hunt and battle of the sexes dynamics depicted earlier, respectively, while the third is an instance where a clear focal point existed alongside a stag hunt situation with fewer players.

11.3. Struggles over the South China Sea

Several ASEAN member states have longstanding disputes with the PRC over substantial portions of the SCS. Even though other ASEAN states are not party to these disputes, these areas are strategically important for maritime trade, air routes, submarine cables, and fishing.[38] ASEAN sought, with limited success, to manage, but not resolve, the disputes with Beijing by attempting to freeze developments, reduce tensions, avoid confrontation, and encourage dialogue until the disputants could directly address their differences.[39] More prominent ASEAN initiatives for handling differences with the PRC in this regard include the 2002 Declaration on the Conduct of Parties (DOC), related statements about implementation efforts, and ongoing negotiations over a Code of Conduct (COC).[40] Limitations to ASEAN's efforts arise from difficulties in overcoming uncertainties and member states' disparate concerns when trying to coordinate around a coherent response to the PRC.

The PRC asserts ownership over a significant portion of the SCS based on claims that it was inherited from the Republic of China, which provides the basis for the "nine-dash line" delineating the Chinese position on PRC maps.[41] Despite not publicly defining the nature of these cartographic markings, Beijing's claims have created separate disputes with Brunei, the Philippines, Malaysia, and Vietnam. These disputes resulted in several instances of the use of force, most notably by the PRC against South Vietnam in 1974 and against Vietnam in 1988.[42] Contestation over the SCS intensified around 2008, after a period of dormancy, culminating in the PRC occupying, reclaiming, and arming several maritime features as the Philippines sought international arbitration to challenge the legal basis for Beijing's claims.[43] Separate but competing Vietnam–Malaysia, Vietnam–Brunei, Vietnam–Philippines, Vietnam–Brunei–Malaysia, and Vietnam–Malaysia–Philippines claims overlap the disputes with the PRC.[44] The nine-dash line also crosses Indonesia's Exclusive Economic Zone (EEZ), extending north from the Natuna Islands.[45]

If ASEAN is indeed interested in establishing a means of managing tensions in the SCS until disputes can be resolved, then member states should hold a common position to bargain collectively with Beijing. This entails laying out a common position that member states consistently hold when engaging the PRC, whether it means adhering to the United Nations Convention on the Law of the Sea (UNCLOS) or some other mutually recognized focal point. There should be a shared effort to monitor and address challenges and support for that position, similar to any collective bargaining situation, asymmetry in individual capabilities relative to the PRC notwithstanding. Member states should also maintain a willingness to impose costs when there are challenges to their common position, even if such sanctions are largely symbolic and meant to apply diplomatic pressure. ASEAN members should likewise maintain the ability and readiness to reward support for the ASEAN position collectively. Such conditions help establish incentives that could encourage Beijing to negotiate and maybe even compromise on some issues, but they are currently absent.

ASEAN's approach to the PRC on the SCS maritime disputes began in the 2000s, featuring a degree of coordination. In 2002, the group and its members came up with the DOC, which they jointly agreed to with the PRC. The DOC outlined the principles of seeking dialogue and cooperation while avoiding actions that could escalate tensions or complicate disputes until a mutually acceptable resolution could be found.[46] The intention of the document was to build trust and confidence among ASEAN member states, as well as within ASEAN. The DOC explicitly lists the UN Charter, UNCLOS, the Treaty of Amity of Cooperation (TAC) in Southeast Asia, the Five Principles of Peaceful Coexistence, and other international law principles as specific frameworks of reference.[47] The TAC, one of ASEAN's foundational documents, and the Five Principles of Peaceful Coexistence, which underpin the Non-Aligned Movement, emphasize respect for territorial integrity, non-interference in domestic affairs, and non-aggression.[48] That Beijing was willing to go along with ASEAN preferences in the 1990s and 2000s to secure legitimacy among its neighbors and a stable external environment for development created an impression of successful coordination that restrained the PRC.[49]

As PRC assertiveness grew alongside its capabilities and economic heft, ASEAN found it increasingly difficult to respond effectively as a whole to Beijing's efforts to pursue its SCS claims. By the end of the 2000s, the PRC stepped up attempts to shore up its position in SCS through increased deployment of paramilitary vessels and harassment and detentions of foreign vessels for intruding into waters it claimed.[50] Some solidarity marked ASEAN's initial response, notably during the 2010 ASEAN Regional Forum meeting in Hanoi, where ASEAN members warned against potentially escalatory behavior.[51] This drew not only admonishment from Beijing at the time but also apparent PRC efforts to either encourage silence or prevent consensus within ASEAN by incentivizing specific members.[52] PRC support was allegedly involved in Cambodian vetoes of language in ASEAN joint statements in 2012 and 2015, as well as in the watering down of another statement in 2015.[53] ASEAN norms and traditions for consensus-building, which allowed for some early coordination, were unable to withstand pressure and side payments from an increasingly powerful and assertive PRC.

PRC pressure and the fear of its consequences prevented ASEAN members from supporting each other and opposing Beijing's initiatives, despite their reservations. In 2008, three ASEAN members submitted representations regarding limits to the continental shelf; however, none supported or joined the Philippines' efforts to clarify the nature of maritime features—on which the claims rested—through independent third-party arbitration.[54] Singapore and Indonesia expressed a desire for consistency with international law, especially UNCLOS, but met with pressure that culminated in the seizure of Singapore's armored vehicles in Hong Kong and, in the case of Jakarta, constant challenges to its EEZ by Beijing.[55] Subsequent ASEAN statements expressing hope for the implementation of the DOC were only possible in 2012, 2016, and 2017, years after the issuance of the original document.[56] There was no overt ASEAN opposition to Beijing's efforts to accelerate the COC drafting talks with language subjecting military activities by non-littoral states in the SCS to agreement by all signatories, despite reservations within the grouping.[57] None of the ASEAN members wished to grant a veto to each other or any other actor, as this would limit their own autonomy.

In the interim, Beijing continued to strengthen its ability to establish control over the waters it claimed in the SCS, eliciting only limited and sporadic responses from ASEAN. Backed by its burgeoning navy, coast guard, and maritime militia, the PRC persisted in the occupation, reclamation, and arming of features in the SCS.[58] Such efforts far outpaced the scale and rate at which other disputants with some capacity, such as Malaysia and Vietnam, were undertaking anything similar.[59] PRC actions persisted despite the concurrent international arbitration process initiated by the Philippines and the ruling by the Arbitral Tribunal in the Hague that the features disputed by Manila and Beijing were not islands under international law.[60] According to the tribunal, the features were legally incapable of the extensive maritime claims made by Beijing; however, Beijing stated that the process was inappropriate and illegitimate and refused to participate.[61]

306   J. I. Chong

Reactions from ASEAN toward PRC behavior were muted throughout the period. The members' responses largely consisted of Hanoi sending vessels to assert its claims and making diplomatic protests over what it deemed excessive PRC behavior.[62] Putrajaya occasionally initiated diplomatic protests, primarily due to domestic pressures to act, while Manila vacillated between accommodation and demonstrating pushback.[63] ASEAN reactions, apart from Indonesian and Singaporean reminders to abide by established precedent and international law, consisted largely of watered-down statements about the importance of regional peace and stability.[64] The group and its member states indicated neither support for nor solidarity with fellow members under pressure from the PRC and were publicly silent on efforts by the U.S. and others to challenge Beijing's claims via Freedom of Navigation Operations (FONOPs).[65]

Behind ASEAN's difficulties in presenting a common front lies the coordination problem stylized by stag hunt dynamics. ASEAN members faced significant uncertainty over whether others would maintain their common stand relating to the SCS disputes, which was necessary for more effective collective bargaining with Beijing. Even if there were some shared will to resist, ASEAN members had to avoid making separate, individual compromises with Beijing for collective bargaining to be effective in managing SCS disputes. Mainland Southeast Asian members had fewer prospects for immediate gains, while those not directly party to the disputes but dependent on maritime access stood to benefit somewhat but not as much as disputant states. Yet, it was also clear to all ASEAN members and other observers that all bore some risk of punishment from Beijing or at least the loss of economic opportunities from opposing PRC claims, with this risk increasing for those acting alone.

Beijing's diplomacy toward ASEAN further complicated existing coordination challenges. Aid, loans, trade, investment, training, and other development opportunities provided to Cambodia, Laos, Myanmar, and Thailand offered incentives for silence, inaction, or even departure from common ASEAN positions. Such attraction proved particularly strong for ASEAN's two poorest and least developed states, Cambodia and Laos, the effects of which supposedly led Phnom Penh to veto joint ASEAN statements on the SCS issues at least twice between 2012 and 2016.[66] Even middle-income Malaysia seemed eager for PRC trade and investments in exchange for silence on its SCS claims and lukewarm support for any shared ASEAN position on the SCS.[67] Singapore's insistence on established international law and precedent drew Beijing's ire, leading to public criticism, supposed non-invitations to the prime minister for key meetings, and the seizure of its armored vehicles transiting Hong Kong.[68] Jakarta's emphasis on UNCLOS, the undisputed nature of its EEZ extending from the Natuna Islands, along with its willingness to impound and sink vessels fishing in the waters it claimed, brought constant challenges from PRC fishing, maritime militia, and coast guard vessels.[69]

The apparent lesson for ASEAN members was that unless a state enjoyed Indonesia's position as Southeast Asia's most populous state and largest economy, Beijing could hold economic interests at stake and impose diplomatic costs that could publicly embarrass a government. These conditions amplified intra-ASEAN uncertainty over coordination on SCS issues, increasing the temptation for individual members to go after their rabbits rather than commit to chasing the stag of a common, collective position. Conditions discouraged individual ASEAN members from acting or convincing states to defy Beijing's preferences on the SCS. The situation concurrently encouraged ASEAN members to second guess whether others would take a stand for collective concerns over managing the SCS disputes in sufficient numbers or pursue their individual interests *vis-à-vis* Beijing. It is, therefore, not surprising that inaction seems to increasingly characterize ASEAN efforts on the SCS, despite the PRC proposing initiatives that many members feel apprehensive about.

11.4. Dealing on Trade

ASEAN seems more ready and able to find common ground over trade cooperation with the PRC, particularly in trade liberalization. Free trade issues enjoy much lower conflicts of interest and higher degrees of certainty within ASEAN. Member states largely agree that they all stand to benefit from freer trade with more partners; hence, they do not view various bilateral and multilateral trade arrangements as mutually exclusive or competitive.[70] ASEAN members are happy to have multiple trade deals with both the same and different partners, with fewer concerns that another member entering an arrangement with the PRC, or any other actor would deprive them of opportunities. Where they need to coordinate is over agreement details—much like in a battle of the sexes game, while outcomes may carry distributional differences, the main concern for actors is to engage in the same activity together.

Proposed by the PRC in 2000, the ASEAN–China Free Trade Area agreement was signed two years later in 2002, with a two-stage implementation process beginning in 2010.[71] Stage one involved older, middle- to high-income ASEAN members—Brunei, Indonesia, Malaysia, the Philippines, Singapore, and Thailand—and the PRC reducing most tariffs in 2010.[72] The remaining newer ASEAN members—Cambodia, Laos, Myanmar, and Vietnam—would follow suit in 2015 during the second, upgraded stage of the arrangement.[73] The agreement saw significant growth in trade between ASEAN and the PRC, with the latter becoming the former's largest single external trading partner in terms of merchandise.[74]

The 2011 ASEAN Summit initiated the RCEP to further liberalize trade in Asia and the Pacific, with negotiations beginning the following year. In 2020, all 10 ASEAN members, along with Australia, China, Japan, New Zealand, and South Korea, concluded an agreement to remove 90 percent of tariffs among the members within 20 years while establishing new rules for trade, electronic commerce, and intellectual property.[75] The RCEP came into effect in 2022 after being ratified by all but Indonesia, Malaysia, Myanmar, and the Philippines.[76] Although the process leading up to its conclusion lasted more than a decade and subsequent ratification did not include all signatories, there was relatively little disquiet among ASEAN members over RCEP. ASEAN members were eager to claim that ASEAN was driving the process, despite observers' claims that Beijing was the real motivating force behind the arrangement, with the intention of shutting out the U.S.[77]

These major trade deals with the PRC overlap with a host of separate bilateral and multilateral trade arrangements ASEAN members concluded among themselves and with the PRC and other partners. Other ASEAN-based multilateral arrangements include the ASEAN Free Trade Area (AFTA), ASEAN Economic Community (AEC), as well as separate free trade agreements between ASEAN and Australia, New Zealand, India, Japan, South Korea, and Hong Kong.[78] Talks are ongoing for an ASEAN free trade arrangement with the European Union, as well as one with the United Kingdom.[79] Bilateral arrangements, such as the Cambodia–China FTA and the Singapore–China FTA, are part of a long list of others.[80] There is also the CPTPP, which includes ASEAN members Brunei, Malaysia, Singapore, and Vietnam.[81] Observers initially touted the Trans-Pacific Partnership (TPP), a precursor to CPTPP, as a U.S. tool for the economic exclusion of the PRC, until Washington unilaterally withdrew participation in 2017 under the Trump administration.[82] The most recent among commercial arrangements that involve a subset of ASEAN members is the IPEF, which includes Brunei, Indonesia, Malaysia, the Philippines, Thailand, and Singapore in a non-binding set of agreements with Australia, Fiji, India, Japan, New Zealand, South Korea, and the U.S.[83]

That ASEAN was able to engage in trade deals with the PRC and other actors with relative ease suggests a strong, shared preference for trade liberalization, despite uncertainties and differences concerning specific arrangements. Whatever time it took to conclude, ratify, and implement ACFTA and RCEP was a function of reaching consensus on specific issues rather than any in-principle reservation or opposition to an agreement.[84] Compromise could be reached on these details, provided that a meaningful agreement on trade liberalization resulted, since this was where intra-ASEAN interests converged. Members making separate and parallel arrangements with Beijing and other sets of actors did not upset efforts at reaching an agreement, since the view was that these relative gains did not significantly disadvantage others. There was little concern among members that other members would derail or significantly undermine trade agreements with the PRC, along with a belief that any concessions would be reasonable, thus creating confidence in committing.

ASEAN–China trade ties carry the qualities of a pure coordination game such as the battle of the sexes, making them far less fraught and prone to vetoes by individual members, even though, with at least 11 parties involved, there exists a much more complicated set of circumstances than a stylized two-actor stag hunt situation. Part of this was due to the presence of a pro-trade focal point prioritizing trade liberalization that did not face significant political opposition from any ASEAN member or within its member states.[85] Moreover, a separate economic bilateral deal with a specific ASEAN member would not detract from a multilateral arrangement. ASEAN members coalesced around the belief that a deal is preferable to no deal, and any associated costs are acceptable, both collectively and individually.[86] Consequently, there was an ability and willingness to give and take both among ASEAN capitals as well as with Beijing, which accompanied a commitment to adhere to and comply with any negotiated solution that emerged.

11.5. Coordination and Confrontation in Indochina

Even if coordination challenges ASEAN faces over security-related issues more closely resemble stag hunt dynamics, they remain more surmountable if a clear focal point for action exists. The high point of ASEAN cooperation remains joint diplomatic opposition to Vietnam's invasion and occupation of Cambodia between 1979 and 1989, before Hanoi joined ASEAN in 1997 and Phnom Penh followed suit in 1999.[87] Opposing Vietnamese actions involved an uneven distribution of risks, costs, and gains among ASEAN members at the time, heightening the temptation for ASEAN members not directly threatened to renege and back away from commitments to cooperate. Yet, ASEAN worked with the PRC and U.S. over a decade to diplomatically isolate Vietnam and the Cambodian government it backed while supporting the opposing local forces, even if this meant working with the murderous Khmer Rouge (KR).[88] A key factor contributing to this sustained cooperative effort was the strong, shared belief among conservative, developmentalist ASEAN leaders at the time that it was necessary to counter further communist expansion in Southeast Asia.[89]

Motivations behind the Vietnamese invasion and occupation of Cambodia were multiple but they conjured fears in ASEAN of an expansionist communist Vietnam after its victory over the U.S. in the Vietnam War and subsequent communist takeovers in Laos and Cambodia. Border disputes, the instability caused by the genocidal KR that came to power in Cambodia in 1975, and friction among rival communist sponsors made the Cambodia–Vietnam relationship increasingly acrimonious in the late 1970s.[90] Moscow supported the Vietnamese Communist Party, while Beijing backed the Khmer Rouge.[91] Events culminated in Vietnam invading Cambodia in 1978 and subsequently occupying the country, forcing the KR from power, and installing the Kampuchean People's Revolutionary Party (KPRP).[92] ASEAN members at the time—initially consisting of Indonesia, Malaysia, the Philippines, Singapore, and Thailand, with Brunei joining in 1984—saw these developments as potentially allowing for analogous forceful replacement of their existing governments with communist regimes.[93]

ASEAN's actions took the form of attempts to deny legitimacy to the government in Phnom Penh and providing material support to resistance inside Cambodia in coordination with the PRC and U.S. efforts to stress Vietnam's limited capabilities. ASEAN members successfully

Herding Cats: Coordination Challenges in ASEAN's Approach to China 311

lobbied the United Nations (UN) to allow the Coalition Government of Democratic Kampuchea (CGDK), composed of those opposed to the KPRP regime, to retain Cambodia's seat against opposition from Vietnam, the Soviet Union, and their allies.[94] Using Thai territory, ASEAN member states clandestinely provided supplies, training, and even arms to CGDK forces inside Cambodia, including the KR, to help sustain their fight against KPRP and Vietnamese forces.[95] Persistent PRC military pressure on Vietnam following their 1979 border war and U.S. economic isolation of Vietnam and Cambodia stretched Hanoi's and Phnom Penh's resources, increasing their dependence on a Soviet Union that was struggling in Afghanistan and facing economic decline.[96] The overall effect of these actions was to "bleed Vietnam white," force its withdrawal from Cambodia, and put an end to ambitions for expansion or exporting revolution.[97]

Successful intra-ASEAN cooperation over Cambodia was not immediately evident at the time, even though the event is today hailed as a high watermark for the organization, given that only Thailand faced an immediate threat from the spillover of conflict in Cambodia, any export of revolution, or a Vietnamese-backed invasion. Other ASEAN members at the time could have left Bangkok to fend for itself, while they focused on issues directly relevant to themselves. There was also ample time over a decade during which distractions or a loss of interest could have led to the deterioration of intra-ASEAN coordination as members peeled away to pursue other objectives. Instead, consistent and steadfast cooperation prevailed both on the ground in Southeast Asia and in international settings, such as the UN, for as long as Vietnam did not withdraw. ASEAN members and the grouping retained significant autonomy and freedom of action on the Cambodia issue despite the power asymmetry in their partnerships with the U.S. and PRC, owing to members being able to maintain clear collective positions.

The consistency and singularity of purpose regarding the Cambodian issue rested on a coalescence of strong anti-communist views among the various ASEAN capitals. The ruling elites of all ASEAN members at the time had either recently begun or were still mobilizing against what they described as domestic communist threats.[98] Anti-communism served as a pillar of legitimacy for these regimes, making it easier to unite against the KPRK's political ideology and its backing from Vietnamese and Soviet supporters. Countering communism in Indochina was simply consistent behavior given how significant an existential threat ASEAN members

312   *J. I. Chong*

made communism out to be at the time; however, the PRC and its KR partner were less problematic compared to the recent Sino–U.S. rapprochement.[99] This provided ASEAN members with a reason to persist on their position, whether dealing with partners such as Beijing and Washington or adversaries such as Hanoi, Phnom Penh, and Moscow.

Of course, other conditions also eased intra-ASEAN coordination on Cambodia. These included the fact that the group consisted of only five, and later six, members, as opposed to ten at the time, limiting the range of interests and making coordination less complicated. ASEAN members at the time were also all at least middle-income states that enjoyed varying, but nonetheless significant, levels of economic success and growing prosperity through different adaptations of developmentalist-style economics.[100] Moreover, they shared conservative, authoritarian tendencies.[101] Such commonalities in outlook and experience further simplified coordination, thereby moderating some of the difficulties typically associated with the stag hunt dynamics in such forms of security cooperation. However, they do not alter the nature of the coordination challenges facing ASEAN in a general sense.

11.6. Alternatives and Implications

The two most competitive alternative explanations for variations in ASEAN's ability to address coordination challenges when engaging the PRC come down to claims about the ASEAN process and the differing natures of disparate issue areas. Proponents of a process-based ASEAN may highlight the fact that the value of ASEAN–PRC engagement lies in continued interaction rather than achieving specific outcomes.[102] Obstacles to reducing friction over the South China Sea are simply teething problems on the arc of greater harmony and more effective cooperation over time. Relations with Beijing will, over time, become less contentious and converge toward the smoother relations observed in trade and responses to Vietnam's invasion and occupation of Cambodia. Even if this were true, such accounts still fail to address why processes play out in markedly different ways over various issues, encountering more complications in some circumstances than others.

Another possibility is that issues exclusively frame the severity of coordination problems, but this explanation does not fully account for the role of focal points in alleviating obstructions to cooperation. Issue areas undoubtedly matter as coordination becomes more difficult when the stakes are higher and uncertainty is more severe, making security-related domains particularly demanding for ASEAN when compared to economic-related ones due to its deals with Beijing.[103] Extended ASEAN cooperation against Vietnam in the 1980s as the grouping dealt with major powers such as China suggests that having clear, common focal points can significantly enhance coordination, even in areas where uncertainty and differing costs are apparent. On issues such as trade, a shared belief in the unassailability of liberalization facilitated agreement. Without a common focal point, it makes already difficult issues such as coordination over an ASEAN position on the SCS even harder.

ASEAN's need for shared focal points to overcome coordination problems, not least when it comes to relations with the PRC, suggests mounting challenges for the group when engaging with Beijing. Divergence among member states has not only increased since ASEAN's expansion in the late 1990s, but it also shows signs of further widening. ASEAN members today differ over not only geography—whether they are mainland or maritime Southeast Asian states with their attendant priorities—they vary over everything, from income, economic structure, and regime type to affinity toward Beijing.[104] Conditions exacerbate existing coordination problems, which are further compounded by the fact that ASEAN members today, at best, share an outlook that revolves around a vague notion of ASEAN centrality and avoiding provocations of both the PRC and U.S.[105] Given the sharpening differences with an increasingly abrasive PRC that is more willing to exploit intra-ASEAN differences, coordination problems over issues tied to Beijing look set to become more intractable, particularly over already contentious security matters.

With intensifying U.S.–PRC rivalry, ASEAN's ability to coordinate on China-related issues is likely to decline further. Despite claiming not to force ASEAN and its members to choose sides, Beijing and Washington are likely to seek ways to complicate cooperation with the each other to preserve or expand their own relative advantages in Southeast Asia. Everything from the use of Beijing's specifications in its Belt and Road Initiative to PRC's insistence on its interpretation of UNCLOS helps entrench Chinese standards in Southeast Asia, encouraging a shift away from previously prevalent U.S. approaches. Washington's promulgation of the global rules-based order it helped develop and sustain concurrently entices ASEAN members away from PRC attempts to introduce new standards and specifications in areas such as economics, law, and technology. These cross-cutting pressures mean that the shearing force on ASEAN will grow as shared interpretations, much less viewpoints, become harder to come by unless ASEAN can establish a widely adopted set of standards for a range of key issues on its own.[106]

The way out of this conundrum for ASEAN lies in taking the initiative to improve its ability to collectively bargain effectively; however, this calls for the reform of ASEAN structures, a prospect that appears unlikely. ASEAN members must either develop and commit to a shared vision that can provide a new focal point or shift decision-making away from the consensus model, where every actor has a veto, all while ensuring their commitment to such initiatives.[107] At the heart of such reforms lies the reduction of coordination problems, particularly of the more serious stag hunt kind. Ideally, these updates to ASEAN should have been undertaken at the time of its expansion, when the external environment was less contentious and more forgiving of mistakes, allowing ASEAN members to experiment and discover a better way forward. Such revisions seem less and less likely in the face of increasingly apparent intra-ASEAN divisions and efforts by Beijing and Washington to push for a Southeast Asia that is amenable to their ever-more incompatible interests, possibly leaving ASEAN in disarray.

A possible contention of analyzing ASEAN through an institutionalized lens is that it ignores the group's normative focus, frames goals that it was never designed to meet, and disregards its successes.[108] The "ASEAN way" of collaboration, which emphasizes consensus-building, non-intervention, and autonomy, certainly allowed the organization to enjoy some ability to shape the tone and nature of regional cooperation.[109] Emphasizing "ASEAN centrality" even enabled a degree of restraint on major powers. These perspectives on norms and cooperation formed the established, default view of ASEAN for some time.

Norms certainly provide a means of overcoming coordination and even collective action problems, not least by creating focal points, incentives, and even expectations for behavior. ASEAN's difficulties in recreating its past success in recent years arise from the fact that its norms were based on the assumption that all major powers, partners, and member states shared an overriding interest in furthering integration in a globalizing world. As major power contestation becomes more acute, such conditions can no longer be taken for granted, as highlighted in the earlier contributions to this feature by Liu and He and Ruonan Liu.[110] The older, normative understanding of ASEAN may have run its course.

11.7. Conclusions

ASEAN appears not fully prepared to handle more complicated engagement with the PRC in a world where it must navigate more carefully between Beijing and Washington. Claims of not wishing to choose sides or hedging appear increasingly like excuses for failing to overcome the coordination challenges necessary for the group's members to work together more effectively.[111] A likely result is an impaired ability to engage in collective bargaining and exercise agency in the face of greater PRC pressure and heightened U.S. demands over relations with Beijing. Adjusting ASEAN to these more complicated circumstances currently presents difficulties, given the fact that there is little impetus for institutional reforms—which are, at any rate, tricky under the best of conditions. Not updating ASEAN over the past two decades of relative stability after the Cold War may mean that the organization is less capable of supporting its members at a time when an effective regional body is most needed in Southeast Asia.

Increasing linkage between economic and security issues could very possibly translate to sharpened uncertainty as well as rising unevenness in the distribution of gains and costs in ASEAN's relations with the PRC, which already contain stark power asymmetries. Stag hunt dynamics and risks may become increasingly prevalent among ASEAN members as they strive to cobble together common positions for engaging with Beijing. Exacerbating these forces include Beijing's efforts to distance ASEAN members over issues where disagreement exists and potential U.S. attempts to appeal to specific ASEAN members to slow down arrangements that could disadvantage Washington relative to Beijing.[112] An absence of clear focal points around which ASEAN members can coalesce adds to the coordination difficulties they face while managing relations with the PRC, especially amid intense U.S.–PRC competition in Southeast Asia.

A less functional and less capable ASEAN may pave the way for less controlled and riskier forms of major power contestation in Southeast Asia. ASEAN helped reduce the acuteness of major power competition for its members during the Cold War by reducing the need to contest for its loyalties and by positioning itself as a partner whose value exceeded the sum of its members. These qualities were evident not only in ASEAN's efforts over Cambodia but also in its earlier attempts to establish a nuclear-free zone and a "Zone of Peace, Freedom, and Neutrality," where members together distanced themselves from the brunt of Cold War rivalries.[113] Today's less cohesive ASEAN faces greater challenges in engaging Beijing—and Washington—on its own terms, which translates into less capacity to buffer and mitigate the playing out of "intense competition" between these two major powers in Southeast Asia.[114] With the PRC and U.S. intensifying their positions in Southeast Asia with less moderation by states in the region, the region may well see greater disarray and even potential for instability.

Endnotes

1. ASEAN, "ASEAN Leaders' Statement on the Application of Timor-Leste for ASEAN Membership," ASEAN Secretariat. https://asean.org/wp-content/uploads/2022/11/05-ASEAN-Leaders-Statement-on-the-Application-of-Timor-Leste-for-ASEAN-Membership.pdf.

2. A. Acharya, "Ideas, identity, and institution-building: From the 'ASEAN way' to the 'Asia-Pacific way?'" *Pacific Review*, 10(3), 319–346 (1997).

3. See Seng Tan, "Consigned to hedge: South-East Asia and America's 'free and open Indo-Pacific' strategy," *International Affairs*, 96(1), 131–148 (2020); H. J. Kraft, "Great power dynamics and the waning of ASEAN centrality in regional security," *Asian Politics and Policy*, 9(4), 597–612 (2017).

4. Kraft (2017), *Op. cit.*; Cheng-Chwee Kuik, "How do weaker states hedge? Unpacking ASEAN States' alignment behavior toward China," *Journal of Contemporary China*, 25(100), 500–514 (2016).

5. J. D. Ciociari and J. Haacke, "Hedging in international relations: An introduction," *International Relations of the Asia Pacific*, 19(3), 367–374 (2019).

6. V. Jackson, "Power, trust, and network complexity: Three logics of hedging in Asian security," *International Relations of the Asia Pacific*, 14(3), 331–356 (2014).

7. K. Stiles, *Trust and Hedging in International Relations* (Ann Arbor: University of Michigan Press, 2018).

8. Tan (2020), *Op. cit.*; Kraft (2017), *Op. cit.*

9. Vannarith Chheang, "Minilateralism in Southeast Asia: Facts, opportunities, and risks," in Bhubindar Singh and Sarah Teo (eds.) *Minilateralism in the Indo-Pacific: The Quadrilateral Security Dialogue, Lancang-Mekong Cooperation Mechanism, and ASEAN* (Abingdon, Oxon: Routledge, 2020), pp. 103–119.

10. ASEAN, "ASEAN Outlook on the Indo-Pacific," ASEAN.org (2021). https://asean.org/asean2020/wp-content/uploads/2021/01/ASEAN-Outlook-on-the-Indo-Pacific_FINAL_22062019.pdf.

11 D. C. O'Neill, *Dividing ASEAN and Conquering the South China Sea: China's Financial Power Projection* (Hong Kong: Hong Kong University Press, 2018); E. Pang, ""Same-Same but different": Laos and Cambodia's political embrace of China," *ISEAS Perspective*, 5 September 2017. https://www.iseas.edu.sg/images/pdf/ISEAS_Perspective_2017_66.pdf.

12 O'Neill (2018), *Op. cit.*; D. Shambaugh, *Where Great Powers Meet: America and China in Southeast Asia* (Oxford: Oxford University Press, 2021), pp. 179–237, 241–251.

13 R. Barber and S. Teitt, "The Rohingya crisis: Can ASEAN salvage its credibility?" *Survival*, 62(5), 41–54 (2020); C. Dunst, "The Myanmar Coup as an ASEAN inflection point," *Journal of Indo-Pacific Affairs*, 4(6), 37–45 (2021); J. Rüland, "Covid-19 and ASEAN: Strengthening state-centrism, eroding effectiveness, testing cohesion," *International Spectator*, 6(2), 72–92 (2021).

14 Kazushi Shimizu, "The ASEAN economic community and the RCEP in the world community," *Journal of Contemporary East Asian Studies*, 10(1), 1–23 (2021); Chien-Huei Wu, "ASEAN at the crossroads: Trap and track between CPTPP and RCEP," *Journal of International Economic Law*, 23(1), 97–117 (2020); The White House, "Fact sheet: In Asia, President Biden and a Dozen Indo-Pacific partners launch the Indo-Pacific economic framework for prosperity," Briefing Room. https://www.whitehouse.gov/briefing-room/statements-releases/2022/05/23/fact-sheet-in-asia-president-biden-and-a-dozen-indo-pacific-partners-launch-the-indo-pacific-economic-framework-for-prosperity/.

15 D. F. Anwar, "Indonesia and the ASEAN outlook on the Indo-Pacific," *International Affairs*, 96(1), 111–129 (2020); N. Sriyanto, "Global maritime fulcrum, Indonesia-China growing relations, and Indonesia's middlepowership in the East Asia region," *Jurnal Kalian Wilayah*, 9(1), 1–19 (2019).

16 C. J. Lai, "Rhetorical traps and China's peaceful rise: Malaysia and the Philippines in the South China Sea territorial disputes," *International Relations of the Asia-Pacific*, 19(1), 117–146 (2019); M. B. F. Manantan, "Pivot toward China: A critical analysis of the Philippines' policy shift on the South China Sea disputes," *Asian Politics and Policy*, 11(4), 643–662 (2019); Chow-Bing Ngeow, "Malaysia's China policy and the South China Sea dispute under the Najib administration (2009–2018): A domestic policy process approach," *Asian Politics and Policy*, 11(4), 586–605 (2019).

17 K. Hewison, "Thailand: An old relationship renewed," *Pacific Review*, 31(1), 116–130 (2018); B. A. Putra, "Comprehending Brunei Darussalam's Vanishing claims in the South China Sea: China's exertion of economic power and the influence of elite perception," *Cogent Social Sciences*, 7(1), 1–13 (2021); Kornphanat Tungkeunkunt and Kanya Phuphakdi, "Blood is thicker than water: A history of the diplomatic discourse 'China and Thailand are brothers,'" *Asian Perspective*, 42(4), 597–621 (2018).

18 Shihlun Allen Chen, "The development of Cambodia-China relation and its transition under the OBOR initiative," *Chinese Economy*, 51(4), 370–382 (2019); Law Kam Yee and Adrian Chiu Chi Yeung, "How weak neighbors manage their relationship with China: The case of Laos," *China: An International Journal*, 18(3), 133–152 (2020); Hong Kong Nguyen, Quan Hoang Vuong, Tung Ho and Thu-Trang Vuong, "The 'same bed different dreams' of Vietnam and China: How (mis)trust could make or break it," *European Journal of East Asian Studies*, 18(1), 93–128 (2019).

19 Dunst (2021), *Op. cit.*; Nian Peng, "Budding Indo-Myanmar relations: Rising but limited challenges for China," *Asian Affairs*, 50(4), 588–601 (2019); Ministry of Foreign Affairs, People's Republic of China, "Wang Yi holds talks with Myanmar's foreign minister." https://www.fmprc.gov.cn/eng/zxxx_662805/202207/t20220704_10714853.html; Su Mon Thazin Aung and Nan Lwin, "What do the official Chinese media's mixed messages on the Myanmar Coup mean?" *ISEAS Perspective*, 74 (2022). https://www.iseas.edu.sg/wp-content/uploads/2022/06/ISEAS_Perspective_2022_74.pdf.

20 J. Sipalan, "As Beijing flexes muscles in South China Sea, Malaysia eyes harder response," *Reuters* (2016). https://www.reuters.com/article/us-southchinasea-malaysia-idUSKCN0YM2SV; "Philippines protests China's 'illegal' South China Sea presence," *Reuters* (2021). https://www.reuters.com/world/asia-pacific/philippines-protests-chinas-illegal-south-china-sea-presence-2021-05-29/.

21 Kai He, "A strategic functional theory of institutions and rethinking Asian regionalism," *Asian Survey*, 56(4), 1184–1208 (2014).

22 *Ibid.*, pp. 1196–1198.

23 *Ibid.*, pp. 1198–1201.

24 O'Neill (2018), *Op. cit.*

25 He (2014), *Op. cit.*

26 ASEAN, "About AEC," Invest in ASEAN. http://investasean.asean.org/index.php/page/view/asean-economic-community/view/670/newsid/755/about-aec.html; ASEAN, "ASEAN agreements: Outcomes and benefits, Invest in ASEAN." http://investasean.asean.org/files/upload/Sec.%203_Envi_1_AEC_Annex%203_Outcomes%20and%20Benefits%20(Aug%20version).pdf; ASEAN, "Economic community," ASEAN Secretariat. https://asean.org/our-communities/economic-community#Highly-Integrated; J. Menon, L. Todd and D. Arujunan, *ASEAN Integration Report*, ASEAN Prosperity Initiative Report No. 1, Institute for Democracy and Economic Affairs (2018). https://www.ideas.org.my/wp-content/uploads/2021/04/Asean_Integration_V9.pdf.

27 S. Destradi, "The finances of the association of Southeast Asian Nations (ASEAN)," in U. Engel and F. Mattheis (eds.) *The Finances of Regional Organizations in the Global South: Follow the Money*, (Abington, Oxon:

Routledge, 2019), pp. 206–221; L. M. Müller, "Governing regional connectivity in Southeast Asia—The role of the ASEAN secretariat and ASEAN'S external partners," Occasional Paper No. 42, Southeast Asian Studies at the University of Freiburg (2018). https://www.southeastasian-studies.uni-freiburg.de/documents/occasional-paper/op42.pdf; R. Stubbs, "ASEAN skeptics versus ASEAN proponents: Evaluating regional institutions," *Pacific Review*, 32(6), 923–950 (2019).

28 S. Limaye, "ASEAN is neither the problem nor the solution to South China Sea disputes," in G. Rozman and J. Liow (eds.) *International Relations and Asia's Southern Tier* (Singapore: Springer, 2018), pp. 95–109.

29 G. Nabbs-Keller, "ASEAN centrality and Indonesian leadership in a contested Indo-Pacific order," *Security Challenges*, 16(3), 21–26 (2020); Kementrian Luar Negari Republik Indonesia, "Bertemu Presiden ADB, Presiden Jokowi Diskusikan Pertembuhan Ekonomi ASEAN 2023," *IndonesiaKini* (2022). https://indonesiakini.go.id/berita/9299725/bertemu-presiden-adb-presiden-jokowi-diskusikan-pertumbuhan-ekonomi-asean-2023; L. M. Müller, "ASEAN centrality under threat—The cases of the RCEP and connectivity," *Journal of Contemporary East Asian Studies*, 8(2), 177–198 (2019); See Seng Tan, "Defence and security cooperation in East Asia: Wither ASEAN centrality?" in Alan Chong (ed.) *International Security in the Asia-Pacific* (London: Palgrave MacMillan, 2017), pp. 61–84.

30 M. Carlson and M. Turner, "Popular perceptions of political regimes in East and Southeast Asia," *Democratization*, 16(2), 377–398 (2009); A. Chang, Yun-Han Chu and B. Welsh, "Southeast Asia: Sources of regime support," *Journal of Democracy*, 24(2), 150–164 (2013).

31 Carlson and Turner (2009), *Op. cit.*; Chang, Chu and Welsh (2013), *Op. cit.*; G. Rodan, *Participation without Democracy: Containing Conflict in Southeast Asia* (Ithaca: Cornell University Press, 2018), pp. 116–210.

32 Rodan (2018), *Op. cit.*, pp. 70–115.

33 E. D. Mansfield, H. V. Milner and J. C. Pevehouse, "Vetoing cooperation: The impact of Veto players on preferential trading arrangements," in E. D. Mansfield (ed.) *The Political Economy of International Trade*, (Singapore: World Scientific, 2015), pp. 265–294; K. Spandler, "Regional standards of membership and enlargement in the EU and ASEAN," *Asia Europe Journal*, 16, 183–198 (2018).

34 D. M. Jones, "Security and democracy: The ASEAN charter and the dilemmas of regionalism in South-East Asia," *International Affairs*, 84(4), 735–756 (2008).

35 M. Beeson, "Can ASEAN cope with China?" *Journal of Current Southeast Asian Affairs*, 35(1), 5–28 (2016); Ian Tsung-Yen Chen and Alan H. Yang, "A harmonized Southeast Asia? Explanatory typologies of ASEAN countries' strategies to the rise of China," *Pacific Review*, 26(3), 265–288

(2013); D. K. Emmerson, "ASEAN between China and America: Is it time to try horsing the cow?" *TRaNS: Trans-National and Regional Studies of Southeast Asia*, 5(1), 1–23 (2017).

36 S. Strangio, "Could ASEAN really cut Laos and Cambodia loose?" *The Diplomat* (2020). https://thediplomat.com/2020/10/could-asean-really-cut-laos-and-cambodia-loose/; C. Quinn, "Myanmar's meaningless five-point consensus," *Foreign Policy* (2022). https://foreignpolicy.com/2022/05/11/myanmar-five-point-consensus-asean/.

37 "Wang Yi tan zhongfang dui jiejue miandian wenti de sange qidai (Wang Yi talks about three expectations for handling Myanmar issues)," Ministry of Foreign Affairs, People's Republic of China, 4 July 2022. https://www.mfa.gov.cn/wjbzhd/202207/t20220704_10714680.shtml; "China, Russia arming Myanmar Junta, UN expert says," DW, 2 February 2020. https://www.dw.com/en/china-russia-arming-myanmar-junta-un-expert-says/a-v60868089.

38 Asia Maritime Transparency Initiative (AMTI), "Maps of the Asia Pacific," Center for Strategic and International Studies. https://amti.csis.org/maps/; Maritime Awareness Project (MAP), "Interactive Map." https://map.nbr.org/interactivemap/.

39 Yee Kuang Heng, "ASEAN's position on the South China Sea and its implications for regional security," in Huang Jing and Andrew Billo (eds.) *Territorial Disputes in the South China Sea: Navigating Rough Waters* (London: Palgrave Macmillan, 2015), pp. 69–81; Le Hu, "Examining ASEAN's effectiveness in managing South China Sea disputes," *Pacific Review* (2021). https://doi.org/10.1080/09512748.2021.1934519; Nehginpao Kipen, "ASEAN and the South China Sea disputes," *Asian Affairs*, 49(3), 433–448 (2018).

40 ASEAN Secretariat, "Declaration on the conduct of parties in the South China Sea," 14 May 2012. https://asean.org/declaration-on-the-conduct-of-parties-in-the-south-china-sea-2/; Hoang Thi Ha, "Pitfalls for ASEAN in negotiating a code of conduct in the South China Sea," *Perspective* (2019). https://www.think-asia.org/bitstream/handle/11540/11007/ISEAS_Perspective_2019_57.pdf?sequence=1; I. Storey, "Assessing the ASEAN-China framework for the code of conduct for the South China Sea," *Perspective* (2017). https://www.iseas.edu.sg/wp-content/uploads/2018/02/ISEAS_Perspective_2017_62.pdf.

41 D. Guifoyle, "The rule of law and maritime security: Understanding lawfare in the South China Sea," *International Affairs*, 95(5), 999–1017 (2019).

42 Ketian Zhang, "Cautious bully: Reputation, resolve, and Beijing's use of coercion in the South China Sea," *International Security*, 44(1), 117–159 (2019).

43 Suisheng Zhao, "China and the South China Sea arbitration: Geopolitics versus international law," *Journal of Contemporary China*, 27(109), 1–15 (2018).

44 AMTI, "Maps of the Asia Pacific;" MAP, "Interactive Map."

45 C. E. Macariag and A. J. Fenton, "Analyzing the causes and effects of the South China Sea dispute," *Journal of Territorial and Maritime Studies*, 8(2), 42–58 (2021).

46 ASEAN Secretariat (2012), *Op. cit.*

47 *Ibid.*

48 ASEAN, "Treaty of amity and cooperation in Southeast Asia," ASEAN Secretariat (1976). https://asean.org/wp-content/uploads/2021/01/20131230235433.pdf.

49 Chin-Hao Huang, *Power and Restraint in China's Rise* (New York: Columbia University Press, 2022).

50 Zhang (2019), *Op. cit.*

51 D. Emmerson, "China's 'frown diplomacy' in Southeast Asia," *East Asia Forum*, 8 October 2010. https://www.eastasiaforum.org/2010/10/08/chinas-frown-diplomacy-in-southeast-asia/.

52 *Ibid.*

53 Mingjiang Li and Yinghui Li, "ASEAN's involvement in the South China Sea disputes: The economics-security conundrum," in G. Houlden, S. N. Romaniuk, and Nong Hong (eds.) *Security, Strategy, and Military Dynamics in the South China Sea: Cross National Perspectives* (Bristol: Bristol University Press, 2021), pp. 215–232.

54 Zhao (2018), *Op. cit.*

55 *Ibid.*

56 ASEAN Secretariat, "Guidelines for the Implementation of the DOC" (2012). https://asean.org/wp-content/uploads/images/archive/documents/20185-DOC.pdf; ASEAN Secretariat, "Joint statement of the foreign ministers of ASEAN member states and China on the full and effective implementation of the declaration on the conduct of parties in the South China Sea" (2016). https://asean.org/wp-content/uploads/2016/07/Joint-Statement-on-the-full-and-effective-implementation-of-the-DOC-FINAL.pdf; Chee Wee Keong, "Joint press briefing on the 14th ASEAN-China senior officials' meeting on the implementation of the declaration on the conduct of parties in the South China Sea (SOM-DOC)," ASEAN Secretariat (2017). https://asean.org/wp-content/uploads/2021/09/14th-SOM-DOC-Co-Chairs-Joint-Press-Briefing-Remarks-As-delivered-18-May-amen.pdf.

57 C. Thayer, "A closer look at the ASEAN-China single draft South China Sea code of conduct," *The Diplomat*, 3 August 2018. https://thediplomat.

com/2018/08/a-closer-look-at-the-asean-china-single-draft-south-china-sea-code-of-conduct/.

58 Zhang (2019), *Op. cit.*

59 *Ibid.*

60 Permanent Court of Arbitration, "The South China Sea arbitration: The Republic of the Philippines v. The People's Republic of China," 12 July 2016. https://pcacases.com/web/sendAttach/2086.

61 *Ibid.*

62 D. Grossman, "Can Vietnam's military stand up to China in the South China Sea?" *Asia Policy*, 13(1), 113–134 (2018).

63 R. C. De Castro, "The limits of intergovernmentalism: The Philippines' changing strategy on the South China Sea dispute and its impact on the Association of Southeast Asian Nations," *Journal of Current Southeast Asian Affairs*, 39(3), 335–358 (2020); Ngeow (2019), *Op. cit.*

64 V. Balakrishnan, "Written reply to parliamentary question," Singapore Ministry of Foreign Affairs, 4 October 2021. https://www.mfa.gov.sg/Newsroom/Press-Statements-Transcripts-and-Photos/2021/10/20211004-Min-written-reply-to-pq2; P. K. Meyer, A. Nurmandi and A. Agustiyara, "Indonesia's swift securitization of the Natuna Islands: How Jakarta countered China's claims in the South China Sea," *Asian Journal of Political Science*, 29(1), 70–87 (2019).

65 Suisheng Zhao, "East Asian disorder: China and the South China Sea disputes," *Asian Survey*, 60(3), 490–509 (2020).

66 O'Neill (2018), *Op. cit.*

67 *Ibid.*

68 D. K. Emmerson, "China in Xi's 'new era': Singapore and Goliath?" *Journal of Democracy*, 29(2), 76–82 (2018).

69 Meyer *et al.* (2019), *Op. cit.*; M. I. Tarigan, "Implementation of countermeasures effort of illegal fishing in Indonesia (case study on sinking the FV Viking vessel)," *Journal of Indonesian Legal Studies*, 3(1), 131–146 (2018).

70 ASEAN, "About AEC," Invest in ASEAN. http://investasean.asean.org/index.php/page/view/asean-economic-community/view/670/newsid/755/about-aec.html; ASEAN, "ASEAN agreements: Outcomes and benefits, Invest in ASEAN." http://investasean.asean.org/files/upload/Sec.%203_Envi_1_AEC_Annex%203_Outcomes%20and%20Benefits%20(Aug%20version).pdf; ASEAN, "Economic community," ASEAN Secretariat. https://asean.org/our-communities/economic-community#Highly-Integrated; J. Menon, L. Todd and D. Arujunan, ASEAN Integration Report, ASEAN Prosperity Initiative Report No. 1, Institute for Democracy and Economic Affairs (2018). https://www.ideas.org.my/wp-content/uploads/2021/04/ Asean_Integration_V9.pdf.

Herding Cats: Coordination Challenges in ASEAN's Approach to China 323

71 ASEAN Secretariat, "Framework agreement on comprehensive economic co-operation between ASEAN and the People's Republic of China Phnom Penh," 4 November 2002. https://asean.org/framework-agreement-on-comprehensive-economic-co-operation-between-asean-and-the-peoples-republic-of-china-phnom-penh-4-november-2002-2/.

72 ASEAN Secretariat, "Agreement on trade in goods of the framework agreement on comprehensive economic co-operation between the Association of Southeast Asian Nations and the People's Republic of China" (2004). https://asean.org/wp-content/uploads/2021/09/Copy-of-ACFTA-TIG-Agreement-_Body-Agreement_.doc.pdf.

73 *Ibid.*

74 Xiaojun Li, "Unpacking China's merchandise trade with ASEAN," *Perspective* (2021). https://www.iseas.edu.sg/wp-content/uploads/2021/06/ISEAS_Perspective_2021_93.pdf.

75 ASEAN Secretariat, "Regional comprehensive economic partnership agreement," RCEP (2012). https://rcepsec.org/legal-text/.

76 ASEAN Secretariat, "Regional comprehensive economic partnership agreement (RCEP) agreement to enter into force on 1 January 2022," RCEP (2021). https://asean.org/regional-comprehensive-economic-partnership-rcep-to-enter-into-force-on-1-january-2022/.

77 M. Cook, "Affirming ASEAN's East Asian centrality," ISEA – Yusof Ishak Institute (2020). https://www.iseas.edu.sg/media/commentaries/affirming-aseans-east-asian-centrality/.

78 Dezan Shira and Associates, "ASEAN's free trade agreements: An overview," ASEAN Briefing (2021). https://www.aseanbriefing.com/news/aseans-free-trade-agreements-an-overview/.

79 European Parliament Think Tank, *Trade Negotiations between the EU and ASEAN Member States*, European Parliament (2020). https://www.europarl.europa.eu/thinktank/en/document/EPRS_BRI(2020)659337; A. Hood and B. Savic, "UK-ASEAN dialogue partnership paves way to potential future trade accord," *Diplomat* (2021). https://thediplomat.com/2021/09/uk-asean-dialogue-partnership-paves-way-to-potential-future-trade-accord/.

80 Ministry of Commerce, People's Republic of China. http://fta.mofcom.gov.cn.

81 US-ASEAN Business Council, "About the CPTPP and RCEP" (2022). https://www.usasean.org/regions/tpp/about.

82 Shintaro Hamanaka, "TPP versus RCEP: Control of membership and agenda setting," *Journal of East Asian Economic Integration*, 18(2), 163–186 (2014).

83 The White House, *Op. cit.*

84 Heng Wang, "Building toward the RCEP? Reflections on the ASEAN-China FTA," in P. L. Hsieh and B. Mercurio (eds.) *ASEAN Law in the*

324 *J. I. Chong*

New Regional Economic Order: Global Trends and Shifting Paradigms (Cambridge: Cambridge University Press, 2019), pp. 46–63.

85 Erin Zimmerman and Diane Stone, "ASEAN think tanks, policy change, and economic cooperation: From the Asian financial crisis to the global financial crisis," *Policy and Society*, 37(2), 260–275 (2018).

86 H. E. McKibben, "What do I get? How do States' negotiation alternatives influence the concessions they receive in multilateral negotiations," *European Journal of International Relations*, 26(3), 896–921 (2020).

87 Lee Jones, "ASEAN intervention in Cambodia: From cold war to conditionality," *Pacific Review*, 20(4), 523–550 (2007).

88 Shaun Narine, "ASEAN and the management of regional security," *Asian Affairs*, 71(2), 195–214 (1998).

89 S. R. Nathan, "MFA press release: Speech by President SR Nathan at the MFA diplomatic Academy's inaugural S Rajaratnam lecture," Singapore Ministry of Foreign Affairs (2008). https://www.mfa.gov.sg/Newsroom/Press-Statements-Transcripts-and-Photos/2008/03/Speech-by-President-S-R-Nathan-at-the-MFA-Diplomatic-Academys-Inaugural-S-Rajaratnam-Lecture-10-Marc.

90 S. J. Morris, *Why Vietnam Invaded Cambodia: Political Culture and the Causes of War* (Stanford: Stanford University Press, 1999).

91 *Ibid.*

92 *Ibid.*

93 M. Alagappa, "Regionalism and the quest for security: ASEAN and the Cambodian conflict," *Australian Journal of International Affairs*, 27(2), 189–209 (2008).

94 Jones (2007), *op. cit.*

95 *Ibid.*

96 R. Yates, *Understanding ASEAN's Role in Asia-Pacific Order* (London: Palgrave Macmillan, 2019), pp. 127–189.

97 *Ibid.*

98 Wen Qing Ngoei, *Arc of Containment: Britain, the United States, and Anticommunism in Southeast Asia* (Ithaca, NY: Cornell University Press, 2019).

99 J. D. Ciociari, "ASEAN and the great powers," *Contemporary Southeast Asia*, 39(2), 252–258 (2019).

100 Yukawa Taku, "Transformation of ASEAN's image in the 1980s: The Cambodian conflict and the economic development of ASEAN member countries," *Southeast Asian Studies*, 49(2), 240–267 (2011).

101 *Ibid.*

102 D. M. Jones and M. L. R. Smith, "Making process, not progress: ASEAN and the evolving Asian Regional order," *International Security*, 32(1), 148–184 (2007).

Herding Cats: Coordination Challenges in ASEAN's Approach to China   325

103 He (2014), *Op. cit.*

104 M. Cook, "Southeast Asia's developing divide," in G. Rozman and J. C. Liow (eds.) *International Relations in Asia's Southern Tier* (Singapore: Springer, 2019), pp. 63–76; Huong Le Thu, "China's dual strategy of coercion and inducement toward ASEAN," *Pacific Review*, 32(1), 20–36 (2019).

105 A. Acharya, "Doomed to dialogue: Will ASEAN survive great power rivalry in Asia?" in *International Relations in Asia's Southern Tier*, pp. 77–91.

106 *Ibid.*; J. S. Amador III, "The continuing erosion of ASEAN centrality," ASEAN Focus (2021), pp. 2–3.

107 S. F. Muhibat, "Embracing change to stay resilient," ASEAN Focus (2021), pp. 4–5; Khoung Vu, *ASEAN Economic Prospects amid Turbulence: Development Challenges and Implications for Reform*, Foreign Policy at Brookings (2020). https://www.brookings.edu/wp-content/uploads/2020/07/FP_20200715_asean_economic_prospects_vu.pdf.

108 Huong Le Thu, "ASEAN: Different Strokes for different folks, but the future should be in sync," *The Interpreter* (2018). https://www.lowyinstitute.org/the-interpreter/asean-different-strokes-different-folks-future-should-be-sync.

109 A. Acharya, "Ideas, identity, and institution-building: From the 'ASEAN way' to the 'Asia-Pacific' way," *Pacific Review*, 10(3), 319–346 (1997); Taku Yukawa, "The ASEAN way as a symbol: An analysis of discourses on the ASEAN norms," *Pacific Review*, 31(3), 298–314 (2018).

110 K. Johnson and R. Gramer, "The great decoupling," *Foreign Policy*, 14 May 2020. https://foreignpolicy.com/2020/05/14/china-us-pandemic-economy-tensions-trump-coronavirus-covid-new-cold-war-economics-the-great-decoupling/.

111 Amador (2021), *Op. cit.*

112 Le Thu (2019), *Op. cit.*; O'Neill (2018), *Op. cit.*

113 R. Emmers, "Unpacking ASEAN neutrality: The quest for autonomy and impartiality in Southeast Asia," *Contemporary Southeast Asia*, 40(3), 349–370 (2018); L. Southgate, "ASEAN: Still the zone of peace, freedom, and neutrality," *Political Science*. https://www.tandfonline.com/journals/rpnz20.

114 R. Emmott, "US, China must manage 'intense competition,' top Biden Advisor says," *Reuters*, 7 October 2021. https://www.reuters.com/world/china/us-china-must-manage-intense-competition-top-biden-adviser-says-2021-10-07/.

© 2025 World Scientific Publishing Europe Ltd.
https://doi.org/10.1142/9781800616318_bmatter

Index

A

abandonment, 209
Abenomics, 16
Abe, Shinzo, 150–152, 157
Afghanistan, 141
air defense identification zone
 (ADIZ), 74, 154, 183
Air-Sea Contact Mechanism, 195
Allison, Graham, 265
"anti-access and area denial"
 (A2/AD), 74
anti-China policy, 221
anti-dumping, 219
Aoyama, Rumi, xviii
ASEAN centrality, 270, 294,
 313–314
ASEAN countries, xx, 51, 54, 265,
 269, 274–276, 281–283, 294
ASEAN Economic Community
 (AEC), 308
ASEAN Free Trade Area (AFTA),
 308
ASEAN Outlook on the Indo-Pacific
 (AOIP), 270
ASEAN–China Free Trade Area
 (ACFTA), 297, 309

ASEAN–China interactions, 293–316
ASEAN–China Special Summit, 279
ASEAN–PRC, 295, 298, 300
Asia Africa Growth Corridor
 (AAGC), 42
Asia-Africa Development Corridor
 Program, 153
Asia-Pacific Economic Cooperation
 Summit, 44
Asia-Pacific region, 39, 109–114, 193
Asian Development Bank (ADB),
 17, 36, 155
Asian Financial Crisis, 302
Asian Infrastructure Investment Bank
 (AIIB), 16, 35, 108, 130, 153, 203,
 206, 237
Asian NATO, 50, 187–188
Assam Rifles, 138
asymmetric perception, 216–221
asymmetric threat perceptions,
 183–188
'*Atma Nirbhar Bharat*' (self-reliant
 India) approach, 135
Australia, New Zealand, and United
 States Security Treaty (ANZUS),
 234

328 *Index*

Australia–China relationship, 231–256
Australia–United Kingdom–United States (AUKUS) relationship, xiv, 112, 141, 202, 213, 235, 279
Australian Defence Force, 251
Australia's Foreign Relations (State and Territory Arrangements) Act 2020, 253

B
Bajpai, Kanti, 100
Balakrishnan, Vivian, 280
balancing, 131
bandwagoning, 131
Bangladesh, Bhutan, India, and Nepal (BBIN) Initiative, 20
Basic Exchange and Cooperation Agreement (BECA), 108
Bay of Bengal Initiative for Multi-Sectoral Technical and Economic Cooperation (BIMSTEC), 20
Beeson, Mark, 234
Belt and Road Initiative (BRI), xv, 16, 19, 21, 33–34, 45, 51, 130, 150, 161, 191–193, 264
Bharatiya Janata Party (BJP), 100, 130
Bhutan, 127
Biden, Joseph R., 34, 70–71, 269
bilateral economic relations, 270
bilateral relations, xiii–xxi, 1–26
Birmingham, Simon, 207
Bishop, Julie, 203, 207
Blinken, Antony, 49
Blue Dot Network, 49
Bochkov, Danil, 98
Bretton Woods system, 55
BRICS, 107, 130
BRI Forum for International Cooperation (BRF), 39

Brunei, 297
Build Back Better plan, 71
Build Back Better World (B3W) initiative, xv, 34, 36, 48
bullying, 272
Bush, George W., 106, 275, 284

C
Cai, Liang, 161
Cambodia, 281, 310, 315
Cambodia–China FTA, 308
Cambodia–Vietnam relationship, 310
Campbell, Kurt, 14
Centre for Contemporary China Studies (CCCS), 136–137
charm offensive, 277
Cheng, Jingye, 204
China, xiii–xxi, 1–26, 293–316
China policy, 105–109
China threat, 105
China–ASEAN relations, 277–278
China–Australia Free Trade Agreement, 236, 254
China–Australia relations, 201–224
China–Bangladesh–China–India–Myanmar Economic Corridor, 40
China–Central Asia–West Asia Economic Corridor, 40
China–IMF Capacity Development Center, 54
China–India relations, 95–115
China–Japan relations, xviii
China–Japan Third-Party Market Cooperation Working Mechanism, 43
China–Mongolia–Russia Economic Corridor, 40
China–Pakistan Economic Corridor (CPEC), 20, 40
China–Singapore (Chongqing) Connectivity Initiative (CCI-ILSTC), 40

Index   329

China–U.S.–Australia triangle, 205
China–U.S. cooperation, 106
China's Southeast Asia Policy, 263–286
Chinese Academy of Social Sciences (CASS), 153
Chinese Communist Party's (CCP's), 13, 37, 238
Chinese factor, 151–154
Chinoy, Sujan R., 99
"Chip 4" alliance, 14
Chong, Ja Ian, xix
Coalition Government of Democratic Kampuchea (CGDK), 311
Code of Conduct (COC), 267, 303
coercion, 272
Cold War, 6, 15, 109, 114, 276, 316
colliding competitors, 84
Communications Compatibility and Security Agreement (COMCASA), 108
Communist Party of China's (CPC's), 192, 275
competition, 5
competitive rivalry, 5, 9–18
Comprehensive and Progressive Trans- Pacific Partnership (CPTPP), 14, 17, 189, 296
comprehensive strategic partnership, 236
Comprehensive Test Ban Treaty (CTBT), 111
confidence-building measures (CBMs), 110, 195
constructive relationship of cooperation, 2
constructive strategic partnership, 2
containment, 131
cooperation, 27
cooperative partnership, xxi, 9–14, 232

cooperative relationship, 8
cooperative rivalry, 9, 14–18
coopetition, 192
countervailing duty, 219
covert, coercive or corrupt, 253
COVID-19 pandemic, xiv, xviii, 2, 23, 69, 79–81, 86, 108, 133, 150, 168, 204, 209, 212, 218, 236, 243, 250, 255, 280
Crawford, T. W., 273

D
Davidson, Philip, 52, 85
debtbook diplomacy, 53
debt traps, 44
decision-making, 301
decoupling, 271
Democratic Progressive Party (DPP), 82
Democratic Security Diamond (DSD), 188
Deng, Xiaoping, 110
Denisov, Igor, 98
dependent variable (DV), 7, 29
Dian, M., 274
Dittmer, Lowell, 180
divergent perceptions, 10
"divide and rule", 274
docking approach, 162–163
Doklam crisis, 18
domestic political factors, 213–216
domestic political interference, 242–244
double-cycle economy, 271
"Dual Circulation" strategy, 193

E
East Asia Summit, 267
East China Sea, 14
East Coast Rail Link, 280
Eastern Economic Corridor, 43
economic NATO, 50

330 *Index*

economic partner, 241
economic security, 190
Enhancing Development and Growth through Energy (EDGE), 45
European Union (EU), 277, 308
Exclusive Economic Zone (EEZ), 303
Export Finance and Insurance Corporation (EFIC), 46
external balancing, xix
extreme competition, 114

F
face-to-face diplomacy, 271
feelings thermometer, 246–248
fifth-generation (5G) network, 243
Fifth Plenary Session of the 19th CPC Central Committee, 193
first island chain, 240
"Five Eyes" intelligence alliance, 187
foreign interference, 243–244, 253–254
fragility, 177
"Free and Open Indo-Pacific" (FOIP), xiv, 34, 44–45, 51–52, 149–169, 188–191
Freedom of Navigation Program (FONOP), 195, 306
free trade agreements (FTAs), 189, 297

G
G2 concept, 106, 114
G20 London Summit, 11
G4 nations, 111
Galwan, 123–145
Gandhi, Rajiv, 96
General Electric, 43
Geng, Shuang, 164–165
geopolitics, 233–235
Gillard, Julia, 22
Gill, Bates, xix

Global Cooperation and Training Framework (GCTF), 191
Global Financial Crisis, 13
Global Gateway plan, 49
global maritime axis, 47, 280
Gokhale, Vijay, 98
'Go West,' 38
gross domestic product (GDP), 192
Group of 20 (G20) country, 233

H
haphazardness, 295–298
hard-line approach, 158–160
Hatda, Pich, 281
hedging strategy, 103, 160–161, 295–298
He, Kai, xvii, 102, 163, 215, 265, 298, 302
Herding Cats, 293–316
Himalayan barrier, 123–145
Hindutva, 100
Hobbes, Thomas, 4, 26
Hong Kong, 79, 218, 248
Hu, Shisheng, 99
Huawei, 13, 18, 135, 204–205, 207, 243–244, 254
Hun, Sen, 282

I
image, 69
India, 105–109
India–China relations, 123–145
India–Pakistan dispute, 107
India–U.S. Civilian Nuclear Agreement, 141
India–U.S. Initiative on Critical and Emerging Technologies (iCET), 113
Indian Air Force, 137
Indian Ocean region, 129, 136–137, 140

Index 331

Indian Ocean Rim Association (IORA), 20
Indo-Pacific concept, xiii–xxi, 1–26, 33–56, 107, 125, 263–286
Indo-Pacific Cooperation Strategy, 277
Indo-Pacific Economic Framework (IPEF), 14, 49, 112, 157, 196, 266, 296
Indo-Pacific Maritime Domain Awareness Initiative (IPMDA), 113
Indo-Pacific Transparency Initiative, 48
Indo-Tibetan Border Police, 138
Indochina, 310–312
Indonesia, 301, 305
infrastructure, 37
infrastructure statecraft, 26, 33–56, 76
Inner Mongolia, 38
interest-threat nexus model, xvii, 7–10, 297
internal balancing, xix, 108
International Development and Security Dialogue, 54
International Labour Organization (ILO), 39
International Monetary Fund (IMF), 17, 124
intimidation, 272
Izumikawa, Yasuhiro, 273

J
Japan, 149–169, 194–196
Japan Bank for International Cooperation (JBIC), 46
Japanese National Security Council, 152
Jervis, Robert, 68–69
Johnson, Christopher, 37

K
Kalyanaraman, S., 98
Kamiya, Matake, 156

Kampuchean People's Revolutionary Party (KPRP), 310
Kant, Immanuel, 4, 26
Keohane, Robert, 5
Khmer Rouge (KR), 310
Kireeva, A., 274
Kishida, Fumio, 15–16, 168, 189
Korean Peninsula, 5

L
Labor Party, 214
Lee, Hsien Loong, 52
Lewis, Duncan, 214
Li, Keqiang, 155
Li, Li, xviii
Liberal Democratic Party (LDP), 155, 190–191
Liberal-National coalition, 214
liberalism, 68
Lin, Minwang, 99
Line of Actual Control (LAC), 100, 131–132
liquefied natural gas (LNG) infrastructure, 46
Liu, Feng, xvii, 102, 163, 215, 265, 302
Liu, Ruonan, xix, 302
Locke, John, 4, 26
Logistics Exchange Memorandum of Agreement (LEMOA), 108
Lou, Chunhao, 100
Lu, Hao, 161

M
"Make in India" campaign, 107
Malaysia, 305
marriage triangle, 181, 196
Mattis, Jim, 47
Mearsheimer, John, 180
Medcalf, Rory, 35
Medeiros, Evan S., 102

332 *Index*

Mekong River Commission (MRC), 281
Memorandum of Understanding (MoU), 46
Middle East, 87
military, 74–75
Minister for Foreign Affairs, 253
Modi, Narendra, 18, 51, 130, 133
Morrison, Scott, 42, 51, 204
Moscow, 310
Mudiyanselage, Harsha Konara, 98
multinational corporations (MNCs), 143
mutual (mis)perceptions, 67–87
Myanmar, 301
Myanmar civil war, 302

N
Nakasone Peace Institute, 184
National Defense Strategy (NDS), 268
National People's Congress, 254
national security, 83
National Security Advisor, 137
National Security Council Secretariat, 137
National Security Legislation Amendment, 203
national security strategy (NSS), 190, 266
National Social Science Foundation of China (NSSFC), 157
NATO, 4, 26, 52, 86, 188
Nepal, 127
New International Land–Sea Trade Corridor, 40
New Zealand, 207, 215
Nikai, Toshihiro, 17
nine-dash line, 303
Ning, Tuanhui, 213
"non-provocative" foreign policy, 180

non-traditional security threats, 84–85
North Korea, 209
Nuclear Non-Proliferation Treaty (NPT), 111
Nuclear Suppliers Group, 129

O
Obama, Barack, 11–12, 44
"one country, two systems" model, 249
order transition, 1–26
Organization for Maritime Security in East Asia (OMSEA), 185

P
Pakistan, 128
Panda, Jagannath P., 100
parallel partners, 84
Partnership for Global Infrastructure and Investment (PGII), 35–36
Pelosi, Nancy, xiv, 26, 82
Pempel, T. J., 37
Pence, Mike, 44, 46
People's Liberation Army (PLA), 132, 137, 240
People's Liberation Army and Navy (PLAN), 129, 184
People's Republic of China (PRC), 231, 293–294
perception, 69
perennial anxiety, 234, 237
Pew Research Center, 217, 271
PHP Institute, 184
pivot to Asia, 163, 182, 275
PLA Air Force, 240
PLA Navy, 240
PLA Rocket Force, 240–241
political psychology, 68
Pompeo, Mike, 45, 47, 279
Pu, Xiaoyu, 99
public attitudes, 244–250

Q

Quad, 48, 70, 106, 112–113, 131, 136, 140, 152, 277, 284
Quad Infrastructure Coordination Group, 49
Quadrilateral Security Dialogue (Quad), 48, 98, 269
Quad Summit, 112
Quality Infrastructure, 42
"Quality Infrastructure" initiative, 42

R

rapprochement policy, 12
Rashtriya Swayamsevak Sangh (RSS), 100
Reciprocal Access Agreement, 23
Regional Comprehensive Economic Partnership (RCEP), 125, 189, 276, 297, 309
regional security environment, 239–242
rivalry, 26
Robertson, Peter, 98
role identity, 4, 26
romantic triangle, 196
Russia–Ukraine conflict, 113, 168, 223

S

Safranchuk, Ivan, 98
Saran, Shyam, 100
Sasakawa Peace Foundation, 184
Schriver, Randall, 54
Schweller, Randall, 236
science, technology, engineering, and mathematics (STEM), 77–78
Second World War, 186
security threat, 241
Self-Defense Forces (SDF), 187
Shanghai Cooperation Organization (SCO) Summit, 18

shared economic interests, 26
Singapore, 297, 305
Singapore–China FTA, 308
Singh, Zorawar Daulet, 99
Sino–Australian relationship, 22–24, 211
Sino–Indian War, 126, 128
Sino–Japanese relationship, 14–18, 149–169
Sino–Japan–U.S. triangle relations, 167
Sino–U.S. relations, 112, 276
Sino–U.S. strategic competition, xxi, 2, 10–14, 26, 33–56
Sixth Tokyo International Conference on African Development (TICAD VI), 151–152
smile diplomacy, 277
South Asian Association for Regional Cooperation (SAARC), 111
South China Sea (SCS), 190, 210, 275, 278, 295, 303–307
Southeast Asia strategy, 265
Soviet Union, 73
special military operation, 86
stability, 177
state-owned enterprises (SOEs), 45
Stoltenberg, Jens, 4, 26
Strategic and Cooperative Partnership, 96
strategic competitor, 44
strategic dependence, 234
strategic partnership, 3, 254
strategic triangle model, 180–181
"String of Pearls" approach, 129
Suga, Yoshihide, 16, 157, 165
"Supply Chain Initiative", 21
systemic pessimism, 237

T

Taiwan Relations Act, 188
technology, 77–79

334 *Index*

Tellis, Ashley J., 106
Terminal High Altitude Area Defense (THAAD) system, 186
9/11 terrorist attacks, 106
Thailand, 297
Third-Party Market Cooperation Guidelines and Cases, 43
third-party markets, 156, 162, 168
Tibetan Special Frontier Force, 132
Tibet Autonomous Region, 106
Tokyo International Conference on African Development (TICADVI), 188
Trans-Pacific Partnership (TPP), 14, 77, 107, 153, 308
Treaty of Amity of Cooperation (TAC), 304
Treaty of Peace and Friendship and Cooperation, 141
Trump, Donald, xiv, 3, 44, 112, 155, 284
Turnbull, Malcolm, 203, 210

U
Ukraine, 13, 124, 142
Ukrainian War, xiv
Umbrella Movement, 248
UN Security Council (UNSC), 104, 111, 129
United Nations (UN), 311
United Nations Convention on the Law of the Sea (UNCLOS), 203, 303, 305, 307, 313
United Nations General Assembly, 250
U.S. Chamber of Commerce, 46
U.S. Development Finance Corporation (DFC), 46
U.S. factor, 95–115
U.S. Overseas Private Investment Corporation (OPIC), 46

U.S. Special Operations Command (SOCOM), 195
U.S.–ASEAN partnership, 272–281
U.S.–ASEAN Special Summit, 267–268
U.S.–China relations, xiv–xv, 34, 70–86
U.S.–Japan Strategic Energy Partnership, 46
U.S.–led coalition, 50

V
Vietnam, 305, 310
Vietnamese Communist Party, 310

W
Walt, Stephan, 8
Wang, Jisi, 81
Wang, Jue, 99
Wang, Lianhe, 211
Wang, Yi, 164–165, 270–271, 277, 279
Warsaw Pact, 52
wedging strategy, 272–281
Wei, Zongyou, 212
Wesley, Michael, 234
White House National Security Council, 47
White, Hugh, 205
Wigell, M., 273
wolf warrior diplomacy, xv
Wong, Penny, 250
Working Mechanism for Consultation and Coordination (WMCC), 97
World Bank, 17
World Health Organization (WHO), 39
World Trade Organization (WTO), 271
World War II, 15, 234, 237, 265
Wuhan consensus, 20
Wu, Lin, 99

X

Xi, Jinping, xv, 18, 34, 37, 42, 71–73, 100, 133, 150–152, 191, 193, 240, 245, 270
Xie, Tao, 206
Xu, Shanpin, 208
Xu, Shaomin, 210

Y

Yang, Bojiang, 158
Yu, Lei, 206
Yuan, Jingdong, 98
Yunnan, 38

Z

Zeng, Jinghan, 234
Zhang, Guoxi, 206
Zhang, Qi, 206
Zhang, Tao, 208
Zhao, Lijian, 166
Zhao, Minghao, xvii–xviii
Zheng, Haiqi, 98
Zhou, Fangyin, xix
ZTE, 13, 135, 204, 244, 254

www.ingramcontent.com/pod-product-compliance
Lightning Source LLC
Chambersburg PA
CBHW061255310325
24273CB00004B/63